Technological Visions

The Hopes and Fears that Shape New Technologies

Marita Sturken is Associate Professor in the Annenberg School for Communication at the University of Southern California and the author of *Tangled Memories: The Vietnam War, the AIDS Epidemic, and the Politics of Remembering* and *Practices of Looking: An Introduction to Visual Culture* (with Lisa Cartwright).

Douglas Thomas is Associate Professor in the Annenberg School for Communication at the University of Southern California. He is author of three books, most recently *Hacker Culture*.

Sandra J. Ball-Rokeach is Professor and Director of the Communication Technology and Community Program in the Annenberg School for Communication at the University of Southern California. She is author of several books, including *Theories of Mass Communication* (with M. L. De Fleur).

Technological Visions

The Hopes and Fears that Shape
New Technologies

Edited by

MARITA STURKEN, DOUGLAS THOMAS,
AND SANDRA J. BALL-ROKEACH

TEMPLE UNIVERSITY PRESS
Philadelphia

Temple University Press, Philadelphia 19122
Copyright © 2004 by Temple University
All rights reserved
Published 2004
Printed in the United States of America

Library of Congress Cataloging-in-Publication Data

Technological visions : the hopes and fears that shape new technologies / edited by
Marita Sturken, Douglas Thomas, and Sandra J. Ball-Rokeach.
    p. cm.
    Includes bibliographical references and index.
    ISBN 1-59213-226-X (cloth : alk. paper) — ISBN 1-59213-227-8 (pbk. : alk. paper)
    1. Technology—Social aspects.   2. Technology and civilization.
3. Technological innovations—History.   I. Sturken, Marita.   II. Thomas, Douglas.
III. Ball- Rokeach, Sandra J.
T14.5.T4396 2004
306.4'6—dc22   2003063392

2 4 6 8 9 7 5 3 1

Contents

Acknowledgments

THE ESSAYS in this volume originate from a set of projects of the Annenberg Center for Communication and the Annenberg School for Communication at the University of Southern California and the Annenberg School for Communication at the University of Pennsylvania. Many of these essays had their first incarnation at the "Technological Visions: Utopian and Dystopian Perspectives" conference held at the University of Southern California in the fall of 1998, which was one of the inaugural activities of the Metamorphosis: Transforming the Ties that Bind Project at USC. The Metamorphosis Project is an inquiry into the transformation of urban community under the forces of new communication technologies, globalization, and population diversity (metamorph.org) and is based in the Communication Technology and Community Program in the Annenberg School for Communication at USC. The essays in this volume also include many contributions that were solicited after the conference in order to address the issue of technological visions through a range of approaches.

We are grateful to these three institutions for their support in the production of this volume and the conference that originated it. Significantly, all three of the sponsoring organizations that made the Technological Visions conference possible were created and have been sustained by the Annenberg Foundation. We are very grateful to the foundation for its ongoing support. We are also grateful to Elizabeth M. Daley, director of the USC Annenberg Center for Communication, who provided both monetary and administrative support; and to Geoffrey Cowan, dean of the USC Annenberg School for Communication, and Kathleen Hall Jamison, former dean of the Annenberg School for Communication at the University of Pennsylvania, who provided important support for the initial conference.

We are indebted to JoAnn Hanley, for her considerable patience and organizational skill, as well as Mary Wilson, Sorin Matei, Jennifer Gibbs, and Elizabeth Gutierrez-Hoyt for their assistance while doctoral research assistants on the Metamorphosis Project.

This project began in the heyday of utopian and dystopian visions prompted by the complex of Internet technologies and their most visible applications. We are indebted to the authors of contributions to this volume for conceiving their projects in ways that escape the short life of "hype." Indeed, this distinguished set of contributors accepted our challenge to speak to the recurring cultural and social issues surrounding proclamations of "communication revolutions" from print to computer-mediated forms. In so doing, they contribute to an elevation of public discourse about new technologies and, thus, fulfilled the editors' vision of an historically grounded, informed analysis of how "new" technologies are imagined, envisioned, and represented.

This volume is a tribute to the philanthropic vision of Walter H. Annenberg, who passed away in October 2002. Through the Annenberg Foundation, Ambassador Annenberg, his family, and colleagues have made significant contributions to the arts, public media, public schools, and higher education. Walter Annenberg's life was dedicated to the importance of education in a changing technological world, and the need to understand communication technologies within broad social frameworks.

Technological Visions

The Hopes and Fears that Shape New Technologies

MARITA STURKEN AND DOUGLAS THOMAS

Introduction
Technological Visions and the Rhetoric of the New

TECHNOLOGIES TAKE on a special kind of social meaning when they are new. As they emerge in various social contexts, modern technologies become the focus of intense political, economic, cultural, and even emotional investment. A so-called new technology is the object of fascination, hyperbole, and concern. It is almost inevitably a field onto which a broad array of hopes and fears is projected and envisioned as a potential solution to, or possible problem for, the world at large. Technological development is one of the primary sites through which we can chart the desires and concerns of a given social context and the preoccupations of particular moments in history. The meanings that are attributed to new technologies are some of the most important evidence we can find of the visions, both optimistic and anxious, through which modern societies cohere. When branded *new*, emergent technologies are, as Sherry Turkle notes in this volume, a kind of Rorschach test for the collective concerns of a particular age.

It is thus the case that technologies in their emergent stages have played a dramatic role in visions of the future and beliefs in the possibility of change. The history of technological development, even in its earliest forms, such as the development of writing in Greek society, has prompted a parallel history of visions about technology, visions of new possibilities and social arrangements, and of loss and nostalgia. Emergent technologies have been the fuel for social imaginings, both of what society should be and of its potential to go farther off course from some ideal path to betterment.

The most recent example of a new technology endowed with both magical and destructive powers is, of course, the Internet. The technological bubble of the 1990s, which was fueled by technological innovation and economic speculation, produced an extraordinary array of hyperbolic proclamations about its potential impact on the world. The Internet, prognosticators stated, would solve the long-standing problems of education, make bureaucracies function better, create a global community through increased connectivity, empower the disenfranchised, and forever alter the roles of consumer and producer. This fantasy of an Internet-driven world was

1

presented as the new hope that promised to connect the privileged few of the world with the underprivileged many.

This idealized embrace of the Internet as a new technology was inevitably accompanied by a darker fantasy about its capacity to transform human relationships. News stories about the Internet portrayed a dangerous world in which criminals and pedophiles took advantage of trusting users, government and corporations slowly eroded privacy and freedom; the media proclaimed correlations between Internet use and higher rates of depression and social isolation. Anxiety about the relatively unregulated nature of the Internet and the increased accessibility of adult material to children in the open arena of the World Wide Web was reinforced by fears that the Internet, as Sarah Banet-Weiser notes in her essay in this volume, was creating a generational divide in which parents were being left behind, thus rendering parental control obsolete.

Visions of technology have a long history of such binary thinking. The visions of technologies as life-transforming, in both transcendent and threatening ways, have been reiterated and embraced again and again throughout history, from the development of the printing press to the computer; from the telegraph to the cell phone; from photography and cinema to television; with new technologies taking the place of more established ones in a seemingly endless cycle. There is little nuance in these characterizations, or, for that matter, much sense of the complex ways in which individuals experience new technologies and integrate them into their lives. Therefore, it remains tragically the case that while technological change continues at a rapid pace, the visions that define it remain caught within a repeating cycle of overly simplistic binary frameworks.

This is particularly the case with communications technologies that have been the object of uniquely powerful visions of social change. James Carey has argued that the power awarded to technology in American culture can be defined in terms of the "transmission view" of communication, a power rooted in religious attitudes. Transmission, Carey argues, has been defined historically in terms of the transportation of ideas and knowledge, a mission that originally carried the "moral meaning" of carrying and distributing a Christian message.[1] The religious tenor of technological visions is thus derived from a kind of messianic investment in the potential of communications media to transform human nature. Carey and John Quirk refer to these optimistic characterizations as evidence of a "rhetoric of the electronic sublime," one that echoes the religious overtones of the embrace of electricity in the nineteenth century, what Leo Marx termed the "electrical sublime."[2] Electricity was embraced as a transformative force, one that promised freedom, democracy, and, by implication, enlightenment. The desires invested in the promise of communication technologies, imbued with this history of religious associations, have thus been particularly overdetermined, precisely because of their capacities to connect people across distances and to create new forms of mobility. Ironically, this relentless optimism in new communication technologies creates an endless cycle of disappointments, since no new technology can possibly fulfill such expectations.

Visions of new technology are highly productive—they impact how technologies are marketed, used, made sense of, and integrated into people's lives. This book is concerned with the impact of these visions of new technologies. These essays address such questions as: Why are emergent and new technologies the screens onto which our cultures project such a broad array of social concerns and desires? Why is technology the object of such unrealistic expectations? What do these visions screen out about contemporary society? How is it possible to think about technologies outside of these frameworks? The essays in this book, which are written by scholars of new media, historians of technology, journalists who report on new technologies, and proponents of digital technology, offer a cautionary approach to the analysis of technology, examining the ways that the visions and metaphors of new technologies in large part create and define the social impact of those technologies. These essays make clear that society's capacity to project concerns and desires on technology operates as a primary form of social denial; the belief that a new technology can solve existing social problems reveals a refusal to confront fully the deeper causes of those problems and the complexity of human interaction.

Visions of technology, whether overly optimistic or anxiously dystopian, consistently award new technologies the capacity to transform. For instance, the belief that communication technologies can promote human connectivity is coupled with the fear that actual human connection has been irretrievably lost. This sense of irretrievability is basic to the power awarded technology in technological visions. Technological change is popularly understood as irreversible—once a technology is used, it is imagined that its effects cannot be undone. There is no turning back, it would seem, from the first moment of "contact" with a new technology, according to these narratives. Once experienced, a technology is imagined to have changed one's way of being in the world forever and to have created immediate kinds of dependencies. Thus, fear of children's contact with computers is not simply about the potential acts those children can participate in with a computer, but the capacity of that computer to transform them into someone else, or, in the least, to provide them with experiences, good and bad, that change them in unalterable ways. This sense of irretrievability thus awards new technologies power in what are essentially technologically determinist ways. Indeed, while technological determinism has long been debunked in academic analysis, it retains a hold in popular discussion and understanding of the impact of technology. The pervasive sense that technologies transform us in irrevocable ways means that idealistic concepts of technology are always accompanied by the anxiety that they will also promote some kind of loss—loss of connectivity, of intimacy, of desire, of *authenticity* in some way.

This sense of loss is often focused on a concern about the impact of new technologies on connectivity and community. New communities are continually made possible by the innovations of new communication technologies, yet, as these new communities form, fears surface that they will undermine existing networks of connectivity, the family and the neighborhood. Since the impact of communication technologies is so often understood as irrevocable, these concerns are magnified. Many of the essays in this book consider the radical nature of a virtual community in response to the popular depictions of the Internet as an isolating force. They grapple with the implications of virtual communities—and what their emergence reveals about concepts of community in general. Is a virtual community one with little social cost, a kind of "community lite"?[3] These essays consider what kinds of ties are created through communication technologies, at what cost, and with what limits. The most recent concern about virtual communities can be seen in fears that current forms of globalization, fueled by communication technologies, have reduced the nation to a mere shadow of its former modern state. Yet, as Carolyn Marvin reminds us in this volume, the nation-state remains firmly in place as an entity for which bodies continue to be sacrificed.

The transformative power awarded to new technologies is directly related to the idea that technologies arise not of the world in which we live but as a force that comes magically from elsewhere, a force seemingly outside of social and political influences. Thus, it is popularly imagined that technology just hurtles forward into the future, with new inventions rising up when their moment has come. Langdon Winner has referred to this as "autonomous technology," the sense that technology is a force unto itself and beyond human control. He writes,

In some views the perception of technology-out-of-control is associated with a process of change in which the human world is progressively transformed and incorporated by an expanding scientific technology. In others the perception focuses upon the behavior of large-scale technical systems that appear to operate and grow through a process of self-generation beyond human intervention. In others still, the matter is primarily that of individuals dwarfed by the complex apparatus surrounding them, which they must employ if they are to survive.[4]

The concept of autonomous technology depicts technology as a force that transcends history, which is just out there, waiting to be discovered by technological innovators. This concept has been essential to defining the ahistorical framework in which technology has been understood. One could argue, in fact, that discussions about technology have been ahistorical throughout history. For instance, utopian visions of the Internet have a tendency to collapse the history of technology into a set of events: beginning with the "invention of fire" proclaimed by John Perry Barlow and others, moving onward to the invention of the printing press, and then skipping over a few centuries to the development of the Internet, understood almost as a predetermined inevitability. Yet, the history of the Internet is infinitely more complex and specific to its time. It emerged from a complex mix of Cold War arms race politics, a post-1960s antiestablishment computer culture, and an increased emphasis on speed and information, which had developed from the nineteenth-century telegraph and the dissemination of television in the postwar era. The ideology of the Internet is the product of a the post-1960s appropriation of resistant cultures into various scientific and technological communities, and a particular Cold War funding relationship between universities and the military; importantly, those ideologies determined not only its structure but many of its uses. As Manuel Castells has written, Internet culture is based in part on a techno-meritocratic culture, which derives its ethic from hacker culture, and a virtual communitarian culture, which finds its roots in 1960s counterculture.[5]

History matters in very important ways to a clearer understanding of technological change. As Asa Briggs notes in this volume, it is only by situating the emergence of new technologies within the history of all technologies when they were new that we can begin to understand them. The ahistorical aspect of technological visions means that many of them borrow from the history of anxieties about life in modern society, yet present these fears as if they are a new and unique threat. Concerns about the impact of the Internet on users, for instance, echo those that greeted the telegraph, telephone, and television. When, for instance, the 1996 Communications Decency Act, an act that was in clear violation of the First Amendment, passed in the U.S. Congress because of political hysteria about pornography on the Internet, it was an echo of congressional hearings in the 1950s about television causing juvenile delinquency. Yet, presented without this historical context, these concerns are magnified within the present, prompting not only a kind of media frenzy, but specific kinds of restrictive and often misguided policy making. Many of the essays in this book situate contemporary discussions of new technology within the history of such discourses, a strategy that inevitably exposes the hyperbole of contemporary technological visions. As these essays suggest, situating discourses of technology within history diminishes in many ways the affective hold of potential stories that can be told about them—this historical framing is a fundamental strategy in examining the limitations of technology and its social impact.

The ahistorical visions of new technologies are directly related to the fact that in the popular imagination, technology is often synonymous with the future. Yet, understanding the future is a matter of prediction, a deeply imprecise activity. History instructs us that there are serious limitations to our ability to predict the effects or uses of new communication technologies, yet tremendous resources are expended on attempts to forecast the future of technology and its potential impact. Policy makers and businesspeople have always had large stakes in predicting the impact of various technologies. As the rate of technological change accelerates, informed discussion about the impact of new technologies does not take place as they are developed but when they are already in use. Whereas technologies such as the telephone and television took years to saturate their markets, new media can accomplish the same task in a matter of months. All of this places an increased premium on prediction. Yet, the landscape of the history of technology is littered with failed predictions, some disturbing, others ironic, many laughable. Often the least visionary comments are made by innovators or inventors of the technology itself (one is reminded of Bill Gates's emphatic insistence that "640K of memory ought to be enough for anyone" or IBM founder Tom Watson's prediction that "someday computers may weigh less than 2 tons").[6]

Prediction is thus an impulse and a dilemma as well as an economic strategy. Moore's Law, computer executive Gordon Moore's now famous 1965 prediction that processor speed would double every eighteen months, has turned out to be true, at least so far, but as Barlow notes, this may be because the computer industry now depends on it being so. Technologies are often used in ways that were unintended by their makers, and are driven by consumer demand, a phenomenon that decades of market research has done very little to decipher. Yet, it is extremely difficult to see in advance the priority that a new technology will acquire within a given society. As David Nye notes in his essay, the telegraph, telephone, phonograph, and personal computer were all thought to be mere curiosities rather than the influential inventions that they became. Many of the essays in this book seek to better understand these predictions in terms of their persistence and insistence in contemporary culture—the predictions of new technologies tell us more about the desires of a particular age than the potentials of the technologies themselves.

These desires are revealed, of course, through the language that is used to talk about new technologies and the images used to represent technology in contemporary media and popular culture. This rhetoric is not simply a means to characterize new technology, rather it serves both to define new technologies and to construct them. Metaphors about computers and the Internet are constitutive; they determine how these technologies are used, how they are understood and imagined, and the impact they have on contemporary society. Similarly, representations of technologies in science fiction not only reflect contemporary concerns about technology, but fuel the visions of technological invention. In putting into play potential images of that future, as Vivian Sobchack writes in this volume, science fiction literature and film create the potentials for particular kinds of technological visions to be pursued or realized.

Yet, the dilemma remains. For how do we talk about and represent contemporary technologies except through metaphors and representations that defined technologies of the past? Transportation is a primary source of technological rhetoric, one that, as we noted earlier, carried religious import. Indeed, Briggs writes that transportation is so integrated into our language that it forms a kind of master metaphor. In his essay, Peter Lyman discusses the implications of the metaphor of the information superhighway, a metaphor that follows the long tradition of transportation as a symbol for technological developments. The railroad was the source of emerging narratives of cultural and social transformation in the nineteenth century, functioning as an icon for the entry of modern society into the world of technology. As Langdon Winner writes in his essay, flying predated the computer as a source of utopian and highly overdetermined narratives of social harmony and individual transformation. The turn-of-the-century vision of the "aerial man" who could fly anywhere in a private plane promised a new enlightened consciousness through the experience of flight. In the 1960s, as Barlow states, transportation was central to visions of the future, which included the prediction of driving at 240 miles per hour in the year 2000. At the time, according to Barlow, moving bodies around seemed much more important than telecommunications. It remains the case, however, that metaphors such as transportation metaphors reveal in many ways the similar inequities of new technologies that replicate those of modern transportation technologies. Richard Chabrán and Romelia Salinas write in their essay that the information superhighway, like traditional highways, drives around certain neighborhoods, circumventing the barrio. Yet, what does it mean for us to really engage with this transportation metaphor? Where is it that we are driving to and what is the meaning of this traffic? Metaphors of transportation imply that new modes of transportation will provide transcendence and that they will lift people out of their worlds and their selves, and take them to new spiritual heights—they are inevitably religious in their implications. The transportation metaphor is finally about the idea that we have a destination, that we are going somewhere, that movement has meaning—that, indeed, is its attraction.

The essays in this book argue that the rhetoric defining technology, and the representations of it, are key to how it is integrated into social lives. Thus, to examine technology rhetorically is a central aspect of understanding its impact in ways that cannot be simply measured. Metaphors such as the information superhighway provide compelling, if not seductive ways to think about technology, yet they also serve to screen out other possible ways of envisioning technological meaning. These visions of technology are thus central obstacles to addressing, as Turkle writes, "our disillusionment with the myths of progress," and to understanding and implementing social change.

As engagements with the disabling aspects of technological discourse, these essays demand that we think about new ways of considering technology's social role, impact, and integration into our lives. They ask us to look beyond, in Turkle's words, the "spin" of technological discourse. This indicates in many ways that we remain stuck, as Turkle notes, in a kind of adolescent pose in relation to technology, embracing the same visions, unable to consider what they indicate about society rather than about technology itself. Contemporary debates demonstrate our childlike relationship to technology, the ways in which we continue to play out our oedipal narratives of technology in an ongoing cycle, caught, it seems, in developmental stages of the Freudian kind. Technology is consistently posed as that which will alleviate our sense of lack and fulfill our needs. Cultural responses to new technologies are thus shaped by both a sense of lack and loss and a hopeful investment in the possibility of resolving that lack and loss in the future.

This book thus aims to intervene in contemporary discourses of new technology, in order to address precisely what that discourse is lacking— historical context, an attention to the effects of rhetoric and metaphor, a realistic assessment of how technologies integrate into contemporary societies and affect the lives of individuals, a complex sense of the practices that individuals use to make meaning with new technologies. The essays in this book engage these issues from a variety of perspectives, and can be read or grouped in a number of ways: those that address technology within a history (Winner, Nye, Sturken, Briggs, Spigel, Sconce, Banet-Weiser, Grossman); those that critique technological rhetoric (Turkle, Lyman, Barlow, Grossman, Thomas, Marvin); those that address issues of technology and community (Gross, Marvin, Hafner, Chabrán and Salinas, Gibbs et al.); and those that are concerned with prediction (Nye, Barlow, Grossman). These concerns overlap in many of these essays, and the essays employ a range of approaches to address them. In what follows, we outline each essay individually:

Sherry Turkle's essay, " 'Spinning' Technology," examines how contemporary rhetoric about the computer and the Internet forms a kind of "spin" that renders complex narratives deceptively simple. For Turkle, the computer is too often thought of as a singular entity, "The Computer" with a capital C, which allows it to be awarded intentionality. In addition, Turkle argues, the Internet allows us to reflect upon contemporary anxieties about human relations and the modernist project. The distinction between understanding that a technology *facilitates* particular kinds of behavior (both positive and negative), rather than *causing* it, is crucial to Turkle's argument. Thus, she writes, it makes more sense to think of the Internet as analogous to speech—it facilitates particular kinds of interaction, some banal, some toxic, some occasionally "life-transforming." The spin about technology hides many contemporary anxieties: our fears that technology is out of control, our concerns about the idea that machines have souls and that the mind is being mechanized. At the same time, it deflects the genuine confusions we feel about the lack of distinction between the real and the simulated, and what kind of "relationship" it is appropriate to have with a machine. Importantly, the spin about technology not only defines its use, but prevents other ways of thinking about technology from being explored.

Turkle's analysis reveals the level of disavowal inherent in technological spin. Likewise, in his essay, "Sow's Ears from Silk Purses," Langdon Winner traces the history of utopian proclamations of technology and what they deny. He examines a commonplace in American public discourse, the announcement of the arrival of new, visionary technologies that promise the rise of a utopian social order. For instance, in the early twentieth century, it was predicted that the airplane would create a new period of human relations, because it would foster the sense that human beings share one sky. Private planes were imagined as the future means by which ordinary people would travel for work and recreation. Winner argues that this overly optimistic, and almost always incorrect, hyperbole (which brands any critical discussion as Luddism) has an effect on how any technology is actually adopted and finds its way into everyday life. Technological optimism is not simply an amusing social flaw, but rather a destructive force that prevents us from addressing crucial questions about how technologies will affect society, democracy, and the environment.

The power awarded technology to transform society can also be seen in its constant association throughout history with spiritual phenomena and the concept of presence. In his essay, "Mediums and Media," Jeffrey Scone argues that electronic technology, beginning with the telegraph, has generated a set of myths about spiritual presence, ranging from ghosts communicating via the ether to the concept of electronic presence in cyberspace. Sconce examines the relationship of the spiritualist movement of the nineteenth century to the emerging electronic technologies of the time, and its accompanying "utopian technophilia." The telegraph, in its seeming ability to separate consciousness from the body, produced a powerful set of spiritualist stories, of spirits speaking through the wires and connecting to, in particular, female mediums. Nineteenth-century concepts of telepresence and an "electronic elsewhere" have been transposed into contemporary concepts of cyberspace as transcendental and transformative. Situating this contemporary rhetoric in relation to previous urges to imagine "electronic presence," Sconce demonstrates the historical continuity of an investment in the powerful concept of presence.

In examining both the overlap and the distinction between modern and postmodern technologies, Marita Sturken argues in her essay, "Mobilities of Time and Space," that our particular moment in time is defined by a tension between modernity and postmodernity. The railroad and the telegraph, as technologies that aided in a compression of space and time in the experience of modernity, can be seen in a continuum with technologies such as the automobile, the freeway, and the Internet that are associated with postmodernism. Thus, many of the concepts of modernity, such as the sense that time is speeded up and that space is collapsed through technology, have been reiterated in postmodernism. For instance, notions of space changed in modernity as technologies enabled people to travel longer distances faster; this is transposed into postmodern nonplaces, such as freeways, airports, and ATM machines, which have proliferated in the past few decades. Similarly, mobile privatization, in which people use devices, such as automobiles, Walkmans, and cell phones, to create private spaces that are also mobile, demonstrates a contemporary emphasis on mobility and connectivity that is continuous with the experience of modernity. Yet, Sturken argues, there are important distinctions between certain concepts of modernism and postmodernism. In particular, the concepts of the body had shifted dramatically from the modern body to the postmodern body as a malleable, digital entity, which can be morphed into new forms and genetically mapped. This has consequences for the way that contemporary science and medicine is practiced and researched.

Historical contextualization can thus change everything about how technologies are viewed. In his contribution to this volume, Asa Briggs discusses the role a historian might play in coming to better understand the ways in which people adopt, accept, and think about new technology. A historian of the British Broadcast Corporation (BBC), Briggs contrasts the history of broadcasting, itself a central shift in the development of communication technologies, with the current belief in the Internet's transformative potential. He situates the contemporary engagement with technology's impact in relation to several older technologies, in particular the railroad, whose importance in helping to usher in the modern age is often overlooked, and the telephone. In assessing the emergence of specific technologies, Briggs argues, it is essential to foreground economics (market-driven and government- and military-based) and politics. The project of history, he argues, is crucial not only to an understanding of technological change, but to the human project itself.

Among the discourses of technology that have long histories, that of mobility has been prominent. Lynn Spigel's essay analyzes the rise of a mobile culture in the 1960s through the marketing of the portable television. The portable TV was sold as a means to take television out of doors, to new places, thus envisioning the viewer within the dual frameworks of the home theater and the mobile home. Spigel demonstrates how television has always been imagined as a medium for movement, through Raymond

Williams's concepts of TV "flow" and the "mobile privatization" by which the television set linked the private family suburban home to the modern city. As Spigel makes clear, these concepts of mobility, which carry with them traditional and highly gendered concepts of public and private, are also central to discourses of the Internet and new media. Spigel critiques contemporary theories, in particular those of Jean Baudrillard, that have declared cyberculture as a kind of liberation from traditional notions of public and private. Rather, the discourse of new technologies replicates gender divisions and reinscribes the divisions of male and female, work and leisure, and public and private, as well as racial divisions along the lines of housing and access. It is precisely the utopian rhetoric of new technology, historically and in the present, Spigel argues, that prevents us from asking larger questions about social change.

The rhetoric of technology is paralleled, of course, by its depiction in contemporary popular culture. The dominant images of technology are visions of science fiction, which, as we have noted, both reflect contemporary anxieties about technology and are constitutive elements in envisioning its future. In "Science Fiction Film and the Technological Imagination," Vivian Sobchack explores how it is that we come to understand the meaning, the "essence," of technology through our experiences with science fiction film. She focuses on the importance of special effects to the affective experience of science fiction, defining several major themes in the history of science fiction films: the equation of high technology with social progress as well as with rationalism and scientific/corporate objectives rather than human emotion; the association of high technology with elitism; and an opposition between technological autonomy and human agency. Sobchack argues that the history of science fiction film has evolved through these parallel themes of effects (special) in relation to affect (feeling), as the genre has changed over time, from representing technology as a wondrous novelty, to a broader "narrative dissatisfaction with technology."

Technology has long been the source of such visions about the future, and predictions about technologies and how they will change the future form some of the primary sources of utopian visions of technology. In his essay, "Technological Prediction," David Nye traces out the history of prediction through the three categories of prediction, forecasting, and projection. Prediction, on which so much of the marketplace rides, is difficult, Nye argues, precisely because the ways that new technologies, from the radio and the gramophone to Viagra and the Internet, will be used are often unforeseen. In addition, a technology's symbolic meanings rather than functional needs may govern its uses. For instance, electrical companies of the nineteenth century did not predict the way that electric light would play a symbolic role in American society, and so were unprepared for such consumption as electrical billboards and Christmas tree lights. Nye argues that the utopian narratives of predictions can be divided into three groupings: natural, that technologies are "natural outgrowths of society"; ameliorative, that new machines will improve everyday life; and transformative, that new technologies will reshape social reality. Dystopian narratives are hegemonic, in the belief that a powerful minority will use them to gain control over others; apocalyptic, with new technologies as "agents of doom"; and satiric, with new devices leading to the reverse of expectations. Nye argues that technological predictions are narratives about the future and our desires for the future, rather than accurate reflections of technological capabilities.

Yet, contemporary cyberdiscourse relies a great deal on prediction. For instance, John Perry Barlow, who is a primary advocate of the uniqueness of the digital age, sets out to define a rhetoric of technology in his essay, "The Future of Prediction." In doing so, he goes about the business of "predicting the present." Drawing from lessons of recent history, Barlow puts forth the thesis that it is the rhetoric of predicting the future that brings it into being, that we "create the future we believe we deserve." Barlow argues, for instance, that Gordon Moore's now famous prediction, Moore's Law, that computer processor speed would double every eighteen months, has succeeded and continues to succeed as a prediction because "the entire computer industry and a good deal of the world economy depend on it continuing to hold." Thus, he states that the future can be invented through setting into motion a vision of what it should and will be. Rather than dismissing the rhetoric of new technology as something to be dismantled, Barlow chooses to embrace it as a means of shaping its future.

Wendy Grossman takes on the Internet predictions made by Barlow and other cyberati, such as Nicholas Negroponte, in her essay, "Penguins, Predictions, and Technological Optimism." A professional "skeptic," Grossman critiques the hyperbole that claims, for instance, that the Internet is equivalent to the discovery of fire. She demonstrates how predictions about the Internet parallel predictions made in the past about other new technologies, such as the belief that the telegraph would, in similar fashion, bring world peace. Grossman reminds us that in the 1950s people thought that domestic robots were the technology of the future and that around 1950, the chairman of IBM thought there would be a world market for only a dozen computers, indeed, that the history of technology is one of failed predictions. Yet, she also makes a compelling argument for the ways in which the Internet does offer new forms of interaction and changing allegiance in terms of citizenship and community. In making her own predictions, Grossman argues that the Internet will remain unimportant for much of the world's population, and that it will be a passive medium for most users—indeed, that its importance will ultimately seem quite limited when eventually seen in the context of a broader history—yet that the radical nature of Usenet will be able to retain public spaces on the Internet.

The rhetoric debated by figures such as Barlow and Grossman has a direct impact not only on how we define new technologies, but also on government policy, according to Peter Lyman, who takes up the issue of metaphors as political rhetoric in his essay. Lyman examines three central metaphors that have influenced political discourse and regulation of the Internet: the information superhighway, the virtual community, and the digital library. As a transportation metaphor, the concept of the information superhighway has the effect of defining the government's role as one of building infrastructure and leaving innovation to the private sector. This has meant that information is understood in terms of commodification, rather than within the framework of a public good. Lyman argues that the metaphor of the virtual community reframes Internet activity within an economy of gift exchange as a collaborative activity, enabling the idea of cooperative institutions in cyberspace rather than the "market vision of the information superhighway." Indeed, the incorporation of concepts of community and gift exchange into Internet culture has had the effect of challenging traditional concepts of the author and intellectual property rights. Lyman's final metaphor, the digital library, suggests that the library should be the model for the Internet as a public domain. Lyman argues that the public library has throughout history served to manage the boundary between markets and communities. Yet, it also reveals the tensions between information management and the libertarian values of the Internet. Lyman's discussion demonstrates the richness with which metaphors create complex associations between the past and the present, and how these metaphors reveal the lag that exists between our understanding of changing technological contexts and the rapidity with which technologies are currently developing.

The importance of metaphor is further examined in Douglas Thomas's analysis of hackers and computer viruses. He sets forth the premise that the predominance of metaphors used to characterize hackers and malicious computer programs such as "viruses" is grounded in a fundamental fear that technology will erase both nature and the body. Hackers have been constituted in the media through a rhetoric of games, addiction, and the hunt, with a particular emphasis, as Thomas describes in the case of Kevin Mitnick, on the hacker's body as out of control. Thomas argues that these metaphors not only frame hackers within the terms of criminality and surveillance, they also encourage everyday users of computers to submit themselves to increasingly complicated systems of social control and regulation. In a similar fashion, the use of the language of biology to describe computer programs as worms and viruses awards each the qualities of agency, cunning, even life. The rhetoric of computer technology thus serves to affirm systems of social control as computer technology in turn operates as a screen onto which anxieties about the body are displaced.

The erasure of the body has of course been central to contemporary discourses of new technology. In her essay, "Peaceable Kingdoms and New Information Technologies," Carolyn Marvin situates the body as the object through which the tensions between globalization and the nation-state can be understood. She argues against the contention that the rise of the Internet will lead to a dissolving of boundaries and borders that will threaten the survival of the nation-state. Tracing the relationship of the nation-state to communication technologies, and examining the concept of the nation as an imagined community, Marvin argues that the essential element of nation-state is not borders, but bodies. Textual communities can be distinguished from bodily communities, she writes, and it is the sacrifice of bodies that ultimately promises loyalty to the nation-state. In understanding communal and national ties, Marvin writes, we must examine their effects upon the bodies of the citizenry, rather than the textual transformations of new technologies. Hence, it is only in relation to bodies, rather than texts, that the so-called revolution of global computing may begin to transform the nation as we know it.

Analyses of community have often looked not only at the concept of the nation but also at the notion of home in uncritical ways, assuming that the relationship to home is a kind of haven for all. In "Somewhere There's a Place for Us," Larry Gross examines the ways that the Internet has functioned as an outlet for lesbian and gay teenagers for whom home is often a contested and difficult place where they cannot discuss their sexuality. Gross argues against the popular image of the Internet as a corrupting influence on youth with its access to pornography and pedophiles. It is, rather, a place where sexual minorities, especially those who are geographically isolated, can build virtual communities that are difficult or impossible for them to develop where they live. Gross traces the role that the various media have played in the formation of gay identity, as well as the ways in which mainstream culture has worked to filter or block access to gay and lesbian material. The use of the Internet to build community is always highly contested, he argues, and is the focus of legal and political battles to restrict Internet content, which has had a direct effect on gay and lesbian sites. Yet, because of the First Amendment, the Internet continues to function as a lifesaving resource for many isolated gay teenagers.

Teenagers and children have long been the source of the most acute anxieties about new technologies. In her essay "Surfin' the Net," Sarah Banet-Weiser argues that children have historically been at the center of debates over sexuality and consumerism, which have found renewed currency in the context of communication technologies. Cultural notions about the innocence of children are primary factors in attempts to restrict activity on the Internet, which in turn serve to infantalize all uses of the Internet. Banet-Weiser contends that the focus on control over children using the Internet replicates earlier debates about children and television, which was blamed in the 1950s for juvenile delinquency. Primary in these concerns about children and technology is the fear that new technologies separate parents and children, that they provide sources of information for children outside of the family and thus make parental authority obsolescent. These fears, of course, help to fuel media hype and industries in filtering software. Banet-Weiser argues that it is important to reframe contemporary discussions about the Internet and children in a way that acknowledges how this technology can be empowering for children, and provide them with a sense of community not only about them but "defined and determined *by* them."

Throughout debates on community and technology, a recurring question has been "what defines a virtual community?" Katie Hafner's essay "When the Virtual Isn't Enough," reflects on the question of what constitutes a virtual rather than a "real-life" community. Hafner contrasts her well-known case study of the WELL—the now famous Bay Area-based online community that has been used by cyberati, such as Howard Rheingold,[7] as an example of the utopian potentials of virtual communities—with the small town in western Massachusetts where her father lived before he died tragically in an airplane crash. In reflecting on cases of life and death, and the experience of mourning both online and in person, Hafner is able to examine the similarities that make the online world appear real, as well as to trace out the differences—differences of proximity, spontaneity, and chance—

that allow her to conclude that the online world will never be able to replicate the experience of community in a real-life, bodily context.

Concepts of community are also directly related to notions of place and geography. Richard Chabrán and Romelia Salinas's essay is a response to contemporary discourses about the Internet that characterize it as a place where identities can be left behind or reconstructed anew. Chabrán and Salinas focus on the notion of place in both global and local spaces, analyzing the ways that digital technology has reconfigured social space. They look at how technological discourses shift when considered in the context of racial and ethnic identity and suggest ways of thinking about the global economy, the information superhighway, and the digital divide in relation to the Chicano and Latino populations within the United States. Chabrán and Salinas demonstrate how the Internet has been used by Latinos as a virtual place in which identity is negotiated, a space where ethnic identity is not erased but affirmed. Through their discussion of community digital archives, online discussion groups, community labs, and artistic engagements with the Web, Chabrán and Salinas give a picture of the complex array of activities that define an emergent Latino community on the Internet. Despite ongoing issues of the digital divide and barriers to access, Latinos have been able to use virtual space as a means to build community, to locate shared spaces, and to counter the erasure of racial and ethnic identities perpetrated by technological discourses.

Contemporary discourses of technological community have relied on the concept of globalization to define the possibility of a new world community connected via communications technologies. In the book's final essay, "The Globalization of Everyday Life," by Jennifer Gibbs et al., a team of researchers at the University of Southern California's Metamorphosis Project evaluates the ways in which the Internet and globalization are affecting people's everyday lives. This project, which aims to evaluate empirically many of the assertions of discourses about globalization and technological change, draws on research in an array of diverse neighborhoods in Los Angeles. The project examines how Angelenos of diverse ethnic origins view the concept of globalization within the framework of utopian and dystopian visions. The study reveals, among other things, the complex networks of connectivity that exist in diasporic and new immigrant communities as well as the ways that people use communication technologies to support these connections. Thus, these communities use communication technologies to support existing social and familial connections across global contexts, rather than constructing new communities online or participating in virtual communities. These researchers thus conclude that while new technologies are making the world increasingly interconnected, and movements of people are bringing diverse peoples together geographically, this has not fostered increased communication between ethnic groups. The Internet does not have a globalizing effect on every people's communication patterns, rather, its meaning is being tailored by everyday people to give it a place in their lives.

In all of these essays, a focus on the visions of technology allows us to see the ways that technology looms over understanding of social change and everyday life. It is the constant perceived presence of technology, in particular communication technologies, that gives technological discourses such tremendous power. It is our goal in this book to begin to chip away at these visions and discourses, to see through their rhetoric, and to understand how they create a particular set of visions of the world and its future. It is through such critical work that we can begin, slowly, to participate in new ways of understanding the role of new technologies in changing social contexts, in clarifying the important yet ultimately limited ways that technology affects our lives. By unpacking the "new" we can hopefully begin to understand the limitations of new technologies and the important aspects of social change that an overinvestment in new technologies serves to mask and screen out.

NOTES

1. James W. Carey, *Communication as Culture: Essay on Media and Society* (Boston: Unwin Hyman, 1989), 15–17.

2. James W. Carey with John J. Quirk, "The Mythos of the Electronic Revolution," in Carey, *Communication as Culture*, 113–41.

3. David Morley, *Home Territories: Media, Mobility and Identity* (New York: Routledge, 2000), 190.

4. Langdon Winner, *Autonomous Technology: Technics-out-of-Control as a Theme in Political Thought* (Cambridge, Mass.: MIT Press, 1977), 17.

5. See Manuel Castells, "The Culture of the Internet," in *The Internet Galaxy: Reflections of the Internet, Business, and Society* (New York: Oxford University Press, 2001), 36–63.

6. See, for example, Ray Kurzweil's *The Age of Spiritual Machines: When Computers Exceed Human Intelligence* (New York: Dimension, 2000).

7. Howard Rheingold, *The Virtual Community: Homesteading on the Electronic Frontier* (New York: HarperPerennial, 1993).

SHERRY TURKLE

1   "Spinning" Technology

*What We Are Not Thinking about
When We Are Thinking about Computers*

THE STRUCTURE OF SPIN

IN THE decades since computers first entered everyday life, authors from the academy and popular media have told many stories about their social impact. Perhaps because academics and journalists are subject to similar market forces, their narratives have shared a tendency to hyperbole. In scholarly circles, studies about technology that report strong effects are more likely to get published; in the popular press, technology stories need to be newsworthy. There is pressure to make complex technologies with complex effects into good or bad news.

Consequently, by the 1990s, writing about computers was dominated by critics and utopians. Titles such as *The Road Ahead, What Will Be,* and *Being Digital* conjured images of untold riches, while computer critics, writing about the same technologies, invoked imminent threat with titles that suggested addiction and soul death: *Trapped in the Net, Caught in the Net, Failure to Connect,* and *Silicon Snake Oil.*[1] Even the postmillennial bursting of the Internet bubble did not so much temper discourse as spawn a new round of apocalyptic pronouncements and comeback narratives. Most recently, the trend toward hype that began with critics and utopians has broadened. It has become a cultural commonplace to use oversimplification about technology as the functional equivalent of political spin—the practice of spinning turns complexity into simple narratives, whether in the realm of political or technological commentary. Contradictory effects are edited out for the news cycle.

The editing that spin requires is facilitated by the use of a simple rhetorical device. This is to portray the object at hand as a monolithic thing, in this case, "The Computer" with a capital C. (In the case of "The Internet," conventionalized spelling has always and quite conveniently endowed it with a capital *I.*) The fact that computers are everywhere, regulating daily rhythms and routines—yet often hidden to view (in the toaster, the bank machine, the alarm clock, the car)—seems to encourage unitary depiction. However, this rhetorical move comes at a cost. The fictive unity of "The Computer" makes it easier to speak of technology as an intentional agent and encourages us to acquiesce in sweeping generalizations about the effects or impact of computer technology on society.

The legal theorist James Boyle, writing about cyberspace and the law, humorously characterized the limitations of seeing the Internet as a causal agent:

> Some time ago, for my sins, I got into some journalists' Rolodexes as a law professor who knew something about the Net. Now, whenever a web-designing cult commits collective suicide, a child is accosted by a pervert in a chat room, or a murderer persuades his victim to turn up by sending an email message, I get a flood of calls looking for the "Internet angle." The trouble is that there rarely is an Internet angle. The murderers, sexual predators and crackpot religions are largely independent of the communications technology they happened to use. One reporter was particularly persistent in trying to get me to cough up an appropriate sound bite. Searching for an analogy, I asked her whether, if I called her up and asked her out on a blind date and murdered her, she would think it was a "telephone-related murder"? She rang off shortly thereafter, probably more convinced of my emotional instability than by my argument.[2]

As a psychologist, I myself get fewer calls about Internet-induced murder than about Internet-induced depression and addiction. But I have had many experiences that give me common cause with Boyle's annoyance. Spinning technology demands the Internet angle in the service of a clean story line. My closest analogy to Boyle's experience with the persistent reporter (one which I unfortunately did not handle with his wit and flair) came in the course of working on a television documentary about the effects of the Internet on family life. One of the case studies in the program was of a mother of three who left her family for a man she met online. I was interviewed at length about the case. During the interview, I explained that the Internet is a powerful medium through which people are sometimes able to work on their personal lives. I felt that what was most central in this story was the troubled relationship of this woman to her family. She described herself as lonely, unhappy, and unable to cope with family issues. When she discovered the Internet, she began to correspond with sympathetic online voices, real people who offered her the companionship she so desperately desired. Eventually, she left home in order to live with one of those real people, a man she claims makes her happy. The Internet made this man known to her. It did not motivate her to want him. In the final editing of the television documentary, my remarks were limited to comments regarding the "compelling" nature of the Internet. My credentials as an Internet expert were used to support the thesis that this woman suffered an addiction to the Internet stronger than that caused by tobacco, alcohol, or heroin.

The language of Internet addiction limits our perspective, deters our asking crucial questions about why some people are able to use online experiences to work through problems and move toward constructive solutions whereas others use online experiences to act out in unconstructive ways. In acting out we stage our old conflicts in new settings; we reenact our pasts in fruitless repetitions. In contrast, working through usually involves a moratorium on action and a deepening of life reflection. Internet relationships provide rich spaces for both acting out and working though. To understand the dynamics of online experience we need to know about people's specific emotional challenges and resources. And we need to know more about specific opportunities and difficulties provided by particular Internet social settings.[3] These questions demand highly detailed answers; online experiences are not generic nor are what people bring to them. When we treat computer-mediated conversation as analogous to heroin (a substance that will always disempower and ultimately destroy its users), such specific psychological and social questions are made to seem irrelevant. But these questions, about the differences among different kinds of Internet users and different kinds of Internet use, are exactly the ones that need close investigation.

In my own studies of Internet social experience, I have found that the people who make the most of their "lives on the screen" are those who approach online life in a spirit of self-reflection.[4] They look at what they are doing with their virtual selves and ask what these actions say about their desires, perhaps unmet, as well as their need for social connection, perhaps unfilled. They use what they learn about themselves in their online lives to improve the "rest of their lives." Neither domain (virtual nor physically embodied) is treated as exclusively real. If we stigmatize virtual media as addictive (and, like drugs, in need of strict control), we will not learn about how to more widely nurture self-reflection within them. A parent whose child is on heroin needs to get the child off the drug. A parent whose child spends a great deal of time on the Internet needs, first and foremost, to be curious about what he or she is doing there. Is the child forming online relationships that are serving developmental purposes? Is the child having specific online experiences that are likely to serve as stepping-stones for emotional or intellectual growth? Do the child's online activities point to things that might be missing in the rest of his or her life? *When contemplating a child at a networked computer, it is more constructive to think of the Internet as a Rorschach than as a narcotic.*

The debate about whether the Internet causes depression, which so preoccupied the media in the late 1990s, depended on a reification of the Internet, on treating it as though it were a single thing.[5] We were not well-served by the terms of the debate. The Internet is a mode of communication. It makes sense to analogize Internet speech to conversation. If we ask, "What is the psychological effect of conversation?" most of us would probably step away from the demand that there be a single correct response. We would answer that some conversations are toxic, others banal, others somewhat hurtful or helpful, and that once in a very long while, a conversation can be life-transforming. This would be true of face-to-face conversations and it would be true of telephone conversations. But it would seem absurd to group all of these different conversations together and conclude that "conversation use" is, on average, mildly depressing. Yet, the prevalent narrative of the "depressing Internet" does just that. This narrative has all the signs of spin, a simplified story that impedes our ability to understand the diverse and complicated ways that computational technology has entered our lives.

Computer technology is in its childhood, perhaps its adolescence. Unfortunately, we behave as though we are trapped in adolescence along with it, with an adolescent preference for absolutes, for seeing things in black and white. In the midst of our tales of love and hate, the computer is clearly being used as a projective screen for other concerns. Often, in our preoccupation with what the computer can do or what the computer is becoming lie unstated questions about what is happening to us, about what we are becoming as we forge increasingly intimate relationships with this machine.

BEHIND THE SPIN

What are we thinking about when we are thinking about computers? What are we trying to not think about when we are thinking about computers? What fears, what anxieties, stand behind the spin?

• *Behind the spin lie our concerns about technology going out of control and about the human costs of technological change.*

Whereas we are reassured by the notion that technology is "just a tool," we are frightened by the increasing complexity of our machines and by the possibility of their autonomy, the idea that they might be out of our control.[6] One cultural response is to create narratives about technology that help to rationalize how it became so powerful or why we feel so weak, for example, by investing stories about technology with a familiar mythic narrative. Earlier generations retold the story of the Industrial Revolution as the second "Fall of Man." These days the narrative of the Fall works its rhetorical power in stories of the "good" and "bad" computer.

In the original Genesis story, Adam and Eve gain knowledge by eating the apple. This delicious fruit has dangerous implications they cannot foresee from their position of ignorance and inexperience. Henceforth, they are expelled from Paradise and destined to lead lives that are, to steal a phrase, "nasty, brutish, and short." The story of the Fall of Man provides a narrative template for a view of our pretechnological universe as idyllic, pastoral, and less physically and mentally regimented than our current mode of life. Historian Lewis Mumford's classic essay on the introduction of clocks in the Benedictine monasteries is written in this genre. The monasteries "helped to give human enterprise the regular collective beat and rhythm of the machine; for the clock is not merely a means of keeping track of the hours, but of synchronizing the actions of men."[7] Mechanical time, according to Mumford, is alien to human life and its specific, natural regularities: "the beat of the pulse, the breathing of the lungs, these change from hour to hour with mood and action, and in the longer span of days, time is measured not by the calendar but by the events that occupy it."[8]

Similarly, when literary critic Sven Birkerts discusses computers and reading in *The Gutenberg Elegies,* he sees the Fall of Man in the history of information technology. For Birkerts, "since World War II we have stepped, collectively, out of an ancient and familiar solitude and into an enormous web of imponderable linkages."[9] And "we feel imprisoned in a momentum that is not of our own making."[10] Precomputer humankind had an elongated time, time that allowed the mind to wander in useful, productive, and unregimented ways, time to read, to ponder, and to think. These days, for Birkerts, with the knowledge *of* computers and the knowledge available *through* computers, we are socialized differently, regimented more, forced to think in nuggets and infobits. In sum, we do not read.

Writers such as Mumford and Birkerts draw attention to how technology has had more than its intended instrumental effects; it has also had subjective effects, often profound and usually unintended. Technology does things for us but also to us, to our ways of perceiving the world, to our relationships and sense of ourselves. Spinning technology through the Fall of Man narrative casts us as the ignorant architects of our own undoing. In this narrative, we make our artifacts but they in turn cast us out into worlds to which we are not suited. The narrative of the Fall reduces the dynamic relationship of people and technology to a story in which technology is the cruel, decisive actor. It was a God with ultimate power who expelled humans from the Garden of Eden. The new narratives of the Fall put technology into that position. They rationalize human passivity in the face of anxiety about technology. They give a sense of inevitability to people's feelings of impotence in the face of our creations.

• *Behind the spin lie competing views of modernist progress with its attendant inequalities of ownership and power.*

Faith in technology is a centerpiece of the modernist conception of progress. In the standard modernist narrative, technology propels us onward and upward. For those who subscribe to this story, computers have to be good (or rather, very, very good) or the modernist project might not be, and then, where would *we* be? Conversely, for those who want to challenge notions of progress (inevitably linked to powerful technologies), computers *have* to be bad because they are represented as the technological ultimate. In Marx's writing technology occupies a complex role: it is both an engine and a platform for the ruling class, a means of dividing people as well as making communism practicable. These days, many utopian and dystopian stories about computers carry the weight of concerns about who owns technology and who is victimized by it. From the position of the haves, technology empowers; from the position of the have-nots, technology imprisons.

In *Mindstorms: Children, Computers, and Powerful Ideas*, mathematician and educator Seymour Papert puts forth a technologically utopian vision for the haves: "In my vision, the child programs the computer and, in doing so, both acquires a sense of mastery over a piece of the most modern and powerful technology and establishes an intimate contact with some of the deepest ideas from science, from mathematics, and from the art of intellectual model building."[11] The language is potent, full of promise. The child gains mastery. The machine is powerful, but the child's contact is joyful and intimate. In contrast, Birkerts writes about our encounter with the machine in the language of the disenfranchised: "Our historically sudden transition into an electronic culture has thrust us into a place of unknowing."[12]

Papert's child is clearly not one of Birkerts's victims, those thrust into a place of unknowing. Papert's child, quite precisely, will reach a place of greater knowing. Papert assumes that his empowered child owns and *con-*

trols technology, while in Birkerts's world passive children and adults are acted upon by "linkages," by forces not of their own making. These versions of the computer future are not research hypotheses as much as political manifestos. Papert wants to mold a computer culture that will conform to his dreams. Birkerts yearns for a predigital world of greater transparency and human control. What keeps the language hot is that both sides are filling old bottles with new wine, recasting the debate on industrialization and its human toll as one about virtuality and its discontents.

• *Behind the spin lie our anxieties about the soul of the new machine and about the mechanization of mind.*

The Marxist tradition sees the costs of industrialization as going far beyond new divisions of power. For Marx, the technologies of the Industrial Revolution also brought a blurring of human and machine. He saw the machine coming to possess "skill and strength . . . with a soul of its own in the mechanical laws acting through it." At the same time that material forces were becoming endowed with life, human life was being "stultif[ied] into a material force."[13]

Marx's language captures an anxiety that stands behind many of our current anxieties about computers: the fear that computers are making people more machine-like while the machines gain "souls." As I have said, an unstated question lies behind our preoccupation about the future of computing. That question is not what computers will be like in the future, but what *we* will be like, what kind of people *we* are becoming. I sit on a park bench with a mother of a six-year-old girl who is playing a question-and-answer game with a computer-controlled robot. The child talks back to the machine when it chides her for a wrong answer or congratulates her for a right one. "My God," says the mother, "she treats that thing like a person. Do you suppose she thinks that people are machines?"

Conversations about computers that play chess, about robotics, about computers that might display judgment, creativity, or affect can lead to heated discussions about the limits of machines and the uniqueness of people. They can lead to such statements as "Simulated thinking might be thinking, but simulated love is never love." The underlying anxiety here lies not in whether machines will come to think like people, but whether people have always thought like machines. For some, the programmed computer suggests that there might be something illusory in our own sense of autonomy and self-determination. For others, it provides an occasion to reject this view and make explicit a commitment to an idea of the human as essentially "not computer." These disagreements are not about technology. They are about people. Mind and yet not mind, the computer is an evocative object that we use to take our own measure.

At different points in history, debates about human nature, about free will and determinism, have been played on different stages, in theology, in psychology, and in philosophy. In the twenty-first century, they will, in part, be played out in debates about machines that think. When we are thinking about computers, we are thinking about ourselves. The increasing complexity of today's computational objects makes us increasingly insecure about our own uniqueness, an anxiety that has made us vulnerable to spin.

WHAT SPIN DEFLECTS

Spin is distracting. Overheated debates about computer addiction and Internet depression keep us from confronting issues raised by contemporary technology that are resistant to the oversimplifications of spin.

• *Spin deflects our new confusions between the real and the simulated.*

Today's children grow up granting new capacities and privileges to the machine world on the basis of its animation. They endow computational objects with properties, such as having intentions and ideas, that were previously reserved for living beings. They devise a new category, "sort of alive," to describe computational creatures, thus blurring the boundary between artifact and flesh. Two stories about children's relationships with computational artifacts serve as illustrations.

The first story describes a moment on a vacation in Italy with my then seven-year-old daughter. On a boat ride in the postcard-blue Mediterranean, she saw a creature in the water, pointed to it excitedly, and said, "Look, Mommy, a jellyfish. It looks so realistic." I told this story to a Disney executive who responded to it by describing the reaction of the first visitors to Animal Kingdom, Disney's theme park in Orlando, which had the uniqueness of being populated by real, that is, biological animals. The first visitors to the park expressed disappointment that the animals were not realistic enough. They did not exhibit the lifelike behavior of the more active robotic animals at Walt Disney World, only a few miles away.

The second story is drawn from my ethnographic work studying children and play. I was at an afterschool center in the mid-1990s, observing a group of seven-year-olds playing with a set of plastic transformer toys

that could take the shape of armored tanks, robots, or people. The trans-
formers could also be put into intermediate states so that a robot arm could
protrude from a human form or a human leg from a mechanical tank. Two
of the children were playing with the toys in these intermediate states (that
is, in their intermediate states somewhere between being people, machines,
and robots). A third child insisted that this was not right. The toys, he said,
should not be placed in hybrid states. You should play them as all-tank
or all-people. He was getting upset because the other two children were
making a point of ignoring him. An eight-year-old girl comforted the upset
child. "It's okay to play them when they are in between. It's all the same
stuff," she said, "just yucky computer cy-dough-plasm."

When Piaget interviewed children in the 1920s and 1930s about which
objects were alive and which were not, he found that children honed their
definition of life by developing increasingly sophisticated notions about
motion, the world of *physics*. In contrast, when I began to study the nascent
computer culture in the early 1980s, children argued about whether a computer was alive through discussions about its *psychology*.[14] Did the computer know things on its own or did it have to be programmed? Did it have
intentions, consciousness, and feelings? Did it cheat? Did it know it was
cheating? Faced with intelligent machines, children took a New World of
objects and imposed a New World Order.

In the course of the 1990s, that order was strained to the breaking point.
Today, children will talk about computers as "just machines" but describe
them as sentient and intentional. The very notion of a machine has been
reconfigured to include an object with a psychology. Faced with the objects of the culture of simulation, children still try to impose order, but they
do so in the manner of theoretical bricoleurs or tinkerers, making do with
whatever materials are at hand, making do with whatever theory can fit a
prevailing circumstance. Different children comfortably hold different theories, and individual children are able to cycle through different theories at
a rapid pace.

My current collection of comments made by children about computational objects suggests a range of theories on the nature of life. When they
play with programmable toy robots constructed of Lego bricks, children's
classifications include: the robots are in control but not alive; would be alive
if they had bodies; are alive because they have bodies; would be alive if
they had feelings; are alive the way insects are alive but not the way people
are alive. When confronted with Sim creatures (screen objects in a popular

game in which the player builds a simulated city), children come forth with a different set of theories: the Sim creatures are not alive because they are just in the computer; could be alive if they got out of the computer; are alive until you turn off the computer and then they're dead; are not alive because nothing in the computer is real; are alive but not real; are not alive but almost-alive; would be alive if they spoke; are not alive because they don't have bodies; are alive because they can have babies; would be alive if they could get out of the computer and onto America Online. What is most notable is the striking heterogeneity of theory, the fluidity of categories.

The new fluidity marks a psychological, cultural, and moral shift that is resonant with new scientific realities. We are at a crossroads at which progress in nanotechnology, genetic engineering, artificial life, and robotics is bringing us closer to technologies of self-replication and natural selection.[15] As they reach adulthood, today's children are not going to approach the issues raised by these technologies with a sensibility that depends on there being one answer that must serve all purposes. They are getting used to cycling through the cy-dough-plasm to far more fluid ways of thinking about life.

• *Spin deflects thinking about what kinds of relationships it is appropriate to have with a machine.*

In the late 1990s, Rodney Brooks, the director of the MIT Artificial Intelligence Lab, developed "Bit," a robot baby. Bit, marketed in 2000 as Hasbro's "My Real Baby," makes baby sounds and has baby facial expressions, shaped by mechanical musculature under its artificial skin. Most significant, this computationally complex doll has baby "states of mind." Bounce the doll when it is happy, and it gets happier. Bounce it when it is grumpy and it gets grumpier. At the MIT Media Lab, Rosalind Picard's research group develops "affective computers," machines that are programmed to assess their users' emotional states and respond with "emotional states" of their own. The Sony Corporation has developed a pet robot dog, AIBO; Matsushita has introduced a robot cat, Tama, designed as a health companion for the elderly. Interactive dolls, affective machines, and robot pets are *relational artifacts*. They are designed to evoke a sense of connection on the part of their human owners. These owners are not simply users, they are conceived of as companions.

During the over two decades in which I have explored people's relationships with computers, and, indeed, throughout the first part of this essay, I have used the metaphor of computer as Rorschach. In this paradigm, the technology serves as a screen that enables people to project their thoughts and feelings, their very different cognitive styles. With relational artifacts, the Rorschach model of a computer/human relationship breaks down significantly. The computational object no longer presents itself as affectively neutral. People are learning that to relate successfully to a computer one has to assess the machine's emotional state. The important questions no longer relate to how the machine works in terms of any underlying mechanical process. Rather, getting along with the technology means taking the computer at interface value, much as one would another person. Perhaps most important, today's children learn very early that some artifacts demand *emotional* nurturance.

Among the first of these relational artifacts to be deployed in the marketplace were virtual pets (such as Tamagotchis) and digital dolls (such as Furbies). What makes them different from earlier computational toys and games is that they have a "life cycle," and therefore demand children's care and nurturance. For example, in order to grow and be healthy, Tamagotchis (little screen creatures) need to be fed, cleaned, and amused. Furbies (cuddly owl-like creatures) simulate learning and loving. Furbies arrive in the child's life speaking "Furbish." They "learn" to speak English. They play hide and seek, communicate with each other, join together in song, and say, "I love you." Furbies add the dimensions of human-like conversation and tender companionship to the mix of what children can anticipate from computational objects. In my research on children and Furbies, I have found that when children play with these new objects they want to know what their state is—not for the sake of getting something right, but rather to make the Furbies happy. Children want to understand Furby language, not to win in a game *over* a Furby, but to have a feeling of mutual recognition. Children are concerned less with how Tamagotchis and Furbies work, or what they really know, and more with the toys' health and well-being. In sum, a new generation of objects pushes on our evolutionary buttons to respond to interactivity by experiencing ourselves as being with kindred others.

In my previous research on children and computer toys, children described the lifelike status of machines in terms of their cognitive capacities (the toys could "know" things, "solve" puzzles). In my studies on children and Furbies, I have found that children describe these new toys as sort of alive because of the quality of their emotional attachments to the Furbies and because of their fantasies about the idea that the Furby might be emotionally attached to them. So, for example, when I ask the question, "Do you think the Furby is alive?" children answer not in terms of what the Furby can do, but how they feel about the Furby and how the Furby might feel about them.

> Ron (6): Well, the Furby is alive for a Furby. And you know, something this smart should have arms. It might want to pick up something or to hug me.

> Katherine (5): Is it alive? Well, I love it. It's more alive than a Tamagotchi because it sleeps with me. It likes to sleep with me.

> Jen (9): I really like to take care of it. So, I guess it is alive, but it doesn't need to really eat, so it is as alive as you can be if you don't eat. A Furby is like an owl. But it is more alive than an owl because it knows more and you can talk to it. But it needs batteries so it is not an animal. It's not like an animal kind of alive.

Traditionally, rag dolls and stuffed animals invited children's projections. The child made of the inert object what he or she wanted it to be, *needed* it to be at a particular developmental moment. Today's robotic pets and dolls do not so much invite projection, as demand engagement. They are not just there to evoke children's emotions; they tell the child what *they* need. In that sense, for the child, they are very much alive, in the sense of having intentions and a personal agenda. Children learn to have expectations of emotional attachments to computers, not in the way we have expectations of emotional attachment to our cars and stereos, but in the way we have expectations about our emotional attachments to people. In the process, the very meaning of the word *emotional* may change.

Over the past five decades, research in artificial intelligence has not succeeded in creating a machine as intelligent as a person; it has not even come close to that. It has succeeded, however, in contributing to a certain evolution of our language in terms of how we use the word *intelligence*. Nowadays, we commonly talk about intelligent machines—machines that play chess or assess mortgage applications. While these feats are wondrous, in the past intelligence indicated a far more complex range of cognitive skills and an ability to perceive the world and its meaning. We now face the prospect of a similar evolution of language in the way we use the words *affect* and *emotion*. Today, children talk about an "animal kind of alive" and a "Furby kind of alive." Will they soon come to talk about a "people kind of love" and a "computer kind of love"? Traditionally, an understanding of a "people kind of love" has been tied to the human experience of the body, of growing up in a family, of loss, of the fragility and the finiteness of life. In our nascent computer culture, "love" might come to mean something else altogether.

Unlike the old AI debates of the 1960s to the 1980s, in which researchers argued about whether machines could be really intelligent, the new discussions about relational artifacts sidestep essentialist arguments about what is inherent in them and instead force us to consider what they evoke in us. When we are asked to care for an object, when the cared-for object thrives and offers us its attention and concern, we experience that object as intelligent, but more important, we feel a connection to it.[16] Rather than debating about whether the new relational artifacts really have emotions, we are challenged to reflect on the issues that are raised by our emotions toward them.[17]

Traditionally, children have had to *project* states of mind onto their toys and dolls. In order to do this, they used as their models the infinitely complex and fluid states of mind of people. We know very little about the psychological implications of children having strong emotional connections with objects that have a limited number of states, even if that limited number of states is sufficient to supply an illusion of life or a deeply gratifying experience. Suppose that one spin-off of the Brooks doll project (let's say, to be launched for Christmas 2010) is a baby stimulator that would hold the attention of a child so that it was as happy interacting with the stimulator as with people. Although we know very little for sure about the implications of such a person/machine relationship, it is possible that it might pose psychological risk to some children, seducing them into the pleasures of a psychological space that offers a simplicity and predictability that the world of people does not.

Another issue to consider is how interacting with relational artifacts may affect people's way of thinking about themselves, their sense of human identity. Children have traditionally defined what makes people special in terms of a theory of "nearest neighbors." So, when the nearest neighbors (in children's eyes) were their pet dogs and cats, people were special because they had reason. The Aristotelian definition of "Man as a rational animal" made sense even for the youngest children. But when, in the 1980s, it seemed to children that smart computers (which spoke, obeyed commands, did math problems, and played tic-tac-toe) were the nearest neighbors, children's approach to the problem changed. In the course of the 1980s, people became special not because they were *rational* animals but because they were *emotional* machines. So, in 1983, a ten-year-old told me: "When there are the robots that are as smart as the people, the people will still run the restaurants, cook the food, have the families. I guess they'll still be the only ones who'll go to Church." *Now in a world where machines present themselves as emotional, what is left for us?*

I have argued that spinning technology enables us to displace our anxieties. If we take strong positions about computers we are sometimes able to avoid direct talk about social inequality, technology out of control, and our disillusionment with myths of progress. Now I am suggesting yet another level of displacement, closer to the dynamics of a fetish. In the psychodynamic understanding of a fetish, attention is commanded by a compelling object so that the fetishist does not need to confront taboo wishes and/or repressed sexual desires. Online pornography and Internet addiction may be safe, "acceptable" causes for concern while there are some things that we don't want to think about *because we find them unthinkable*. And most central among these may be the question "What kind of relationship is it appropriate to have with a machine?" *The question is real enough to be worth fleeing from—not because we have built machines that have intelligence or emotions, but because of the emotions that our machines evoke in us.* But, as with all histories that involve fetishes—objects about which we feel passionate because we cannot face the underlying issues from which they shield us—we ultimately will have nowhere to hide.

NOTES

Acknowledgments: I acknowledge the help of my research assistants, Jennifer Audley, Olivia Dasté, Rachel Prentice, and Robert Briscoe. This material is based upon work supported by the National Science Foundation under Grant No. 0115668. Any opinions, findings, and conclusions or recommendations expressed in this material are mine and do not necessarily reflect the views of the National Science Foundation.

1. Bill Gates, *The Road Ahead* (New York: Viking Penguin, 1995); Michael Dertouzos, *What Will Be* (New York: HarperCollins, 1997); Nicholas Negroponte, *Being Digital* (New York: Alfred A Knopf, 1995); Gene I. Rochlin, *Trapped in the Net: The Unanticipated Consequences of Computerization* (Princeton, N.J.: Princeton University Press, 1997); Clifford Stoll, *Silicon Snake Oil: Second Thoughts on the Information Highway* (New York: Doubleday, 1995); Jane M. Healy, *Failure to Connect: How Computers Affect Our Children's Minds—For Better and Worse* (New York: Simon and Schuster, 1998); Kimberly S. Young, *Caught in the Net: How to Recognize the Signs of Internet Addiction and a Winning Strategy for Recovering* (New York: John Wiley and Sons, 1998).

2. James Boyle, "Foucault in Cyberspace: Surveillance, Sovereignty and Hard-Wired Censors," *University of Cincinnati Law Review* 177 (1997). See also <http://www.wcl.american.edu/pub/faculty/boyle/Boylebio.htm> (visited June 30, 2002).

3. In one study of the Internet and depression, the extent to which Internet resources were shared with people in an individual's "offline" life was another important and very specific variable. See R. Kraut, S. Kiesler, B. Boneva, J. Cummings, V. Helgeson, and A. Crawford. "Internet Paradox Revisited" *Journal of Social Issues* 58 (2002): 49–74.

4. Sherry Turkle, *Life on the Screen: Identity in the Age of the Internet* (New York: Simon and Schuster, 1995).

5. The debate about the Internet and depression is an interesting case of how academics and journalists each seemed under pressure to report a complex unfolding story as a relatively simple news story, the trademark of spin. The original study was conducted at Carnegie Mellon University. See R. Kraut, M. Patterson, V. Lundmark, S. Kiesler, T. Mukophadhyay, and W. Scherlis, "Internet Paradox: A Social Technology That Reduces Social Involvement and Psychological Well-being?" *American Psychologist*, 53, no. 9 (1998). Further work from this study, the HomeNet study, would clarify that the paradox of the Internet as a social technology is that it increases social well-being only when used in conjunction with traditional social technologies. See Kraut et al., "Internet Paradox Revisited."

6. Langdon Winner, *Autonomous Technology* (Cambridge, Mass.: MIT Press, 1977).

7. Lewis Mumford, "The Monastery and the Clock," in *Technics and Civilization* (New York: Harcourt, Brace and World, 1934), 13–14.

8. Ibid., 62.

9. Sven Birkerts, *The Gutenberg Elegies* (New York: Fawcett Columbine, 1994), 15.

10. Ibid., 20.

11. Seymour Papert, *Mindstorms: Children, Computers, and Powerful Ideas* (New York: Basic Books, 1980), 5.

12. Birkerts, *The Gutenberg Elegies*, 21.

13. Karl Marx, quoted in Simon Schaffer, "Babbage's Intelligence: Calculating Engines and the Factory System," *Critical Inquiry* 21 (Autumn 1994): 206.

14. Sherry Turkle, *The Second Self: Computers and the Human Spirit* (New York: Simon and Schuster, 1984).

15. On this point, see, for example, Bill Joy, "Why the Future Doesn't Need Us," *Wired* 8, no. 4 (April 2000).

16. Even with computers that are far from the relational artifacts I am describing here, people anthropomorphize machines and tend to treat them as if they were people. For example, if users do a task on computer A and then are asked to rate the experience on computers A and B, they give the experience a higher rating on computer A than on computer B. In other words, people seem to not want to insult the computer to its "face." Byron Reeves and Clifford Nass, *The Media Equation* (Stanford, Calif.: CLSI, 1966).

17. A discussion of this issue goes beyond the scope of this essay, but I am thinking particularly of David Winnicott's ideas about the transitional object. See David Winnicott, *Playing and Reality* (New York: Basic Books, 1971).

2   Sow's Ears from Silk Purses

The Strange Alchemy of Technological Visionaries

IT BEGINS in the early nineteenth century and continues uninter-
rupted to the present day. Announced with enormous enthusiasm from
widely diverse sources, it has become one of the most cherished and enduring themes in American public discourse. The fact that it is always mistaken,
always associated with faulty expectations and destructive policies, does
not prevent it from cropping up again and again. Indeed, it would seem
that its very falsehood is the source of its enduring appeal, an implausible
dream we desperately want to come true *this time* even though it has so
often disappointed us in the past.

To be specific: the arrival of any new technology that has significant
power and practical potential always brings with it a wave of visionary
enthusiasm that anticipates the rise of a utopian social order. Surely the
coming of this machine, this new device, this technical novelty will re-
vitalize democracy. Surely its properties will foster greater equality and
widespread prosperity throughout the land. Surely it will distribute political power more broadly and empower citizens to act for themselves. Surely
it will cause us to cultivate new and better selves, becoming larger and
more magnanimous people than we have been before. And surely it will
connect individuals and groups in ways that will produce greater social
harmony and a relaxation of human conflict. From the coming of the steam
locomotive, to the introduction of the telegraph, telephone, motion pictures,
centrally generated electrical power, automobile, radio, television, nuclear
power, guided missile, and the computer (to name just a few), this has been
the recurring theme: celebrate! The moment of redemption is at hand.

One finds a vision of this kind in a speech given by the chemist Denison
Olmstead before the American Association for the Advancement of Science
in 1855: "My object is to prove that science [by which he also means the technologies made possible by scientific knowledge] in its very nature, tends to
promote political equality, to elevate the masses; to break down the spirit of
aristocracy; to abolish all those artificial distinctions in society; to raise the
industrial classes to a level with the professional." Olmstead praises steam-

boats, railways, the telegraph, factories, and chemical engineering because they tend to "equalize the gifts of heaven, and to produce social equality among men." The bounty that springs from science and industry, he argues, is so rich and overflowing that it will inevitably generate an egalitarian society, "rendering the conveniences and elegancies of life accessible to the many instead of the few."[1]

Echoes of Olmstead's panegyric have been heard in every generation since the mid-nineteenth century. The specific varieties of science and technology linked to the vision have continually changed, as developments once heavily touted have lost their luster (e.g., Ford's assembly line) and new hopefuls are added to the portfolio. But there is always great confidence that a democratic utopia lies just around the bend. In the early twentieth century, for example, many of the redemptive qualities people nowadays attribute to the computer and the Internet were strongly associated with the coming of aviation. In 1915 Henry Woodhouse, editor of *Flying*, the *Wired* magazine of its day, argued that the airplane would eliminate the barriers that had always divided mankind, bringing what he called a "new period of human relations." Fundamental in the new era would be growing recognition that all people of the world share the same sky, one made universally accessible by mechanical flight. This realization would bring about a "peaceful social revolution," an era of unity, cooperation, and peace on the planet. Writers on aviation were strongly convinced that a society of aviators would be "a society at once more democratic, egalitarian and cultured."[2] Many predicted that everyday folks would not only use airplanes for travel, but for a wide variety of work and recreation activities. Real estate agents would take to the air to show potential buyers how a property looked from the sky; salesmen would move from town to town in airborne showrooms hawking their wares; college teams would compete in air races, drawing crowds equivalent to those at football games.

As is often true of such visions, the political edge of the fantasy focused on social problems associated with a previous stage of technological development, in this case the monopoly power of the railroads. Widespread use of airplanes, some believed, would help cleanse the political corruption that railroads had brought to Washington, D.C., and the state legislatures. Competition from this new means of transportation would lift the burdens of "railroad rebates, overcharges, discriminations and the evils which our capitalistic system of distribution has brought upon us." Anticipating a prominent theme in today's writings on networked computing—disintermediation, the elimination of middle men—one enthusiast argued that airplanes offered "the realm of absolute liberty; no tracks, no franchises, no need of thousands of employees to add to the cost."[3]

Even feminist authors of the time exulted in this vein. Charlotte Perkins Gilman's article in *Harpers* in 1907 predicted an elevated, enlightened self-hood for those who experience flight. The "aerial" man, she wrote, "cannot think of himself further as a worm of the dust, but [only] as a butterfly, psyche, the risen soul."[4] Gilman's text makes it perfectly clear that the category of man also includes women like herself.

In my own childhood, visionaries in this grand tradition attached similar dreams to nuclear power, the peaceful atom that would provide clean, safe electric power—energy too cheap to meter. Again, this development was uniformly portrayed as a source of social equality, prosperity, and social harmony. Cartoon propaganda films of the 1950s regaled school children with images of a Disneyesque friendly atom in the same classrooms that instructed them in the "duck and cover" drills and primed them for nuclear war. Indeed, there was a direct connection between the two kinds of instruction. The beneficence of electrical power from atomic plants was simply the positive outgrowth of ongoing preparations for thermonuclear holocaust. Splitting the atom, we were supposed to understand, had a very good side along with an obviously bad one. But on balance, this teaching implied, nuclear technology was clearly a boon to humankind and cause for celebration. In that light, antinuclear peace activists of the 1950s were routinely dismissed as "kooks."

As redemptive technologies touted in a given period have lost their utopian allure, American publicists have always been ready to embrace new ones. Thus, many of the grand hopes associated with the atomic age soon migrated to the launch pads of intercontinental rocketry of the 1960s and the world-transforming possibilities of the space age. Well into the 1970s there were many who believed that "The High Frontier" of space colonies would prove the salvation of technological society rife with social and environmental problems.[5]

Today, of course, few people devote their energies to exploring the horizons of yesterday's utopias in nuclear power, space exploration, or television. Following accidents at Three Mile Island and Chernobyl as well the economic meltdown of the U.S. nuclear power industry, the atomic dreams of the 1950s were heard as mere clicks on the Geiger counters of historical background radiation. Similarly, as the exorbitant costs and minimal benefits of space colonization became obvious, proposals to spend billions of federal dollars on manned space probes were quietly shelved, leaving it to

Hollywood to mimic once grandiose dreams as *Star Trek* and *Star Wars* illusions. In the same vein, who can do anything but wince when reminded of the lofty expectations announced at the birth of television about democratizing education and revitalizing political participation? By now, commercialization of programming has removed television as anything vaguely associated with education at any level. Political pathologies involved in the absorption of the public sphere by television have been lavishly documented by Neil Postman, Robert McChesney, James Fallows, indeed, a whole generation of media scholars—the rise of sound bites, spin doctors, and attack ads; the excessive modeling of political speech on entertainment as we "amuse ourselves to death"; the corruption of democracy as politicians accept money from special interests in order to purchase TV ads for the next campaign; and the increasing cynicism of citizens whose only exposure to political life is via the tube.

But never mind. Once the early returns have come in and the formerly new seems tired and old-fashioned, the focus quickly shifts to other objects of fascination. Hence, at the turn of the millennium, visions of impending redemption emphasize the promise of digital communications and networked computing. As one widely read manifesto on "the new technology" explains, "It will enhance our leisure time and enrich our culture by expanding the distribution of information. It will help relieve pressures on urban areas by enabling people to work from home or remote-site offices . . . It will give us more control over our lives, enabling us to tailor our experiences and the products we use to our interests. Citizens of the information society will enjoy new opportunities for productivity and entertainment."[6]

As is typical in the grand tradition of techno-enthusiasm, the operative verb tense in such projections is *will*. These things *will* happen. If there were ever a comprehensive history of the rhetoric of technological utopia, an appropriate title for it would be "The Triumph of the Will." The very language used to convey the message insists that wondrous blessing on the horizon is ineluctable. So great is its power and glory that any demand for negotiations about exactly which technology will be introduced, by whom, and in what form is mere impudence. Only a fool would ask to see the fine print, examine the blueprints, or check the credentials of the planners.

I am not suggesting that attempts to imagine a better future for humankind or to link that vision to particular technologies are always ill-conceived. On the contrary, the world needs people able to indulge extravagant and unlikely visions and to link them to the full range of economic, social, institutional, artistic, political, and technical means that might help the world achieve them. We need the great imaginers, thinkers with the audacity of Jean-Jacques Rousseau, Robert Owen, Jane Addams, Martin Luther King Jr., E. F. Schumacher, Hazel Henderson, and other lovable visionaries of past and present. In our time, for example, a wonderfully sane map of the future of global society is sketched in Dalai Lama's *Ethics for The New Millennium,* a philosophy in which the power of science and technology is guided not by the craving for wealth or the mania for innovation, but through a strong commitment to relieve the suffering of others. The Dalai Lama asks us to consider what our policies and technologies look like if guided by an ethic of compassion.[7] That standpoint, however, is far removed from the shrill, redundant, increasingly pathetic proclamations of impending salvation that seem to crop up whenever new technology is on the rise, especially in the United States.

I would have no quarrel if the visions of techno-enthusiasts were simply the musings of writers and thinkers notable for extravagant but unreliable predictions. What typically happens, however, is that rosy utopian fantasies are projected as the standard cover story for patterns of technological and social change that sometimes involve enormous problems, ones that need to be confronted directly and early on in their development, without all the rhetorical anodynes and comforting illusions. As the public comes to accept extravagant projections as a plausible map of future outcomes, the possibility for serious research, thinking, and debate on the emerging technology's social, environmental, and political dimensions seems hardly worth doing. If there are relevant alternatives that might be explored, they soon disappear in the clouds of optimistic chatter that inform public understanding of the matter. Historians from Perry Miller to David Nye have labeled such visionary exuberance *the technological sublime,* the sense of awe, power, and spiritual transcendence that has arisen in people's hearts as they see a locomotive, massive steel bridge, city lit by electricity, or (today) the dancing icons on a Web page.[8] As it enters into our decision making and public policy, however, a better term for the phenomenon would be *the technological ridiculous.*

Techno-enthusiasts of the past two centuries have begun their musings with a valid and important insight: the coming of any powerful new technology offers an occasion for rethinking who we are and what kinds of social institutions we will have. Making any new technology involves "making" the kinds of people who will use it. From the 1880s onward, for example, many of the most potent technological systems have been ones predicated on installing processes of rapid throughput. Such processes quickly transform materials into finished goods, achieving a faster flow of materials, energy, and information than earlier means of production and distribution had made available. By themselves, however, the new mines, oil wells, factories, refineries, and networks of transportation and communication would have done little to change the world. Also required was a social milieu fundamentally altered in ways that could accommodate the flows generated. Especially in its initial stages, changes of this kind required enormous social pressure, campaigns in advertising, public relations, education, and public spectacles to induce people to use the great bounty of industrial throughput and to accept assumptions and expectations that were expected of consumers in mature, industrial societies.[9] Habits informed by the scarcity most people knew from earlier times had to be discredited and replaced by new beliefs, new channels for satisfaction. Well into the 1920s, most Americans had been raised with strict standards of thrift, frugality, and modest use. People still recall stories about their great-grandmothers who never threw anything away and whose well-organized closets included a box labeled: "String: too small to use." But the creation of "modern society"—the dynamic, rapidly changing, industrial social order of the mid-twentieth century—required that industrial corporations, designers, advertisers, journalists, educators, and the media apply their ingenuity to sell people on notions of selfhood and social relationships presupposed by all the new appliances, vehicles, foods, chemicals, and household conveniences. Among these ideas were some unprecedented commitments.

The notion of planned obsolescence and throwaway goods, for example, was upheld as a wonderful step forward in the standard of living. From automobiles to candy wrappers, the good life was to be found in buying and using up products as rapidly as possible. Cars that could easily last two decades if kept in good repair, for example, were regarded as obsolete and ready for the junkyard after four or five years. Being able to view the objects of everyday life as temporary and disposable became a de facto requirement of citizenship in the "modern age."

In the same vein, consumer goods were promoted as a means of symbolic communication, a way of demonstrating one's identity and social standing. Corporate design and advertising prepared a set of codes that enabled people to draw fine distinctions between the status value of owning, for example, a Chevrolet, Pontiac, Buick, Oldsmobile, or Cadillac. As a family's income increased, it was expected to buy that family's way up the ladder of social display.

During the same period, personal and family mobility was affirmed as a sign of prosperity. Being on the go, moving from one job to another, one town to another, one house to another was upheld as a necessary and desirable way to live. Being rooted in a particular community for a lifetime and watching successive generations sink similar roots came to be regarded as stultifying, a prescription for languor and boredom.

In addition, the idea that spending more, consuming more, and discarding more was widely promoted as the best path to a good life. No longer was saving money or building things that would last a long time regarded as a virtue. Commitment to economic growth in the mode of rapid throughput required that there be a relatively short interval between the time goods left the factory and the moment they arrived at their final destination: the landfill. In the same vein, personal well-being presupposed that people adapt their expectations to the rapid throughput of income, materials, energy, and refuse.

The industrialists, designers, advertisers, journalists, and educators who first promoted such practices in the middle decades of twentieth-century society did not rely solely on the utility of new products and services as their primary selling point. Their representations of modernism drew heavily upon utopian images of personal power and even spiritual transcendence associated with the use of automobiles, appliances, household chemicals, and other material goods. Newspaper and magazine advertisements for cars and gasoline in the 1920s and 1930s showed happy drivers speeding down highways with no other vehicles in sight; "There's Always Room Out Front," an ad for Ethyl proclaimed.[10] The same publications showed women in clean, shining, gadget-filled kitchens fulfilling their destinies as well-equipped "homemakers." The man of the family was often portrayed as successful executive looking proudly down from his skyscraper office upon the well-ordered city below. In the New York World's Fair of 1939, imagery of this kind reached apotheosis, showing a "World of Tomorrow" far removed from the miseries of the Great Depression, a world of superhighways, radiant metropolises, robot servants, and happy, suburban middle-class bliss. In futurist tableaux of this period, the social construction of technologies like the passenger automobile and the automatic dishwasher was accompanied by the construction of novel self-images, personal identities, social ideals, private and public values, as well as spiritual attachments. At the heart of these supposedly democratic developments was the creation of a new historical agent, one that would rise to unchallenged prominence in the late twentieth century: the insatiable consumer.

It is important to recall the alternatives set aside as this new match between production and human living was set in place. One might have built a mature technological order in which thrift, durability, preservation of natural things, the creation of walkable communities, and a bioregional, ecological approach to supply and production were the central commitments. In his writings of the late 1930s Lewis Mumford imagined an advanced technological society predicated on principles and institutions of that kind.[11] But America did not move in that direction. Instead it raced headlong into the vision proposed in modernist projections—the cities, suburbs, single-family homes, automobiles, highways, and shopping malls that dot our landscape today. There was nothing historically inevitable about any of the material structures and social patterns of modernism. They were particular social and cultural commitments affirmed at a particular moment in time, choices about what the "good life" ought to include, choices embedded in a collection of contingent technological styles. That world—still our world—might have had different features.

During periods of intense technological change (perhaps all periods will have this quality from now on) a key question is at stake: what forms of selfhood and social organization will be chosen, and who is empowered to decide? The reason technological utopianism is destructive is that it deflects people from addressing such questions in ways that are distinctly their own. Insofar as we believe the stories about enhanced democracy, equality, personal fulfillment, and world harmony—all depicted as something that flows automatically from the simple adoption and use of new instruments—we relinquish our ability to engage with the urgent decisions at hand. Transfixed by supposedly optimistic utopian dreams, we do not study the choices that face us or the consequences they entail. Neither do we investigate and or discuss publicly the options available in the areas of activity in question, leaving the key decisions to others, people who may not have our best interests or the long-term well-being of the planet anywhere in their plans.

The results of this approach to the continual reweaving of technical and social practice are observed in a number of festering dystopias: the automobile and urban/suburban sprawl; television and its vast wasteland of mindless entertainment; chemical/mechanical intensive agriculture and the destruction of both topsoil and the family farm; decades of "technological revolutions" in K–12 education and the gradual decline of the nation's schools—and the list goes on. America's experience with nuclear power offers an especially poignant story. For three decades the nation believed the utopian vision of inexhaustible energy and widely shared wealth. Only later did the bad news emerge: the exorbitant economic costs of building the plants along with unsolved problems of nuclear safety and radioactive waste disposal—conditions not acknowledged in the print of Faustian bargain. Histories of the period point out that many of those who planned the nuclear power system were aware of problems that eventually surfaced in unhappy ways. But persons in the industry who were concerned about what seemed to be erroneous projections about economic costs, safety, and waste disposal were encouraged by their colleagues to remain silent, to go along with the program and hope that the problems would be solved in the fullness of time.[12] An attitude of that kind is still the unspoken motto for today's technological visionaries. Don't ask. Don't tell.

Those who raise impertinent questions or insist on calling attention to some of the less attractive features of social innovations that have a technological component are quickly labeled "antitechnology" or "Luddite," with the strong implication that they are unsympathetic to the suffering of the world's populace and the need for technological improvements on all sides. Thus, in the early 1960s, Rachel Carson was denounced as a foe of chemical science and technology when her writings called attention to damage caused by the excessive use of DDT and other pesticides. Today social activists who insist that caution be used in the introduction of genetically modified foods, that, for example, consumers be informed which products have been bioengineered and which have not, are called "Luddites" by corporate spokespersons who want to see biotechnology in agriculture proceed as rapidly as possible. In a similar vein, a person is bound to branded "antitechnology" if he or she suggests that introducing computer-based instruction into the schools may not be the panacea for education its proponents believe it to be and that the policy needs further testing before huge sums are invested in electronic equipment. Over many decades the tendency to label voices as either "pro" or "anti" technology has contributed to a breakdown of speculation, research, and debate on many crucial policy choices. As the twenty-first century begins, this barrier to intelligent inquiry appears to be growing even larger.

It is interesting to speculate about which blunders the lure of technological utopianism presents to us today. A consistent unfulfilled promise of technological utopia is that of equality, social leveling, and widely shared power over decisions. That is, of course, one of the consistent dreams of today's theorists of cyberspace and the digital society. As Nicholas Negroponte explains, "I guess I have too many of those O (for optimistic) genes.

But I do believe that being digital is positive. It can flatten organizations, globalize society, decentralize control and help harmonize people."[13] A century and a half after Denison Olmstead made similar predictions about the era of iron and steel, the enduring dream is announced as if it were something entirely new.

But the actual development of systems of computing and communication points in a far less favorable direction. As digital technology expands, sources of news, music, movies, journalism, and other varieties of information—the sources most people usually encounter—are managed and marketed increasingly by a handful of large, very powerful corporations. Thus, what was heralded as an information explosion intrinsically populist in essence, looks increasingly to be an information implosion characterized by an unprecedented concentration of control over mass media and an increasingly obvious digital divide between the information-rich and information-poor. An appropriate moment to have focused on issues in this domain was the "reform" of telecommunications policy during the mid-1990s. The American public might have seized the opportunity, studying and debating the regulations proposed for the Telecommunications Act of 1996. Of course, those with powerful economic interests at stake knew exactly what opportunities for media mega-mergers the legislation held in store. In this instance corporate lobbyists drafted whole passages of the legislation that Congress obligingly passed and President Clinton signed into law. But few people in the general populace took much notice of how the rules that govern competition in telephone, radio, television, cable, Internet, and related industries were being altered in ways that would affect present and future generations. In the years that followed, an unprecedented concentration of ownership and control moved ahead rapidly as one multibillion-dollar firm merged with another.[14]

Not surprisingly, many of the reports in newspapers and magazines and on television that interpreted the reshaping of the realm in telecommunications did not emphasize the enormous political and economic power plays involved. Instead, they charmed the public with the always appealing, well-rehearsed themes of techno-enthusiast vision. The new communications regime, we were told, would be a boon for democracy because it would make more information more accessible through the workings of the free market. In the right-wing manifesto, "Cyberspace and the American Dream: A Magna Carta for the Knowledge Age," issued by the Progress and Freedom Foundation in 1994, Esther Dyson and her colleagues argued that there was no need to fear the consolidation of power in media giants, much less any need for government to regulate competition among the major players. "If Washington forces the phone companies and cable operators to develop supplementary and duplicative networks, most other advanced industrial countries will attain cyberspace democracy—via an interactive multimedia 'open platform'—before America does, despite this nation's technological dominance."[15] In this vision the guarantor of "democracy" is simply the rapid creation of networks of broadband communications. All that is necessary to achieve it is liberation from the "rules, regulations, taxes and laws laid in place to serve the smokestack barons and bureaucrats of the past." When that is accomplished we will see the "creation of a new civilization, founded in the eternal truths of the American Idea." But, in the view of Dyson and her colleagues, no dedicated effort is needed to achieve equality, community, and democratic self-government, for such blessings flow automatically from the new digital pipeline.

Today as one boots up one's Web browser, who can fail to notice the staggering profusion of moving advertisements, pop-up menus, and devices for automatically channeling what people do in cyberspace, methods that now threaten to make the Internet not the great boon for populist communications that the visionaries predicted, but yet another dystopian nightmare—an amplification of cable TV with myriad opportunities for on-line sales and the expansion of consumerism. Along its present course the Internet seems likely to reproduce (not eliminate) long-standing economic inequalities, to amplify (not reduce) levels of stupefaction through mass media, to jeopardize (not protect) the privacy of personal information, and to further erode (not reverse) drastically declining citizen participation in elections and other political roles. Perhaps it is not too soon to compare the widely proclaimed vision of a utopia through networked computing to the failed technological visions of the past and their beguiling but ultimately hollow predictions of equality, harmony, freedom, and personal transcendence. After all, what ever happened to the apotheosis for democratic society promised by the industrial factory? By the automobile? By mechanized agriculture? By broadcast television? By nuclear power? By the space age? And, can we now add, by the Internet?

A colorful story from the history of American technology offers an appropriate metaphor for the situation that confronts us. An old adage insists, "You can't make a silk purse from a sow's ear." In the early twentieth century, however, one of the nation's most successful chemical engineers, Arthur D. Little, set out to disprove it. Using the ears from a sow named "Sukie" (whose participation in the experiment seems to have been less than voluntary), Little prepared a chemical mixture that he then spun into an artificial silk. From there his assistants succeeded in weaving and sewing an attractive purse (Figure 2.1). Little used this wonderful accomplishment as an example to advance his Horatio Alger-style philosophy of life. "When chemistry puts on overalls and gets down to business," he wrote, "things begin to happen that are of importance to industry and to commerce. New values appear. New and better paths are opened to reach the goals desired."[16] Indeed, in Little's view, success awaits us at every corner. Today, of course, the accomplishments of electrical rather than chemical engineering are the ones that hold the great fascination for many people. But the underlying dreams mirror Little's project remarkably well.

As one compares the content of visionary proclamations to the eventual results of technological change, it seems that we have long been engaged in transformations of different kinds, taking technologies that once had enormous basic potential, turning them into entities whose wider social, politi-

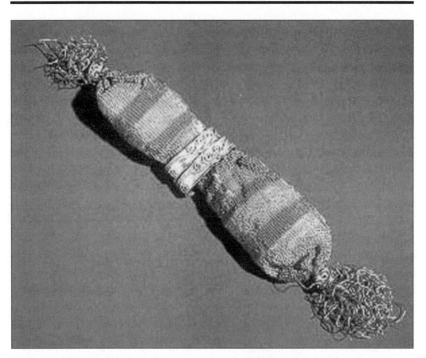

Figure 2.1 *Silk Purse From a Sow's Ear* by Arthur D. Little. Reprinted with permission from the Smithsonian Institution, photo no. 81-13888 CS.

cal, and environmental dimensions are ugly to behold. What seemed at the outset to be a lovely silk purse has often ended up a sow's ear, a deformed creation that mocks democratic purpose and resists remaking. Perhaps it is time to affirm that we have heard the false promises and hyperbolic speculations too often, that it is time for this strange alchemy to cease. Let us seek better ways of talking about technical devices, more reliable ways of imagining their possibilities and problems. Most of all, let us find ways to include a broader spectrum of the populace in shaping the new tools and systems as they come along, rather than indulging outworn fantasies of immaculate technological conception.

Notes

1. Denison Olmstead, "On the Democratic Tendencies of Science," in *Changing Attitudes Toward American Technology*, ed. Thomas Parke Hughes (New York: Harper & Row, 1975), 144–54.

2. Quoted in Joseph Corn, *The Winged Gospel: America's Romance with Aviation, 1900–1950* (New York: Oxford University Press, 1983), 38.

3. Quoted in ibid., 35. The theme of disintermediation in the new institutions of digital technology is explored in Andrew Shapiro, *The Control Revolution: How the Internet is Putting Individuals in Charge and Changing the World We Know* (New York: Perseus Books, 1999).

4. Quoted in Corn, *The Winged Gospel*, 39.

5. See, for example, Stewart Brand, ed., *Space Colonies* (New York: Penguin Books, 1977). By the mid-1980s Brand and many of his colleagues at the *Coevolution Quarterly* and *The Whole Earth Review* had invested their hopes in space technologies of a different kind, the computer technologies that gave rise to cyberspace.

6. Bill Gates (with Nathan Myhrvold and Peter Rinearson), *The Road Ahead*, rev. ed. (New York: Penguin Books, 1996), 284.

7. His Holiness The Dalai Lama, *Ethics for The New Millennium* (New York: Riverhead Books, 1999).

8. David E. Nye, *The American Technological Sublime* (Cambridge, Mass.: MIT Press, 1994).

9. These developments are discussed in Terry Smith, *Making the Modern: Industry, Art and Design in America* (Chicago: University of Chicago Press, 1993), and Roland Marchand, *Advertising and the American Dream: Making Way for Modernity, 1920–1940* (Berkeley: University of California Press, 1985).

10. The ad is reproduced in Marchand, *Advertising and the American Dream*, 362.

11. See Lewis Mumford, *Technics and Civilization* (New York: Harcourt, Brace, 1934) and *The Culture of Cities* (New York: Harcourt, Brace, 1938).

12. The story is told in Irvin C. Bupp and Jean-Claude Derian, *Light Water: How the Nuclear Dream Dissolved* (New York: Basic Books, 1978).

13. Nicholas Negroponte, "Being Digital—a book (p)review," *Wired* 3, no. 2 (February 1995): 182.

14. A discussion of this issue in historical context is given in Robert McChesney, *Rich Media, Poor Democracy: Communication Politics in Dubious Times (The History of Communication)* (Chicago: University of Illinois Press, 1999).

15. Esther Dyson, George Gilder, George Keyworth, and Alvin Toffler, "Cyberspace and the American Dream: A Magna Carta for the Knowledge Age," *Release 1.2*, August 22, 1994 (Washington, D.C.: Progress and Freedom Foundation); <http://www.pff.org/position.html>.

16. Arthur D. Little, "On the Making of Silk Purses from Sow's Ears," a pamphlet (Cambridge, Mass.: Author, 1921).

3   Mediums and Media

WITHIN A five-year span in the 1840s, the American public witnessed two of the most remarkable moments in telecommunications history. On May 24, 1844, friends and observers gathered with Samuel B. Morse at the Supreme Court in Washington, D.C., to participate in the first official test of an electromagnetic telegraph line. Miss Ellsworth, the daughter of the commissioner of patents, had the honor of choosing the first words to be transmitted by this new technology. Morse sent her chosen message, "What hath God wrought?" to his associate Alfred Vail in Baltimore, who then sent the message back to Washington for confirmation. In the ensuing years, the telegraph rapidly expanded as a commercial operation, and in the following decade, its lines quickly crossed the continent. By 1861, the telegraphic network had outraced the transcontinental railroad to California. By 1866, a reliable cable reached across the Atlantic to England and beyond.

For a world that had waited weeks to receive messages from across the ocean, and days to receive messages from across the nation, the ability to contact London from New York in only seconds must have truly tested the limits of credulity. Even more astonishingly, the electronic circuitry of the telegraph made possible the instantaneous exchange of messages in the complete absence of physical bodies. This sense of disembodied communion was unprecedented and the most provocative quality of the celebrated new medium, inspiring many commentators to declare Morse's invention the most momentous innovation in human history. In the first of a series of such glowing predictions about electronic media, many believed telegraphic technology would lead to nothing less than a utopian age. "The world, it has been said, will be made a great whispering gallery," wrote one telegraph enthusiast, "I would rather say, a great assembly, where everyone will see and hear everyone else. The most remarkable effect, if I may judge from my own narrow thought, will be the approach to a practical unity of the human race; of which we have never yet had a foreshadowing, except in the gospel of Christ."[1]

In the midst of such utopian technophilia, only four years after Morse's public debut of his remarkable invention, the family of John and Margaret

Fox went to bed for the evening in their small cottage in Hydesville, New York, a tiny village just southeast of Rochester. For a number of months previous to the night of March 31, 1848, the family had endured many sleepless evenings punctuated by a series of unexplained disturbances in their home. Previous tenants had also complained of the incessant rappings and knockings in the cottage, but despite frequent attempts to discover and eliminate the source of these sounds, the noises continued unabated. On this particular night, John, Margaret, and their two young daughters slept together in the parents' bedroom. The rapping sounds were particularly violent that night, and though Mr. and Mrs. Fox tried to get their children to ignore the noises and go to sleep, the daughters amused themselves by imitating the commotion. Finally, the youngest daughter, Kate, said aloud, "Here, Mr. Split-foot, do as I do." Kate then clapped her hands three times, which instantaneously triggered three of the mysterious raps in apparent response. Kate's sister, Margeretta, did the same and also elicited three of the mysterious knocking sounds. Suspecting an unseen intelligence behind the rappings, the children's mother engaged the invisible entity in dialogue. Eventually, by rapping its answers in response to the questions of Margaret Fox, the spirit correctly counted to ten, identified the ages of the Fox children, and numbered how many of the Fox family were still alive and how many were dead. Later, the spirit responded to more complex questions by rapping once for "yes" and twice for "no."[2]

Occurring in an era of vast social and technological change for the nation as a whole, the mysterious rappings in upper New York State helped spark a religious and political movement that would become known as modern spiritualism. Within a decade, the movement would attract thousands of avowed believers, souls searching for spiritual truth who now turned to the century's other most remarkable telecommunications device—the clairvoyant medium. Inspired by Kate Fox's ghostly "telegraphic" exchange in her parents' home at Hydesville, spiritualism eventually included among its members Harriet Beecher Stowe (who claimed that *Uncle Tom's Cabin* had been dictated to her by "spirit" authors), Horace Greeley, James Fenimore Cooper, and even President and Mrs. Lincoln (who are said to have conducted seances in the White House).[3] As spiritualism expanded into a national and international phenomenon, it assumed many forms and intersected with many other practices and beliefs, so much so that providing a brief overview of the movement is almost impossible. In its most basic form, however, spiritualism was a philosophy that believed the dead were in communication with the living through mediums who channeled the spirit world. From their abode in the "seventh heaven," the spirits reassured those on earth that their loved ones lived on in the afterlife. In seances across the country, the telegraphic spirits proclaimed "the joyful tidings that they all 'still lived,' 'still loved,' and with the tenderness of human affection, and the wisdom of a higher sphere of existence, watched over and guided the beloved ones who had mourned the dead, with all the gracious ministry of guardian angels."[4]

Within this five-year period, the United States thus saw the advent of both the electromagnetic and spiritual telegraphs, technologies that stand as the progenitors of two radically different histories of telecommunications. Most technological timelines credit Morse's apparatus as ushering in a series of increasingly sophisticated electronic communications devices over the next century, inventions developed in the rationalist realm of science and engineering that revolutionized society and laid the foundations for the modern information age. The "Rochester knockings" heard by the Fox family, on the other hand, inspired the modern era's occult fascination with seances, spirit circles, automatic writing, telepathy, clairvoyance, Ouija boards, and other paranormal phenomena. The historical proximity and intertwined legacies of these two founding mediums, one material and the other spiritual, is hardly a coincidence. Certainly, the explicit connections between the two communications technologies were not lost on the spiritualists themselves, who eagerly linked spiritualist phenomena with the similarly fantastic discourses of electromagnetic telegraphy. As spiritualist belief crossed the country along with the unreeling cables of the telegraph companies, spiritualist books such as *The Celestial Telegraph* and periodicals such as *The Spiritual Messenger* frequently invoked popular knowledge of Morse's electromagnetic telegraph to explain their model of spiritual contact. "You send a telegraphic dispatch from New York to London through the medium of the Atlantic Cable," wrote one spiritualist. "Break the Atlantic Cable, and all communication must stop through that medium. Break the laws that are favorable to mediumship in spiritual affairs, and all communication through that channel must likewise cease."[5] One account even suggested that electromagnetic telegraphy itself was the result of spiritual intervention. Said a "spirit" from the other side when channeled through a medium in 1874, "Morse, of himself, could not have fashioned the magnetic telegraph. His mind was reaching out for thought that would help him in his work, and, as the mental action of your sphere is visible to the denizens of this, those who had been watching the workings of his mind suggested, through a familiar process of mental impression, that which enabled him to shape the invention into a form of practical utility."[6]

American spiritualism presented an early and most explicit intersection of technology and spirituality, of media and mediums. Enduring well beyond a fleeting moment of naive superstition at the dawn of the information age, the historical interrelationship of these competing visions of telegraphic channeling continues to inform many speculative accounts of media and consciousness even today. Many of our contemporary narratives concerning the "powers" of electronic telecommunications have, if not their origin, then their first significant cultural synthesis in the doctrines of spiritualism. Although the idea of a spiritual telegraph may seem ludicrous today, the contemporary legacy of the spiritualists and their magical technology can be found in sites as diverse as the "psychic friends" network, Baudrillard's landscape of the hyperreal, and Hollywood's current tales of virtual reality come alive and run amok. A century and a half after Kate Fox's initial exchange over a ghostly wire, American culture remains intrigued by the capacity of electronic media to create seemingly sovereign yet displaced, absent and parallel electronic worlds.

In suggesting the limitless possibilities of flowing electrical information, telegraphy's apparent ability to separate consciousness from the body placed the technology at the center of intense social conjecture, imaginative cultural elaboration, and often contentious political debate. In these at times volatile struggles, the discorporative power of telegraphy and the liberating possibilities of electronic telepresence held a special attraction for women, many of whom would use the idea of the spiritual telegraph to imagine social and political possibilities beyond the immediate material restrictions placed upon their bodies. Significantly, from the earliest moments of the movement, spiritualists associated the powers of mediumship most closely with women, and especially teenage girls. Through a unique convergence of social, scientific, and spiritual logics, women appeared to be "naturally" suited for the mysteries of mediumship. As Ann Braude writes in her history of the movement, "Americans throughout the country found messages from spirits more plausible when delivered through the agency of adolescent girls. . . . The association of mediumship with femininity was so strong that it was not dispelled by the contravening evidence of the existence of male mediums."[7] When men did manifest mediumistic powers, they were said to embody the feminine qualities that made such otherworldly contact possible. As one spiritualist noted, "it may be observed that ordinarily the feminine mind possesses, in a higher degree than the masculine, two important requites of elevated mediumship: first, it is more religious; and, secondly, it is more plastic."[8]

Several excellent histories of spiritualism have discussed the complicated politics of gender involved in the movement's rise and fall during the nineteenth century. There has been relatively little discussion, however, of spiritualism as a popular discourse on gender *and* telecommunications, one that produced the modern era's first fantasies of discorporative electronic liberation. Long before our contemporary fascination with the beatific possibilities of cyberspace, feminine mediums led the spiritualist movement as wholly realized cybernetic beings—electromagnetic devices bridging flesh and spirit, body and machine, material reality and electronic space. Then, as now, such fantastic visions of electronic telecommunications demonstrate that the cultural conception of a technology is often as important and influential as the technology itself. As James Carey argues, the telegraph not only served as the material foundation for a new communications network, it also "opened up new ways of thinking about communication within both the formal practice of theory and the practical consciousness of everyday life. In this sense the telegraph was not only a new tool of commerce but also a thing to think with, an agency for the alteration of ideas."[9] In contrast to Morse's material technology of metal, magnets, and wire, the spiritual telegraph could only exist in the mortal world as a fantasy of telegraphic possibility. In an era when the technology of the telegraph physically linked states and nations, the *concept* of telegraphy made possible a fantastic splitting of mind and body in the cultural imagination, demonstrating that electronic presence, whether imagined at the dawn of the telegraphic age or at the threshold of virtual reality, has always been more a cultural fantasy than a technological property.

Understanding our own culture's continuing interest in fantastic forms of electronic telecommunications requires examining more closely the historical context of telegraphy's technological advent and conceptual influence. What was the cultural environment at mid-century that allowed spiritual telegraphy to thrive? How did the women mediums channeling this telegraphy use the mysteries of telepresence as a means of social empowerment? Finally, what became of the technological and cultural power of the medium by the end of the century? I believe such an analysis of this founding spiritual technology will demonstrate that our own era's fascination with the discorporative and emancipating possibilities of the looming virtual age is in many ways simply an echo of this strange electronic logic, a collective fantasy of telepresence that allowed a nation to believe over 150 years ago that a little girl could talk to the dead over an invisible wire.

ELECTROMAGNETIC MYSTERIES

When Samuel Morse and Kate Fox opened contact with Baltimore and the Beyond in the 1840s, they did so at a time when there were few distinctions made between what would shortly become the antithetical domains of physics and metaphysics. Lacking this modern distinction, the spiritualists' initial conceptualization of "celestial telegraphy" was not so much a misapplication of technological discourse as a logical elaboration of the technology's already supernatural characteristics. Talking with the dead through raps and knocks, after all, was only slightly more miraculous than talking with the living yet absent through dots and dashes; both involved subjects reconstituted through technology as an entity at once interstitial and uncanny. In reviewing the appeals of spiritualist literature, what must have attracted the belief of many converts was spiritualism's ability to provide a technically plausible system of explanation for these seemingly occult occurrences, transforming the supernatural into the preternatural. People had claimed to talk to ghosts before 1848, of course, but as interest in spirit phenomena spread in the wake of the "Rochester knockings," the first apostles of the movement, whether attempting to legitimate and thus conceal an elaborate hoax, or more innocently, genuinely searching for a credible system of explanation, sought a logic and language appropriate to understand rationally this seemingly irrational phenomenon.

In a bid for such authority, spiritualism attempted to align itself with the principles of electrical science so as to distinguish mediumship from more superstitious forms of mystical belief in previous centuries. It was the animating powers of electricity, after all, that gave the telegraph its distinctive property of simultaneity and its unique sense of disembodied presence, allowing the device to vanquish previous barriers of space, time, and, in the spiritualist imagination, even death. More than an arbitrary, fanciful, and wholly bizarre response to the innovation of a technological marvel, the spiritual telegraph's contact with the dead represented, at least initially, a strangely "logical" application of telegraphy consistent with period knowledges of electromagnetic science, the experimental frontiers of physics/metaphysics, and the vicissitudes of a highly unstable (and highly gendered) force known as "nervous energy."

The scientific study of the relationship between such nervous energy, electricity, and the divine "spark of life" began with research by the Italian scientist, Luigi Galvani. Historians are unclear as to the exact date of Galvani's discovery (sources cite 1771, 1780, and 1790). It is also ambiguous whether the momentous discovery belongs to Galvani or his wife. In any case, someone in Galvani's household sometime in the late eighteenth century noticed that a pair of frog legs, sitting on a table near an electrical generator, twitched violently when touched by a metal knife. Inspired by this odd phenomenon, Galvani immediately began his famous experiments on muscular motion and "animal electricity." Though scientists had earlier speculated about the relationship of electricity and organic energy, Galvani's book, *Effects of Electricity on Muscular Motion*, inspired a flurry of related research in the early part of the next century.[10] Though their theories were often in disagreement, scientists and physicians were convinced that electricity was in some way related to the "vital force" of life.

Experiments concerning electricity and muscular motion became increasingly ambitious and baroque in the new century. In 1803, Galvani's nephew, Giovanni Aldini, performed galvanic experiments on beheaded criminals and amputated human limbs. His most spectacular demonstration occurred in London when, in front of a large crowd, he performed many such experiments on a criminal who had just been hanged. "A powerful battery being applied, very strong contractions were excited, the limbs were violently agitated, the eyes opened and shut, the mouth and jaws worked about, and the whole face thrown into frightful convulsions."[11] Aldini was eventually able to compel corpses to lift heavy weights, roll their eyes, and extinguish candles with their breath, all through the animating principles of electricity. Others mounted similarly gruesome public exhibitions.[12] It was within the context of such public spectacle showcasing electricity's relationship to the body that Mary Shelley wrote *Frankenstein*, the most famous literary account of electricity and life's vital force. In the novel's preface, Shelley describes the genesis of her literary creation and the now infamous pact made between her, Lord Byron, Polidori, and her husband to write competitive horror stories. "Many and long were the conversations between Lord Byron and Shelley, to which I was a devout but nearly silent listener. During one of these, various philosophical doctrines were discussed, and among others, the nature of the principle of life, and whether there was any probability of its ever being discovered and communicated."[13] "Perhaps a corpse would be re-animated," continues Shelley, "galvanism had given token of such things: perhaps component parts of a creature might be manufactured, brought together, and imbued with vital warmth."[14]

Similar mysteries and experimental activities surrounded the phenomenon of magnetism. The figure who would prove to be most influential in this regard for the spiritualists was the German physician, Franz Mesmer. In the late eighteenth century, Mesmer was interested in the therapeutic possibilities of magnets. After witnessing the dynamics of priest and patient during a Roman Catholic exorcism in 1776, Mesmer became convinced of the theory of animal magnetism. This theory maintained that magnetic fluid, much like electrical fluid, pervaded the world, and that by altering this invisible substance through looking, touching, and a passing of hands, the diseased body of a patient could be brought back into alignment with this force. Under therapy, patients applied water taken from large "magnetized" tubs, and as "mesmerized" subjects, some reported religious visions and even contact with the dead.

Such intense interest in Mesmerism was not limited to France. Theories of animal magnetism, often combined with theories of animal electricity, occultism, and phrenology, were also common in England and the United States during this period, as reported in journals such as *The Magnet* and *The Phreno-Magnetic Vindicator.*[15] Edgar Allen Poe's gruesome story, "The Strange Facts in the Case of Monsieur Valdemar," exploited this fascination with Mesmerism as a power both factual and fantastic that somehow linked science and spirit. In this tale, a man is mesmerized at the point of death and then kept in a state of limbo for a number of weeks. After the man begs to be allowed to die, the trance is at last broken and the man's body instantly decomposes into a pool of "liquid putridity." The shocking conclusion of this tale depended on the reader's familiarity with the cryptic links hypothesized between invisible yet palpable forces such as electromagnetism and the greater mysteries of life itself.[16]

Thus was electromagnetic science the quantum physics of its day, a frontier of inquiry bordering science and spirit that raised more questions than it answered. In this age of accelerated discovery, invention, and hypothesis, an increasingly sizable reading public not only learned of new technologies and scientific principles (some often quite dubious), but also participated in more sweeping speculation about the constitution of the body and its relationship to the material and spiritual worlds. This is the context in which the American public theorized Kate Fox's enigmatic rappings. Already a fertile terrain for the speculative adventures of popular culture, the mysteries of electromagnetism would become in the spiritualist mind a foundational science in a grand theory of technology and consciousness. Conceptually energized by the example of the telegraph, spiritual science would promote the wonders of physical discorporation and a dream of social emancipation, all to be realized through the telecommunicative wonders of electronic presence.

THE "SCIENCE OF THE SOUL"

The strange technologies of spiritualism, both the flesh and blood medium in her parlor and the celestial telegraph in the invisible spirit world, were perhaps the most literal and dramatic expressions of what James Carey and John Quirk have termed the century's "electrical sublime."[17] Importantly, spiritualist faith in mediums and celestial telegraphy went beyond a mere utilitarian application of the telegraph as a metaphor. Critical to articulating a convincing technological (and thus "scientific") fantasy of mediumship, spiritualist doctrine clearly stated that the spiritual telegraph was in fact a "real" (albeit invisible) technology. Anyone who doubted the reality of the spiritual telegraph *as a telegraph* needed only to look at the example of Samuel Morse himself, who, once dead, became a frequent and proficient interlocutor from the spirit land, turning his mind back to mortal earth to continue uplifting the world that his material technology had already revolutionized.[18] Perhaps the most sincere testament to the technology's concrete existence in the heavens came from Horace Greeley, editor of the *New York Herald*. An early supporter of spiritualism, Greeley offered $2,000 a month to any medium who could furnish him with news from Europe in advance of the more terrestrial modes of communications (this being, of course, in the days before the Atlantic cable).[19]

Significantly, within the century's general celebration of technology, the spiritualists concentrated almost exclusively on electronic technologies of telecommunications. Inspired by the example of the telegraph and convinced of its parallel existence in the world of the dead, many spiritualists described a host of ever more elaborate yet completely functional "spiritual technologies" that could be found in the afterlife, each of them centered on the wonder of telepresence and disembodied electrical contact. In many respects, spiritualist fantasies of disembodied communication and living technologies greatly resembled the fantastic devices of the then emerging genre of science fiction, another arena of popular culture that demonstrated an interest in the discorporative powers of telegraphic technology. Indeed, in many cases it would be difficult to differentiate between these two discourses of scientific possibility. Within later spiritualist literature, for example, mediumistic accounts of adventures on Mars and Venus were not uncommon, while science fiction throughout the century frequently imagined the astonishing possibilities to be realized through the telegraphic liberation of mind and body. A particularly interesting author in this regard was Robert Milne, a Scottish writer born in 1844 who settled in San Francisco, where he penned a number of extraordinary tales detailing seemingly paranormal telegraphic phenomena. One tale in particular is of interest as a vivid fantasy of telegraphic discorporation. In "Professor Vehr,'s Electrical Experiment," a young man visits the famous Professor Vehr who has been experimenting with electronic telepathy. Vehr tells the young man that he has invented an apparatus that allows one to "see" anywhere in the world. Worried because he has not heard from his fiancée in many months while she travels in Europe, the young man asks if he can use the device to find her. Vehr agrees and places the mental traveler inside a complicated electronic apparatus, bearing a "marked resemblance to the known characteristics of a Leyden jar" with what looked like "ordinary telegraphic wires."[20] Once inside the device, the young man holds a telegraph wire in each hand. Vehr then taps the wires into a telegraph line outside his window. The professor explains the process to the young man's friend in a passage that explicitly links the century's technological and spiritual fixations:

> "That is the first effect of moderately strong charge of static electricity in the human frame," explained the professor. "It induces a highly wrought condition of the nerves, which in their turn act upon the ganglion of the brain; that, in its turn, reacting again, through the duplex series of nerves, upon the wire held in the left hand, which brings the holder into communication with whatever object enthralls his attention at the time of the trance. The experiment is, in effect, clairvoyance reduced to an art, the mesmeric trance accomplished by scientific means and conditioned by the recognized and accepted laws of electrical science."[21]

Through the machine, the young man sees another man courting his fiancée in New Orleans. His telegraphic consciousness returned to the room of Professor Vehr, the young man is despondent about his imminent romantic loss and his sense of helplessness. Vehr then agrees to debut his latest innovation. This time by attaching his apparatus to the telegraph line, Vehr is able to discorporate and transmit the young man to New Orleans, where he quickly defeats his rival. But, in an ending much less utopian than most spiritualist literature, when Vehr tries to bring the reunited couple back across the wires, they disappear into the vast electronic elsewhere, never to be seen again.

While authors such as Milne realized the era's telegraphic fantasies in science fiction, a number of respected scientists sympathetic to the spiritualist cause developed theories and performed experiments in an attempt to provide empirical proof of spiritualist principles. One writer even posited a simultaneous existence of the material and spiritual worlds within the human body, arguing that the soul itself was an electromagnetic phenomenon trapped by material flesh.

> It is easy to conceive, then, that the magnetic essence of *all* the particles and compounds of the body, associated together, must necessarily form *an interior, magnetic and invisible body,* in the same manner as the association of the particles themselves forms the outer and visible body. Moreover, as the pervading and surrounding essence of each of these particles must correspond in nature to the particle itself, and may be called the spirit of the particle; so this interior, magnetic body, if it could be tested by spiritual chemistry, would be found to consist of what may be termed spiritual carbon, spiritual nitrogen, spiritual calcium, and so on to the end of the category composing the *physical* body. At death the particles of the visible body collapse, and this interior, vitalizing and magnetic body, exhales forth in its united form, its various parts maintaining their mutual affinities as before; and could we then see it as it is, we would find it to possess spiritual bones, muscles, heart, lungs, nerves, brain, &c., and that it still preserved all the *general* features of its original mould, though in a vastly improved state. [22]

The author proposed that this "spirit body," or what we commonly think of as the soul, would then recognize itself in a new spirit world, "abounding with scenery, organizations and other objects corresponding to its own essence and affections; and then would commence a life sevenfold more intense than that enjoyed while in the flesh!" [23] Just as Mary Shelley had thirty years earlier conceived of a material body stitched together from limbs stolen from the grave and then animated with jolts of electricity, this spiritualist constructed his own Frankenstein, one powered by spiritual electricity that eerily resided within each person as an invisible doppelganger waiting to emerge at the moment of death. Thus did heaven, the afterlife, and the soul become theorized, spatialized, and concretized phenomena subject to scientific inquiry and validation.

History prepares us, then, for the opening comments in physicist Frank J. Tipler's 1994 book, *The Physics of Immortality.* Tipler introduces his book by arguing that "theology is a branch of physics," and even more provocatively, "physicists can infer by calculation the existence of God and the likelihood of the resurrection of the dead to eternal life in exactly the same way as physicists calculate the properties of the electron."[24] Replacing telegraphic metaphors with those from the computer age, Tipler continues: "It is necessary to regard all forms of life—including human beings—as subject to the same laws of physics as electrons and atoms. I therefore regard a human being as nothing but a particular type of machine, the human brain as nothing but an information processing device, the human soul as nothing but a program being run on a computer called the brain."[25] Tipler's theories, of course, are conceptual cousins to the long-standing fantasy in science fiction and contemporary cyberculture that human consciousness (and presumably the soul as a by-product of that consciousness) might one day be downloaded into a powerful computer. For many, then as now, metaphysics are apparently most convincing when supported with some form of mathematics. Operating within a larger general fascination for the possibilities of electronic telecommunication, the spiritualists found the telegraph to be a most logical and appropriate instrument of social and even material deliverance. The miraculous "disembodying" presence evoked by Morse's technology suggested the tantalizing possibility of a realm where intelligence and consciousness existed independently from the physical body and its material limitations, be they social, sexual, political, mortal, or otherwise.

The Negative Female

As one might imagine, such emancipating possibilities were of particular interest to women, who from Kate Fox onward served as the ideological and technological core of the movement. Communication with the spirit world required more than a mere telegraph, be it electromagnetic, celestial, or otherwise. Spiritual contact also depended on the equally enigmatic technology of the medium, a complex receiver who channeled the mysteries of spiritual electricity through the circuitry of another unfathomable entity in nineteenth-century science—the female body. Like the telegraph, women presented many Victorians with "a machine they could not understand," making "feminine" physiology and psychology an equally imaginative field of scientific speculation, especially when such conjecture intersected, as did seemingly all aspects of nineteenth-century life, with theories of electromagnetism. Exploiting the scientific ambiguities surrounding both electromagnetism and their own bodies, female mediums would make strategic use of "telepresence" as an avenue for empowerment and emancipation.

Electrical theories of femininity were almost as old as electrical theory itself. As with most other totalizing accounts of cosmos and consciousness, electromagnetic principles of the early nineteenth century gradually informed the study of ever more complicated phenomena. In the process, electromagnetic discourses soon infiltrated discussions of life sciences beyond galvanism and biology to pervade emerging disciplines such as psychology and anthropology. More important for the tenets of spiritualist belief, electromagnetic theory also entered increasingly into debates over sex and gender. In *Animal Electricity; or the Electrical Science,* for example, published the same year that Morse debuted the telegraph in Washington, James Olcott proposed that "electrified" women were the agents responsible for the evolution and diversity of the world's races. While Olcott engaged in abstract theorization, others tested the mysteries of gendered sensitivity and electromagnetism in a more empirical manner. An important figure in the spiritualists' eventual electromagnetic model of mediumship was Baron Charles Von Reichenbach, whose work seemed to provide experimental proof of enhanced feminine sensitivity. His earliest experiments involved placing "cataleptic" and "feeble-brained" teenage girls in dark rooms and then exposing them to a magnet. After performing this experiment on some twenty-two young women, Reichenbach concluded that "those sensitive persons, who are so in a high degree, perceive in the dark, at the poles of powerful magnets, a luminous appearance of a waving, flamelike nature, less or more according to the degree of their diseased sensibility, or more or less perfect degree of darkness."[26] In other words, Reichenbach believed that girls with a "diseased sensibility" could perceive a flickering aura around magnets, a force that was neither wholly electrical nor magnetic (interestingly, "disease" in this scenario led to an increase rather than a diminution of this allegedly feminine trait, suggesting that femininity in itself was regarded as a diseased state).

Olcott and Reichenbach incorporated electrical theory into the related and more widespread patriarchal belief in Victorian society that women, although physically and mentally inferior, were in some sense more sensitive than their male counterparts. Surveying the Darwinian tradition in gender psychology that dominated the century, Cynthia Russett observes that women were routinely distinguished from men by their "powers of intuition, of rapid perception, and perhaps of imagination."[27] Women also displayed their strength of emotion, as well as a " 'refinement of the senses, or higher evolution of sense-organs,' and rapidity of perception and thought, expressed in 'intuitive insight' and 'nimbleness of mother-wit.' "[28] It should be noted, however, that these seemingly "positive" traits related to perception were, at the time, "held to stand in inverse ratio to high intellectual development, since the latter induced reflection and this in turn retarded perception."[29] Ironically, these negative qualities attributed to women were to become the foundation of their spiritual authority. As Judith Walkowitz notes, "spiritualists deemed women particularly apt for mediumship because they were weak in the masculine attributes of will and intelligence, yet strong in the feminine qualities of passivity, chastity, and 'impressionability.' "[30]

Spiritualism and its eventual antagonists in medical science shared a brief but crucial moment of common intellectual heritage in these early accounts of feminine physiology. Although their theoretical concerns would eventually diverge, both the spiritualists and the pioneers of scientific neurology, inspired by the electrifying examples of galvanism, attributed much importance to the nervous principle that governed a telegraphic model of the nervous system. Both paradigms thought mediumistic women to be particularly vulnerable to the vicissitudes of the mysterious forces of nervous energy, a form of organic electricity that one commentator described as "an intermediate agent by which mind acts on matter, and which is itself neither mind nor matter."[31] As the more sensitive of the sexes, women were believed to have an unstable abundance of such energy, especially as adolescents. As this same author writes in diagnosing the "generally young, . . . inexperienced, and female" mediums of spiritualism, "they are just that class whom we ordinarily speak of as persons of high nervous temperament, of an acute mental organism. It is the very class of persons in whom the nervous principle is active, from whom we seem to see the nervous energy thus flowing off."[32]

As the two entities most closely associated with the mysteries of the life force, women and electricity were deeply imprecated in Victorian questions of spirituality. Building on a larger Victorian ideology of the ineffable moral purity and higher spirituality of women, the spiritualists would go on to produce a theory linking electromagnetism and femininity in a divine alliance. If communication with the dead were possible, reasoned most, then women, having brought life into the world through their "receptive reproductive economy," would be the most likely candidates for bringing the living spirits back onto the mortal plane through their exquisite sensitivity.

Appropriately, while Morse's telegraph carried news of banking, commerce, and other concerns of the masculine sphere, the spiritual telegraph addressed issues of vital concern to women. Mediums frequently strayed into such political territory during trance sessions, public events where the medium would enter a trance state and channel the words of a departed soul eager to comment on the mortal world's political landscape. Channeling such a spirit for an audience in New York, for example, Emma Hardinge challenged the audience to improve the fate of the city's 6,000 prostitutes. "The six thousand women are *'outcasts.'* Where are the six thousand men? In your saloons, and halls of legislature, your offices of trust, and places of honor, chanting the hymn of model America's 'fraternity,' whilst gibing demons cry 'Amen.' "[33] Communicating at seances through the circuit of telegraph and medium, the spirits of a higher and more refined plane of existence repeatedly argued that women needed to be liberated from the "limited education that restricted the development of their intellects, from unjust laws that denied them access to their property and custody of their children, from unequal marriages that subjugated them to men, and from economic restrictions that forced them into dependence."[34]

Such advocacy, however, did not necessarily brand these women (and men) as extremists. Within the context of spiritualism's model of electronic presence, women mediums and trance speakers were able to raise feminist issues and debate them freely without necessarily challenging directly the overall social order.[35] In a complex and somewhat ironic process of ideological negotiation, spiritualism empowered women to speak out in public, often about very controversial issues facing the nation, but only because all understood that the women were not the ones actually speaking, at least not women who were still alive. "Mediums presented not their own views but those of the spirits who spoke through them," notes Braude. Both in drawing rooms and large auditoriums, "the essential passivity of women was asserted in a public arena, displayed before thousands of witnesses."[36] Women could thus only assume such an active role in spiritualist thought and practice through their fundamentally passive natures, a constitution electrically inscribed in their enhanced sensitivity.

Existing at the fringes of Victorian science's understanding of electricity, femininity, and spirituality, the medium occupied a strategic political and intellectual space that allowed her to intervene in the public sphere through a combination of supernatural and technological discourses, a model legitimated by the equally incredible yet incontrovertible evidence of the telegraph. While the technology of the telegraph transformed America into a wired nation, the *concept* of telegraphy enabled endless displacements of agency, projecting utopian possibilities onto a disembodied, invisible community and recasting an often radical political agenda as an act of supernatural possession. The telegraph, spiritual or otherwise, not only made one interlocutor physically absent, but also placed the ultimate source of transmission in irresolvable ambiguity. Spiritualism as a movement exploited this intrinsic mystery of electronic telecommunications to make possible both new means and new forms of political discourse. In a sense, spiritualist women exploited the indeterminacy of telegraphy's electronic presence to "throw their voice" both physically and politically in a most complex form of ventriloquism. Arguably, such a masquerade would have been impossible without the provocative example of Morse's telegraph and its powers of disembodiment. For a brief moment at least, spiritualism presented a unique and even subversive articulation of femininity, electricity, and technology, recasting women's physical and mental inferiority into a form of technological authority—an expertise frequently invoked in support of women's rights, abolitionism, and other radical causes.

Hysterical Telegraphy

The importance of telegraphy as a conceptual construct is especially apparent when considering that telegraphic metaphors not only gave structure to spiritualist belief, but also presided over the movement's eventual delegitimation and extinction. Ironically, the empowering model of telegraphic technology would eventually be turned against the spiritualists, leading to a new articulation of femininity and electronic disassociation that would serve to restrict the autonomy of women (often quite literally). In opposition to the liberating fantasy of corporeal transcendence harbored by the spiritualists, emerging (and often competing) sciences such as neurology and psychiatry employed telegraphic knowledge to articulate their own theories of feminine physiology and psychology. As the century unfolded, critics of spiritualism increasingly aimed these rationalist sciences at mediumistic women in an attempt to place their bodies back under medical and thus political control. As Walkowitz observes, "special female powers also rendered female mediums vulnerable to special forms of female punishment: to medical labeling as hysterics and to lunacy confinement."[37]

Sharing the premise that women possessed a unique sensitivity, the emerging science of neurology sought its own explanations as to the electrical relationship of consciousness and the body. Spiritualism and its medical antagonists developed rival theories to address what both paradigms saw as a very specialized and highly telegraphic relationship between gender, consciousness, and electricity.[38] While the spiritualists believed a woman's surplus (or imbalance) of nervous energy made her a more receptive candidate for receiving the higher electromagnetic transmissions of the spirits, medical science felt this surplus led instead to dysfunctions of the body where the nervous system, as a great telegraphic network, was overtaxed by the variable intensity of this flow. While mediums viewed themselves as channeling invisible streams of spiritual electricity, a capacity enabled by the more plastic and religious feminine mind, many physicians of the period saw women as extraordinarily prone to electrical dysfunctions of the nervous system. This was no idle debate. For its advocates, celestial telegraphy led to revelation, enlightenment, and, in many cases, the elevation of feminine voices in a resoundingly patriarchal society. The collapses of nervous telegraphy, on the other hand, led to the seemingly ubiquitous nineteenth-century maladies of hysteria and neurasthenia. What the spiritualists saw as mediumistic phenomena, medical science labeled as mania and insanity. This telegraphic breakdown of the nervous system brought with it stigmatization, institutionalization, and even death.

When confronted with an overtaxed nervous system, mediumistic or otherwise, the physician's task was to restore this economy through the precise application of electrical flow.[39] As one theorist wrote, "If there is an induced current so acting as to diminish the normal current, then effects, such as paralysis, or anesthesia are produced; if it acts so as to increase the nerve force, then such phenomenon as excessive motor activity or hyperaesthesia is the result."[40] John Haller and Robin Haller describe the logic behind such "electrotherapeutics."[41] "The use of electricity on the neuron, it was believed, restored 'conductibility' which, due to prostration, had become resistant to the nerve current. By exciting the nerve tissue, a condition of 'electrotonos,' or a change in nerve excitability, occurred, in which the neuron found newer paths of transmission for its nervous impulses."[42] As physicians adopted electricity as a popular treatment for a variety of physical complaints in the second half of the century, it became especially important in treating mental and nervous disorders. "We like it," wrote one asylum director, "find it beneficial in most cases, valuable in a majority, and indispensable in certain forms of hysterical insanity, in primary dementia, and neurasthenia."[43] For many physicians, belief in mediumistic abilities was both cause and symptom of a disordered nervous economy, a condition that would eventually lead to full hysteria. In this regard, Charcot compared spiritualists to children, writing of the movement, "it indicates clearly the danger there is, especially to persons nervously predisposed, in superstitious practices, which unfortunately have for them so great an attraction, and in that constant tension of mind and imagination to which those are brought who apply themselves to spiritistic performances and the search of the marvelous, an occupation in which children take so much delight."[44]

Spiritualism's struggle against the nonbelievers, medical or otherwise, suggests that as a popular fantasy that quickly captured the public imagination, telegraphic disembodiment made possible new avenues of social liberation even while extending old and more familiar relations of gendered power. Within an already dynamic field of social struggle, the electrical animation of telegraphic presence significantly informed increasingly antagonistic regimes of knowledge, producing theoretical spaces (and technological models) that could generate either calls for social change and political reform or criteria of insanity and institutionalization. Mediums became complex and contested "devices," linking for some the living and the dead, science and religion, masculine technology and feminine spirituality, while for others signifying the fundamental fragility of women and their inability to adjust to the modern world and its many wonders. Operating at the provocative fringes of religion and rationalism, spirit and science, mediums presented themselves as a "technology" constructed from and yet in conflict with the more colonizing embodiments of traditional religion and rationalist science. In doing so, they walked a fine line between empowerment and institutionalization. One might say, whereas the spiritualists imagined telegraphic technology as a means of transcending material existence in an out-of-body experience, medical science employed telegraphic metaphors to reground consciousness within the bodies of women who were thought to be out of their minds.

In the months after the "Rochester knockings," the Fox sisters and their mother traveled extensively to provide public demonstrations of the spirit phenomena. Skeptics examined the women and their communications repeatedly, but could not definitively account for the source of the rappings. Their disbelief did little to dampen enthusiasm for the growing movement. In a letter published in the *New York Herald* in April 1851, however, a relative of the girls claimed to know the true source of the manifestations. Kate Fox, the youngest of the Fox daughters, allegedly explained to this relative that she produced the raps by cracking the joints in her knees and toes, a skill both she and Margeretta had mastered as children by pressing their toes against the footboard in bed. Despite this admission and numerous counterattacks, the movement continued to flourish. In 1888, fully grown and somewhat down on her luck, Margeretta made a public confession of the less than paranormal source of the manifestations (according to some, because she had received money to do so). Interestingly, Margeretta recanted the confession no sooner than she had issued it, placing the matter once again in some degree of ambiguity.[45]

Started as a girlish prank, perhaps, the spirit manifestations rapidly assumed a public life of their own. In a period distinguished by the mysteries of electricity, an emerging turbulence in the politics of gender, and an overall utopian enthusiasm for technologies of deliverance, this unlikely juxtaposition of toe joint and telegraph helped articulate what would eventually become a fully developed fantasy of electronic transmutability. Through images of discorporation, anthropomorphization, and even cybernetics, spiritualism produced the media age's first "electronic elsewhere," an invisible utopian realm generated and accessed through the wonders of electronic media. The conceptual appropriation of telegraphy by spiritualism (and medical science) suggests that as telegraph lines stretched across the nation to connect city and town, town and country, they also stretched across the nation's imagination to interconnect a variety of social and cultural spheres. For the spiritualists, the bodiless communication of telegraphy heralded the existence of a land without material substance, an always unseen origin point of transmission for discorporated souls in an electromagnetic utopia. Each time a medium manifested occult telepresence, be it through rappings or spirit voices, planchette readings or automatic writing, she provided indexical evidence of a social stage continually displaced and deferred that held the promise of a final paradise. Such unbridled enthusiasm for the wonders of an "electronic elsewhere" would have no real equal until the emergence of transcendental cyberspace mythologies in our own cultural moment.

By the end of the nineteenth century, spiritualism as a science was for the most part discredited, but spiritualist belief survived to inform cultural fantasies surrounding the next century's new telecommunications marvels. The "electronic elsewheres" imagined in connection with wireless, radio, and television, however, would be much more sinister and disturbing than the spiritualist fantasies of electronic utopia. As telegraphy gave way to wireless, and as the nineteenth century gave way to modernity, new articulations of telepresence were to be more anxious than beatific, suggesting a realignment in the social imagination as to the powers and possibilities of electronic telecommunications.

NOTES

1. Ezra Gannett, *The Atlantic Telegraph: A Discourse Delivered in the First Church, August 8, 1858* (Boston: Crosby, Nichols & Co., 1858), 13.

2. Through a series of yes-no questions, the family learned that the eerie interlocutor was the ghost of a peddler who had been murdered by a former occupant of the house years earlier. Later, by rapping out the alphabet, the spirit identified himself as "Charles Rosna," and claimed that his bones could be found buried in the basement of the home.

3. Some spiritualists claim that Lincoln's contact with the movement and its socially progressive spirits guided the president into issuing the Emancipation Proclaimation. They point out that Lincoln had not been an abolitionist at the beginning of his presidency.

4. Emma Hardinge, *Modern American Spiritualism* (New Hyde Park, N.Y.: University Books, 1970). 39. Originally published in 1869.

5. J. H. Powell, *Mediumship: Its Laws and Conditions; with Brief Instructions for the Formation of Spirit Circles* (Boston: William White and Company, 1868), 21.

6. *The Spirit World, Its Locality and Conditions, by the Spirit of Judge John Worth Edmonds, Late a Prominent Citizen of New York, Given Through the Mediumship of Wash. A. Danskin, and Published at the Request of the First Spiritualist Congregation, of Baltimore* (Baltimore: Steam Press of Frederick A. Hanzsche, 1874), 7.

7. Ann Braude, *Radical Spirits: Spiritualism and Women's Rights in Nineteenth Century America* (Boston: Beacon Press, 1989), 23.

8. John Murray Spear, *The Educator: Being Suggestions, Theoretical and Practical, Designed to Promote Man-Culture and Integral Reform, with a View to the Ultimate Establishment of a Divine Social State on Earth* (Boston: Office of Practical Spiritualists, 1857), 163.

9. James W. Carey, "Technology and Ideology: The Case of the Telegraph," in *Communication as Culture* (Boston: Unwin Hyman, 1989), 204.

10. Galvani's work as well as a summary of period experiments by other scientists can be found in Margaret Glover Foley's translation of Galvani's *Commentary on the Effects of Electricity on Muscular Motion* (Norwalk, Conn.: Burndy Library, 1953).

11. John Bostock, *An Account of the History and Present State of Galvanism* (London: Baldwin, Cradock and Joy, 1818), n.p.

12. See Fernand Papillon, "Electricity and Life," *Popular Science Monthly* 2 (March 1873): 532–33. One experimenter, in choreography worthy of the Grand Guignol, compelled a corpse "to point at one or another of the spectators."

13. Mary Shelley, "Frankenstein," in *Three Gothic Novels* (New York: Penguin Books, 1968), 262–63.

14. Ibid., 263.

15. For an account of phrenology's impact in this period, see Roger Cooter, *The Cultural Meaning of Popular Science: Phrenology and the Organization of Consent in Nineteenth-Century Britain* (Cambridge: Cambridge University Press, 1984).

16. The vagueness of animal magnetism and animal electricity as physical forces was not lost on period commentators. Many critics lampooned the often inarticulate theories of these emerging "sciences" in cartoons, editorials, and popular literature. For example, in Elizabeth Inchbald's play, *Animal Magnetism: A Farce in 3 Acts*, written in 1792 and performed well into the next century, an inept doctor hopes to learn the science of animal magnetism from a visiting expert, La Fluer. In the following exchange, La Fluer explains the principles behind Mesmeristic science.

La Fluer: You know doctor, there is an universal fluid which spreads throughout all nature.

Doc: A fluid?

La Fluer: Yes, a fluid—which is—a—fluid—and you know, doctor, that this fluid—generally called a fluid, is the most subtle of all that is most subtle— Do you understand me?

Doc: Yes, yes—

La Fluer: It ascends on high, [looking down] and descends on low, [looking up] penetrates all substances, from the hardest metal, to the softest bosom— you understand me, I perceive?

Doc: Not very well.

Later in the play it is revealed that practitioners of Mesmerism have an uncanny romantic influence over women, an example of what has survived as the only vestigial meaning left for the phrase, "animal magnetism." See Elizabeth Inchbald, *Animal Magnetism: A Farce in Three Acts* (New York: Publisher unknown, 1809).

In his study of Mesmerism in prerevolutionary France, Robert Darnton argues that animal magnetism, along with many other fantastic theories, fed a growing public fascination with popular science at the end of the century. "The reading public of that era was intoxicated with the power of science," writes Darnton, "and it was bewildered by the real and imaginary forces with which scientists peopled that universe. Because the public could not distinguish the real from the imaginary, it seized on any invisible fluid, any scientific-sounding hypothesis, that promised to explain the wonders of nature." See Robert Darnton, *Mesmerism and the End of the Enlightenment in France* (Cambridge, Mass.: Harvard University Press, 1968), 23.

17. James W. Carey and John J. Quirk, "The Mythos of the Electronic Revolution," in *Communication as Culture*, 121.

18. For an account of Morse's contact with earth, see "The Skeleton in the Fox Cottage," by P.L.O.A. Keeler, in *Hydesville in History*, ed. M. E. Cadwallader (Chicago: The Progressive Thinker Publishing House, 1917), 53.

19. Reverend H. Mattison, *Spirit-Rapping Unveiled! An Expose of the Origin, History, Theology, and Philosophy of Certain Alleged Communications from the Spirit World by Means of "Spirit Rapping," "Medium Writing," "Physical Demonstrations," Etc.* (New York: J. C. Derby, 1855), 67.

20. Robert Milne, "Professor Vehr's Electrical Experiment," *The Argonaut*, January 24, 1885, in *Into the Sun and Other Stories: Science Fiction in Old San Francisco*, ed. Sam Moskowitz (West Kingston, R.I.: Donald M. Grant, 1980), 87.

21. Ibid., 89.

22. William Fishbough, "Laws and Phenomena of the Soul. Number One," *Spirit Messenger and Harmonial Advocate* 1, no. 6 (November 20, 1852): 1.

23. Ibid.

24. Frank J. Tipler, *The Physics of Immortality: Modern Cosmology, God and the Resurrection of the Dead* (New York: Doubleday, 1994), ix.

25. Ibid., xi.

26. Charles von Reichenbach, *Physico-Physiological Researches in The Dynamics of Magnetism, Electricity, Heat, Light, Crystallization, and Chemism, in Their Relations to Vital Force* (New York: Partridge and Brittan, 1851), 34.

27. Cynthia Russett, *Sexual Science: The Victorian Construction of Womanhood* (Cambridge, Mass.: Harvard University Press, 1989), 40.

28. Ibid., 42.

29. Ibid.

30. Judith Walkowitz, "Science and Seance: Transgressions of Gender and Genre in Late Victorian London," *Representations* no. 22 (Spring, 1988): 9.

31. Traverse Oldfield, *"To Daimonion," or the Spiritual Medium. Its Nature Illustrated by the History of its Uniform Mysterious Manifestation when Unduly Excited. In Twelve Familiar Letters to an Inquiring Friend* (Boston: Gould and Lincoln, 1852), 24–25.

32. Ibid., 39.

33. Emma Hardinge, *America and Her Destiny: An Inspirational Discourse* (New York: Robert M. DeWitt, 1861), 12.

34. Braude, *Radical Spirits,* 56.

35. As Braude writes, "mediumship gave women a public leadership role that allowed them to remain compliant with the complex values of the period that have come to be known as the cult of true womanhood" (ibid., 82). The cult of true womanhood, as described by Braude and others, asserted that women were characterized by "purity, piety, passivity, and domesticity," and were thus particularly suited for religious and spiritual matters (ibid.). See also Barbara Welter, "The Cult of True Womanhood: 1820–1860," *American Quarterly* 18 (Summer 1966): 151–74.

36. Braude, *Radical Spirits,* 85.

37. Walkowitz, "Science and Seance," 9.

38. S.E.D. Shortt, "Physicians and Psychics: The Anglo-American Medical Response to Spiritualism, 1870–1890," *The Journal of the History of Medicine and Allied Sciences* 39 (1984): 339–55; and Edward M. Brown, "Neurology and Spiritualism in the 1870s," *Bulletin of the History of Medicine* 57 (Winter 1983): 563–77.

39. A. H. Newth, "The Galvanic Current Applied in the Treatment of Insanity," *Journal of Mental Science* 19 (April 1873): 79–86.

40. A. H. Newth, "The Electro-Neural Pathology of Insanity," *Journal of Mental Science* 24 (April 1878): 78.

41. John S. Haller and Robin M. Haller, *The Physician and Sexuality in Victorian America* (New York: Norton, 1974), 13.

42. Ibid.

43. George M. Beard, "The Treatment of Insanity by Electricity," *Journal of Mental Science* 19 (October 1873): 356.

44. J. M. Charcot, "Hysteria and Spiritism," *Medical and Surgical Reporter* 59 no. 3 (July 21, 1888): 68.

45. Frank Podmore, *Mediums of the 19th Century* (New Hyde Park, N.Y.: University Books, 1963).

MARITA STURKEN

4   Mobilities of Time and Space

Technologies of the Modern and the Postmodern

IN THE 1926 film *The Crowd*, directed by King Vidor, a young man, John Sims, ventures to New York City, a place he sees as the land of opportunity. There he fully becomes a citizen of modernity, his life ruled by the clock (Sims and his fellow clerks, all assigned a number and seated in rows of identical desks, watch the clock carefully and race to the door when its hands hit 5) and dictated by the space of the modern city. Vidor's New York is dominated by crowded streets, oppressively tall skyscrapers, and the relentless traffic of cars, trolleys, and trains. It is a city in which modern life is defined not only by the crowd—the sense of living always surrounded by strangers, crowding in, pushing, staring—but also by the presence of technology in all aspects of life, by the towering skyscrapers that cast shadows on the sidewalks, and by the dangers of transportation technologies. Sims's young daughter is hit and killed by a truck while running across the street, and in his despair Sims leans out over a railroad bridge and contemplates jumping down in front of a train. Technology and its perils are omnipresent in modern life, the film seems to say, making the decision between living and dying so incremental, so potentially accidental. Vidor uses a mobile cinematic style to portray the city—gliding up the sides of skyscrapers, creating complex montages of the chaos of urban streets, and painting interiors as spare, cold spaces of alienation. In the final shot, Sims and his family sit watching a film in a movie theater. As the camera pulls away from them, as if traveling backward toward the screen, they are lost in a sea of laughing faces—elements of the masses watching mass entertainment. Their individuality lost, they are absorbed into the crowd.

Vidor's film can be situated at a particular moment in the early twentieth century, after the tragic and disastrous events of World War I, when the world of modernity was portrayed increasingly by artists, writers, and filmmakers as one of alienation, anxiety, and violence, a life threatened rather than improved by technology and industrialization. This was a time during which the experience of modernity was questioned and greeted with increasing ambivalence. It followed the turn of the century, when the

71

experience of modernity had been emphatically embraced. As the nine-teenth century turned into the twentieth, there was in Euroamerican cul-ture a sense of standing at the precipice, embracing the future, a posi-tion both exciting and terrifying. This had been the height of modernity, with its combination of optimism with anxiety, an embrace of the new coupled with a fear of losing the past. It was primarily through the ex-perience of modern technologies that this sense of promise and fear was produced.

Today, at the turn of the millennium, much of the industrial (and postin-dustrial) world finds itself at a particularly important juncture. This is not, as is often argued, defined by the replacement of modernity by postmoder-nity. Rather, it is a time defined by the tension between the two. The world-view of most of the industrialized world remains relentlessly modern in its valuing of science, technology, growth, and progress. Yet these modern sensibilities are integrated with an increasingly postmodern sensibility—a sense of cynicism and fatigue with modernity's hurtling forward into the future, a world increasingly defined by the digital, the computer, and the virtual. Life appears to be speeding up and compressing downward at the turn of the millennium, with a sense of decreasing control over the speed of daily life. Yet, this feeling of life speeding out of control is a deeply modern one, one that prevailed throughout the twentieth century. This mo-ment in history is thus defined specifically by the tensions of living with both the heightened qualities of modernity and the shifting worldview of postmodernism.

Technologies, in particular communication technologies, have been cen-tral to definitions of both modernity and postmodernity. Indeed, the expe-rience of modernity has been associated so powerfully with the emergence of industrial technologies that the equation of the two is often taken for granted. Can we ever think of modernity outside of a framework of tech-nological development? The modern is the mechanical, the industrial, and its attendant belief in progress, and the modern subject a technologized subject, whose worldview, way of being, and daily life is shaped by the integration of technology into the fabric of life—the figures of *The Crowd*. The primary symbols of modernity—railroads, skyscrapers, subways, the urban cityscape—are themselves technological artifacts. Importantly, these technologies did not create the modern condition, rather they emerged from the changing set of social imperatives and relations that constituted this condition.

There are important parallels between the turn of the century and the turn of the millennium, particularly in terms of the intensity of technological change. The period around 1900 saw the invention of the phonograph, radio, cinema, the airplane, the automobile, the telephone, and the X ray, all of which remain important today. The end of the twentieth century witnessed the development of satellite technology, digital imaging, fax, cell phones, the Internet, and the extremely rapid expansion of the World Wide Web. Whereas the world of the turn of the century was focused on the industrial and the mass media, today's world is understood in terms of the postindustrial, globalization, and media convergence. Increasingly, large numbers of people live in a world of digital technology, virtual space, and genetic codes, one defined by computer technology. Whereas the modern was mechanical, the postmodern is decidedly electronic.

Yet, the modern and the postmodern are not as incompatible or different as such descriptions might indicate. The idea of technologies facilitating connectivity, for instance, has been central to both moments in history. While the telegraph prompted proclamations about world peace and the end of human conflict in the nineteenth century, the Internet is now declared to be the first step in a new world understanding. The telephone and television were both seen as potentially jeopardizing family cohesiveness and undermining parental authority, just as the Internet is seen to render parents powerless. The ways that these narratives are perpetuated from one technology to the next makes clear, in many ways, how contemporary society remains both modern and postmodern.

It is the aim of this essay to examine this relationship between technology and definitions of the modern and the postmodern. The term *postmodernism* has been hotly contested and debated, the subject in the 1980s and 1990s of numerous treatises on its usefulness, or not, as a term.[1] Many have argued that what is termed *postmodernism* is, in fact, deeply imbricated within the modernist project and is an example of late modernism, radical modernism, or, supermodernity. It is my goal in this essay to argue that while aspects of the modern and the postmodern overlap, there are sometimes useful distinctions between the two, which can be most clearly delineated in relation to technologies and how they are experienced, used, and integrated into daily life. Examining both the distinctions and overlap between modern and postmodern technologies can, in turn, help us to understand this particular moment of history. I begin with a chart:

MODERN—POSTMODERN
national/international—global
hierarchical social structure—network society
mechanical—electronic
industrial—postindustrial
urban city—suburban sprawl, megalopolis
geographical space replaced by social space—nonplace
Cartesian space—virtual space
standing in a crowd—social isolation
surrounded by strangers—mobile privatization
circulation of traffic in city—Internet "traffic" and packet-switching
city strolling, the flaneur—Web surfing
time as measurable—time as global
time as linear—time shifting
analog clock/watch—digital clock/watch
railroad—rapid speed trains (TGV and Shinkensan)
telegraph—Internet
subway—freeway
airplane—space shuttle
automobile as transportation—automobile as style
radio—Walkman
photograph—digital image
typewriter—computer
typewriter keyboard—computer mouse
television—multimedia/DVD/TiVo
cinema—virtual reality
telephone—cell phone
space travel—travel inside the body through fiberoptics
the body as a circulatory system—the body as a genetic map
tuberculosis and antibiotics—AIDS and retroviruses
representation—simulacrum
autonomous subject—multiple and fragmented subjectivities
war of guns, bombs, machines—virtual/cyberwar
wars as conflicts between nations—terrorism

There is, of course, pleasure in charting oppositions. Indeed, mapping and charting are crucial urges of modernity. However, my intention here is to demonstrate a set of continuums rather than binary oppositions between modernity and postmodernity. As oppositions, many of these distinctions between modernity and postmodernity cannot hold. Yet, seen as a set of continuums, which then constitute different focuses in modernity and postmodernity, these binaries can help us to see the shifting terrain and tensions between the two. I thus present this chart as a point of departure for considering what qualities are shared between the modern and the postmodern, and when distinctions between the two matter, in relation to time, space, concepts of mobility, and notions about the body.

THE MODERN EXPERIENCE OF TIME

There is perhaps no concept that embodies more profoundly the experience of modernity than that of speed. It has been noted by Lewis Mumford and others that the desire for speed emerged in the thirteenth century and became "insistent" by the sixteenth century.[2] Time became something new in the emerging modern world of Europe in this era, and by the nineteenth century was codified in irrevocable ways. The modern world of the nineteenth century prized synchronization, standardization, efficiency, and the predictability that this produced. This new experience of time replaced a premodern time that was dictated by region, by the cycle of the earth around the sun and the seasons of the year. Modern time was a new form of mechanical time, not so much observed as measured.

The concept of time as uniform and measurable was facilitated by new modern technologies. The mechanical clock had been invented in the fourteenth century, but until the end of the nineteenth century, town clocks could vary significantly from region to region. The standardization of time in the late nineteenth century was prompted primarily by the railroad and the telegraph and furthered as well by needs of military planners. Thus, two technologies were instrumental in the marking of time into specific time zones across the globe. Historian Stephen Kern writes:

> Despite all the good scientific and military arguments for world time, it was the railroad companies and not the governments that were the first to institute it. Around 1870, if a traveler from Washington to San Francisco set his watch in every town he passed through, he would set it over two hundred times. . . . The day the railroads imposed a uniform time, November 18, 1883, was called "the day of two noons," because at midday clocks had to be set back in the eastern part of each zone—one last necessary disruption to enable the railroads to end the confusion that had so complicated their functioning and cut into their profits.[3]

The mapping of the world into different time zones was a particularly global act of the nineteenth century. The designation of Greenwich, England, as the center of standardized time looked, in the nineteenth century, quite commonsensical. England was conceived as the center of the world, and the international date line was designated in the middle of the Pacific Ocean, imagined by the Europeans as an empty space, a safe place to bear the inconvenience of time skipping forward a day. Yet, from the perspective of late twentieth- and early twenty-first-century global capitalism, this mapping has had profound consequences, certainly unanticipated by the nineteenth-century proponents of uniform time. The day begins in the world not in Europe but in Asia. More important, the economic day begins in Asia, giving Asian markets significant influence on the rest of the global markets. On New Year's Day, 2000, the twenty-four-hour celebration presented a global mapping of the world in twenty-four time zones, facilitated by live and global television coverage, and beginning on a small island in the Pacific. The coverage of the millennium could be seen as an explicit embrace of connectivity in terms of globalization and the emerging postindustrial global economy, but its framework came from the desire to synchronize time in the modern era.

The railroad demanded a new kind of measurable time and also embodied the forward march of time that is so central to the modern worldview. Indeed, the railroad has often been characterized as the most quintessential technological artifact of modernity. The railroad changed the landscapes that it traversed, both literally, as hills were tunneled through and gradations smoothed out for the tracks, but also in terms of how the traveler experienced it. In his classic study, *The Railway Journey*, Wolfgang Schivelbusch writes that the railroad reconfigured the landscape that was viewed from its window, conquering nature so to speak, and speeding up the experiences of looking. Schivelbusch writes that nineteenth-century travelers who had not adjusted to the mode of industrial travel were "not able to develop modes of perception appropriate to the new form of transportation," and many of them, such as Flaubert, wrote about the oppressive tedium of train travel.[4] The speed of the train created a monotonous landscape that could not be subject to contemplation, rendering it, in effect, "a new landscape." Similarly, French philosopher Paul Virilio argues that the nineteenth and twentieth centuries defined the era of acceleration. He states, "Up until the nineteenth century, society was founded on the brake. Means of furthering speed were very scant."[5] With the Industrial Revolution, Virilio argues, society passes from the age of brakes to the age of the accelerator, in which "power will be invested in acceleration itself."

The railroad was the dominant symbol of acceleration. It not only codified time and sped it up in the nineteenth century, it also collapsed time in greatly reducing how long it took people to travel long distances. In its linearity, the railroad thus operates as a primary metaphor for the meanings of modernity—it moves forward, it designates time as linear, and it restructures time and space as it hurtles toward the future, toward new places, toward destinations. As Peter Lyman notes in this volume, metaphors of transportation have been used throughout history to designate new technologies, including the current metaphor of the superhighway. The railroad as an icon of modern progress set this symbolism in motion.

Speed is, of course, central to communication technology. In contemporary media, the live and the instant have taken on even greater value, and information is increasingly considered to be of less value when it is not instant. Yet speed is also an indicator of volatility and the potential for chaos.[6] Contemporary characterizations of the turn of the millennium and the postmodern experiences often deploy speed as a central characteristic of our era. With contemporary technologies such as live television, satellite broadcast, and the Internet, instantaneity and speed have only increased in importance. Thus, any distinction between modern and postmodern concepts of speed is negligible, simply one of degree. However, on the quality of linear time moving forward, there is an important distinction. Modern time marches forward, implying that each movement and minute toward the future is an improvement, a testimony of the importance of progress. Modern literature and art begin to question this linearity, and in the postmodern context, no such faith in linear progress remains. In postmodernism, time is something to be played with, to be shifted, reversed, and fast-forwarded. Thus, it could be argued that a postmodern sensibility is closer to Walter Benjamin's famous notion of hurtling toward the future, yet, at the same time, involves a questioning of the very notion of moving forward, or of progress, at all.

MODERN AND POSTMODERN SPACE

Like the railroad, the telegraph was a defining new technology of the nineteenth century. Invented in the late eighteenth century and electrified in the 1830s, it was a primary force in the increasing speed with which information traveled over distances. It was thus influential in the collapsing and reconfiguring of space that defined the modern experience. If information could travel quickly, the meaning of that information changed. In his study of the telegraph, *The Victorian Internet*, Tom Standage describes some of the early uses of the telegraph to apprehend criminals, send gambling information, and relay public news.[7] Information was defined by the telegraph as having a higher value if it was transmitted across a distance.

In this sense, the telegraph can be seen as a device that both collapsed distance and changed the meaning of the space between various points. The capacity of the telegraph to transfer information across space meant that distance was not as central an obstacle to human interaction. Standage tells several stories of couples who pursued romance or married over the telegraph, stories that were written up in the press as "The Dangers of Wired Love" or "Making Love by Telegraph."[8] Thus, overcoming distance was embraced as a means to greater human connection. By extension, the telegraph was often understood within utopian terms as a medium through which world peace and reconciliation would be popular—one of the first technologies, in fact, to be thought of in global terms. Speed of communication was thus defined as an improvement in comprehension and reconciliation—the belief that the faster the messages were received, the more like-minded those communicating would become.

Space that is traveled through or traversed by wires is compressed, and takes on a different form. It becomes, in the words of Schivelbusch, an "in-between space"—not a destination. He writes, "On the one hand, the railroad opened up new spaces that were not as easily accessible before; on the other, it did so by destroying space, namely the space between points. That in-between, or travel space, which it was possible to 'savor' while using the slow, work-intensive eotechnical form of transport, disappeared on the railroads. The railroad knows only points of departure and destination."[9] As such, the railroad transformed certain areas into in-between places, places now designated with no purpose, distinct from railroad destinations. Similarly, places that the telegraph traveled through became in-between places.

This distinction between space and place is central to the modern experience. As distances were quickly traversed and spaces were transformed by the increased mobility of the modern citizen, time and space were increasingly disconnected. Anthony Giddens argues that modernity reconfigured space in two important ways: it separated time and space, and created a distinction between space and place. If place defines a locale or specific geographical location, space is a more abstract concept, referring to social space as well as conceptual space. Giddens writes,

> In pre-modern societies, space and place largely coincide, since the spatial dimensions of social life are, for the most of the population, and in most respects, dominated by "presence"—by localised activities. The advent of

modernity increasingly tears space away from place by fostering relations between "absent" others, locationally distant from any given situation of face-to-face interaction. In conditions of modernity, place becomes increasingly *phantasmagoric*: that is to say, locales are thoroughly penetrated by and shaped in terms of social influences quite distant from them.[10]

This separation of space from place was fostered by and in turn fueled the development of the modern technologies of the telegraph, railroad, telephone, and radio.[11]

If modernity was characterized by a separation of space and place, in postmodernity, there is an emphasis on the proliferation of nonspaces—airports, freeways, bank machines. For instance, Margaret Morse analyzes freeways, malls, and television as the "locus of an attenuated *fiction effect*, that is, a partial loss of touch with the here and now," a distraction.[12] As nonspaces, freeways, malls, and television produce a kind of dislocation, a displacement, which in turn fosters a kind of detachment. Morse situates the freeway as a new form of mobile subjectivity, yet her analysis demonstrates the similarities between the modern experience of the railroad and the contemporary freeway. The observation that "perhaps no aspect of the freeway experience is more characteristic than the sudden realization that you have no memory of the past ten minutes of your trip" is analogous to Schivelbusch's observation that nineteenth-century railway travelers could not "read" the landscapes that they traveled through.[13]

The postmodern concept of the nonplace thus bears a contiguous relationship to the modern sense of space as compressed, traveled through, removed from actual places. The experience of nonplaces, spaces of waiting and transition such as airports, is not simply one of distraction or detachment. It is also about a kind of solitary subjectivity—not of social relations so much as an emphasized singularity. Marc Augé writes, "The space of non-place creates neither singular identity nor relations; only solitude, and similitude."[14] In addition, as many theorists have pointed out, what count as "nonplaces" for some are places of work and even homes for others.[15] Hence, concepts of postmodern space have had a tendency to ignore issues of class and privilege in relationship to space.

The collapsing of space and emergence of nonplaces demonstrate in many ways overlapping concepts of space in modernity and postmodernity. However, there are some important distinctions between ways of imagining space in both, and this has primarily to do with the concept of the virtual. The space of the modern city is crowded and compressed, yet, at the same time, the modern experience is about an embrace of the horizon,

a sense of space as potentially infinite. Whereas in feudal and agrarian societies, the horizon evoked danger, mystery, and the unknown, in the era of
modern science, the horizon signifies possibility, the capacity to look farther,
into the future, and, importantly, the capacity of imaging technologies, such
as photography, to allow the human eye to see farther, beyond the horizon,
in aerial views, and through microscopy into the human body itself.

Modern space is both crowded and infinite; it is also tangible and measurable. Yet, the postmodern emergence of nonplaces also indicates an important shift toward, if not an ease with, the experience of virtual space.
While the wireless radio and telegraph were modern media that produced
experiences of virtual space, and were thought of in the mystical terms of
the "ether," the increased role of virtual space has been primarily fostered
by computer technology, specifically the Internet and wireless technologies of computers and mobile phones. Virtual space is antithetical to what
is commonly thought of as physical space. It cannot be touched; it cannot, more important, be measured. Concepts of space in modernity were
shaped in many ways by concepts of Cartesian space—the idea, derived
from Descartes, that space can be defined and mapped mathematically. A
Cartesian grid measures three-dimensional space along three axes, each intersecting the others at ninety degrees. In its design, it is a rationalist and
scientific way of conceiving space—space is defined through its mathematical measurability.

Yet virtual space defies the laws of Cartesian science. It cannot be seen or
mapped. It exists in an abstract state. A bank machine uses the language of
customer service, but one's experience of it bears no relation to entering a
bank building. A Web site on the World Wide Web may be experienced as a
place (a "site") in virtual space, complete with "rooms" and "pages," but it
exists on multiple computer screens and is physically stored on a computer
server. People wearing virtual reality headsets may see the space before
them as a physical space, but it cannot be mapped in Cartesian terms, any
more than it can be "seen" within the computer that stores it. In traditional
terms, virtual space is "invisible."

I would argue that the experience of virtual space, and the related experience of simulations, constitutes a significant shift away from the modern
experience into postmodernism. This is not simply because these spaces are
of increasing importance in information exchange and social interaction,
but also because of the increased *ease* with which they are integrated into
daily life. The rapid pace with which the World Wide Web diffused into
American culture and has now become an important force worldwide is

an indicator of the social and cultural shifts that enabled this embrace—the moment when the virtual was no longer a threat but rather a comfortable space for occupation.

Mobility and Connectivity

The changing concepts of space and time in the modern and the postmodern are deeply connected to the experience of mobility in modernity. In the so-called premodern world, mobility was not only rarely an option for most citizens, it was also not a value. The world outside was one to be feared, imagined as the source of a potentially infinite number of terrors. Yet, beginning with the world navigations of the fifteenth century and moving into the Scientific Revolution, European culture not only began to map beyond its horizon, but also to regard travel in increasingly positive terms. This was aided by the spoils of colonization and the ideology of racial superiority that this fostered. Thus, travel outward from Europe affirmed concepts of other cultures as more childlike and primitive in comparison to European societies, and established concepts of other races as "other" to European whites.

By the era of the railroad, mobility was a primary factor of modern life. Modern subjects were supposed to be mobile—to move from small towns into the big city, to travel by train for long distances, to take trolleys and subways from their homes to their places of work. The modern city was designed to be walked or ridden through, to be seen on the move. Cities like Paris were reconfigured to allow for mobility, as Baron Haussmann razed the city to create the wide boulevards for modern transportation systems, using the railroad as his guide. Thus, Schivelbusch argues, *circulation* was a primary value of nineteenth-century life. The streets of the modern city primarily serve traffic, rather than operating as forums for neighborhood life.[16] The commerce of the emerging consumer society was also based on mobility. The urban consumer walked past advertisements and went window shopping, and the modern department store was designed for shoppers to circulate past displays without a particular destination. Schivelbusch writes:

> The nineteenth century's preoccupation with the conquest and mastery of space and time had found its most general expression in the concept of circulation, which was central to the scientistic social notions of the epoch. . . . The century's social organisms were replicas of events in both the biological and the traffic sphere. In other words, the nineteenth

century saw the health and vitality of social institutions and processes as dependent on a functioning circulatory system.[17]

He goes on to note that whatever was seen as part of circulation was regarded as "healthy, progressive, constructive" and all that was detached from it was seen as "diseased, medieval, subversive, threatening." In this framework, mobility is not only an important value, it is essential to the life of the city and its capacity to survive. While theorists of postmodernism often define mobility in the negative terms of detachment and derealization, within the modern city it was experienced as the life blood, the city's reason for being. Yet, at the same time, circulation and mobility were also experienced as the dangers of the modern city. As Ben Singer writes, modernity "was conceived as a barrage of *stimuli.*"[18] There was a public fascination with accidents and a proliferation of stories about the dangers of modern machines in the nineteenth century. The public saw the railroad as the site of potential (if not actual) destruction, a machine of death, and, as *The Crowd* demonstrates with its tragic scene of the young girl hit by a truck, the modern city street was risky and potentially violent in its mix of humans and machines. The modern "accident" was understood in technological terms.

Transportation systems mobilized the modern citizenry, and in turn had an effect on the ways of traversing the city on foot. The quintessential modern city dweller was, in Charles Baudelaire's concept, a flaneur who strolled the city streets in a kind of detached state, an observer who walked without destination or purpose. The flaneur is a figure defined by mobility, and indicative of changing concepts of vision. Anne Friedberg writes that new forms of visual display emerged in the nineteenth century that were based on the idea of a visual experience as a form of travel.[19] Dioramas, in which audiences sat before elaborate sets with changing backgrounds, each rotated every fifteen minutes, were advertised as a form of travel—through which, for example, Parisians could imagine that they had traveled to the Great Pyramids and had seen faraway places. Panoramic paintings were designed to be viewed not from one position, but by a mobile viewer. Panoramas filled a 360-degree space that viewers would then walk along to see the full view, and were designed to be only partially in view from any given viewpoint, so that the viewer would have to move in order to see all. These early visual forms, which anticipated the development of cinema as a moving picture at the turn of the century, indicate a new kind of modern vision. Indeed, modern art of the late nineteenth and early twentieth centuries, especially futurism and Cubism, was preoccupied with depicting speed and motion, and the ways that vision was mobile, ever changing.

As the circulation of the modern city changed the social dynamic of neighborhoods, new forms of social interaction were created by the mobile modern citizen. People saw each other in passing, caught glimpses of strangers on the move, and experienced a fleeting impression of other members of the "crowd" in urban streets. Baudelaire wrote a well-known poem to a passer-by, *A une passante (To a Passer-by)*, in which he catches a mere glimpse of a majestic but mourning woman, amid the deafening noise of the street. She returns his gaze and is lost in the crowd: "A flash . . . then night!—O lovely fugitive, I am suddenly reborn from your swift glance; Shall I never see you till eternity?"[20] Modern artists and writers thus portrayed the relentless mobility of the city as a source of isolation and separation from others.

Forms of mobility in postmodernism tend to operate much more in the realm of the virtual than in the space of the modern city. Hence, the flaneur of modernity has been transformed into the computer user who surfs the Web, who "browses" online while actually sitting before a computer. These forms of mobility thus increasingly take place in spaces in which people are "seen" as electronic addresses and monikers, subject to various forms of technological surveillance.

Toward the latter half of the twentieth century, there emerged through a new group of technologies a different kind of mobility, one that created yet another set of social interactions and isolation. This has been famously referred to by Raymond Williams as "mobile privatization." He wrote, "at most active social levels people are increasingly living as private small-family units, or, disrupting even that, as private and deliberately self-enclosed individuals, while at the same time there is a quite unprecedented mobility of such restricted privacies."[21] Williams was interested in the ways that television aided in the idea of the private suburban home, which was connected to the broader social sphere via the mobile television image. He saw the automobile as a form of mobile privatization, each "shell" moving "in comparable ways but for their own different private ends."

The technologies that allow people to create private spaces that are also mobile have, of course, proliferated to an even greater extent in the late twentieth and early twenty-first centuries. The Sony Walkman or Discman allows the listener to create a private space even while walking through or riding the crowded mass transportation systems of modern cities.[22] Like the automobile, these technologies are designed to allow mobile persons to feel separated from their surroundings, as well as their fellow passengers. Yet, other mobile technologies such as the mobile phone are not simply about isolation from those around us, but rather about reconfiguring connectivity—allowing one to connect to others elsewhere while separating one from those in the same place. A cell phone is designed to allow one to be connected (privately) to others while mobile. It thus transforms in dramatic ways the experience of the telephone, which was traditionally rooted in place, a telephone number designating not a user, but a particular location. While mobile phones have been the source of much scorn, as symbols of the relentless time frame of work and connectivity at the expense of human relationships, it is important to recognize that they are simply devices that do not in and of themselves define particular kinds of behavior or conversation. For instance, some of the most moving stories of how people in the World Trade Center or on hijacked airplanes responded on September 11, when they knew they were doomed, come to us from cell phones.

Yet, the concept of mobility is deeply fraught with questions of access. The mobilities of people around the globe have always taken place within hierarchies of movement—such as the difference between those who move by choice versus those who move as refugees, for instance. Doreen Massey terms these distinctions a "power-geometry" in which individuals have very different relationships to their own movements and varying access to the technologies that enable movement.[23] The concept of the postmodern nomad is thus dependent on privilege and class.

How people are connected to others is related to various forms of social organization. In recent years, the concept of networks, and the social organization of networks, have gained a central place. Manuel Castells defines a network as a set of interconnected nodes, an open structure that is able to expand without limits. He writes that "as a historical trend, dominant functions and processes in the information age are increasingly organized around networks," creating a network society, which is "characterized by the preeminence of social morphology over social action."[24] Castells argues that there were three independent processes that came together at the end of the twentieth century to make the network dominant: the increased globalization of capital and the management flexibility it requires, the demands for individual freedom and open communication, and the advances in computing and telecommunication technology.[25] These conditions, and the shifting social concepts of connectivity, organization, and individual rights that accompanied them, allowed the Internet to take hold so quickly in the 1990s, precisely because it enabled network forms of interaction. The valuing of mobility, which began in modernity, thus enabled a set of changes in social structure by the end of the twentieth century. A network is dependent on mobility—the mobility of capital, information, and bodies.

MODERN AND POSTMODERN BODIES

The world imagined by Castells and theorists of the virtual, in which human interaction is organized through networks and terminals, is often a world in which bodies appear strangely absent. This is a typical quality of technological discourse. Though modern fears of technology were prompted by concerns about how machines were injuring and killing human bodies, utopian concepts of modern technology rarely considered bodies in their formulations. Modern technology was often understood as an extension of the body, as a means through which the body could be strengthened, and modern machines were often conceived in the language of morphology—as having arms, legs, and the like. Yet, for the most part, in modernism, the distinction between the human body and the machine, even when it is a robot, was clear—they are separate and boundaried entities. Not so in postmodernism, in which the very concept of a body's boundaries is under question. Thus, it is in relation to the body that we can see perhaps the greatest distinction between modern and postmodern concepts of technology.

It is with the emergence of cybernetics in the post–World War II period that concepts of the body in relation to technology begin to change. In the postwar period, machines and computers are increasingly seen as embodying human characteristics, such as intelligence, and the integration of bodies and machines begins to emerge as a new value. The cyborg, a cybernetic organism that is part human and part machine, was imagined by scientists Manfred Clynes and Nathan Kline in 1960 as a means of improving the human capacity to withstand the rigors of space travel, with systems regulated by feedback and homeostasis.[26] The cyborg has since come to operate as a primary postmodern metaphor for a contemporary relationship to technology—the ways in which many people increasingly experience technologies as integrated into their bodies, the increased sense of a lack of boundary between machine and body. In her highly influential essay, "The Cyborg Manifesto," Donna Haraway writes that the boundaries between animal and human, organism (human and animal) and machine, and physical and nonphysical have been "thoroughly breached." She states, "Late twentieth-century machines have made thoroughly ambiguous the difference between natural and artificial, mind and body, self-developing and externally designed, and many other distinctions that used to apply to organisms and machines. Our machines are disturbingly lively, and we ourselves frighteningly inert."[27]

The currency of the cyborg metaphor in turn has prompted the development of new kinds of mobile technologies that are less separate from the body—wearable computers, tiny headphones for cell phones and Walkmans. In the postmodern context, there is thus an ease with imagining that the body has no distinct boundaries, that technologies such as pacemakers can be embedded in bodies without changing their human status, and that the body itself is changeable, mutable, in essence a work-in-progress. While in modernity, the body was considered to be stable in some way, something one was stuck with, in postmodernism, bodies are understood to be easily transformed. One can change one's gender (through cross-dressing and surgery), one's race (through skin tone and colored lenses), one's appearance and shape (through gym workouts, plastic surgery, and liposuction), and one's genetic makeup.

Concepts of the body are irrevocably tied into concepts of identity, and here too, distinctions between modernity and postmodernity are worth considering. Concepts of identity in modernity are related to the fears of individuality that characterize the urban modern experience—living among strangers, distinguishing oneself from the crowd. Yet, modern identity is also fundamentally rooted in Enlightenment concepts of the subject as autonomous, singular, stable, and fully conscious. The postmodern subject is much more fragmented and multiple. For instance, as Sherry Turkle argues, engagements with the Internet often involve role playing and a recognition that one can construct one's identity in multiple ways.[28]

The discourse of postmodern technology thus has a tendency to portray the body and identity as separable entities, often erasing the body and rendering it absent. A fascination with virtual reality and identity in relation to online technology has translated into a remarkable set of assertions about how the body can be left behind. The idea, for instance, that in role-playing as someone else online, people can experience life as if they are not situated within their actual bodies, has not only been a part of cyberati discourse but also a marketing tool for Internet services. In a well-known 1999 ad, for instance, MCI declared that the Internet was a place without race, gender, or infirmities. Implicit within these characterizations is the idea that one can interact with others without one's body, that one's thoughts, way of being, and emotions are somehow disconnectable from one's body.

Some of the most significant shifts in concepts of the body, however, are the result of new medical techniques in the late twentieth century. Medical models of the body in modernity had clear distinctions between the body and foreign entities, such as bacteria and viruses. In the postwar era, and a shift toward a postmodern view, medicine increasingly began to see the body as a kind of system, with communication technologies operating increasingly as metaphors for how the body functions—the brain thought of as a communication center, sending messages to the various organs and muscles, for instance. The immune system emerged as a primary model in the 1960s with cybernetic notions of self-regulating system governed by homeostasis.

By the late twentieth century, the body was also imagined through the framework of genetic science. Interestingly, the Human Genome Project, the massive project to map the human genome, combines deeply modern notions of science with the postmodern view of the body as easily changeable as a digital file. The Genome Project is, no doubt, about the search for origins in a distinctly modern way. The belief in the capacity to retrieve and understand those origins, and to chart them, is rooted in a modern Cartesian belief in mapping as a rational means to understanding. In this model, the body is encoded genetically, with DNA as its primary code, and it is the role of science to learn to read that code. This language comes directly from digital technology, which encodes information, such as text and images, mathematically so that it can be transported and transformed. The genetic body is imagined as a kind of digital information. It is one of the primary features of digital technology that it allows information to be exchanged, transformed, and reconfigured, and these qualities are thus transferred onto the body. The postmodern digital body is defined as profoundly alterable, easily morphed—its genetic makeup changed, its "instructions" for being now rewritten by science.

These technological metaphors, through which the body is imagined, point in many ways to a kind of disavowal of the current global crises of disease and death that Western medicine has done little to stave off. The modern medical "miracles" of antibiotics and vaccines, which eradicated many diseases worldwide, have since given rise to new, more virulent and systematic diseases. For instance, AIDS, as a retrovirus, rescripts the genetic makeup of the cells its inhabits, it is no longer a foreign entity as defined by modern science.[29] The current global health crisis is thus a reminder that the metaphors of the easily retooled postmodern body are deeply inadequate to define actual human bodies, and a reminder as well of the extent to which bodies are fragile entities—not systems or technologies.

Modernity and Postmodernity after September 11

The events of September 11 demonstrated in striking ways the tensions both of and between modernity and postmodernity. The terrorist attacks on that day made clear in tragic ways that a nostalgia for a supposed premodern existence can still hold tremendous symbolic power. The primary targets that day, the twin towers of the World Trade Center, were quintessential symbols of modern architecture. The sleek, straight lines of the towers unashamedly replicated the bold statements of modernism, of metal reaching in both arrogance and optimism for the sky. Yet, as objects of scorn prior to their destruction, the towers also had seemed to indicate modernism's last gasps. It was almost as if, as emblems of modernism's waning influence, the towers had to overstate themselves, to be not just tall but the tallest buildings (at least for a short while) and to be not just one building but two.

Paradoxically, though they were motivated by a profound hatred of not only of the United States and the capitalist world it symbolizes but also of the symbols of modernity, the terrorists deployed the tools of modernity in their destruction. Two jet planes, emblems of the modern optimism of air travel, the liberating narrative of man conquering the skies, destroyed two modern skyscrapers as symbols of engineering prowess and the secular belief in technological progress (as two other planes were aimed at the symbols of the nation). This was not the image of postmodern virtual warfare, of cyberwar, imagined by such theorists as Paul Virilio and Jean Baudrillard. The attack was visible, hugely spectacular, not virtual; it was thick with the tools of modern warfare.

Yet, there were aspects of September 11 that now seem to be distinctly postmodern. Despite the mundane aspects of the businesses that actually existed within them, the two towers were symbols of the emerging global capitalism, and those businesses had created, in the aftermath of the 1993 WTC bombing, broad electronic networks to safeguard their records in case of a cataclysmic event (though none imagined anything on such a scale). Cell phones and other forms of electronic and mobile communications (precisely because they were attached to users, not places) were absolutely central to how much is known about that day, to the tragic final words of family members, and to the decision of passengers to take one plane down rather than let it become a weapon. And it is now known that failed communication networks were also tragically responsible for many firefighters losing their lives. Communication technologies and networks were thus central to the response of the attacks. In addition, biotechnology and genetic science has been important to the aftermath, as DNA identification has been central to the long and painful task of identifying bodies and body parts.

The attacks on September 11 were a criminal act, carried out not by a nation declaring war, but by a network—the quintessential organizing framework of postindustrial capitalism and postmodernism. The cell organization structure of the al Qaeda network, a new kind of terrorist organization, is highly decentralized—just as difficult to take down as the Internet, since when part of each is disabled, decentralization allows the other parts to continue to function. This is a much darker aspect of the network society than the Internet, which marks the potential for new kinds of global conflict. Nevertheless, the attacks provoked the very modern response of a declaration of war.

Just as the violence of World War I forced a rethinking of the beliefs in modern technology, so this event, as other contemporary acts of violence, should demand a reconsideration of the investment in postmodern fantasies of leaving physical bodies behind and embracing the virtual. As Walter Benjamin wrote of the aftermath of World War I: "A generation that had gone to school on a horse-drawn streetcar now stood under the open sky in a countryside in which nothing remained unchanged but the clouds, and beneath those clouds, in a field of force of destructive torrents and explosions, was the tiny, fragile human body."[30] Like the wars that it has been used to justify, as well as other acts of violence upon the human body, September 11 reminds us that the human body remains fragile in ways that biotechnology cannot alter. The shard of a body may be identifiable through postmodern technology, but it remains testimony to the immutability, the vulnerability, and the intangible uniqueness of the human body itself.

Notes

Acknowledgments: I would like to thank Dana Polan, Sarah Banet-Weiser, and Sandra Ball-Rokeach for their comments and suggestions.

1. See, for instance, Fredric Jameson, *Postmodernism, or, The Cultural Logic of Late Capitalism* (Durham, N.C.: Duke University Press, 1991); Jean-François Lyotard, *The Postmodern Condition: A Report on Knowledge*, trans. Geoff Bennington and Brian Massumi (Minneapolis: University of Minnesota Press, 1984); and David Harvey, *The Condition of Postmodernity* (Cambridge, Mass.: Blackwell, 1990). Anthony Giddens argues against many of the distinctions between modernity and postmodernity that are made by these theorists in *The Consequences of Modernity* (Stanford, Calif.: Stanford University Press, 1990), Chapters 4 and 5.

2. Lewis Mumford, *Technics and Civilization* (New York: Harcourt, Brace, 1934), Chapter 1.

3. Stephen Kern, *The Culture of Time and Space: 1880–1918* (Cambridge, Mass.: Harvard University Press, 1983), 12.

4. Wolfgang Schivelbusch, *The Railway Journey: The Industrialization of Time and Space in the 19th Century* (Berkeley: University of California Press, [1977] 1986), 58.

5. Paul Virilio and Sylvère Lotringer, *Pure War*, trans. Mark Polizotti (New York: Semiotext(e), 1983), 44–45.

6. Kern notes that an acceleration of time was key to the ways in which a series of events culminated, not inevitably but rapidly, into World War I. He writes that ultimatums with short time frames played an important role in the escalation toward conflict: "a great many factors led to the breakdown of peace, but the sheer rush of events was itself an independent cause that catapulted Europe into war" (*The Culture of Time and Space*, 262). Ironically, the new dependence on modern communication technologies aided in altering the tenor of diplomacy. This demonstrated a tragic belief in technology that would soon be shaken by its highly destructive deployment on the battlefield. Hundreds of telegraph messages were sent between the Russian tsar and the German kaiser in last-minute negotiations to avert war, yet, Kern argues, the telegraph ultimately only aided in the failure of diplomacy, which had had a tradition of slow exchange.

7. Tom Standage, *The Victorian Internet: The Remarkable Story of the Telegraph and the Nineteenth Century's On-line Pioneers* (New York: Berkley Books, 1998).

8. Ibid., 134–39.

9. Schivelbusch, *The Railway Journey*, 37–38.

10. Giddens, *The Consequences of Modernity*, 18–19.

11. This distinction between space and place has a slightly different emphasis than the distinction that Michel de Certeau makes in *The Practice of Everyday Life*.

12. Margaret Morse, "An Ontology of Everyday Distraction: The Freeway, the Mall, and Television," in *Logics of Television: Essays in Cultural Criticism*, ed. Patricia Mellencamp (Bloomington: Indiana University Press, 1990), 193.

13. David Brodsley, *L.A. Freeway: An Appreciative Essay* (Berkeley: University of California Press, 1981), 41, discussed in Morse, "An Ontology of Everyday Distraction," 203.

14. Marc Augé, *Non-places: Introduction to an Anthropology of Supermodernity*, trans. John Howe (London: Verso, 1995), 103.

15. See, for instance, David Morley, *Home Territories: Media, Mobility, and Identity* (New York: Routledge, 2000), 176; and John Tomlinson, *Globalization and Culture* (Chicago: University of Chicago Press, 1999), 111–12.

16. Schivelbusch, *The Railway Journey*, 183.

17. Ibid., 194–95.

18. Ben Singer, "Modernity, Hyperstimulus, and the Rise of Popular Sensationalism," in *Cinema and the Invention of Modern Life*, ed. Leo Charney and Vanessa R. Schwartz (Berkeley: University of California Press, 1995), 73.

19. Anne Friedberg, *Window Shopping: Cinema and the Postmodern* (Berkeley: University of California Press, 1993).

20. Walter Benjamin analyzes this poem in *Charles Baudelaire: A Lyric Poet in the Era of High Capitalism*, trans. Harry Zohn (London: NLB [Verso], 1973), 45.

21. Raymond Williams, *The Year 2000* (New York: Pantheon, 1983), 188.

22. For a discussion of the Walkman as a cultural form, see Paul du Gay, Stuart Hall, Linda Janes, Hugh Mackay, and Keith Negus, *Doing Cultural Studies: The Story of the Sony Walkman* (Thousand Oaks, Calif.: Sage, 1997).

23. See Doreen Massey, "Power-Geometry and a Progressive Sense of Place," in *Mapping the Futures*, ed. J. Bird et al. (New York: Routledge, 1993), and *Space, Place, and Gender* (Minneapolis: University of Minnesota Press, 1994).

24. Manuel Castells, *The Rise of the Network Society* (Malden, Mass.: Blackwell, 1996), 467.

25. Manuel Castells, *The Internet Galaxy: Reflections on the Internet, Business, and Society* (New York: Oxford University Press, 2001), 2.

26. Manfred Clynes and Nathan Kline, "Cyborgs in Space," in *The Cyborg Handbook*, ed. Chris Hables Gray (New York: Routledge, 1995), 29–33.

27. Donna Haraway, "A Cyborg Manifesto: Science, Technology, and Socialist-Feminism in the Late Twentieth Century," in *Simians, Cyborgs, and Women: The Reinvention of Nature* (New York: Routledge, 1991), 152.

28. Sherry Turkle, *Life on the Screen: Identity in the Age of the Internet* (New York: Simon and Schuster, 1995).

29. See Marita Sturken, *Tangled Memories: The Vietnam War, the AIDS Epidemic, and the Politics of Remembering* (Berkeley: University of California Press, 1997), chapter 7.

30. Walter Benjamin, "The Storyteller: Reflections on the Work of Nikolai Leskov," *Illuminations* (New York: Schocken Books, 1969), 84.

ASA BRIGGS

5   Man-made Futures, Man-made Pasts

COMPLEX QUESTIONS relating technology to social and cultural change are not simply a matter of drawing sharp, even absolute, contrasts between utopians and dystopians. The way we answer the questions depends not only on our background, temperament, and experience, and on the particular disciplines that we represent, but on the societies and cultures to which we belong. Within each culture and society there are no agreed-upon answers. Technology prompts different preoccupations and different responses. The range of technological acceptance varies. So, too, do the surrounding rhetoric and even the relevant institutional structures.

I approach such questions not as a technologist, an economist, an anthropologist, a psychologist, a creative artist, or a philosopher, but as an historian. This means exploring origins, charting events and processes, and examining context before turning to controversial issues—which are seldom absent in the history of technology—and considering and assessing technological choices and outcomes relating in particular to the media. By discipline as well as by background and temperament, I am as much interested in the future as I am in the past. I believe that historical perspectives encompass past, present, and future. Continuities and discontinuities must both be identified.

I am aware of the essential importance of being interdisciplinary in thinking about the issues. I have spent a great deal of my academic life trying to put forward the claims of interdisciplinarity in universities in both teaching and research.[1] There are far too many universities that are still highly departmentalized, concerned solely with disciplines, not with problems or opportunities, too many also that ignore the experience of other institutions that have attempted to create interdisciplinary structures and procedures. What I say or write as an historian about the relationship between technology and social, including educational, change depends not only on my zeal for this cause but on my role in planning Britain's innovative Open University and on an international scale the Commonwealth of Learning, based in Vancouver.[2] Every historian is influenced consciously or unconsciously by personal experience in dealing with both the recent and the distant past, and this accounts for the deliberately autobiographical emphasis in this essay.

Historiography, which is concerned, if not solely, with historians' autobiographies, has become richer, however, than the kind of historiography that figured prominently in Cambridge, England, when I was studying history there. It has had to pay more account to context and in doing so it has inevitably become more comparative. I have found it interesting, therefore, to compare my own origins and development as an historian, born one year before the founding of the BBC, with the autobiographical account given by Robert A. Rosenstone, who was brought up, as he puts it, "in the Dragnet School of History," and who wrestles with the basic issues arising out of "postmodern history."[3] Rosenstone says little about the teaching of history or about the institutional history of education, and it was within that context that I applied the word *convergence* to the circumstances of the 1960s before it had become a buzz word applied to digital technology in the 1980s and 1990s.

In the 1960s demand for a broadening of access to education in Britain coincided with the advent of an applicable technology, television. That particular technology, dear to the heart of then British Prime Minister Harold Wilson, was not treated, however, as a panacea once Wilson had passed the planning of an Open University on to others. They identified different modes of learning, including traditional modes, like the tutorial (every student had an individual tutor), the use of the mass media, with radio (cheaper and in some ways more effective than television) and carefully planned, produced, and packaged kits of printed materials.

The Open University, therefore, very quickly became something more than a "University of the Air," as Wilson called it, a term used in the University of Southern California long before it was used in Britain. Its Planning Committee, of which I was a member, pressed for the new name. It recommended also that the university employ a battery of learning techniques. There were intimations of the language of the Internet when its first chancellor, Lord Crowther, former editor of *The Economist*, proclaimed that the Open University would be as "open to ideas and to methods" as it would be to students. Different courses required different approaches, as did different students, learning at their own pace. The university lived up to its expectations and developed its course planning through interdisciplinary teams, including educational technologists. Both history and technology figured prominently in its first prospectus and have ever since.

One of the most striking of its early courses, very carefully programmed, was "Man-Made Futures."[4] The teaching team noted that "whereas once the direction of technological change seemed to be inevitable or decided by private interests, there is now a growing belief that alternative directions can and should be the subject of open debate." "The timing" should be added to the word *direction*. Lags between innovation and diffusion vary and have been the subject of detailed research, much of it pursued long before the 1960s, with one of the more recent and most interesting studies introducing the term *suppression* into the analysis.[5] In examining *man-made pasts*, a term that I am using in this essay to complement rather than to contrast with the term *man-made futures*, chronology and timing always have to be charted as carefully as possible, complex though the task may prove to be. It often involves unraveling secrets.

There are milestones or landmarks in man-made pasts that look different as vantage points in time change. Whatever the vantage point, however, one of the big differences between the study of man-made futures and of man-made pasts is that there are no events in scenarios of the future. In the fleeting present, the word *historic* is often applied both to present events, including sporting as well as political events, and to innovations before they have reached even the first stages of diffusion. *Historic* is nevertheless a perilous word, overused in the media at a time when the historic past is neglected and concern for chronology is often dismissed as obsolete.

There are cultural differences between the United States and Britain in their approaches to such questions, but it is pertinent to ask whether the differences between the two, far from being structural (or traditional), are merely a matter of time, another lag. There remain bigger cultural differences between the United States and Britain, taken together, and France than there have been between the two, taken separately.

It was imaginative French writers, like poet and professor Paul Valéry, who died in 1945, rather than British and American academic writers, who first explored the cultural ramifications of the speed of change through technology. However, since 1974, when the Open University's "Man-Made Futures" course was first offered, communications technology has changed so fast in the United States, Britain, and France that, whatever our stance, we can hardly keep mental pace with it. Within the classic media trinity—information, education, and entertainment—technology has influenced information and entertainment more than education, although at least as much has been said and written about the effects of the Internet and the Web on educational access and advance as on information and more than on entertainment. Within industry, communications technologies undoubtedly represent the most dynamic sector in contemporary technology—the word *glamorous* is often used to describe them—just as the exploitation of sources of energy (steam, electricity, water, nuclear power) once did and just as bioengineering has already begun to do and will do in the future.

Yet enthusiasm about communications technology is natural, in relation to achievement and, stronger still, to potential. It, too, must be seen in perspective, however, and financial and economic factors, particularly the so-called Wall Street factor in the United States, which influence its development must be considered as carefully in charting its changing fortunes as the surrounding debate about its influence. In understanding both words and action, history is relevant. Using every kind of source, not least ephemera, verbal and visual, it must take account of foregone alternatives and discarded hype. Much that now seems new turns out to be old. For example, in contemplating the digital technology behind globalization—and the ample rhetoric surrounding it—we quickly appreciate how little there is in the rhetoric that is completely new. During the 1980s, when viewdata systems were being advertised and when enthusiasm for cable television reached a peak, the rhetoric was not dissimilar. Very different interests were involved, however, and there could be a variety of political orientations.

A century earlier, in the Britain of the Marquess of Salisbury, the last nineteenth-century British prime minister—and a very conservative and aristocratic prime minister at that—was talking the language of the global when he told members of the Institution of Electrical Engineers in London (the year when it took on that title and, of greater importance, the centenary year of the French Revolution): "You have by the action of the electric telegraph combined together almost at one moment the opinions of the whole intelligent world with regard to everything that is passing at that time upon the face of the world."[6] Globalization is not a new concept even if the word is. And there was a Marxist strand in the historiography, going back to the *Communist Manifesto* of 1848.

The fact that at that particular point in a continuing communications revolution, the telegraph, as an instrument of globalization, could be so enthusiastically conceived of by a conservative who was also a great believer in technical innovation, warns us to be careful about thinking too simply about "the globe" exclusively in a twenty-first-century American manner. The adjective *global* itself is one of many words associated with communications that demand historical charting. When the final volume of the *Oxford English Dictionary* first appeared in 1928 after years of preparation—it was based on five million quotations—it gave as the only meaning of the word *global* "pertaining to or embracing the totality of a group of items, categories or the like." The geography was left out. It was not until the publication of a 1972 *Supplement* that *global* was defined primarily as "relating to, or involving the whole world."

The geography had always been there, however, since "the age of discoveries." Salisbury was just as aware of the importance of trade routes in the politics of empire as postimperial thinkers and writers were a century later. In the second case, "electronic colonialism" became a target, and it was the politics of information flow (and entertainment), not technology, that introduced globalization into UNESCO. History has layers, as important a concept as lags. While in the late nineteenth century man-made pasts were often conceived of as the triumph of the civilized over the primitive, with anthropology, not sociology, reinforcing the move toward "progress," in the late twentieth century they were reorganized and re-presented in terms of exploitation and repression. Economics, and later sociology, were of increasing importance in shaping reactions to technology from below or from the periphery.

The chronology of industrialization, charted by Marx, has been significant too in this connection. The British textiles industry depended on imports of raw cotton from the United States before America had begun its own process of industrialization, while the cultivation of raw cotton itself depended on black slave labor brought in from Africa in a triangular trade that linked continents. The suspicion and criticism of technology in Britain, still not dissipated, goes back to the smoky atmosphere of the early nineteenth century, when industrial workers made much of the comparison between their own exploitation and that of blacks working in slave plantations.

There were signs then, as there are now, of a love-hate relationship between the British and technology, with steam power—bridges were good, machines were bad—having quite different meanings for different groups of people. It was in this early industrial setting, indeed, that the word *Luddite* made its first appearance in history in relation to a particular place on the map, Nottingham. It was a word that was to be carried across the world, however, and used in extended fashion every generation since, sometimes with the adjective *intellectual* attached to it. Thus, bitter critics of the Internet have been at great pains to deny that they are latter-day Luddites. In consequence, informed twenty-first-century commentators on the relationship between man-made pasts and man-made futures are aware, as they contrast

British and other national attitudes toward technology, that many of the factors associated with attitudes toward technology in Britain must be related to social, cultural, and above all economic, history and not to the inherent characteristics of technology or, indeed, of any particular technology.

In different phases of the story of technological advance, the same technology, mechanical or electrical, has been used in different ways in different societies, for a variety of reasons and with a variety of consequences. Radio technology, for example, produced three quite different systems of broadcasting: state-organized, for propaganda purposes; commercially driven through advertising and integrated into the market economy; and public service broadcasting, claiming its autonomy, free from both propaganda and market-driven economics. There had been as big a difference in relation to telegraphy between Britain and France and, indeed, in relation to the railroad, with France on the one hand and the United States on the other, because of different attitudes toward state authority.[7] In practice, the systems are best perhaps thought of as ideal types, and how each system worked requires independent historical examination.

It was while looking at such differences that I became involved in more general studies of the relationships in different countries between radio and society, and later television and society, and subsequently in the media as a group. Some of the history is common, as are the words used to describe and to chart it: the word *convergence*, for example, has been used as much in relation to technology in Britain as to technology in the United States. Some of this history, however, is distinctive, and remains so.

A fundamental issue relating to our present situation concerning digital technology, which brings with it the convergence of words, numbers, sounds, and images and the multinational organizations dealing in them, is whether its global spread through the Internet and World Wide Web will introduce a totally new phase in communications history. Will globalization prevent, permit, or encourage different societies to maintain degrees of social and cultural difference between themselves (as broadcasting to a considerable extent did) or will they all in some kind of way, as yet imperfectly definable, become the same? There are many signs that differences remain and will remain, although comparing Japan and China may be more fruitful in this connection than comparing Britain with the United States or both with France, and comparing Africa with Asia may be most fruitful of all.

My interest in identifying how and why local, regional, and national histories diverged was heightened in the late 1950s, after I was asked by the director-general of the BBC to write its history and given full access to all its rich archival resources. I became deeply involved in what proved to be a protracted undertaking, which did not end until the early 1990s, by which time I had written more than a million words. Throughout I was anxious to keep my own autonomy and refused to be described as the BBC's official historian.

Even before I turned to the history of broadcasting, I had became interested in what became computer technology—the word had not yet passed into common language—during the war, when I was very fortunate as a young soldier to work at Bletchley in the Hut 6 team that was breaking Enigma. As cryptographers, using embryonic computers—we did not call them such—in what became an Anglo-American team, we knew that we could not break enemy messages without using computer techniques. Yet we saw the technology as purely instrumental. We were too busy to think too much about the future, although where the world was moving as the war ended—and that obviously concerned some of us deeply—did not seem to us then, as far as I can clearly remember, to depend on computerization. We knew of Alan Turing, but I do not think that any of us thought or dreamed about personal computers—or miniaturization. There was even less time to think about the past. In an extremely short period of training to become cryptographers we worked first with coded messages from the distant past. Working on them seemed, from the start, totally irrelevant. So did the history of cryptography during World War I.

I gave my first broadcasts during the war when I was in uniform. They were Forces Educational Broadcasts, part of a pioneering series that included history as one of the subjects. I had no idea then that I would be invited thirteen years later to write the history of British broadcasting. By then I had spent six months at the Institute for Advanced Studies in Princeton, in 1953, where we talked more about mathematics and physics—and computers—than about history, and more about Oppenheimer and McCarthy than either. I met American operating broadcasters then for the first time and realized that they were in a quite different context from British broadcasters. From the start of my work on the BBC in 1957 I was anxious to do more than write the history of an organization that had been remarkably rapidly transformed into a national institution, often compared with the Church of England, a comparison made by the Archbishop of Canterbury himself, who emphasized the rapidity of the technological, social, and cultural transformation: "We woke, so to speak, to find [wireless] in our presence and affecting us all."[8] What we woke up to hear, however, depended on where we were.

When I started writing what I deliberately called *a* history rather than *the* history of the BBC, I had unique institutional archives at my disposal—archives of the kind that are largely missing in the United States—but few books of any value except autobiographies, including that of John Reith with whom I had to cooperate closely. Of the 222 items cited in Elihu Katz's *Social Research in Broadcasting* (1977), admittedly a selective list, only nineteen were published before 1960, the year when J. T. Klapper's *The Effects of Mass Communication* appeared in America. I had to work largely on my own therefore, and it was through the writing of five volumes of BBC history, culminating in a volume called *Competition*, published in 1995 (the BBC period that I covered ended in 1974), that I became more and more interested in the themes discussed in this book.

Apart from the years of World War II, a war of words, the period in its history that interested me most was between 1922 and 1927, when the initials BBC stood not for British Broadcasting Corporation but for British Broadcasting Company. Reith, a thirty-four-year-old Scot, was appointed its first general manager; it was his personality and ideas that shaped a new organization that was, largely for technical reasons, a monopoly, and to which he did not hesitate to attach, for entirely cultural reasons, the adjective *brute*. It was he too who determined that the company, which paid a dividend limited by law to 7.5 percent, should be converted into a public corporation, a new form of organization, totally outside the business complex.

It was not Reith's gloomy autobiography, *Into the Wind*, that impressed me when I started writing my history but his then unpublished *Diary*, his personal notes to me, and, above all, the book he wrote in 1924 with unbelievable speed, *Broadcast Over Britain*. It was not only the Reithian philosophy in the book that is fascinating to peruse and contemplate—Reith had not then had his name converted into an adjective—but his personal perspectives. The first chapter of the book was called "In the Beginning," and he was to claim for the rest of his life that "early days are crucial ones in either individual existence or corporate organisation." When he started working for the BBC with a staff of four, "there were no sealed orders to open . . . very few knew what broadcasting meant: none knew what it might become . . . There was no precedent, no store of experience to be tapped . . . Fortunately we were vouchsafed a measure of vision."[9]

I have kept these lines in mind when I have looked at all subsequent changes in communications technology, which have never followed a straight line but have always raised questions of what was, what might be, and, indeed, what should be. I have found it interesting, therefore, to compare what Reith had to say about broadcasting with what American pioneers of the computer and later of the Internet and World Wide Web have had to say about futures that were still in the making. The magazine *Wired*, which quickly became an icon, warned politicians in 1997 that they should not dream of talking to "digital citizens" about the past, or the present for that matter: "All they want to know about is tomorrow."[10]

The story of the origins and development of *Wired* is as interesting and essential reading for an historian of media as the history of the BBC's *Radio Times*, first published in 1923, and it is well told, if not definitively or in its complete context, by Robert H. Reid in his *Architects of the Web*.[11] Reid deals, like Reith, with "early days," in Reid's case, "one thousand days that built the future of business." Yet, like Reith in *Broadcast over Britain*, he was writing about them in the same decade as they happened. Moreover, before starting on his book he had been employed by Silicon Graphics, a pioneering business venture that played a big part in the development of Silicon Valley. He knew personally many of the people he was writing about. His book carries with it, therefore, a sense of involvement rather than a sense of perspective. There was much about the likely future of the Internet after those thousand days that was uncertain, as it still is. So there was about broadcasting in 1924.

The Internet and the World Wide Web appeared late in my own life as an historian, although I was delighted when the Open University conferred an honorary doctorate on Tim Berners-Lee, whose achievement as creator of the Web was described by *Time* magazine, leaping across man-made pasts, as "almost Gutenbergian."[12] It was an attractive adjective, for although Gutenberg centenaries had been regularly celebrated, until the 1960s nobody bothered very much in looking at the impact of printing, certainly not in the way that we have looked at it since the rise of television. Gutenberg had hovered in the background, but until Marshall McLuhan, that superb word spinner, there was no "Gutenberg galaxy."

Such leaps forward in the history of technology obscure, for instance, the importance of the railroad. There was a marked shift of perception of time and space with the advent of railroads, revealing in itself if only because through their inherent characteristics locomotives on their tracks forced a reconsideration of direction too. Yet railroads could not have been as strategically placed as they were in history if there had not first been a power revolution—the development of steam power, which Marx saw as *the* crucial turning point in the whole of human history. The railroad posed all the questions that are being posed in this book of essays, including ones that relate not only to power—or distance—but to speed.

Transportation should never be left out of the history of communication. Railroads were the most controversial of all innovations. To some people, perhaps most, they symbolized progress; to others, like Dickens, they symbolized death.[13] Disasters were always publicized even when the novelty had disappeared and railroad systems, complete with timetables, had treated railroad travel not as an adventure but as a routine. There was also a big difference in the way railroads were perceived in different countries. The folklore of the railroad—and the songs and pictures associated with it—was as different in the United States and in Britain as early radio broadcasting was. For a British traveler in the United States, writing in 1851, there seemed to be some natural affinity between "the Yankee keep moving nature and a locomotive engine . . . Whatever the cause, it is certain that the 'humans' seem to treat the 'engine', as they call it, more like a familiar friend than as the dangerous and desperate thing it really is."[14]

Transportation predictions, among the most common instances of predictions, provide a wealth of images, including "fellow travellers," "on the track," and "the other side of the track." It was the imagery of the highway, however, not of the railroad, that hit the headlines in 1993 when President Bill Clinton and Vice President Al Gore preached "the technogospel" of the information highway first in California and then in Washington, D.C., on the latter occasion with a huge photograph of the planet as a backdrop.[15] The shift of image was doubtless related to the automobile. One of my favorite transportation predictions that went astray was a remark in *Harper's Magazine* in 1902 on the eve of one of the biggest changes in transportation in the twentieth century: "The actual building of roads devoted to motor cars is not for the near future, in spite of many rumors to that effect." How near is near? In Britain, where similar sentiments were expressed during the decade before World War I, cars were still being described as "horseless carriages" and the costs of running a garage compared to those for running a stable. Another prediction related to airplanes. It had been demonstrated, an "expert" pontificated, that "no possible combination of known substances can be united in a practical machine by which man shall fly long distances through the air."[16] Whole anthologies of such comments have been assembled.

The people who have made quotable dogmatic statements, some of them very distinguished people, include Bertrand Russell, and even H. G. Wells, who could never have been described as ignorant about science and technology. And they were progressive writers, not conservatives. (Why have so many conservatives celebrated new technologies?) A dominating dogmatic strain in prediction seems to me to be as worthy of study as the utopian and the dystopian strains. Experts, with astronomers prominent among them, claim to know more than they really can about the shapes of the future. Meanwhile, popular newspapers and periodicals of various kinds, conservative and radical, general and specialized, present fantastic pictures of the future, many of which are tinged by value judgments that are explicable in terms not of technology but of the contours of societies and cultures.

For those of us who are interested in what futures might be as well as what they will be, these pictures offer through free play of the imagination, as does science fiction, an entry into fascinating worlds. They are a preparation for a cyberworld. Yet just as future scenarios have no events in them they also usually leave out the economics which can never be left out of any "real" world and which dictates much that goes on in cyberspace. There can be no total "free play." In William Gibson's *Neuromancer* (1984) there were glimpses of "the green cubes of the Mitsubishi Bank of America, and high and very far away . . . the spiral arms of military systems forever beyond . . . reach."[17]

A fascinating period in relation to the history of prediction was just a little over a century ago during the last decades of the nineteenth century, which I have written about in some detail elsewhere.[18] It was claimed in *The Engineer* (1889), the year when Salisbury gave his address, that the long line of isolated ripples of past discovery seemed to be blending into a mighty wave, some magnificent generalization, something, perhaps, of an anticlimax. The times were propitious then for prediction. Just at the time when often specialized expert magazines and periodicals were being brought into existence to convey information, magazines of fantasy designed for a wide nonprofessional reading public, already a viewing public too, were exploring what the likely shape of the future would be.

It is revealing to compare the content and the language of *The Electrician* with a popular paper in England like *Answers*, designed for a mass audience, or to study the pages of *Lightning*. For a writer in *Answers* in 1894, simplifying a complex history of pedigrees and traditions, Edison, from whose workshops many inventions made their way into the world, was a "mighty genius." He had not only "reproduced the human voice for all time" but with his kinetoscope had devised a machine "which enables us to look on at a scene that may have taken place 20,000 miles away; to reproduce in fact [an interesting use of the word *fact*] a battle in all its details, a stage play, any great public occurrence or [something of an anticlimax] a bicycle race from start to finish."[19] In the following year *Science Siftings* quoted Alexander Graham Bell, who had been carrying out experiments on selenium and reached the conclusion that "telephoning by means of a beam of light will be commercially practicable."[20]

The most interesting of the media studies that I carried through in parallel to writing my BBC history was on the early history of the telephone, a subject of as intense interest to the late nineteenth-century students of man-made futures as broadcasting. In 1882, six years after Alexander Graham Bell had demonstrated his first telephone, the *Electrical World*, a responsible periodical, having described the role of the Post Office in the management of telephones in Britain, concluded that "this is as much as may be said about the telephonic system as it is at present." Yet, it went on, "What it may develop into is a different matter, and just now there are signs that this wonderfully versatile appliance may be converted into uses for which at first it seems ill-adapted. We are not referring to the project of tapping the stage and the pulpit telephonically or of laying on operatic music, like gas, for the use of every householder."[21] *The Electrician* was concerned instead about the relationship between local and distant point-to-point communication, a subject that was to gain in importance.

It was precisely those activities that did not interest *The Electrician* which interested me when I wrote an article in 1976, the centennial year of Bell's invention, on "The Pleasure Telephone: A Chapter in the Pre-history of the Media," where I began by describing how at Salisbury's great house, Hatfield, guests were amazed in their rooms to hear the Marquess's "spectral voice" reciting nursery rhymes through a "mysterious instrument on a neighbouring table."[22]

I was drawn to the subject of the telephone by Ithiel de Sola Pool, who in the same year invited me to become associated with his MIT project on the telephone, which was supported by the National Science Foundation (NSF). I already knew MIT, for I had been fortunate enough to be awarded the Marconi Medal in its first year, along with Dr. Wiesner, MIT's president, and I had already turned my attention to the angles of divergence in different societies and cultures between people's predictions of what a particular technology, impossible fully to isolate, would produce and what actually happened. Without using the terms *man-made pasts* and *man-made futures*, I was seeking to relate them to each other. Why was there divergence? The telephone was a relevant communications device to investigate.

It was apparent to me from the start that it is not only technology that is involved. I still treasure the orientation memoranda that Pool sent round to his collaborators, the first of which (January 7, 1976) raised the same issues that I was raising in my research as a Marconi Fellow. Why were Bell, Vail and their associates such good predictors? "After a couple of years of uncertainty," Pool noted, "they abandoned the notion of a broadcast system in favor of a point-to-point system. They anticipated that the network would grow into a universal service to cover the country and even be international. They recognized the advantages of a system that rented equipment rather than sold it."

Pool put forward four hypotheses (he liked doing this) to account for their success as predictors: they were "particularly bright men"; "they were men who combined technological expertise with practical economic and business sense"; "they were men who were spending eighteen hours a day, year after year, thinking about these matters"; "they had had a dream, and being in charge of the system they made it happen according to their dream. It wasn't a matter of prediction but rather of action." "Several of these propositions may be true," Pool concluded, "but depending upon the weight we attach to each of them we would proceed differently in a technology assessment," the end product of the project which the NSF requested.

The short orientation memoranda contained interim assessments, interesting in themselves, written by Pool before his general assessment was completed. Thus, when in his first memorandum he set out the second hypothesis he distinguished between the "technical expertise of Bell, Vail and their associates" and "the journalistic speculation that went into starry-eyed fantasies about things that were either technically or economically possible"; and in the third he referred once more to journalists, those who were "spending two weeks writing a piece off the cuff."[23] Clearly, however, before Pool assessed the telephone, he had already assessed journalists.

His fifteenth orientation memorandum showed how far his ideas about the telephone assessment had proceeded. Like the writer in *The Electrician*, he was talking now not of the telephone as an invention but of a "telephone system." He had already been influenced by Colin Cherry, who had been made the first Henry Mark Pease Professor of Telecommunication at Imperial College London, and who was to be awarded the Marconi Medal in 1978: the title of his inaugural lecture had been "Telecommunication as a Social Science."[24] "The technology assessment of the telephone," Pool wrote, "is the assessment of a large system, resulting from a considerable number of major inventions." "The telephone itself," he declared, "is only one of them and would have been compatible with a very different system if the other inventions had been different." Cherry had mentioned "the crucial role of the switchboard." Pool mentioned the development of copper wire and later coaxial cable, and the chronological relationship between the telephone, radio, telephony, and broadcasting.

It was at that point in his research strategy that my own research became relevant to the project, although it was not of immediate interest to Pool that I wanted to go back to the beginnings, "the couple of years of uncertainty." I immersed myself in scattered American and Canadian Bell archives relating to this early period, including advertisements. "The history of the telephone," one pioneering Bell historian, who got no further than an article, wrote, "can be as fascinating as a novel and as amusing as an anthology of Stephen Leacock and Mark Twain."[25] I came to the conclusion that he was right.

Early comments on an invention are essential pieces of evidence. For some commentators Bell's demonstration of the telephone at Salem was "Salem witchcraft." Because the telephone had first been demonstrated in the United States there were British descriptions of it as "another American humbug." There seemed to be an ethical dimension too. What should happen to someone caught swearing over the telephone? What if criminals made use of it? There is always ambivalence about such matters in the case of any new communications invention. Yet Bell commentators noted quietly and approvingly how, despite such controversy, there were individuals in small communities, "local merchants or men who had other business interests," who were becoming Bell agents and setting up switchboards in their offices.

Pool himself was not looking for "fun" in the telephone. Instead he produced his lucid "retrospective technology assessment," which he presented to the NSF in June 1977 and which referred again on its first page to an hypothesis. "For a successful technology assessment, economic and technical expertise must simultaneously be brought to bear. Support for the hypothesis is the principal lesson for our case study of the telephone and its effects upon society. Banal as that conclusion may seem, many current technology assessments make little use of economic analysis." Nonetheless, there was more history than economics in the assessment, which pointed to later studies by Pool and to the publication of his *Technologies of Freedom*, which begins with the sentence "Civil liberty functions today in a changing technological context" and has more politics in it than either history or economics.[26]

I agreed with Pool—and still do—that it is essential to bring both economics and politics into the picture. Given that there are usually technological options, whether one option or another is chosen depends on investment decisions, many market-based, some governmental, in that case often involving military considerations, some both, all related to estimates of costs and likely profits. We know that politics and policy calculations come into the reckoning in every country where these decisions have had to be made. Some are pragmatic decisions, or claim to be. Is that claim tenable?

In conclusion, I would like to return to the specific role of the historian in looking at the questions I have raised, not least because other specialists have provided useful insider accounts of how they think and work. During the course of my own lifetime as a professional historian, historians have had to come to terms with the fact that there is no absolute past, a conclusion they reached before futurologists were talking about futures. One of the great historians of the twentieth century, Marc Bloch, who wrote a book entitled *Le Métier d'Historien*, translated into English as *The Historian's Craft*, thought about these matters a great deal while he was in a concentration camp near Lyons in France in World War II.[27] Tragically before he had time to complete his book he was taken out from his cell and shot in an open field, one of the victims of the Nazis. Sadly, he would have had no difficulty in predicting his own fate and, sadly for us, what he could not do was to finish the seventh part of his book, which was concerned with what he called "pre-vision." It is a word to remember, related as it is to the word *vision*, another word that figures prominently in the history of communications. It is difficult, however, to reconstruct what he would have chosen to write about in the seventh part of his book.

Bloch was a brilliant analyst of past events and processes, including those of the Middle Ages, but there is very little detail in his book about tendencies, trends, and forecasts relating to the late twentieth century. Nevertheless, he believed that history is not the science of the past—there is just one science of men in time, *une petite science conjecturale*—and that the faculty of understanding the living is the master quality of the historian whether he is dealing with the people of the past or with people still to come. That is a comment that has often rung through my mind. So too has his description of pre-vision as a mental necessity. There was no hint of prophecy.

The first of his possible subheadings for the seventh unwritten section of his book was "The Ordinary Errors of Pre-vision," and in noting what it might say he chose his examples from economic fluctuations and, significantly, from military history. Other headings were "The Role of Conscious Awareness in Relation to Pre-vision," a sign of how extremely interested Bloch was in Freudian approaches to unawareness in relation to pre-vision; "The Paradox of Pre-vision in Human Affairs," which raised issues similar to those raised by the sociologist Robert Merton when he examined "self-fulfilling prophecy"; and "Short-Term Pre-vision and Long Term Pre-vision," the span of time with which the historian is concerned. "Regularities," the way in which history goes round or through routines as well as moves through clusters of innovatory change, was another heading, as was "Hopes and Uncertainties," written before the label *age of uncertainty* was attached to the 1970s and 1980s. There were to be surprises as well as uncertainties in the late twentieth century, like the fall of the Berlin Wall in 1989, in which communications played an important part.

I prefer to think within such a framework when I examine the relationship between man-made pasts and man-made futures, aware that the way in which communications technology has developed since the 1880s and 1890s has made it possible to write history as a whole in a different way from what was previously possible. Indeed, it would not have been possible to write the social and cultural history that I have written without communication technology, any more than it would have been possible to break Enigma messages (regularly and quickly) without "computers."

This was recognized before the twentieth century began by people who were talking about Edison's inventions and their likely impact. With the kinetoscope in mind, a writer in 1895 put it this way:

> The advantage to students and to historians of our changes in the capacity to present and to record will be immeasurable. Instead of the dry and misleading chronicle tinged with the exaggerations of chroniclers' minds [and they provide us with many of the stories, of course] our archives will be enriched by the vitalised pictures of great national scenes, instinct with all the glowing possibilities which underlay them.

There was an obvious element of rhetoric there, and there was an over-optimistic trust in "the glowing possibilities." Twenty-first-century rhetoric, abundant in all discussions of technology, must always be examined very carefully.

It is impossible for us now to think of history simply as chronicle or to judge historians by the quality of their narratives. The twentieth and twenty-first centuries are recorded in words and pictures—from above and from below—in a way that no previous century ever has been, and in consequence historians look at the world as it is in a different way from pre-twenty-first-century historians looking at their world. Perceptions have changed. And new problems arise when television and film present history in new ways and when boundaries between "fact" and "fiction" that were clearly defined for Bloch, are, like much else, now blurred. There are status changes too. Academic professors of history have a different status as history moves out of universities through an always changing media world, a world in which they can establish global reputations, becoming "celebrities" in the process. To consider the historiography in all this is a formidable task that involves far more than technology.

NOTES

1. Asa Briggs et al., *Interdisciplinarity, Problems of Teaching and Research in Universities* (Paris: OECD, 1972), 185–253.

2. Asa Briggs, *The Collected Essays of Asa Briggs, vol. 3: Serious Pursuits, Communications and Education* (Urbana: University of Illinois Press, 1991), 386–414.

3. Robert A. Rosenstone, "The Future of the Past: Film and the Beginnings of Postmodern History," in *The Persistence of History: Cinema, Television and the Modern Event*, ed. Vivian Sobchack (New York: Routledge, 1996), 201–18.

4. Nigel Cross, David Elliott, and Robin Roy, *Man-Made Futures: Readings in Society, Technology and Design* (Open University Milton Keynes, 1974).

5. Brian Winston, *Media, Technology and Society: A History: From the Telegraph to the Internet* (New York: Routledge, 1998), 9–15.

6. The quote is from *The Electrician*, November 8, 1889. Salisbury was addressing the first annual dinner of the Institute of Electrical Engineers.

7. Patrice Flichy, *Dynamics of Modern Communication* (Thousand Oaks, Calif.: Sage, 1995), 41–57.

8. Quoted in Briggs, "Prediction and Control, Historical Perspectives," in *The Collected Essays of Asa Briggs*, 100.

9. John C.W. Reith, *Broadcast Over Britain* (London: Hodder and Stoughton, 1925), 23.

10. Jon Katz, "Birth of a Digital Nation," *Wired* 5, no. 4 (April 1997): 49.

11. Robert H. Reid, *Architects of the Web: 1,000 Days That Built the Future of Business* (New York: Wiley, 1997).

12. Joshua Quittner, "Tim Berners-Lee," *Time*: The Time 100 The Most Important People of the Century (March 29, 1999). Accessed at <http://www.time.com/time/time100/scientist/profile/bernerslee.html>, 3.

13. Asa Briggs, "The Imaginative Response of the Victorians to Railways," in *On the Move: Essays in Labour and Transport History*, ed. Chris Wrigley and John Shepherd (London: Hambledon Press, 1991), 60–61.

14. Benjamin A. Botkin and Alvin F. Harlow, *A Treasury of Railroad Folklore* (New York: Crown, 1953), xi, 2.

15. Mark Slovka, *War of the Worlds* (New York: Basic Books, 1995), 89.

16. Simon Newcomb, *Side-Lights on Astronomy and Kindred Fields of Popular Science* (New York: Harper and Brothers, 1906), Chapter 22. Online at <http://onlinebooks. library.upenn.edu/webbin/gutbook/lookup?num=4065>.

17. William Gibson, *Neuromancer* (New York: Ace Books, 1984), 52.

18. Asa Briggs and Daniel Snowman, eds., *Fins de Siècles: How Centuries End: 1400–2000* (New Haven: Yale University Press, 1996), 157–235.

19. *Answers*, November 10, 1894.

20. *Science Siftings*, July 6, 1895.

21. See Robert V. Bruce, *Bell: Alexander Graham Bell and the Conquest of Solitude* (Boston: Little, Brown, 1973).

22. Briggs, *The Collected Essays of Asa Briggs*, 77.

23. All of the Pool quotes in these paragraphs are from unpublished memoranda, Massachusetts Institute of Technology, Department of Political Science. These are from my personal archive.

24. Colin Cherry, *The Age of Access: Information Technology and Social Revolution, Posthumous Papers of Colin Cherry*, ed. William Edmondson. (London: Croom Helm, 1985), 3.

25. G. L. Long, "History Can Be Fascinating," undated article in the Canadian Bell Archives.

26. Ithiel de Sola Pool, *Technologies of Freedom* (Cambridge, Mass.: Belknap Press, 1983), 1.

27. Marc Bloch, *The Historian's Craft*, trans. Peter Putnam (New York: Vintage, 1953). For the discovery of lost passages in Bloch, see M. Mastrogregori, "Marc Bloch's Interrupted Manuscript," in *The European Legacy* 3, no. 4 (July 1998).

Lynn Spigel

6   Portable TV

Studies in Domestic Space Travels

In 1967, the Sony Corporation tuned consumers in to a new inno-vation in product design, a 5-inch mini-portable TV that it called "drive-in television." The ad for the set shows a man and a woman parked at a drive-in theater, watching their new mini-portable receiver while tenderly embracing under the blanket of night (Figure 6.1). The advertising copy explains: "For smooching 'n watching, this tiny Sony operates off your car lighter. . . . you get a picture that's perfectly brilliant. Even with a police-man's flashlight shining in."[1]

Sony thus used the popular conception of the drive-in movie—as a semi-private and even illicit space for dating—to promote television watching as an erotic experience to be had outside the home. However, the advertiser staged this scenario of unmarried sex with full awareness of the fact that most consumers were buying TVs for more traditional household uses. As-suring the reader that the portable set could also be watched by nondriving smoochers, Sony was more interested in selling a particular fantasy about television spectatorship in domestic space than in making people actually watch TV in their cars. In other words, the slogan "drive-in television" was directed less at a concrete practice for watching television than at a mode of imaginative experience. The slogan encouraged consumers to experience TV—and domestic space itself—as a vehicle for transport through which they could imaginatively travel to an illicit place of passion while remaining in the safe space of the family home.

Although a quirky example, this ad is symptomatic of the more gen-eral cultural sensibility surrounding television and family life in the late 1950s through the 1960s. In this "second wave" of television installation, when most American households already had one receiver, marketers were looking for ways to convince the public to replace old living room consoles or else install additional sets throughout their homes. While early design and marketing presented television as living room furniture, by the end of the 1950s manufacturers broadened their design schemes to include (and even emphasize) nondecorative uses for TV. As *House Beautiful* announced

110

Figure 6.1 TV gets wheels in this 1967 ad for a mini-portable set (© Sony Corp.).

in 1958, "For Ten Years the TV set has pretended to be furniture, which it is not." In place of the furniture model, *House Beautiful* recommended the purchase of a Philco Predicta, which, it claimed, "may be placed anywhere in the room."[2] While this was offered as pragmatic advice, the idea of moving television sets around the house gave way to much more fantastic visions. Instead of the sedentary viewing protocols that the console implied, portable receivers were marketed as marvelous new "space age" toys that promised audiences a more masterful, even active, relation to everyday life at home. As opposed to their 1950s predecessors, which were promoted as "home theaters" that promised family togetherness and shelter from the evils of urban life, ads for portable sets pictured TV as a vehicle that would drive people away from their mundane domestic lives and into a world of active adventure and romantic (if not sexual) quests.

This essay explores the cultural significance of portability and the related technologies of miniaturization and remote control. In an effort to revise some of the more abstract theories on technological change (and especially Baudrillardian-based arguments which claim that television and new satellite-based technologies have obliterated conventional boundaries between public and private spaces and have changed human subjectivity completely), this essay addresses the rise of mobile culture in historical and material terms. Examining the way portable sets were promoted in advertisements and popular magazines aimed primarily at the white middle class, I focus on how marketing and design strategies relate to changing ideals of middle-class family life in the 1960s.[3] While advertisements, magazine articles, and other vehicles of popular culture obviously do not reflect directly how people experience television or how they use it in their everyday lives, such sources do provide an intertextual context—a set of interrelated texts—through which people learn about new technologies. They help to establish a horizon of expectations, and at moments of technological transition they also help to establish a set of possibilities for how we use communication technologies and how we think about them in our everyday lives. In the 1960s, the promotional rhetoric around portable television demonstrates the way in which this new technology was designed for and predicated on broader ideological transitions in American family life. These changes revolve around a shift from the Eisenhower era's emphasis on nuclear family consumer lifestyles to the Kennedy era's ideal of "New Frontierism," which stressed active citizenship, physical fitness, adventurousness, and "movements" of all kinds.

In fact, the concept of movement permeated all levels of television culture in the 1960s—not just the set itself. Movement and portability were written into television's aesthetic form, especially with the advent of mobile cameras. Remote news gathering and location shooting allowed television to shed itself of its overwhelmingly theatrical and static sensibility. By the early 1970s, movement seemed so basic to television's cultural form that cultural theorist Raymond Williams devised the word *flow* to characterize not only the programs themselves, but their scheduling by networks (he spoke of the way programs led into one another) and their reception by audiences.[4]

Movement was also a major narrative motif of program content and news images. From the famous footage of the Kennedy motorcade to the news reports of civil rights marches to the trip to the moon in 1969, television was replete with travel narratives of every sort, from the political to the sublime. Meanwhile, series programming such as *Route 66* (1960–64) and *The Fugitive* (1963–67) showed men on the run who moved away from their homes in search of their identity and/or freedom. Even genres as unlikely as the family sitcom began to stress notions of mobility and related ideas of sexual liberation from housework and suburban domesticity. As the classic family sitcoms like *Leave It to Beaver* (1957–63) increasingly vanished from the airwaves, the domestic comedy began to feature fantastic households populated by witches, genies, and robots who were able to perform the technological feats of portability and remote control with their special supernatural powers. In programs like *Bewitched* (1964–72), the mundane tasks of housekeeping became opportunities for displays of women's liberation as housewife/witch Samantha Stephens twitched her nose to wash the dishes and then flew off to lunch in Paris.[5] In ways such as these, television's technological and cultural form took on a keen fascination with movement that was intimately connected to notions of social progress and mobile family lifestyles.

Thus, more than simply an object form, the portable TV was the material manifestation of broader conceptual frameworks for television and family life in the 1960s. As a cultural sensibility rooted in the continual relocation of household objects and human subjects in and out of the home, portability came to represent larger social anxieties about postwar transformations in the relationship between public and private spheres. Like the ad for "drive-in television" with its allusion to promiscuous sexuality, these anxieties were mostly rooted in sexual difference and the reigning ideals of

femininity and masculinity that have worked to sanction (and even legal-
ize) the division of spheres since the Victorian period.

This essay, then, begins with the material object, portable TV, in order
to unravel the cultural significance of portability and its relationship to the
gendered divisions of private and public spaces. In particular, I am concerned with the way ads and magazines represented domestic space and
how these media encouraged people to experience their daily lives through
new transistorized forms of portable and remote control technologies. I also
want to show how sexual difference and the ideological divisions between
private/feminine and public/masculine spheres still inform the way we
think about new electronic technologies and that most recent metaphor of
portable culture—the information superhighway. With this in mind, I end
the essay by considering the way portable culture has recently manifested
itself in a new domestic ideal—the home office—which, despite its apparent "liberating" notions of working mothers and domestic dads—is still a
highly gendered, and also racialized, paradigm for everyday space.

From Home Theater to Mobile Home

In the 1950s, when television was hailed as a new "entertainment" and
"information" medium, two central and often connected conceptual frameworks were written into its cultural logics and narrative forms. These frameworks, which I will refer to as "theatricality" and "mobility," were constitutive of virtually all statements about TV, statements generated by the
industry, advertisers, policy makers, artists, critics, and social scientists and
engineers. Theatricality and mobility have not only permeated, but in fact
are generative of, television's object and cultural form.

During the period of its early installation after World War II, popular
writers, intellectuals, and corporate executives spoke of television as both
a "home theater" that brought spectator amusements into the living room
and a "window on the world" that would imaginatively transport viewers
across the globe. Over the course of the last fifty years, theatricality and mobility have continued to generate the ways we speak about television and
the related technologies of cable, satellites, and most recently, the Internet.
Consumer magazines such as *Home Theater* still package television through
notions of theatricality, while terms like *surfing* or *information superhighway*
serve as the contemporary version of a much older fantasy about travel to
distant locales that telecommunication has historically offered its publics.
Theatricality and mobility have also been generative of the "statements"

that television makes, both at the level of its programming and at the level of its material design and object form. Live "Golden Age" anthology dramas are famous for their adaptations of legitimate theater, and even 1990s dramatic formats still aspire to theatricality (think, for example, of *ROC*'s live performances or the 1997 season premier of *ER*, which was shot live as it unfolded on stage). Meanwhile, since the radio age, broadcast programs have also promised audiences a sense of mobile transport to distant locales. In the case of television, media events premised on this transportation model range from *See It Now*'s demonstration of the 1951 co-axial cable hook-up of East and West Coasts to the *Pathfinder*'s recent satellite transmissions from Mars.

Given the fact that broadcasting was developed in the United States for household uses, it is perhaps no coincidence that theatricality and mobility have also been central metaphors for the middle-class home and bourgeois family.[6] Since Victorian times, the theater was a central organizing principle for domestic architecture and family relations. Architects, plan-book writers, religious leaders, domestic engineers, women's magazines, and books on interior decor variously imagined the bourgeois home as a stage on which a set of highly conventionalized social roles were played by family members and guests alike. This theatrical conception of the home and human subjectivity within it carried through from the Victorian era to modern housing design. In her work on modernist architect Adolph Loos, Beatriz Colomina has shown that exclusive client-built homes of that genre that were organized around notions of residence based on the performative nature of everyday life and related notions of visual pleasure.[7] Although presented through mass production economies and designs that appealed to middle-class tastes, the housing designs of the postwar suburb echoed these earlier modernist homes, foregrounding theatricality and visuality as central structural principles. In this respect, as I have argued previously, television was the popular activity par excellence through which the home theater was envisioned.[8] The arrangement of television in domestic space was guided by theatrical principles of set decoration and optimal audience pleasure, and television itself was often promoted as a substitute for theatergoing in the public sphere.

While the home theater continues to define modes of domestic architecture and electronic culture even today, by the end of the 1950s this metaphor for domesticity and domestic communications began to make way for a new set of metaphors that pictured the house as a vehicle for transport, or what I am calling a "mobile home." At a time when Americans were obsessed with the possibility of satellite technologies and outer space travel, this mobile model of domesticity was especially realized in images that depicted the home as a rocket.[9] Drawing from previous streamline styles, but tailoring these to the penchant for space flight, ads for all sorts of remodeling products—from Armstrong flooring to Scotchguard fabrics—showed consumers how to sweep away the tacky remnants of 1950s domesticity and make way for decor that gestured toward the planets. Everything from kitchen dinettes to family cars to toothpaste containers mimicked outer space fashions. While obviously a marketing gimmick devised to make people buy new domestic trappings, the gimmick was probably effective because it tied what is typically devalorized as feminine, decorative, trivial pursuits to the so-called higher masculine goals of national supremacy and citizenship. In other words, this new and improved family home validated itself through appeals to progress; no longer a place of insular stasis, the home was now a motor for change. Mimicking the ideals of Kennedy's New Frontier, and especially his emphasis on space travel as a sign of ultimate national progress, this space age home gave private life a public purpose.

It was in this context of a new ideal of mobile domesticity and progressive family lifestyles that portable television—and a whole new way of watching TV—were introduced to the public.[10] To understand the specific dynamics at hand, I want to turn now to the promotional rhetoric that welcomed in the portable sets.

Breaking Up the Family Circle

In its first incarnation, television was primarily marketed as a family activity. Programming was typically developed and scheduled with family audiences in mind. By the end of the decade, this family circle notion of television changed in several ways. First, as new forms of sponsor-network relations evolved and as Nielsen rating measurements changed, networks began to move away from the singular focus on family audiences and aggregate ratings toward the idea of demographics and audience shares. Networks increasingly developed prime-time programs with individual demographics in mind, attempting to draw in, for example, so many women ages eighteen to forty-nine by targeting them with programs that suited their (as opposed to their family's) tastes. While this focus on demographics did not happen overnight (many shows of the 1960s were still marketed with family groups in mind), the general trend in the industry favored a conception of the audience as an individual consumer type rather than a family unit.

So too, this trend favored socially mobile consumers over the stable family group, and in this sense, mobility was not simply a metaphor, but was also integral to the economic logics of the industry.

In this industrial context, the family console planted in a central living space gave way to portable receivers that could be watched by individuals and moved throughout the home.[11] In 1963, *Good Housekeeping* estimated that "portables are the most popular models today, comprising about 60 percent of all sets sold."[12] The U.S. Census bears this out. From 1955 to 1969, the sale of black-and-white portable and table-top receivers rose dramatically, peaking at mid-decade as color sets (of all models) began to rise in popularity. Meanwhile, the sale of black-and-white consoles sharply declined; by mid-decade consoles were sold primarily in color models. Overall, this meant that by 1969 over twice as many portable and table-top models were sold than were consoles (7,606,000 versus 3,442,000).[13]

Although advertisers still marketed television—especially the color models—as a family medium, they also sought to convince people to watch television alone (and thus to buy more than one TV).[14] One novel marketing twist was the increasing emphasis on what numerous manufacturers called "personal" viewing. As opposed to the family theater of the early 1950s, by the end of the decade manufacturers began to promote solitary room-to-room viewing with advertisements showing Mom, Dad, and the kids separately enjoying TV programs on their very own portable receivers.

Despite the rhetoric of festive good fortune and affordable prices, advertisers did recognize the potential psychological risks entailed in their new campaigns to make television watching a solitary, as opposed to a family, experience. Anticipating this consumer resistance, a 1965 ad for Panasonic portables asked, "Can a personal TV get too personal?"[15] While Panasonic reassured potential customers that portable TV could never be too private, the ad nevertheless expressed the anxieties inherent in the transition from a model of television viewing based on the family theater to the portable model of TV spectatorship based on individualized reception. As this ad suggests, the sentimental family iconography that depicted television in the 1950s could not easily be displaced by the spectacle of self-centered, even narcissistic, viewing. Instead, manufacturers for portable television had to respect the residual cultural sensibilities surrounding television. They had to introduce the new "personal TV" as something compatible with, rather than antithetical to, 1950s cultural ideals of family entertainment.

In this regard, advertisers promoted portable TV as a remedy for family fights over program choices on the living room console. An ad for Admiral

TV, for example, presents two portable receivers, one with a man and the other with a woman on screen. With the TV couple smiling, and the sets rubbing against each other in such a way as to suggest a physical, if not romantic, relation, the ad told consumers to "Meet the Happy Mediums" by purchasing two sets[16] (Figure 6.2). This advertising strategy followed the logic of more eccentric contraptions marketed in the early 1950s—devices such as the "Dumont Duoscope" (a set with two separate picture tubes that would display two separate channels simultaneously so that people could sit together while watching different programs). But while such contraptions were mainly marketed as ways to maintain the ideals of family harmony while allowing for individual privacy and tastes, the "his and hers" marketing strategy for portable sets was much more concerned with demonstrating the pleasures—even autoerotic pleasures—to be achieved through watching TV alone.

This point is especially demonstrated by a 1964 ad in the Admiral campaign that used this "his and hers" strategy when telling consumers to "Make a date with a Playmate," its 11-inch portable model. The ad shows two Playmate portables, one held by a male hand and the other by a female hand. As in the previous example, the sets are positioned side by side, suggesting a sense of intimacy between the TV couple. Continuing with its romantic innuendoes, Admiral suggested that the Playmate could be taken anywhere, even the bedroom, where consumers could listen to their favorite program with the Playmate's "private pillow" earphone.[17] A clear instance of product differentiation, such promises of promiscuous "playmate" dates and "private pillow" pleasures made the portable distinct from the family console.

More generally, manufacturers suggested that portable TV was perfect for bedroom viewing, and numerous ads contained hints of the secret desires and solitary (if not masturbatory) pleasures that portable TV would bring to the home. So prevalent was this idea that even mattress and bedding companies made use of the portable TV when advertising their wares. For example, in 1957 Wamsutta Mills advertised its "Supercale" sheets by showing a woman turning in for the night with a copy of *TV Guide* in her bed and a portable receiver resting on a near-by dresser.[18] Here as elsewhere, the "bedroom" TV became a sign of personal indulgence, an object that spoke more to narcissistic pleasure than to the 1950s emphasis on companionate marriage.

While the narcissistic identification and autoerotic desire encouraged by such ads was presented as a positive goal for the consumer, this also had

Figure 6.2 Two TVs are better than one. (© Admiral Corp.)

more negative, depressing implications. In fact, portable TV was sometimes used metonymically as a kind of short-hand symbol for the perceived crisis of failed passion and dead-end marriage. At a time when divorce rates were climbing,[19] women's magazines and popular weeklies presented articles (typically told from a woman's point of view) in which a husband's loss of sexual interest was represented via the image of a portable receiver. In its January 1970 issue, *Good Housekeeping* capped off this decade-long trend with a story entitled "Can Love Live with Indifference?" A large photograph on the first page showed a husband fast asleep in bed, while his wife, sporting a sexy nightgown, stares, with furrowed brow, at her portable set. The caption reads, "Night after night my husband turned away from me. Hurt, baffled, frustrated—I couldn't believe he was the same man I married."[20]

Whether presented as a luxurious tool for personal indulgence or a depressing comment on romantic estrangement, such images of portable TV should be seen in the context of a more general move away from the suburban family ideals that had been so integral to marketing campaigns for television sets in the early 1950s. While the television industry still targeted the family as its primary consumer unit, it nevertheless revamped its images of ideal families, appealing to domestic consumers in markedly changing terms. Trading in its 1950s emphasis on domestic interiors and sedentary family circles, the industry represented family life in terms that engaged ideals of freedom, sexual liberation, personal achievement, and participation in public affairs, ideals that were integral to both Kennedy's New Frontier and the various social movements of the 1960s.

Privatized Mobility

At the most basic level, the move away from domestic enclosures was written onto television technology itself. Names like the General Electric "Adventurer," the Zenith "Jetliner," and the RCA "Globe Trotter" spoke to the new emphasis on active leisure and imaginary travel away from home. Television manufacturers especially drew on the public's burgeoning interest in space travel. In 1960, Motorola spoke of its "astronaut portable," while a host of manufacturers boasted of "space age" performance and style.[21] As the case of the "Drive-In Television" suggests, advertisers also encouraged consumers to imagine portable sets as earthbound vehicles, not only cars but also motorcycles and boats.

Not only did advertisers recommend uses, they also designed the set itself in ways that conjured up travel away from home. Numerous manufacturers made portable cabinets look like luggage. In 1959, Philco claimed that its portable was "handsomely encased . . . in leather-like vinyl simulating natural saddle, white or black alligator."[22] Making the visual comparison more emphatic, the Philco ad placed the portable receiver next to an actual suitcase. Portability thus opened up a whole new set of cultural fantasies about television and the pleasure to be derived from watching

TV—fantasies based on the imaginary possibility of leaving, rather than staying, home.

In ways such as this, the stress on mobility made portable television (or at least the fantasies surrounding it) quite different from its 1950s console predecessor. While early advertising promised viewers that TV would strengthen family ties by bringing the world into the living room, representations of portable receivers inverted this logic. Rather than incorporating views of the outdoor world into the home, now television promised to bring the interior world outdoors. In this regard, we might say that what Raymond Williams referred to as communication technology's capacity for *mobile privatization*—its promise to link the private family home with the modern industrial city—was now inverted into a related ideal of *privatized mobility.*

Williams developed the concept of mobile privatization in order to explain television's rise as a technology and cultural form. In this context, Williams uses the idea of mobile privatization to describe the inherent paradox entailed in two contradictory yet intimately connected modes of modern social life: geographic mobility (realized through technologies of communication and transportation) and privatization (realized through domestic architecture and community planning). He locates the roots of this paradox in the changes wrought by the Industrial Revolution. After industrialization, people no longer experience a rooted existence in small agricultural communities. Instead, in a society organized around large urban centers, people live in a highly mobile world where communities are joined together through transportation and communication systems. At the same time, since industrialization, there has been an increased emphasis on the ideology of privacy, an ideology that materialized in the private family home. Nevertheless, the private family has always depended on the public sphere for funding, maintenance, and information about the world. Broadcasting, Williams argues, serves as the resolution to this contradiction insofar as it brings a picture of the outside world into the private home. It gives people a sense of traveling to distant places and having access to information and entertainment in the public sphere, even as they receive this in the confines of their own domestic interiors.

In the 1960s, the paradox of mobile privatization that Williams described still structured the statements that people made about television. However, the inversion I refer to as "privatized mobility" characterized a peculiar shift of emphasis. Now, rather than experiencing the domicile as a window on the world that brought public life indoors, the resident experienced the home as a vehicular form, a mode of transport in and of itself that allowed people to take private life outdoors.

In fact, privatized mobility extended beyond the case of television per se; it was written into architectural styles and decorative practices. This period saw the rise of the mobile home as new a design for middle-class suburban lifestyles. Differentiating itself from the trailer's previous associations with Depression-era and wartime hardships, the term *mobile home* was coined in the mid-1950s "to refer to a place where respectable people could marry, mature, and die."[23] A popular mode of everyday life, the mobile home perfectly encapsulates the contradictions of portable culture. While most people living in these homes did not use them for travel, the homes nevertheless were promoted in ways that negotiated cultural ideals of travel, adventure, outdoorsy-ness, and personal freedom with the values of home ownership, a stable family life, and suburban community.

For the more traditionally house-bound consumer, a host of "indoor-outdoor" products boasted of their ability to transform domesticity (and the civilizing customs it implied) into rustic, outdoor lifestyles. In 1966, *Ladies Home Journal* included an article on a new line of sleeping bags that allowed for an "indoor camp-out." The *Journal* told readers that the sleeping bags were "an adventure for the whole family . . . the ideal campsite, of course, the floor." The accompanying photograph to this indoor-outdoor fantasy was a domestic scene in which two children nestled up next to each other in their bandanna-patterned sleeping bags, while Dad, lying in his own bag, watched a miniature portable TV.[24]

In tune with this indoor-outdoor aesthetic, numerous ads for television sets promoted TV's ability to merge domestic space with the world outdoors. In the early 1960s, Motorola's advertising campaign for hi-fi, table, and portable models featured brilliantly rendered upper-class homes that incorporated dramatic landscapes into the living room. Sporting the slogan, "Fresh from Motorola," the ads depicted the home as a nature retreat (Figure 6.3). A 1963 ad shows a house made entirely of glass and shaped like a perisphere.[25] The glass home functions as a series of views through which we see hillsides, an ocean, and two large rocks near the shore. The seaside motif continues thematically into the interior space as a rock formation occupies the center of the living room where it forms a kind of altar for a TV set. Steps of flagstone and vegetation lead up to a hi-fi/TV console.

Other ads in this "Fresh from Motorola" series depict the activity of television watching as a kind of outdoor sport. A 1963 ad for a portable model

Figure 6.3 In this 1963 ad, indoor and outdoor space merge as TV goes back to nature. (© Motorola Corp.).

shows a woman watching TV in a dome-shaped all-glass pool house that lies adjacent to her markedly modernist home in the background.[26] Placed at the edge of the pool, the portable set is tuned to an exercise program that pictures a female figure stretching her body. Meanwhile, in the foreground of the ad, a woman dressed in a leotard imitates the action on screen. This ad for the portable model thus carries the Motorola series to its logical extreme. Portability allows the woman literally to carry her television pleasures outside the home, where she becomes an active, rather than a passive viewer. Her body, just as the receiver itself, is placed in motion.

In ads such as these, portability is more than a technological contraption; it serves to define not only the receiver but also the experience of television spectatorship itself. Portability is thus portrayed as a conceptual design for living—a mode of experience—that became the dominant model for television culture in the 1960s. Distinct from the sedentary domestic culture of the 1950s, and the passive model of spectatorship implied by the "home theater," portable TV assumed an active viewer, a mobile subject. As Zenith proclaimed in 1964, portables were "for people on the go."[27] Moreover, whereas the early cultural expectations for television and its live production practices emphasized TV's ability to simulate the experience of "being at the theater," the 1960s model of portability emphasized television's ability to simulate adventures in the great outdoors.

Some manufacturers even sold their sets with special "weather-resistant" attachments. RCA named its 1967 portable model the "Sport," and marketed it with a removable "snap-on sunshield" that would "filter [sun] for better daylight viewing, inside or out."[28] This indoor-outdoor motif was continued in that same year by Admiral, which promoted its "snap on 'Sun Shield' TV."[29] A 1967 ad for the RCA "Jaunty" used an even more unlikely accessory. The ad shows a pair of flippers and a snorkel mask laying next to a portable TV whose screen depicts a woman who looks like she's been diving. Thus, whether through marketing gimmicks or advertising metaphors, advertisers encouraged consumers to think of television as an active outdoor sport.[30]

Despite the promise of exotic outdoor fun, it seems unlikely that actual consumers took these advertisements literally. Nor does it seem likely that people assumed advertisers intended them to do so. In fact, in 1963 *House Beautiful* reported that "research has shown that for whatever reasons, portables are seldom moved."[31] From this point of view, it seems most probable that what advertisers assumed the public wanted the *fantasy* (as opposed to the actual possibility) of being somewhere else while watching TV at home.

In this sense, such sales come-ons evoked what Margaret Morse has called television's capacity to "derealize" space. Morse argues that television is one of several postwar phenomena that encourage people to experience the lived environment in a state of distraction so that they are no longer "present" in the material spaces they occupy (she uses the shopping mall and the freeway as additional examples).[32] Ads for portable television promoted this derealization of space as an ideal state of consciousness, as a highly pleasurable form of experience. Even if most people actually watched their portable receivers at home, the ads supplied a new kind of "psychical reality" for television, giving the public a fantasy of TV watching as an active, and markedly nondomesticated, mode of experience that took place in an imaginary space, outside the material contours of the home.

In addition to its promise of imaginary transport to another spatial realm, advertisers promised that the portable TV would allow spectators to manipulate space, to convert the "here and now" into the "there and then," to make "presence" into "absence," "home" into "not home." Manufacturers boasted of the portable's capacity for multiple hook-ups, telling consumers they could plug it into cigarette lighters in cars and boats, as well as conventional household sockets. Moreover, the portable television's capacity for electrical conversion allowed advertisers to evoke a range of contradictory meanings and uses for television. With its "indoor-outdoor" convertible sockets, portable TV could appeal to people aspiring to conventional family ideals, or just as easily to consumers who embraced the nonfamilial, "liberated," and even countercultural lifestyles of the 1960s.

Liberated Viewers

Representations of the "mobile home" and the fantasies of portability it contained were predicated on a new set of gender and generational relations that were tied to the movements of the day, especially the sexual revolution. Advertisers often represented their imaginary television outings as social relations apart from the family unit; and they often displayed television in scenes that evoked youth culture and/or sex out of wedlock.

For example, a 1965 ad for the Zenith "Voyager" shows a group of young people gathered on a beach at night, barely dressed and watching TV as the tide comes in.[33] In that same year, RCA-Victor claimed its "Sportabout" portable was just right "for the action crowd." The ad shows a young man and woman on motor scooters, with 19-inch portables rigged onto the back of each bike.[34] Sony's 1967 ad campaign for its 5-inch portable took this "swinging youth" ethos to its provocative extreme. One ad in the campaign promotes the Sony "Sun Set" model by showing people watching it in a nudist colony (Figure 6.4). Calling it the "Sony for Sun-Lovers," the ad includes twelve naked men and women watching the mini-portable while resting in tall grass that hides the more private parts of their anatomy. Sony, however, used this visual censorship as a way to provoke—as opposed to diminish—the reader's sexual interest in the scene as the advertiser went to great lengths to direct our visual attention to what we were not allowed to see. For example, the ad draws attention to female genitalia by having women modestly hide their body parts. Meanwhile, a male nude towers over the scene, holding a bar bell and flexing his sizable biceps. Sony thus encouraged consumers to imagine the activity of watching TV as an erotic, and emphatically nonfamilial, pastime. Of course, as with these ads more generally, Sony was quick to remind people of the convertible nature of this fantasy, telling readers, "there's nothing to stop you from going indoors and watching the Sun Set after the sun goes down."[35]

In cases such as this, the move away from family life that was built into the symbolic apparatus of portability was accompanied by new images of male and female viewers quite different from the Moms and Dads of the 1950s home theater. The representation of gender roles in promotional materials for television underwent a marked shift, even if these ads preserved the middle-class family as a dominant design for living.

Representations of female viewers embraced the ethos of liberated lifestyles. While Sony's nudist colony was the most extreme example of the marketing of the sexual revolution, other ads also incorporated new sensibilities about women's social and economic equality. In the context of the widespread popularity of Betty Friedan's *Feminine Mystique* (1963), advertisers addressed women, not only as housewives, but as people expecting to achieve some degree of economic and professional success.

The association of portability with women's liberation and economic mobility was crucial to the promotion of portable receivers from the start. As early as 1957, *House Beautiful* ran an ad for Magnavox portables that displayed a young woman in graduation cap and gown on screen. At a practical level, Magnavox most likely recognized the market for portable receivers among the growing number of young people living away from home in college dorms. But at a symbolic level, the ad implies that the

The Sony for Sun-Lovers

If you're a person who hates to stay indoors watching television on a bright sunny day, we've got the perfect set for you. Because with the all-transistor Sony Sun Set, you can go outdoors and watch television on a bright sunny day.

The secret is the screen. Instead of a conventional white screen, the Sun Set has a special black screen that cuts down the glare. Which means that the picture

won't fade out unless it's supposed to. And since it plays off AC current as well as rechargeable batteries, there's nothing to stop you from going indoors and watching the Sun Set after the sun goes down.

The Sun Set

Figure 6.4 No longer a family group, the ideal TV spectator is now going "back to nature" in this 1967 ad for a Sony portable (© Sony Corp.).

portable receiver is imbued with the values of women's liberation—particularly its emphasis on the pursuit of professional careers over what Betty Friedan derisively called "occupation housewife." Condensing the set's ability to be carried outdoors with the growing emphasis on girls' achievements before marriage, the caption boasts that the portable "promises performance that surpasses many ordinary 'stay at home' sets."[36]

Ironically, then, while Friedan had vehemently attacked advertisers for creating stereotypical images of women, advertisers co-opted burgeoning sentiments of women's liberation and turned them into consumer lifestyles. In this regard, ads for portable TV especially resonated with the new sexual freedoms of career girls promoted in Helen Gurley Brown's *Sex and the Single Girl* (1962). Equating liberation with sex appeal, they presented slender, modern-looking women who wore mini-skirts and other "mod" garb. As in the "Fresh From Motorola" ad for pool-side TV, advertisers often presented women in action poses that evoked athletic lifestyles. And, unlike the ads from the 1950s, which typically presented family groups and domestic milieus, these ads often contained solitary female figures set against abstract backgrounds or negative, empty spaces.

In images such as these, the new woman's increased corporal "mobility" and athleticism typically also served to evoke her economic mobility, discretionary income, and consumer choices. A perfect example is a 1966 issue of *TV Guide* that promoted the new fall line-up of state-of-the-art television sets.[37] On the cover, apparently running toward the reader, is a woman dressed in an orange mini-skirt, accessorized with white shoes, white gloves, and a white hat that looks ambiguously like an English bobby hat and a space helmet. The final and most eccentric touch to this already odd ensemble is a small-screen portable television set that the woman holds in her outstretched arms, as if it were a purse. The visual metaphor used here—portable TV as a woman's purse—is the 1960s version of a much longer history of visual culture (movies, fairs, museums) in which women's spectatorship has been linked to shopping. In this particular version, the new woman's corporal mobility is conflated with both her economic mobility and her (implied) sexual freedom.

To be sure, this advertising imagery resonated with television programming of the time, which increasingly promoted new models of femininity that spoke to the reigning ethos of sexual liberation. Despite censorship concerns at networks, housewives had more athletic bodies and wore revealing clothing like Capri pants (*The Dick Van Dyke Show*, 1961–66) or harem garb

(*I Dream of Jeannie*, 1965–70) in place of aprons. The single-girl sitcom was especially concerned with movement away from the family, and as if to underscore the centrality of this theme, some of these shows foregrounded it in their credit sequences. For example, *That Girl* (1966–71) portrayed single woman Ann Marie literally moving away from her suburban family home to live by herself in the city. The credit sequence showed Ann frolicking through the streets of Manhattan amid a series of moving vehicles. Following *That Girl*, the breakthrough "new woman" sitcom, *The Mary Tyler Moore Show* (1970–77), took this to its logical extreme. The famous credit sequence showed Mary Richards driving from her small town home to the thriving city of Minneapolis, where she turns her engagement ring in for an exciting career in television. In ways such as these, both the technological apparatus and some of the most popular new programs it delivered associated women's liberation with a move away from traditional ideals of family life in the 1950s suburb.

The idea of mobility and travel away from home was also associated with a more active style of masculinity. By the end of the 1950s, and especially in the early 1960s, male spectators shed the family man status of their early 1950s predecessors. In the context of the New Frontier's emphasis on physical fitness and do-gooder countrymen—as well as the more countercultural romanticization of beatniks and playboys—male spectators were often represented as sportsmen and adventurer seekers. In 1960, RCA-Victor promoted its "Sportabout" line of portable sets by displaying a procession of male figures (cut off at the waist) carrying the sets across a two-page advertising spread. The first man in line was dressed in a formal black suit, carrying a television set as if it were briefcase. The second man was dressed in white pants and tennis shoes, and his portable receiver looked like a gym bag. Finally, the third man was dressed more ambiguously, in a sporty shirt with formal black pants and shoes, so that the portable TV functioned more ambiguously as both brief case and gym bag. In this way, the ad encouraged the reader to imagine TV not simply as a sedentary pastime, but rather as the perfect marriage of work and leisure. So too, the image of male bodies dressed for success and proceeding purposefully across the page imbued the ad with a sense of progress and potent masculinity. The ad's copy associates these pictorial allusions to potent masculinity with the technological capacity of the set itself, calling it a "big time performer" and claiming it is "high in picture power."[38] Other ads balanced this brand of rugged masculinity with the family man image that had more traditionally been used to market TV. Addressing men as both husbands and adventurers, GE told the male consumer to "bring your wife and your wanderlust to your GE Dealer's."[39]

As with the case of women, these images of new masculinity resonated with characters on television itself. Heroes such as Richard Kimble (*The Fugitive*), Tod Stiles and Buz Murdock (*Route 66*), Paladin (*Have Gun Will Travel*, 1957–63), or Kelly Robinson and Alexander Scott (*I Spy*, 1965–68) lived apart from women, straying far away from domestic lifestyles. Even if these heroes were often involved in romantic interludes or melodramatic plots about human morality, they nevertheless provided a distinct departure from the family man of 1950s television. As one critic of the period argued, "many of television's most highly rated dramatic series have created an essentially womanless society, and in so doing have defined a provocative breed of male hero. . . . [whose] behavioral sterility, so aggressively explored by the European avant-garde in the last decade or so, is a natural for television." Claiming this hero was a reaction against previous radio and television programs that represented men as lovable boobs ruled by their overly "superior" wives, he argued that TV's new womanless hero was an expression of a man's desire for "liberation," a "sublimated yearning for one's wife to be dispatched."[40]

The association of television's new virile avant-garde hero with the rejection of domesticity was clearly, and at the time, unabashedly misogynistic. For our purposes, such associations have particular relevance to the more general dynamics of portable culture, beyond the case of programming per se. Portable television technology carried with it a host of highly gendered meanings about private and public life. Indeed, despite the emphasis on heroic men and emancipated women, the cultural fantasies of 1960s television were by no means revolutionary. Anxieties about sexual difference and the power dynamics between men and women still provided the source material for representations of television and the activity of watching TV.

This is particularly notable with regard to the way domestic labor and leisure were represented. Although female spectators were depicted as upwardly mobile and less house bound, promotional rhetoric surrounding portable TV still often reproduced stereotypical housewife roles. In fact, even the Sony nudist colony ad, with its explicit allusions to sexual liberation, still found it necessary to have one of the female nudes knitting while watching from her place in the sun. More generally, even while women were not typically pictured in family scenes, in the few ads that did show family groups, women spectators tended (like their early 1950s predecessors) to perform child-rearing functions (such as helping the child move the TV) or else household chores (such as serving snacks or wheeling the portable cart as if it were a snack cart).

That said, however, portrayals of housewife spectators were never simply about feminine submission to male authority in the home. Instead, such images were complicated by the fact that women spectators actually worked—that is, they took active and productive roles while watching television. Conversely, male spectators typically sat passively and were even rendered as what we now call the classic "couch potatoes." In this regard, even while male spectators might have been given the luxury of total relaxation, these scenarios belied subtle reversals of gender power in the home. Whereas Western culture typically associates men with activity and women with passivity, these images of housewife spectators and their lazy male husbands often reversed that hierarchy so that women were decidedly in the active role while men were presented as passive subjects, not only "victims" of TV, but also at the mercy of their more industrious wives.[41]

By the mid-1960s, when the advertising industry increasingly used ironic humor as a sales strategy, representations of lazy male spectators sometimes took on sinister tones. In these cases, the male spectator was not simply represented as a lazy lounger; instead he was shown to be thoroughly humiliated and degraded. Sony TV was especially brutal in this regard. A 1965 ad shows an overweight, balding, large-nosed man in polkadot pajamas who is lying in bed with a 5-inch "lightweight" Sony TV resting on his stomach. The bold print title caption reads, "Tummy Television," and the copy continues, "The 5 inch Sony [is] for waist sizes 38 to 46." Just in case anyone imagined that this man might have anything to do in bed except watch his Tummy TV, the ad claims, "So that your wife can sleep, we also include a personal ear plug."[42] Several months later, Sony followed up with an ad for its 4-inch model. Visually comparing the smallness of the set to the largeness of a man's pot belly, the ad shows the same male model slumped in a chair, smoking a cigar, while the mini-TV sits perched on its handle on the man's thighs. Because the TV looks as if it is actually crawling up the man's legs, the ad draws attention not only to his protruding stomach, but even more provocatively to his crotch (in fact, the receiver seems headed for his genitals). The humorous juxtaposition of the miniature TV and the man's anatomy is further emphasized by the boldface caption that reads "Pee Wee Tee Vee"—a slogan which, in not too subtle ways, also suggests the diminutive size of the man's genitals (at least in comparison to his pot belly) (Figure 6.5). In short, it seems unlikely that Sony could have

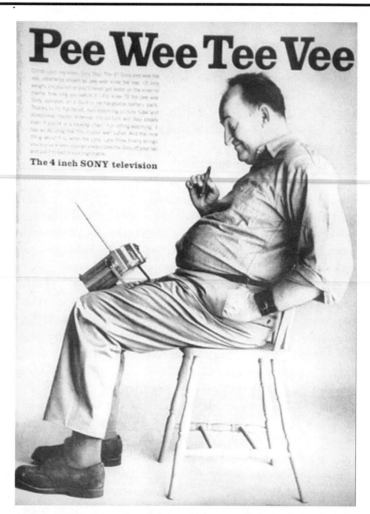

Figure 6.5 In this 1965 ad for a Sony mini-portable, masculinity is obviously the butt of the joke (© Sony Corp.).

intended this ad to be read in any other way than as a humiliating joke about the male spectator's out-of-shape and decidedly unphallic body.[43] The enigma this ad poses, of course, is why Sony assumed that this depressing image of masculinity would make people want to buy television sets. Because images such as these are more associative than they are literal, it seems useful to explore this enigma in relation to a final set of cultural fantasies surrounding portability and miniaturization—fantasies of mastery over technology.

While I have been arguing that portability implied an active relation to television, it is nevertheless true that this could easily turn onto its opposite—complete and utter human stasis.[44] The transistorized technology of portable TV not only allowed the human subject to move the set in and out the home, it also perfected TV technology to the point where human movement was accomplished by the set itself. The portable set was often marketed with a remote control, a device that came wrapped in a set of ambivalences about the relation of "man" to machine. On the one hand, advertisers promoted the ease and comfort offered by automation, demonstrating how viewers could dominate domestic space and time by commanding the set to perform instantaneously from remote locales. Metaphors of flight were especially applied to the remote accessory, as product names like Admiral's "Super Son-R" promoted the idea that the viewer was a pilot navigating a ship through the airwaves.[45]

Yet, despite these action-adventure fantasies of domestic space travel and mastery over distance, the remote control brought with it the nagging fear that technology would render the human body completely immobile, passive, even redundant. Lazy spectators sat transfixed by the tube as their remote controls performed the human function. At its most extreme, and sometimes in quite humorous and self-aware terms, advertisers staged fantasy scenarios of sadomasochism in which man and machine reversed roles of aggressor and victim, master and slave. Not surprisingly, in these terms, the ads had explicit sexual content.

From this point of view, we might better understand Sony's derisive representations of passive male spectators and their "Pee Wee Tee Vees." Sony chose to express the cultural ambivalence about automation by way of a joke that would address anxieties about mastery, a joke that had both a psychological and a social dimension. On the one hand, with its focus on the relative size of male body parts versus TV components, Sony's "Pee Wee Tee Vee" humorously rendered social anxieties about technology as castration anxieties about male power. In addition, on a more pragmatic level, these ads voiced the paradox of mastery over technology: when people produce sentient machines, human intelligence and productive labor become less and less necessary.

Such master-slave fantasies thus pervaded all aspects of television culture during this period—from the literal technology to the more conceptual issues of control over social life, sexuality, and human subjectivity. Their legacy is still felt today in ads for that ultimate vehicle of portable culture—the computer.

FROM MOBILE HOME TO HOME OFFICE

What interests me about all these representations is what they say not only about the past but also about the present. I want to turn now to some speculations on the mobile culture of today, and the lessons that we might learn from the 1960s.

I began researching the portable television set in response to my frustration with theories of television and new media that make rather grandiose claims about information society and cyberculture—especially work inspired by Jean Baudrillard. I am particularly thinking of Baudrillard's essay "The Ecstasy of Communication," in which he argues that we have experienced a complete break with Victorian logics of private and public spheres, and with that the end to Freudian-based models of subjectivity and scenarios of sexual difference. The break, he argues, comes with the introduction of television and then satellite technologies which, he claims, make it impossible to experience home and public life as separate. Rather than experience the home as a private theater on which individuals play roles in scenes, now we are forced into an "obscene" world where private secrets and public information are one and the same.[46] Although his views are sometimes prescient of our worst information society nightmares, Baudrillard speaks in fantastic terms that are probably intended more to shock than to explain material circumstances and process of change. Still, insofar as this brand of fantastic rhetoric has become a kind of cultural cache for cyberenthusiasts and doomsday predictors alike, I think it is important to note that Baudrillard considers this historical shift in wholly ahistorical terms, omitting all of the material details through which these changes were experienced at the time. His work has been taken up in overly literal and deterministic ways as people envision complete historical annihilations of familiar binaries and ideologies like public and private, male and female, unconscious and conscious.

By looking at representations of home and technology from this period, we see a very different picture. While the case of portable television does reveal an historical shift in cultural sensibilities regarding domesticity and domestic technologies, this shift was never simple nor was it fully achieved. Instead, representations from this period exhibit profound ambivalence about the changes they envisioned. Even as they glorify emerging conceptions of a new space age mobile family, they hark back to residual ideas about gender roles and the division of spheres that can be traced to Victorian times.

Our present-day world of mobile communications is still structured around these binaries of space and sexual difference, although there are some obvious changes. While the "Drive-in Television" represented its period's focus on mobile forms of domestic leisure, today's information superhighway is organized around the problem of work. In relation to this changing emphasis, new metaphors of home abound.

Recent ads for Web sites and computers repeat central themes of portable culture, but search for new twists. Given the fact that the computer industry has not been as successful as the television industry in selling its products for domestic use, it is perhaps not surprising that advertisers are still experimenting with their sales pitches.

The most typical new configuration is the home office—a hybrid site of work and leisure where it's possible to make tele-deals while sitting at home in your bathrobe. Promoted in magazines like *Home Office* and *Mac Home*, the home office is a space of high-tech computer workspaces staffed by single moms or stay-at-home dads who keep Pampers next to modems.

Even while it combines traditional forms of male and female labor, and even while men and women are both shown as home workers, the home office most typically appears as a masculine extension of the feminine sphere. Furnishing the home office is presented as a paramount dilemma. Should it re-create the sterile antifeminine spaces of modern industrial design, or should it flirt with feminine flair? The merging of (male) productive labor and (female) reproductive labor poses questions for old modernist ideas about form and function. Frills and hard drives don't mix.

The problem, however, is not simply decorative. The merging of productive and reproductive labor is also riddled with conflicts about male and female roles. These home offices are utopian solutions to tensions felt in everyday life, and their miraculous mergers of private and public, male and female, productive and reproductive work, are simply the wish-fulfillment of the advertising industry, which knows that people actually have a much harder time merging these divisions in practice. Indeed, these advertising images are meaningful precisely because people still experience their lives through these gendered divisions and are taught to believe that they should be able to overcome these divides through personal achievements. These ads are less a testimony to a sexually liberated world than a symptom of a culture that tells people they should and can do everything at once.

Computer companies advertising a number of different new technologies often make use of gender divisions in ad copy. In 1997, for example, Princeton Graphics (a computer hardware company) advertised its "Arcadia Home Monitor" in clearly gendered terms.[47] The Arcadia monitor merges traditional TV and computer screens, and in so doing promises to merge traditional modes of work and leisure. However, when advertising the new single-screen system, the company reverts to old lessons about femininity and masculinity and their traditional relations to public/work and domestic/leisure. Introducing the "birth of Arcadia," the ad uses a two-page layout to show how the computer monitor and TV set have evolved into the one Arcadia system. Occupying the center of the layout is a huge-screen Arcadia monitor. The left border of the left hand page shows a vintage Philco TV set and gives a brief history of TV set design, leading up to the Arcadia digital TV. The right hand border of the right page shows a vintage computer display and gives a brief history of computer design leading up to full-motion video monitors. The birth metaphor is then carried through as these old technologies figuratively become the mother and father of digital TV. Or as the caption tells us, "Its Mother was a TV. Its Father was a Monitor." The image that dominates the center of the Arcadia screen and the page's layout underscores the point. An old woman appears on the left side of the screen and an old man on the right. Thus, according to the rhetoric of the ad, the new technologies that merge home entertainment with the public world of work are still rigidly divided into gendered categories. Here as elsewhere, TV is represented as a mode of leisure associated with feminine pursuits while computers are presented as masculine. In fact, as this split-page layout so clearly suggests, even as TV sets and computers increasingly merge into one home screen, this singular screen does not obliterate the distinctions between male and female, work and leisure, public and private that were associated with the older technologies. Instead, this new home screen incorporates these sex-related binaries to such a degree that they reappear in a "birth" narrative which promises consumers that while technologies generate change, the traditional heterosexual family remains the gene pool of all mutations.

In ways such as these, images of high-tech homes are organized around familiar divisions of public and private spaces and the gendered divisions that entails. Even if these ads play with these divisions and offer communication technologies as utopian solutions to them, they nevertheless assume that their readers recognize the ideological distinctions between spheres and sexes. Indeed, the prevailing consumer discourses on new technologies aimed at the white middle class continue to present tableaux in which domestic subjectivity is presented though the logics of sexual difference and related divisions of public and private spaces, even if these logics are updated for a computer age.[48]

HOUSING PROJECTS AND SOCIAL MOBILITY

While no doubt a new design for living, the mobile home of the 1960s, and its more recent manifestation as the home office, does not necessarily provide radically new identities for its residents. Even if binaries of private and public, labor and leisure, masculine and feminine have transformed, this is not the same as complete obliteration. Instead of a complete collapse of private and public spheres, what we are faced with is a much more contradictory environment where different models of domesticity exist in emergent, residual, and dominant forms. Indeed, while I have been mapping a series of housing models, it should be clear that the home theater, the mobile home, and the home office do not simply march in a straight historical timeline. Instead they are ideal forms that present distinct possibilities for living that are emphasized in different degrees in specific social contexts.

Given this, it is probably the case that most of the target consumers for the new communication technologies live in very hybrid situations, drawing on models of home that carry with them a host of different historical associations. The living room TV provides a home theater. Desktop computers and fax machines decorate the home office. Mobile telephones, boom boxes, and lap tops continue with themes of portable culture by allowing us to work not only at home, but in cars, on planes, and even, as AT&T tells us, on the beach. In other words, people simultaneously experience different historical styles of domesticity and domestic communications.

Moreover, while I have been dealing with a particular consumer demographic—the white middle class—and a particular cultural ideal—the suburban family lifestyle—it is of course the case that other groups experience home and technology in markedly different ways. In the 1960s, when white middle-class culture was represented through appeals to mobile family lifestyles, mobility meant something very different for people of color and working-class people. While, for example, the federally funded highways built in the postwar period were designed to bridge suburb and city (thus mostly benefiting whites), they often cut through working-class and ethnic communities, destroying homes and businesses.[49] Meanwhile, as bell hooks has argued, for black Americans travel has been less a romantic metaphor of liberation than it has a constant threat. Black migrations and even everyday transportation have historically been accompanied by acts of white terrorism.[50] Discriminatory seating practices on buses fueled the civil rights movement in the mid-1950s, while the movement itself was predicated on the turn away from a social system that had disenfranchised entire communities. Obviously, this politicized notion of movement was worlds apart from the images of mobile family lifestyles meant to counteract white middle-class angst about sedentary family life.

So too, this different articulation of movement was central not only to transportation technologies such as cars, buses, and freeways but also to communication technologies. In the 1960s, when suburban homes and household appliances mimicked the imagery of outer space and satellite technologies, venues of black culture continually attacked the space race on the grounds of its racist logic. As I have demonstrated elsewhere, while popular media aimed at whites imagined outer space as the "final frontier" for family values, the black press saw the space project as a racist waste of tax dollars that would be better spent on housing in the inner city.[51] In 1969, playing on *Apollo 11*'s victory cry, the black magazine *Ebony* called the moon landing "one small step for 'The Man,' and probably a giant step in the wrong direction for mankind."[52]

Today, as the computer industry makes its way into the American home, similar discrepancies emerge. In 1998 the city of Oakland and IBM announced their plans to wire a thirty-year-old housing project for the future. Built in the era of civil rights on the flatlands of Oakland's West side, the project—known as the Acorn Complex—is being transformed into a high-tech company town. Individual apartments will be equipped with computers; the complex will include a high-tech learning center; and residents will receive computer training courses that they can take in their homes. Those who successfully complete the course will be certified by IBM and given jobs with local companies. According to the *Los Angeles Times*, the high-tech project is viewed with ambivalence by the community. While some residents embrace the project as a way to "level the computer playing field" and to give people jobs, the newspaper also reported the more skeptical comments of a professional critic who asks, "Could somebody tell me how some glitzy, multimedia gizmos are going to solve the problem of rats and cockroaches in Oakland's municipal housing?" Meanwhile, for its part, IBM speaks as the voice of social justice. A company spokesman told the *Times*, "This obviously isn't going to be a huge profit generator for us. . . . But we've always been a good corporate citizen."[53]

How are we to make sense of the present conditions of everyday life in the wake of cybermedia? The case of the Acorn Complex poses some radically different possibilities. New media as a cure for poverty and the failures of civil rights? New media as a detour through which real destitution goes unchecked? New media as corporate good will—or more cynically put—as a public relations ploy? Whatever the case, IBM's vision of the home office as company town is radically different from the visions of personal freedom and family bliss offered in middle-class consumer magazines.

For reasons such as this, deterministic treatises on technology and its radical effects on daily life are at best simplistic. Now circulating through a host of both utopian and dystopian speculative fictions, technological determination obscures larger social questions about how we get our ideas of home and family life in the first place. Even if technology is one component contributing to change, social engineering in the form of housing policies, welfare, family planning, transportation, and the like are fundamental in their impact on the structures of everyday life (and communication technologies are intricately involved in the formation of these policies and their implementation).

That said, it is still the case that technology and our ideas about it do contribute to the network of forces through which ideologies and practices of everyday life are constituted and achieved. The statements generated about new technologies in popular culture engage the public in dialogues not only on technological change itself, but also on larger issues of home and family life. The portable culture ushered in at the dawn of the 1960s has helped to redefine and also prefigure the various high-tech housing designs of the present. But while this culture was predicated on movements of all kinds, it seems hasty to say that the utopian rhetoric of progressive change at the heart of portability has transformed the world and our perceptions of it in quite the ways that contemporaries predicted. It seems equally hasty to embrace the dystopian nightmares offered today by cyberfiction and numerous theoretical accounts of postmodernity.

Instead, at a time of technological change, it might in the end be useful to think about what is not being said about new technologies. We might consider those "structured absences" through which discourses on new technologies evade crucial topics for debate. These topics would certainly include questions of housing and media policies that tend to go unaddressed in both consumer advertising and cyberfictions. Promotional rhetoric and speculative fictions about new technologies have typically kept these more fundamental questions at bay. Insofar as the discourse on new technologies has essentially been aimed at the people who can buy them—most typically the propertied class—it has tended to deal mostly with the issues that concern these class interests. As we have seen in the case of portable TV, this technology became a fetish object that stood in for larger social anxieties related to middle-class family life. Even more pervasively, the history of technological innovation demonstrates that a litany of new communication forms, from the telegraph to the computer, were ushered in with similar fears about social life and utopian statements about the future.[54] The fact that this discourse on technological innovation is highly conventionalized and formulaic begs us to consider what is at stake in this compulsion to repeat the same ideas, even as the society itself has noticeably changed.

In this respect, it seems to me that since the nineteenth century and continuing through to today, this utopian (and dystopian) rhetoric about new technologies has served to derail us from asking larger questions about how social change might occur in the first place. Technologies alone will surely not decide the fate of housing and family life, nor will they tell us how to communicate with media and for what social good. Paradoxically, in this sense, while the culture of portability has been based on an obsession with movement, progress, and travel through space, the statements it generates tend to keep the people exactly where they are.

Notes

Acknowledgments: This is a shortened, revised version of Lynn Spigel, "Portable TV" published in *Welcome to the Dreamhouse: Popular Media and Postwar Suburbs* (Durham, N.C.: Duke University Press, 2001), 60–103. Copyright, 2001, Duke University Press. All rights reserved. Used by permission of the publisher. Thank you to Alison Trope, who assisted me for a Web site project that initiated this study; Heather Osborne, who assisted me with research; and Jeffrey Sconce and Jan Olsson for their editorial suggestions.

1. *Life*, June 6, 1967, 103.

2. *House Beautiful*, October 1958, 181.

3. This essay is based on an examination of every issue of *Life, Ladies Home Journal, Good Housekeeping, House Beautiful*, and *Better Homes and Gardens* from 1956 to 1970. While *Life* addressed a family consumer, and often directly addressed the man of the house, the other magazines were aimed specifically at women. The readership base for these magazines included a range of lower- to upper-middle-class readers, but their representations of the home often spoke to a middle-class dream of luxurious living rather than representing the lived realities of any one social group. The magazines all also assumed their reader was white, and ads promoted products in

specifically racialized terms. *Life* contained the greatest number of full-page ads for portable television during this period, and that is reflected in this analysis. Note as well, that *Ebony* often advertised portable television sets with ads identical to those found in the other venues, and occasionally by using the same ads but inserting a black viewer.

4. Raymond Williams discusses flow in *Television, Technology, and Cultural Form* (New York: Schocken, 1975), Chapter 4.

5. By 1966 all of the classic nuclear family sitcoms were off the air, replaced by broken family sitcoms (in which a mother or father was missing) or else fantastic sitcoms. For more on these programs, see my "From Domestic Space to Outer Space: The 1960s Fantastic Family Sitcom," in *Close Encounters: Film, Feminism, and Science Fiction*, ed. Constance Penley et al. (Minneapolis: University of Minnesota Press, 1991), 205–35.

6. See my "From Theatre to Space Ship: Metaphors of Suburban Domesticity in Postwar America," in *Visions of Suburbia*, ed. Roger Silverstone (New York: Routledge, 1997), 217–39.

7. Beatriz Colomina, "Intimacy and Spectacle: The Interiors of Adolf Loos," *AA Files* 20 , 1990, 5–15; and Beatriz Colomina, "The Split Wall: Domestic Voyeurism," in *Sexuality and Space*, ed. Beatriz Colomina (Princeton, N.J.: Princeton Papers on Architecture, 1992), 73–128; For her book-length study, see Beatriz Colomina, *Privacy and Publicity: Modern Architecture and Mass Media* (Cambridge, Mass.: MIT, 1996).

8. Lynn Spigel, *Make Room for TV: Television and the Family Ideal in Postwar America* (Chicago: University of Chicago Press, 1992).

9. These depictions had very different meanings for white and black America. See my "White Flight," in *The Revolution Wasn't Televised: Sixties Television and Social Conflict*, ed. Lynn Spigel and Michael Curtin (New York: Routledge, 1997), 47–72; and my "Outer Space and Inner Cities: African American Responses to NASA," in my *Welcome to the Dreamhouse*.

10. It should be noted that portable television and the ad pitches for it harked back to earlier product designs and ads for portable radio. See Michael Brian Schiffer, *The Portable Radio in American Life* (Tucson: University of Arizona Press, 1991).

11. The first ads I found for portable models were in the mid- to late 1950s, but campaigns proliferated in the early 1960s. Philco introduced the first transistorized portable in 1959. It was named the "Safari." See Schiffer, *The Portable Radio in American Life*, 193.

12. "A Buying Guide for Television Sets," *Good Housekeeping*, September 1963, 154.

13. My calculations are based on the U.S. Bureau of the Census, *Statistical Abstract of United States*, No. 1167, "Manufacturers' Sales and Retail Value of Home Appliances: 1955–1969" (Washington, D.C.: U.S. Government Printing Office, 1970), 729.

14. In 1960, 13 percent of U.S. households had more than one TV. By 1970 that figure rose to 33 percent, and in 1972, 44 percent. Lawrence W. Lichty and Malachi C. Toppings, *A Source Book on the History of Radio and Television* (New York: Hastings House, 1975), 522.

15. *Life*, December 10, 1965, R11.

16. *Life*, April 15, 1966, 3.

17. *Life*, July 10, 1964, 42. Similar ads for Admiral Playmates ran in *Ladies Home Journal*, December 1963, 44.

18. *House Beautiful*, May 1957, 38.

19. While divorce rates were reduced after a postwar peak they began to rise steadily and steeply again by 1965. See Elaine Tyler May, *Homeward Bound: American Families in the Cold War* (New York: Basic Books, 1988), 4–8.

20. *Good Housekeeping*, January 1970, 28.

21. *House Beautiful*, September 1960, 36.

22. *House Beautiful*, May 1959, 62.

23. See Kenneth T. Jackson, *Crabgrass Frontier: The Suburbanization of the United States* (New York: Oxford University Press, 1985), 262.

24. Margaret White, "Indoor Camp-out," *Ladies Home Journal*, June 1966, 76–77.

25. *Life*, March 29, 1963, 40–41.

26. *Life*, January 25, 1963, 64–65.

27. *Life*, May 15, 1964, 54–55.

28. *Life*, July 21, 1967, 14.

29. *Life*, February 10, 1967, 18. General Electric also advertised its "play any-where" TV with a pair of sunglasses resting nearby. *Life,* June 11, 1965, 125.

30. *Life*, July 7, 1967, 65.

31. "A Buying Guide for Television Sets."

32. Margaret Morse, "An Ontology of Everyday Distraction: The Freeway, the Mall, and Television," *Logics of Television: Essays in Cultural Criticism*, ed. Patricia Mellencamp (Bloomington: Indiana University Press, 1990), 193–221.

33. *Life*, September 17, 1965, 67.

34. *Life*, April 30, 1965, 20.

35. *Life*, July 14, 1967, 61.

36. *House Beautiful*, June 1957, 14.

37. *TV Guide*, September 18–24, 1996, cover.

38. *Life*, May 30, 1960, 78–79.

39. *Life*, June 11, 1965, 125.

40. Joseph Golden, "TV's Womanless Hero," *Television Quarterly* 2, no. 1 (Winter 1963): 14–15.

41. For more on this see my *Make Room for TV*, Chapter 3.

42. *Life*, March 5, 1965, R4.

43. *Life*, October 8, 1965, 118.

44. In these terms, the ads surrounding portable TV provide a textbook case of the central dynamics at work in the uncanny. In his essay on the subject, Freud describes the uncanny as the ambivalent sense of the *Heimlich* (that which gives a feeling of being at home or familiar) and the *Unheimlich* (that which is not home, which is hidden from view and provokes fright). He then goes on to analyze the uncanny as a literary phenomenon, foregrounding two central plot points that give rise to the uncanny, one that revolves around a disturbance of vision and the other automation (or the coming alive of inanimate objects). From this point of view, the ads for portable

television and remote control seem like postwar versions of the central dynamics staged in tales of the uncanny. Offering consumers the possibility of being home and not being home at the same time, and presenting the TV set itself as a machine come to life, the ads take the frightening aspects of the uncanny and turn them into the stuff that technological utopias are made of. Despite that, however, and in line with the general ambivalence at the heart of the uncanny, all the elements in these ads easily transform into opposites until technological utopia becomes technological dystopia. For the essay, see Sigmund Freud, "The 'Uncanny,' " in *Psychological Writings and Letters*, ed. Sander L. Gilman (New York: Continuum, [1919] 1963), 120–53.

45. *House Beautiful*, June 1961, 10.

46. Jean Baudrillard, "The Ecstasy of Communication," in *The Anti-Aesthetic: Essays on Postmodern Culture*, ed. Hal Foster (Port Townsend, Wash.: Bay Press, 1983).

47. *The Web*, May 1997, 104 and back inside cover.

48. In this respect, despite Baudrillard's claims to the contrary, Freudian notions of subjectivity still dominate representations of domesticity. This is not to say that people really are Freudian subjects or that Freud's theories of human subjectivity are ultimately true. Rather, my point is about discourse, that Freudian principles of theatricality and assumptions about sexuality are still generative of the statements we make about subjectivity in popular discourses on new technologies.

49. For an analysis of the discriminatory practices around transportation, see Robert D. Bullard and Glenn S. Johnson, *Just Transportation: Dismantling Race and Class Barriers to Mobility* (Garbiola Island, B.C.: New Society Publishers, 1997).

50. bell hooks, *Black Looks: Race and Representation* (Boston: South End Press, 1992), 165–78.

51. See my essays "White Flight" and "Outer Space and Inner Cities" in *Welcome to the Dreamhouse*. David Nye points out that opinion polls of the times showed many Americans—including whites—were skeptical of the space race. See his *Narratives and Spaces: Technology and the Construction of American Culture* (New York: Columbia University Press, 1997), 147–60. But, my point here is that the popular culture aimed at whites typically glorified space as a place for family values, while popular media aimed at blacks criticized it as a distraction from more important social problems—especially unfair housing policies in inner cities.

52. Steven Morris, "How Blacks View Mankind's 'Giant Step,' " *Ebony* (September 1970), 33.

53. Greg Miller, "Home-Wired Bound," *Los Angeles Times*, February 9, 1998, D3, D6.

54. See, for example, Carolyn Marvin, *When Old Technologies Were New: Thinking about Electric Communication in the Late Nineteenth Century* (New York: Oxford University Press, 1988); Catherine L. Covert, "We May Hear Too Much: American Sensibility and the Response to Radio, 1919–1924," in *Mass Media Between the Wars: Perceptions of Cultural Tension, 1918–1941*, ed. Catherine L. Covert and John D. Stevens (Syracuse: Syracuse University Press, 1984), 199–220; James W. Carey and John J. Quirk, "The Mythos of the Electronic Revolution," *American Scholar* 39, no. 1 (Spring 1970): 219–41 and 39, no. 2 (Summer 1970): 395–424; Daniel J. Czitrom, *Media and the*

American Mind From Morse to McLuhan (Chapel Hill, N.C.: University of North Carolina Press, 1982); Susan Douglas, *Inventing American Broadcasting, 1899–1922* (Baltimore: Johns Hopkins University Press, 1987); Cecilia Tichi, *Electronic Hearth: Creating an American Television* Culture (New York: Oxford University Press, 1991); Spigel, *Make Room for TV*; Jeffrey Sconce, *Haunted Media: Electronic Presence from Telegraphy to Television* (Durham, N.C.: Duke University Press, 2000).

Vivian Sobchack

7 Science Fiction Film and the Technological Imagination

From the 1950s to the present day, the science fiction (SF) film has given concrete narrative shape and visible form to America's changing historical imagination of the special—and social—effects of "new" technologies, and to the ambiguities of being human in a world in which advanced technology has altered both the morphology and meaning of social and personal existence. Indeed, one can regard the film genre of SF as a popular and poetic mapping of American culture's ambivalent romance and disenchantment with a life-world become increasingly technologized since World War II. As a popular and poetic cartography, however, the films are less interested in adhering to standards of scientific and technological accuracy or actuality than they are in visualizing and foregrounding our technological *imagination*. That is, although the genre's narratives of experimentation, invention, and exploration are based superficially upon scientific and technological discourse and focused upon the *objectivity* of the scientific attitude and the instrumental effects of technology, their deeper interest is in how science and technology *subjectively* transform our experience and imagination and thus affect our daily lives in a variety of meaningful ways. Thus, within the guise of narratives and visions that pretend to objective speculation about our increasingly technologized future, most SF films not only dramatize but also visualize our subjective fears and desires about technology not as it might be in the future but as we experience it in the present. In this regard, it is worth citing Martin Heidegger's famous statement in "The Question Concerning Technology" that "the essence of technology is nothing technological."[1]

We could say, then, that the essence of the SF film's technological imagination is nothing technological and that, rather, the essence of the genre is the phenomenologically felt meaning of technology: the social investments and affective charge that together in-form our present technological experience and make of it something at once intensely personal and deeply historical. Nonetheless, the SF film—as a *cinematic* genre—must concretize the affect-laden and ambivalent technological imagination of a particular historical period in visible and objective images wrought by technology. That is, the SF film represents and foregrounds the less visible and subjective meanings and affects of our relation *to* technology *through* technology in what we call "special effects." These special effects appear as privileged instances in the narrative but they also point behind and beyond the film's story to the grounding technology that allows these special imaged instances to exist at all—even when the narrative is dystopian and critical about the social effects of technology. Thus, audiences find their dreams of and desire for technology piqued and satisfied twice over watching SF: once in the specificity of the narrative with its special effects moments of affective payoff in story and spectacle, and once again outside the narrative in various media texts from *Cinefantastique* to television shows and movies that not only objectively document the genre's enabling technologies but also subjectively respond to and celebrate our affectively charged technological (and technical) wonder and desire to know "How'd they do that?" Special effects in the SF film, therefore, are not special merely because they are effects: they are special because they are also entailed with—and concretely embody—particular affects associated with our relationship to novel forms of high technology such as wonder, desire, aesthetic pleasure, anxiety, and fear.[2] This concrete embodiment of our historically and socially meaningful (and feeling-full) relations with technology insofar as they are achieved through technology is, in fact, what makes these effects significantly, rather than trivially, special. As such, and in forms ranging from tacky and low-budget evocations of spaceship controls and televisual communications devices such as the triangular and intergalactic (and definitely television-like) "Interociter" from 1955's *This Island Earth* to flyer saucers and robots and the most advanced (and computergraphically costly) "terminators," special effects as both process and product are the SF genre's (and the audience's) fetish objects, the ones we long for and wait for, the ones that stand in for—both exposing and covering up—our larger and more socially grounded fascinations with and anxieties about technology.

In this regard, in a provocative essay entitled "Making Culture into Nature," Michael Stern asks "What makes an effect 'special'?" since, as he points out, everything in *any* film is "an 'effect'—something fabricated, made."[3] In the SF film, he argues, it is the genre's foregrounding of certain of the cinema's own technological and formal features as they are embodied by certain secondary figural images that is central to the SF narrative. That is, certain technological capacities of the cinema (particularly new ones) are mobilized and highlighted, but also are narratively disguised as wondrous and fictional, as literally and concretely enacting "the possibilities, delights, and terrors of glamorous new technologies: space flights, death rays, matter transmitters, cloning, living on the moon or at the bottom of the Pacific"[4]— to which we might add (in the present historical moment) the virtual spaces of computers, the quick changes of form and identity wrought by warping and morphing, and the altered visions and states of being enabled and alienated by new perceptual technologies. Emphasizing this double movement of foregrounding present cinematic technology while simultaneously displacing its presence onto a narratively future (or fictional) technology, Stern also argues that SF special effects serve a particular *ideological* function. That is, the genre's films tend to celebrate and promote *the desire for new technologies* that is so necessary to contemporary capitalist and consumer society while simultaneously effacing (or "naturalizing") not only the *grounding* technological effects of cinema (such as "mere" editing) but also the narrative effects of older and more socially pervasive (and often problematic) technologies (such as automobiles). The SF film, by focusing our attention and desire on new visions of technology, in effect (a telling pun here) transforms our vision of present technologies, as Stern says, "from cultural artifacts into natural objects."[5] Thus, even when SF narratives are thematically and dramatically at their most cautionary, dystopic, or apocalyptic in regards to new technology and its social or personal effects, insofar as the films use and privilege the latest and most spectacular technologies to create the narrative's foregrounded special effects, they are also—in both effect and affect—promoting a particularly technological imagination and selling a dream of technological promise and progress.

Nonetheless, the overarching affectivity of special effects in the SF film and the genre's ongoing celebration and fetishistic display of technological innovation and progress (whether manifest in the narrative or latent in the cinematic technology) are *historically informed*. We can see quite literally on the screen and across the history of the genre not only transformations in technology itself, but also transformations in our culture's affective relations with it. Narratively, these transformations and displacements of special affects (our desires and anxieties related to technology) into special effects (technologically-achieved images and images of technological achievement) are frequently as broad and unsubtle as some of the clunkier and can-opener-like robots found in low-budget SF films of the 1950s like *Tobor the Great* (1954). Affectively, however, they are just as frequently as poetic and complex as the icy biotech laboratory that makes replicant "eyes" in *Blade Runner* (1982)—their concrete explicitness resonant with the more inchoate expressions of desire and anxiety that surround technology and pervade popular culture at a particular historical moment.

Furthermore, it is important to recognize that both these special and effective technological images and images of technology are not only *reflective* of the technological achievements and affective imagination of their contemporaneous cultural moment; they are also *co-constitutive* of them. That is, there is a *reciprocal* relationship between the technological imagination and desire represented *on* the screen and that figured *off* the screen in other areas of our culture. As Annette Kuhn points out, "representations may have effects of their own, can themselves impinge upon the realm of the social."[6] Hence, on the one hand, we can see real scientific discovery and technological innovation certainly influencing both the representational modes and the fictional narratives of the SF film. Images of the moon or of planets no longer have to be painted by an astronomical artist as they were in *Destination Moon* (1950); they can now be filmed photographically. Space ships no longer look like V2 rockets and the new hot and applied science of biotechnology now clones dinosaurs in *Jurassic Park* (1993) as well as it clones laboratory sheep like Dolly. On the other hand, however, it is equally true that the special effects and the affective technological imagination of SF movies also have real-world consequences. One need only remember that the first American space shuttle—the *Enterprise*—was named after (and perhaps carried the same ideological baggage as) the flagship of the SF television series *Star Trek*. Or that President Ronald Reagan used references to and the rhetoric of *Star Wars* to name and naturalize his Strategic Defense Initiative—a Cold War-like plan for global satellite surveillance. Or, just as significantly, that the Department of Defense—which first started the Internet and developed computer-graphic simulations for military training— now looks to and eagerly borrows hardware and software developed by the entertainment industry. Thus, quite literally, the models and simulations we see in our fictional representations frequently serve as the impetus and model for future social action.

If we look back across the history of the American SF film since the 1950s as well as across its narrative representations of technology and its affective effects (what I am here calling the films' "technological imagination"), we can identify a number of key *themes* and their materially—and emotionally—concrete *transformations* over time. And while space here does not permit more than a quick (and somewhat reductive) historical gloss on the genre, I hope nonetheless that such a gloss will suggest possibilities for more extended and specific historical analysis of the reciprocal relationship between real technology and imagined technology, between cultural and narrative desires and anxieties surrounding technology, between the SF films' special effects and affects.

There are four major themes related to technology that emerge with the film genre in the 1950s and then undergo figural and dramatic transformation as both effect and affect in the generic and social history of the SF film. The first is the equation of post–World War II high technology with both futuristic novelty and social progress. The second is the equation of high technology with a rationalism and objectivity connected to the scientific and corporate—rather than to human and individual subjectivity and emotion. The third is the association of the "high" in high technology with elitism of both an intellectual and institutional kind. And the fourth is an opposition between the effective instrumentality of high technology and the affective agency of human biological being in general, and between technological automatism and autonomy and human agency and self-identity in particular. These four themes emerge in their initial form when SF first coalesces as a film genre in the context of a postwar world forever transformed—both by the 1945 explosion of the atomic bomb and its unprecedented devastation of Hiroshima and Nagasaki and by the more benign introduction of high technology first into American popular consciousness and then progressively into daily cultural life. In the Cold War society of the 1950s, politicians spoke of the need for technological superiority in the arms race at the same time people were buying modern home appliances, wearing miracle fabrics, and "living better through chemistry." The period and the films' major technological signifiers were the rocket, the atomic bomb, the television set, and the imposingly inscrutable Cray computer; and their major institutional signifiers were the imbrications of science and technology in a novel military-industrial complex and the newly organized postwar economic formation of corporate and consumer society.

The SF films of the period thus mark the very *novelty* of technology and its social effects by figuring technology as *literally new*. That is, dramatizing this first theme, spaceships and flying saucers not only borrow upon the spareness and sleekness associated with a contemporaneous modern design meant to convey intense but spare functionalism and rational instrumentality, but also all the machines and devices we see are as shiny and bright as if they'd just come out of their packaging. This is so whether the films are optimistic or cautionary about technology: for example, both *The Day the Earth Stood Still* (1951) and *Forbidden Planet* (1956) figure their spaceships and gadgetry in sleek, bright, and shiny images bent on evoking progressive technological wonder (and wonder at technological progress) even as they worry overtly in the narrative about technology overwhelming and annihilating us. In this regard, only the low-budget SF films that couldn't afford spectacular effects can be seen in a literally negative relation to technology. (A paucity of special technological effects or the use of a cardboard instrument panel that looks less impressive than the dashboard of one's car do not offer technological wonder or promise technological progress.)

However, if we trace the history of this theme of technological novelty from the 1950s through to the present moment, we find foregrounded at the narrative level a progressive *degradation* of technology as novel and progressive. Although there are exceptions (1968's *2001: A Space Odyssey* being, perhaps, the most ironic), the shiny bright and aseptic technosphere of the 1950s—clean, wonderfully functional, and hardly used—is transformed through time. Indeed, between 1968 and 1977, technology becomes figured in a variety of ways that increasingly undermine both literally and metaphorically the affective hope of a brighter and better future and the equation of technology with novelty and progress. In the less sanguine visions of early 1970s films like *Silent Running* (1972), technology—as well as the future—is tarnished and grungy for the first time: dirty, dysfunctional, and disappointing. By the late 1970s and in the benign SF worlds of Lucas and Spielberg, technology becomes tamed and domesticated, either under control or nicely settled into like old slippers. (Think here of Luke Skywalker's beat up jalopy of a hovercraft or the nearly junked state of Han Solo's *Millennium Falcon* in 1977's *Star Wars*, both futuristic images of technology that are seen as nearly obsolete, ready for trade-in if only one weren't a teenager or particularly fond of the old thing.) And by the decade's end, prominently marked by the figuration and effects of *Alien* (1979), technology becomes explicitly dissociated from social progress. Indeed, through the 1980s and 1990s, technology is increasingly figured as not only literally exhausted (think of all those wondrous ducts and the atmospheric pollution in *Blade Runner* and *Brazil* [1985]), but also retrograde. Hence, the emergence of what has been called tech noir: the coupling of technology not with a progressive future, but with an historical (if affectively nostalgic and eroticized) postwar (film generic) past. Thus, in *Dark City* (1998), alien technology looks positively Victorian while the human world seems stuck in a darkness born of the 1940s and in *The Matrix* (1999), old-fashioned telephones and the detritus of earlier low-tech culture speak to a lost reality underlying the imagined future.

Although, of course, there are always some exceptions, what we have seen over the genre's history is the general waning of the particular special affects and effects that charged technological narratives in the 1950s with the emotional meanings of unceasing and wondrous novelty, social progress, and hope for a shiny and brighter future. Increasingly, and parallel to the increasing rapidity with which the new becomes obsolete in the genre's present extracinematic context, new technology in recent SF narratives is always already old and superseded, always already relegated to the kid's closet in the bedroom (pace *Close Encounters* [1977] and *E.T.: The Extra-Terrestrial* [1982]), or always already trashed on the junk heap of history. Thus, whereas the special affect associated with less-than-brand-new technology figured in the dystopian SF films of the late 1960s and early 1970s was an angry—and in the films literal—disillusionment based on affective (and social) expectations unfulfilled, most recently there has been what we might, perhaps, call a new re-signation to technology, a new affective charge based on a very different set of associations and expectations surrounding its presence and its effects. The great irony in this historical transformation of special affect in SF, however, is that the genre has increasingly mobilized—and invented—new technologies to *represent* this narrative dissatisfaction with technology. Thus, underneath and still grounding the genre's narrative trajectory of technological disappointment and disillusionment is the medium's technological progress in constructing new illusions. More recently, in fact, with the rerelease and promotion of nine or so seconds of brand-new digital effects in the old *Star Wars* or the completely digital characters in the new episodes (*Star Wars: Episode 1: The Phantom Menace*, 1999; *Star Wars: Episode II: Attack of the Clones*, 2002), the SF film genre seems excessively marked by a desperate desire for technological novelty. Indeed, the anxious and overbearing hype surrounding such technological novelty seems to be trying to forestall what will nearly always be a deep disappointment: the "been there, seen that" disengagement of affect that increasingly characterizes our culture's stance in the face of the new.

The second theme that emerges at the genre's popular beginnings is the equation of high technology with rationalism and objectivity. Here the affective charge takes form in sleek and modern instrumentalism, functionalism, and aseptic asceticism. Hence not only the minimalist geometry of 1950s rockets and saucers, the clean lines of consoles, and the mathematization figured by formula on blackboards, and on meters, dials, and rheostatic devices, but also the privileged but suspect sterility of corporate scientific and technological enterprise (reaching its apotheosis in the spare and progressively decontaminated levels of the underground laboratory in *The*

Andromeda Strain [1971], but beginning in the many white coats and scientific labs in 1950s SF). Indeed, rationality and sterility as associated affects of the technological imagination of the 1950s are in direct contrast to earlier generic figurations of a more hysterical, romantic, ultimately individualist, and hardly ascetic affective relation to scientific and technological enterprise. Here, we can think of the suspect and gothic science and alchemy of the 1930s horror film, best characterized by an hysterical Henry Frankenstein reproducing on his own in the basement of his castle. Or of the praiseworthy individualism, garage inventions, and entrepreneurial gadgetry (often "thrown-together" and "made out of paper clips") of market capitalism that are fetishized in 1940s biopics about the likes of a young Thomas Edison or Alexander Graham Bell.

In the 1950s, proper scientific and technological innovation comes not out of the closet or garage or gothic basement and not from a single individual: rather, it comes from an institution that privileges an above board and well-lit communal effort as well as efficiency, cleanliness, asceticism, order, and reason. This narrative figuration and privileging of anti-individualistic and antientrepreneurial science and technology, however, were also affectively informed by anxiety—not only anxiety about fitting into an increasingly corporate culture, but also about the possibly negative effects of a lack of affect that was perceived to mark the culture's intellectuals and technocrats. Increasing rationalism and antihumanism coupled with anti-individualism: these were the American doubles of the perceived affective effects of communism. Thus, many of the films of the period that really didn't engage corporate science and technology directly spoke nonetheless of popular ambivalence about the special effects and affects of communal rationalism and the waning of humanism. As one of the humans taken over by the alien pods in *Invasion of the Body Snatchers* (1956) puts it, trying to convince others to join him in the alien collective consciousness: "Love, desire, ambition, faith—without them life is so simple." Without them, however, you turn into either a fifth column alien pod or an "organization man" in contemporary American corporate culture.

Both the desire for and the anxiety about rationalism and objectivity have been radically transformed since the 1950s. In the wake of widespread disenchantment in the 1960s with the social effects and secrecy surrounding the institutional incorporation of science and technology into the military-industrial complex and a rationalized security state, in the wake of a low-tech and irrationally rationalized war in Southeast Asia, in the wake of domestic problems never addressed or resolved and often caused by high technology, the SF film, from the 1970s on, has moved farther and farther away from the affective turn ons and special effects wrought by the conjunction of rationalism and high technology. Instead, and increasingly, the genre has embraced an imagery and affectivity that—extroverted in special effects—is more about subjective or spiritual epiphany than about rational deduction, and less about the affective charge of high technology than about the affective charge of what we might call a "technological high." In this regard, the special effects "star gate" light show that appealed to the intellectuals and rationalists in the audience of the adult SF film *2001* also appealed to a younger generation who saw the same figuration as an euphoric trip of consciousness-raising enhanced by drugs and the desire for something less cold and clinical than rationality.

By the late 1970s and thereafter, technology and its affective charge had little to do with the rational: think of the carousel or chandelier-like euphoric affect and magic effected by alien technology in Spielberg's *Close Encounters of the Third Kind* and *E.T.*, the transcendent technological transformations of death and religious discourse in *Cocoon* (1985), and—rationalism and Scully aside—the sheer desire "to believe" that pervades the always skeptical, but always committed *X-Files*. Indeed, special effects technology is now rarely linked to rationalism or objectivity and this disassociation, to great extent, explains the slippage of SF proper into the increasingly reenergized and popular genre of fantasy where—in films as dramatically dependent on high technology such as *What Dreams May Come* (1998), *Pleasantville* (1998), the *Harry Potter* films (2001, 2002), the *Lord of the Rings* trilogy (2001, 2002, 2003), and all the quasi-SF/fantasy comic book films such as *X-men* (2000), *Spider-Man* (2002), and *Hulk* (2003)—rationalism and objectivity are never issues, although the relationship between special effects and special affects most certainly is.

The third theme that emerges in the 1950s is the association of the "high" in high technology with elitism of both intellectual and institutional kinds. This association has also been radically transformed over time. In the 1950s, high technology was the province and in the possession not of the general public but of public institutions: the military, universities, governmental and corporate research institutes, and think tanks. In the early 1950s, most people had never dealt with a computer and were just beginning to embrace the television set as part of their home furnishings. Thus, high technology was considered concretely—literally—as "high": out of the reach of any but the elite, and too bulky, too expensive, too complex to be absorbed by the general public as just another domesticated consumer commodity.

Hence, attached to the understanding and possession of high technology in the 1950s are not only connotations of elitism, but also those involving both class and secrecy: the feeling that a technocracy was at work and not always in the public interest of a popularly conceived populist democracy.

Social and technological history and the history of high technology, of course, changed these notions. One need only think of television or (already an "oldie") the digital watch to summarize the historical movement and material pervasion of high technology into the "low" life of everyday popular culture over the years between 1950 and 1980. Once mystical and elite, television quickly became our "familiar" while—even more rapidly—the novel and expensive digital watch became the momentary and cheap fetish object of sidewalk vendors selling nearly valueless commodities for under a buck. Similarly, once signaling the size and opacity of the military-industrial complex as well as a cold computer sentience we really didn't want to contemplate (the kind of computer sentience that—on its own—forged American-Soviet relationships against human intervention in 1969's *Colossus: The Forbin Project*), the immovable and inexpressive Cray computer became radically humanized over time and popularization. Those Crays turned into Macs and then PCs (an even more diminutive and familiar name for an already "personal" computer), brought down to size, affordable cost, and domestic appropriation. Thus, the familiarity of video games and a certain relaxation of computer gravity and accountability. Thus, we move over time from the (ir)rational psychosis of HAL in *2001* and the confident Cray-like Colossus of *The Forbin Project* to the petulant and jealous PC in *Electric Dreams* (1984)—the latter not only a personal companion, but also jealously neurotic and romantically competitive with the woman upstairs for its user's attention. This is technology brought low and comprehensible, familiar and appropriated, but also recalcitrant in ways that are not about disparities between the elite and the popular or between human and technological consciousness, but about comprehensible spats—whether comical or anxiety-producing—in which the human and technological reduce each to the other in affective concern and scale.

The fourth theme that has undergone significant transformation in the SF film is the initial opposition of technology as an other—both effectively and affectively—to the biologically human in general, and to human agency and self-identity in particular. Beginning in the 1950s, the SF technological imagination figured technological consciousness and effect as opposed to human biological consciousness and affect. The difference between human being and technological artifact—between, for example, Robby the Robot and Dr. Morbius or Commander Adams in *Forbidden Planet*—was clear cut. There was no affective nor technological need in the 1950s to complicate the boundaries between a robot that looked like the offspring of the Michelin tire man and a juke box and real human beings with agency and emotions. Robby was not a simulacrum of human being, merely a mechanical servant given certain markers of human frailty so as to be accommodating and comic: pride, chattiness, et al. While certainly the progenitor of C3PO of 1977's *Star Wars*, Robby never challenged the nature and ontological status of human being. Like most of the sentient robots to follow for the next decade, Robby's consciousness was not confusing, even as its mimesis of the human was quite delicious. In the late 1960s and early 1970s, however, we can see a change in machine intelligence and its relation to human being. Throughout *2001* but particularly in its death scene, dysfunctional spaceship computer HAL is dramatized as having more personality than the mission's human astronauts, while the ultrasophisticated and mobile computer in *Demon Seed* (1977) not only wants to take over the world but also wants a child (raping its human creator's wife to produce a hybrid techno-biological baby).

From the 1980s to the present day, in both our culture and our films, we can see an increasing confusion between and conflation of the technological and biological, of algorithmic and analogic consciousness, of flesh and prostheses. Thus, our most recent SF films question—in both desire and fear—just what it means to be human, and what constitutes embodiment, consciousness, memory, and perception in an age not only of computers but also of biotechnology. Here we might think not only of the *Terminator* trilogy but also of Spielberg's *A.I.: Artificial Intelligence* (2001), in which robotic children and gigolos are imprinted to "feel" more passion than do their "natural" human counterparts. The once clear—and affectively oppositional— dichotomy between the human body and technological artifact, between subjective consciousness and objective representation, between direct experience and mediated experience, has collapsed in the last several decades. These distinctions made in the 1950s no longer hold and, over time and technology, both the special effects and special affects of the SF film have come to focus on the ambiguous nature and, more recently, the shifting morphology and location of human identity and subjectivity. Indeed, computer-graphic warping and morphing stand as merely the most current technological effects charged with significant and special cultural affect.[7]

Particularly from the 1980s on, using and narratively foregrounding both new *perceptions of technology* and new *technologies of perception*, SF films have dramatized malaise, euphoria, and irony about the technologically transformed nature of human consciousness, perception, identity, memory, and embodiment—all of which we now intimately and popularly recognize (like Arnold Schwarzenegger) as, in the deepest ways, always already constructed and mediated by technology. Previous forms of identity—including those of private memory and direct or unmediated experience—are "terminal" in an age of media simulation, microchips, biotechnology, cosmetic surgery, and body-building. Indeed, in SF films (and paralleled in contemporaneous culture), the special effects of new technologies do not merely ground narratives, but *generate* them and their technologically altered characters. *Blade Runner* gives us genetically created replicants who are "more human than human" in their passion for life, memory, and meaning. *Videodrome* (1983) fuses—and confuses—human bodies with VCRs and real perception with the hallucinatory perceptions of new mind- and gender-bending modes of television. *The Terminator* (1984) graphically displays the technological capacity for self-repair and the fragility of human flesh, while its sequel nearly ten years later, *Terminator 2: Judgment Day* (1991), has nearly given up the flesh altogether, privileging not Schwarzenegger's or Sarah Conner's buffed-up bodies, but the total liquidity and mutability of the morphing T1000. *Robocop* (1987) explores the persistence of memory—and thus the remnants of humanity—in a programmed cyborg, but this human memory is figured primarily through replayed *video* images. Both *Total Recall* (1990) and *Strange Days* (1995) *commodify* memory: memories are bought, sold, and experienced through new technologies of perception and consciousness for recreational purposes, but also interrogate and re-create what identity and subjectivity mean when both are able—through technology—to be objectified, circulated, and experienced by others. And, more recently in *Dark City*, through both form and narrative, warping and morphing affectively effect the ungrounding and complete destabilization not only of memory and identity, but also of place and space. It is hardly surprising, then, that the hugely popular *The Matrix* and its sequels (2002, 2003) take this ungrounding even further to question overtly the very nature of what we experience as "reality." Since the 1950s, then, transformations in the technological imagination of the SF film have figured the boundaries of body and consciousness, machine and artificial intelligence, technological and human perception as becoming, by today, almost completely fluid and reversible rather than hierarchically mimetic and oppositional—and this to both highly pleasurable and disturbing degrees.

Responsive to and partially constitutive of the technological imagination of its contemporaneous culture, the SF film is always technologically and historically in a state of transformation in regard to its major themes, its narrative figures of technology, and its special effective and affective modes of technological figuration. Indeed, at this particular historical moment, its transformations and affective charge have moved (and transformed) it both across genres and across screens. As we have seen, over time, the desire for transformation through technology has generically detached itself from visions of rationality and progress and attached itself (with some anxiety) to more subjective states of technological being. At the present moment, however, much of this desire for and belief in the power of technological transformation has—without apology—relocated itself from the SF film to the even more fluid genre of fantasy. Here, while foregrounded in spectacular special effects, new technology is itself finally naturalized. That is, it is no longer necessary to explain it or explicitly tie it—*as technology*— to the narrative it blatantly enables and grounds. As the SF film naturalizes old technologies, so the fantasy film goes a step further and naturalizes new technologies. In 1998, using the latest in computer graphic effects, *What Dreams May Come* and *Pleasantville* exemplified the disassociation of technology from both science and rationality, indeed from technology itself. Here we saw technology associated not with science but with pure affect: with the wish and desire to undo death, with extremes of emotion that colorize an otherwise drab and unimaginative world. Most recently, computer graphic effects have been put not in the service of science and technology but, quite overtly, in the service of magic (the *Harry Potter* films) and myth (the *Lord of the Rings* trilogy). As Stern suggests in his ideological critique of the SF film—but here *in the genre of fantasy even more so*—we see constructed and legitimated "a world in which technology is an abstract category of effects without any specific social and political context," a world in which technology is foregrounded as "magical" and "socially ungrounded."[8] The technological imagination is itself naturalized in fantasy: effaced, technological effects disappear into pure affect.

Nonetheless, the SF technological imagination—foregrounded as such— still exists on the screen and in popular consciousness. As evidenced most recently by *The Matrix*, the SF film is still a way for cinema to show off and promote its latest technologies in narratives highlighting technology— along with more ineffable and nontechnological variations of "the force." Indeed, at the beginning of the new century, the genre is still successful at the box office. Even if this is so, however, the cinema is a technology that primarily expresses (and partially constitutes) the twentieth century—not the twenty-first. Thus, no longer quite satisfied with screen effects and affects as they exist in twentieth-century cinema, SF—having already figured futuristic immersive technological effects and affects—has increasingly detached itself from the technological limitations of cinema itself to "real-ize" these new effects and affects in other media. That is, the genre has moved to CD-ROMs, interactive Internet games, and theme parks offering immersive SF adventures simulated in the perceived depth and motion of virtual reality. Here the technological affect connected with technological effects has a great deal to do with the stimulation of intensified physical sensations and/or with a sense of agency and control. As the premises of the SF film have literally moved, so have its special effects and affects been technologically transformed and in turn have transformed our sense of the technological. In sum, SF—as a film genre—now faces a technological future that already exceeds the very mechanisms and industry that gave birth to and nurtured its original technological imagination.

NOTES

1. Martin Heidegger, "The Question Concerning Technology," trans. William Lovitt, in *Martin Heidegger: Basic Writings*, ed. David Farrell Krell (New York: Harper & Row, 1977), 317.

2. An introduction and elaboration of this idea of the transformation of special effect into special affect can be found in Vivian Sobchack, *Screening Space: The American Science Fiction Film* (New Brunswick, N.J.: Rutgers University Press, 1997), 281–92.

3. Michael Stern, "Making Culture into Nature," in *Alien Zone: Cultural Theory and Contemporary Science Fiction Cinema*, ed. Annette Kuhn (London: Verso, 1990), 67.

4. Ibid., 69.

5. Ibid.

6. Kuhn, *Alien Zone*, 53.

7. For elaborations of both the technological history and cultural significance of morphing, see the essays in *Meta-Morphing: Visual Transformation and the Culture of Quick Change*, ed. Vivian Sobchack (Minneapolis: University of Minnesota Press, 2000).

8. Stern, "Making Culture into Nature," 70.

DAVID E. NYE

8   Technological Prediction
A Promethean Problem

TECHNOLOGICAL PREDICTION is a vast area, which I divide into three parts: prediction, forecasting, and projection. We predict the unknown, forecast possibilities, and project probabilities. I use these three terms to correspond to the division, common in business studies of innovation, between what James M. Utterback terms "*invention* (ideas or concepts for new products and processes), *innovation* (reduction of an idea to the first use or sale) and *diffusion* of technologies (their widespread use in the market)" (table 8.1).[1] Prediction concerns inventions that are fundamentally new devices. This is a more restrictive definition than the Patent Office's sense of invention, for that includes innovation, which I treat as a separate category. What is the distinction? As I use the terms, the incandescent electric light was an invention, the creation of new kinds of filaments were innovations. The telephone was an invention, but the successive improvements in its operation were innovations, for they improved an already existing device. There are relatively few inventions, which are fundamental breakthroughs. In communications these would be the telephone, electric light, radio, television, mainframe computer, personal computer, and the Internet. While prediction concerns such inventions, forecasting concerns innovations, which are quite numerous by comparison. Innovations are improvements and accessories within the systems that breakthrough inventions make possible. The third term, projection, which I will discuss only in passing, concerns the future sales, profits, market share, and so forth of new models of established technologies.

Table 8.1   Three Forms of Technological Prognostication

Prognostication	*Device*	*Time Frame*	*Status*	*Central Figures*
Prediction	invention	long term	unknown	inventor
Forecasting	innovation	medium term	possible	engineers, entrepreneurs
Projection	new model	short term	probable	designers, marketers

This is a crude division, and of course there are gray areas among prediction, forecasting, and projection, which might also be thought of as points on a continuum. Yet these distinctions are not merely a matter of semantic convenience. If one looks at the time frames involved, prediction deals with the long term or indefinite periods, while forecasting focuses on immediate choices about getting a new device perfected, into production, and into the market. Those making projections are forced to work with the shortest time frame, because they deal with new models of devices that are already competing in the market. It follows from these observations that the people centrally involved in prognostication change depending upon which category one is dealing with. Inventors, futurologists, and some academicians speculate about fundamental breakthroughs; they predict them or debunk their possibility. But once a workable device exists, venture capitalists, engineers, and consultants busy themselves with its possibilities. And finally, when new models of familiar devices are being created, designers and marketers become central. While aesthetics lies beyond the concerns of the present essay, I believe it could be argued that a considerably different aesthetic characterizes invention, innovation, and product development, emphasizing, respectively, technical elegance, functionalism, and beauty.[2]

Turn on your television, and you mostly hear forecasting and projection, not prediction. For example, a technology guru on CNN recently announced that voice recognition will be the next big thing in computers because then keyboards can be done away with, and small computers that respond to verbal commands can be embedded in useful objects everywhere.[3] Machine speech recognition is already used by telephone companies; its possible extension and development to replace computer keyboards is a forecast.

As this example suggests, technological predictions and forecasts are in essence little narratives about the future. They are not full-scale narratives of utopia, but they are usually presented as stories about a better world to come. The most successful of these little narratives are those that present an innovation as not just desirable, but inevitable. As public relations people are well aware, when investors and consumers believe such stories, they can become self-fulfilling. Selling stories of the wonders to come has been popular at least since the great World's Fair in Chicago a century ago,[4] and they became the stock-in-trade of some magazines, on certain television shows, and at Disney's "Tomorrowland." To put this another way, inventors and corporate research departments create not only products but compelling narratives about where these things will fit into our lives. Inventors need to do this if they want to get venture capital, and companies need to market such scenarios to get a return on investment.

I will return to the question of narrative at the end of this essay, after examining six propositions about predicting technological innovation. I offer these as more than mere examples, yet as something less than a fully developed theory. My examples come both from the history of electrification as well as more recent communications technologies.[5]

1. Prediction is difficult, even for experts.
George Wise, an historian now working at the General Electric research labs in Schenectady, wrote his doctoral thesis on how well scientists, inventors, and sociologists predicted the future between 1890 and 1940. Examining 1,500 published predictions, he found that only one-third proved correct, while one-third were wrong and another third were still unproved. Technical experts performed only slightly better than others. Many methods were used, including intuition, analogy, extrapolation, studying leading indicators, and deduction, but all were of roughly equal value.[6] In short, technological predictions by any method proved no more accurate than flipping a coin. This result may surprise laypersons, but it is what a business historian, or an historian of technology, would expect.

If prediction has proved extremely difficult, what about forecasting? Surely that ought to be easier, because it deals with already existing technologies and relies on existing trends. Anyone interested in computers has heard of Moore's Law, formulated in 1965, which predicted, quite accurately, that computer memory would double roughly every eighteen to twenty-four months.[7] Yet there are also many famous failures of forecasting by professionals: demographers, sociologists, and biologists. No one saw the post–World War II baby boom coming. American birth rates had fallen steadily for more than a century, and demographers were surprised when this decline did not continue. In the 1960s a great many sociologists, seeing how much the workweek had shortened since the late nineteenth century, projected that automation would reduce the average American's work time to under twenty-five hours by century's end. Congress even held hearings on the coming crisis of leisure, which never came. Instead, the average American today is working more hours than in 1968.[8] Paul Ehrlich, in *The Population Bomb*, predicted in the early 1970s that it was already too late to save India from starvation.[9] He did not foresee the tremendous increases in Third World agricultural productivity. Social trends are difficult to anticipate. General forecasting is risky, failure common.

Technological forecasting is little better. In 1905 few investors forecasted that the new automobiles would replace trolley cars.[10] Street traction had grown tremendously in the previous fifteen years, and it was expanding into long-distance competition with the railroad. The automobile was still a rich man's toy, and no one predicted the emergence and impact of the automotive assembly line. In the 1930s, when only one in a hundred people had actually been up in an airplane, a majority of Americans apparently expected that soon every family would have its own plane.[11]

In 1954 Lewis Strauss, head of the Atomic Energy Commission, told the National Association of Science Writers that their children would en-joy "electrical energy too cheap to meter."[12] IBM once thought the main computer business would always be mainframes and waited seven years before competing directly with Digital Computer's minis.[13] Later, Apple mistakenly thought there was a market for the Newton. In 1991 MIT Press published *Technology 2001: The Future of Computing and Communications*. It contains fourteen articles by leading figures in the field, but none of them discussed the Internet, which does not appear in the index. Nor does "cy-berspace" or "World Wide Web." This failure of foresight was by no means unusual. The researchers at Microsoft did not foresee the sudden emergence of the World Wide Web either.

Third are failures of technological projection, which is to say failures when looking into the future for products already in the market. Clearly, projection can be expected to work reasonably well when the economy is stable. The total demand for widgets will most likely also be stable, as well as extrapolations based on growth rates *may* prove accurate. But even a market that is stable overall is full of competing products, and expanding and contracting firms. In the 1950s Ford thought there was a market for the Edsel.

And as the world stock markets of late have reminded us, business con-ditions are seldom stable for long. In the 1960s American utilities expected growth in electrical consumption to double in the next decade. This seemed rational, because it had doubled during each of several previous decades. The utilities did not foresee that the energy crises and slow growth of the 1970s would trigger a move toward conservation.[14] The energy crisis like-wise caught American car makers unprepared, as they had projected con-tinued demand for large cars and had few energy-efficient, small vehicles for sale in 1973.

As these examples suggest, any trend that seems obvious, and any pat-tern that seems persistent, may prove unstable because of changes in the economy, changes in technology, or some combination of social and technical factors. As the mathematician John Paulos put it, "futurists such as John Naisbitt and Alvin Toffler attempt to 'add up' the causes and effects of countless local stories in order to identify and project trends." But "interactions among the various trends are commonly ignored, and unexpected developments, by definition, are not taken into account. As with weather forecasters, the farther ahead they predict, the less perspicacious they become."[15]

It is not just futurists who stumble. Business historians have found that innovations rarely come from the established market leaders, who suffer from what is sometimes called "path dependency." As James M. Utterback notes, an established firm is usually too committed to a particular conception of what its product is. This idea is embedded in its manufacturing process and its managerial hierarchy. When a major innovation appears, the leading firm understands the technology, but remains committed to its operating system. IBM and the PC is a good example. At first IBM did not take the threat seriously enough, and Apple's products, as well as several others, were on the market for at least four years before IBM entered the field. IBM then was clever enough to license others to manufacture its system.

In most cases, when an innovation such as the PC appears, established industries redouble their commitment to the traditional product and production process that has made them market leaders. They make incremental improvements in manufacturing, and yet nevertheless lose market share to the invader. One might think that this pattern would not occur in fast-changing electronic industries, where innovations come so frequently that there is little time for routines and habits to blind participants to the advantages of the next change. But Utterback cites a comprehensive study of the photolithographic alignment manufacturers, who supply semiconductor firms. During the successive invention and development of five distinct generations of machines, in no case did the market leader at one stage manage to retain its top position at the next.[16] Each production system seems to gain a technological momentum[17] inside the firm, preventing it from moving swiftly to adopt competing innovations.[18]

2. New technologies are market-driven.
Another reason that forecasts and predictions are so hard to make is that consumers, not scientists, often discover what is "the next big thing." The new drug Viagra was originally developed without reference to sex, but the college students who served as guinea pigs discovered what consumers

would like about it. To put this general point in a negative way, just because something is technologically feasible, don't expect the public to rush out and buy it. You can lead a horse to water, but you can't make it drink. Consumers have to want the product. There have been many mistaken investments in machines that work but which the public did not want. The classic case perhaps is the picture phone marketed by AT&T in the 1970s. It was technologically feasible, but few people bought it. Yet while some apparently reasonable technologies fail to sell, quite a few people do unexpected things. They buy Japanese electronic pets, for example.

Histories of new machines tend to focus on the process of invention, and to suggest that research and development drives the market. This is usually not so, even in the case of inventions that in retrospect seem fundamental to contemporary society: the telegraph, telephone, phonograph, and personal computer. When such things first appear, creating demand is more difficult than creating supply. At first, Samuel Morse had trouble convincing anyone to invest in his telegraph. He spent five years "lecturing, lobbying, and negotiating" before he finally convinced the U.S. Congress to pay for the construction of the first telegraph line, which ran from Washington to Baltimore. Even after it was operating he had difficulties finding customers interested in using it.[19] Likewise, Alexander Bell could not find anyone to buy his telephone, and so he reluctantly decided to market it himself.[20] And at first Thomas Edison found few commercial applications for his phonograph, despite the sensational publicity surrounding its discovery.[21] He and his assistants had the following commercial ideas a month after it had been shown to the world: to make a speaking doll and other toys, to manufacture speaking "clocks . . . to call the hour etc. for advertisements, for calling out directions automatically, delivering lectures, explaining the way" and, almost as an afterthought at the end of the list, "as a musical instrument."[22] A century later, in the mid-1970s, the personal computer, when first shown to a group of MIT professors, seemed rather uninteresting.[23] They were unable to think of many uses for the prototype machine and they suggested that perhaps the personal computer would be most useful to shut-ins.

In short, the telegraph, telephone, phonograph, and personal computer, doubtless four of the most important inventions of the communications revolution, were initially understood as curiosities.[24] Their commercial value was not immediately clear. It took both investors and the public time to discover what they could use them for. Eventually, all of these inventions became the basis for extremely large corporations, and each of these inventions stood at the center of a technological system. As people became familiar with these four technological systems they built them into both their daily lives and their profit-making schemes.

How these four different systems of communication developed is beyond the scope of this essay, but it is worth emphasizing that machines do not sell themselves. Entrepreneurs have to study the markets and decide where their best opportunities are. This focus on the market also characterized the construction of the American electrical system between 1880 and 1940, establishing a foundation for the functioning of other modern communication systems.[25]

Electricity had to compete with other sources of light and power. As a motive force, electricity competed with compressed air, the steam engine, and the internal combustion engine. As a source of heat, it had to compete with coal, gas, and oil; and as a light source, it competed with gas and kerosene. Given these competitors, electrical utilities did not target all markets at once. Utilities, most of which were private, found that expansion made the most sense as a sequence that began with the central city in the 1880s. There, department stores, hotels, clubs, and prestigious addresses provided a compact and wealthy market. These customers were willing to pay a premium for a glamorous new form of lighting that was clean and safe compared to its competitors. Second, after 1888, was the street car, which carried electricity toward the urban periphery. Briefly, in the 1890s street railways were the largest consumers of electricity. Streetcars replaced horsecars and spread farther out into the hinterland. They cost no more to run, traveled faster, and were far cleaner. Third, came intensive factory electrification. It began in the 1880s with lighting in industries prone to fire such as textile mills, but only at the turn of the century did most factories adopt electric motors. Lowering the price of electricity for large customers was a crucial factor in winning this market away from steam engines. Fourth, once these large customers were well established, utilities could achieve economies of scale in their power plants. With peak use during the daylight hours, after 1910 utilities focused on domestic lighting and power as a way to balance the load and use excess generating capacity. Fifth, electricity came to the farm. While about 10 percent of American farmers managed to obtain electricity before the 1930s, either because of proximity to interurban trolley or utility lines or because they purchased their own generating equipment, most had to wait until the government got into the power business in the Roosevelt years. Rural customers came last in America because electricity was primarily understood as a commodity, not as a state-supplied service. In contrast, most western European farmers already had electricity when the New Deal programs went into effect. Similarly, the telegraph, telephone, phonograph, radio, television, and Internet all have been developed through private investment in the United States.

One general observation about marketing a new technology: private utilities at first had to provide not only electricity but considerable education and support service as well. People simply did not understand the new force of electricity. Most of the competent electricians worked for the utilities, and they had to provide wiring, safety checks, and advice on the proper use of appliances. This was an unavoidable cost of introducing an unfamiliar system.[26] Gradually, such services disappeared, and the responsibilities of the utilities ended at the meter. Likewise, people today need more support and service for computers than they usually get. Who has not cursed the poorly written software manual or incomprehensible instructions for a new VCR? Who has not been frustrated by recorded messages on the telephone, or hung up after being on hold for long periods?

3. Innovations proliferate rapidly.

In contrast to the small number of fundamental inventions that become the basis for entirely new systems of communication, most innovations plug into an existing system. Once one has built the electrical grid, the telephone network, or more recently the World Wide Web, next comes the proliferation of new application technologies or innovations. For example, as the electrical grid spread across the country, small manufacturers rushed in with a stunning array of new products: electrified cigar lighters, model trains, Christmas tree lights, musical toilet-paper dispensers, and shaving cream warmers, as well as the objects we now take for granted, such as toasters, irons, refrigerators, and washing machines. As electric devices proliferated, the large manufacturers, Westinghouse and General Electric, like the computer hardware makers of today, soon found it impossible to compete in every area. This is even more the case with software development. Once several million PCs and Macs were in place, programmers created the software equivalent of the earlier appliances, in the form of programs that help us to compose music, do our income taxes, make architectural drawings, encrypt messages, write novels, and so on.

And to reiterate the previous point, the average consumer plays a leading role in the market for such innovations. As a journalist has noted, "The rapid growth in scanner sales, and the equally rapid price drop, have been driven by home users, not businesses. Home users also drive the sales of color printers, sound cards, high-speed modems, external cartridge drives, and video accelerator cards."[27] The most recent example of the same phenomenon is video mail, making it easy for people to take snap shots or short videos and send them to friends over the Internet. Some of these programs can reduce a one-minute video to only 500 K, which can be downloaded in less than ten seconds.

It generally happens that selling the basic hardware for a communication system ceases to be as profitable as selling software and services. People now spend far more money on things that use electricity than on the electricity itself, and this disproportion has been increasing since the 1920s.[28] Something similar happened with the telephone. AT&T began with an absolute monopoly and expanded slowly during the period when no one could compete. During the 1890s, however, their patent protection ran out, competitors appeared, the market doubled and redoubled in size, and the cost of telephone calls began to drop.[29] The intensity of telephone use and the number of applications still continue to increase a century later. Where once the telephone bill reflected a simple transaction between a customer and the phone company, now a wide range of commercial relations take place through the telephone, including the 800 and 900 area code numbers, Internet and e-mail providers, fax machines, and mobile phones. As with the electrical system, the telephone now provides the infrastructure, or even the main platform, for many businesses that were not anticipated.

If we look at the computer, the same pattern is evident. Once the new infrastructure of PCs was in place, software developers, like the independent appliance makers or the telephone service providers, could move in. The cost of computer memory has long been falling, but the cost of much software remains high. From the manufacturing point of view, software development remains expensive because programs keep increasing in complexity.[30]

Today, the proliferation of new technologies is taking place within the established market frameworks of the electrical grid, the telephone, television, the PC, and the Internet. What makes this a particularly rich period of innovation is the synergy made possible by this mix of networked systems. Many possibilities are latent or only partially developed, putting a premium on forecasting for the near future.

4. The best design does not always win.
Even if we can accurately foresee the coming of a new technology or innovation we cannot be sure about what design will win a place in the market. Perhaps failure was obvious for the air-conditioned bed, the illuminated

lawn sprinkler, and the electrically sterilized toilet seat, all marketed in the 1930s,[31] but it was by no means obvious that Betamax, the technically better machine, would lose out to VHS in the home video market. Here, not technological excellence but marketing was the crucial ingredient. JVC, the Japanese electronics firm that had developed the VHS system, made alliances with other manufacturers and allowed them to license the right to produce it.[32] Perhaps the most familiar recent example of a superior machine capturing only a small part of the market is that of the Apple Macintosh line of computers. Here again the decision to "go it alone" appears to have been a decisive mistake.[33] A somewhat different example is the case of FM radio, which is better for short distances than AM, but languished virtually unused for a generation.[34] In this case, patent ownership was less central than RCA's enormous investment in AM transmission.

Finally, consider an example from the electrical industry, that of district heating versus individual home heating. A century ago most power stations were near the center of town, and they routinely marketed excess steam heat to apartment blocks, office buildings, and department stores. Since then district heating has failed to capture much of the American market,[35] in contrast to Scandinavia, where district heating is common, saving energy, lowering pollution levels, and reducing the cost of home heating. American social values emphasized individualized technologies, so that every house had its own heating system. My point is that if the technologies are shaped by the market, the market in turn is inflected by social and political values. This brings me to my fifth point.

5. The uses of new products are hard to foresee.

Even if we predict which new technologies are possible and which designs will thrive in the market, we may fail to foresee how they will be used. Thomas Edison invented the phonograph, but he failed to see that it would primarily be used to play music. He thought his new invention would be an aid to businessmen, who could dictate letters to the phonograph, and he did not focus on music and entertainment even as late as 1890.[36] As a result, competitors grabbed a considerable share of the market.

A second example. Between 1900 and 1920 the new technology of radio was understood by government and industry to be an improvement on the telegraph. They expected it to be used for point-to-point communications. When radio stations emerged after World War I as a consumer-driven phenomenon, the electrical corporations were surprised, and moved quickly into the new market.[37] In both the case of the phonograph and the radio, the public used these new technologies less for work-related ends than to have fun.[38] Likewise, many children use PCs less to write papers and pursue education than to play computer games, visit strange Web sites, and explore alternative identities. These activities may or may not be educational; my point is that most were not anticipated.

Another example of unanticipated use is the higher-than-expected consumption of electricity in refrigerators, which so puzzled a California utility that they hired anthropologists to find out what was going on.[39] They discovered that families used the refrigerator for much more than food storage. It was also a place to hide money in fake cabbages, to protect photographic film, to give nylon stockings longer life, to allow pet snakes to hibernate, and to preserve drugs. At times people opened the refrigerator and gazed in without clear intentions, mentally foraging, trying to decide if they were hungry, often removing nothing before they closed the door again. The anthropologists concluded that the refrigerator, and by extension any tool, "enters into the determination of its own utilities, suggesting new ideas for its own definition . . . and [it] threatens to take on altogether new identities."[40]

A study of how computers have actually been used to change the production process reached a similar conclusion.[41] Shoshona Zuboff found that while executives and managers expected to gain more control over the workforce through computerizing all aspects of factory production, often something quite different occurred. Computers actually were used to make the firm more transparent, less hierarchical, more democratic. They quantified what had been subjective and revealed much of what had been secret or unarticulated, for both workers and managers. The computer, which managers had expected to increase their power, instead transformed and in some ways weakened their authority. As with the refrigerator in the home, the computer in the factory enters into the determination of its own utilities, suggesting new ideas, taking on unexpected functions.

The Internet offers a final, stunning example of this principle. This communication system was first conceived as part of Cold War defense, and it was initially used only by military planners and scientists. They developed a decentralized design so that messages could not easily be knocked out by a war. But this same feature made it difficult if not impossible to monitor and control the Internet. The developers did not imagine such things as Amazon.com, pornography on the Net, downloading music to a PC, or most of the other things people are using the Internet for today.

In short, when considering the phonograph, the radio, the refrigerator, and the Internet, we can see not only that technologies conceived for one clearly defined use acquire other, unpredicted uses over time; we can also see that engineers and designers tend to expect new devices to serve a narrow range of functions, while the public has a huge range of intentions and desires and often brings far more imagination to new technologies than those who first market them. This brings me to my final proposition.

6. A technology's symbolic meanings may determine its uses.

Too often we think of the history of technologies in purely functional terms. But even so prosaic a device as the electric light bulb had powerful symbolic meanings and associations from its inception. Edison's practical incandescent light of 1879 was preceded by many forms of "impractical" electric lighting in theaters, where it was used for dramatic effects. A generation before Edison's light bulb even began to reach most homes after around 1910, it was appropriated by the wealthy for conspicuous consumption, used to illuminate public monuments and skyscrapers, and put into electrical signs. As a result, by 1903 American cities were far more brightly lighted than their European counterparts; Chicago, New York, and Boston had three to five times as many electric lights per inhabitant as Paris, London, and Berlin.[42] Intensive electric lighting of downtown American cities far exceeded the requirements of safety. The Great White Way and its huge signs had become a national landmark by 1910. Soon, postcards and photographs of every illuminated city skyline became common across the United States. In New York, during World War I when wartime energy saving darkened Times Square, the citizens complained that the city seemed "unnatural"! People demanded that the giant advertising signs be turned on again, and they soon were, with new slogans selling war bonds.[43]

This intensive use of lighting in the United States was in no sense a necessity, and the European preference for less advertising was not temporary or the expression of a "cultural lag." Today many European communities continue to resist electric signs and spectacular advertising displays. At the 1994 Winter Olympics in Norway, the city council of Lillehammer refused Coca-Cola and other game sponsors the right to erect illuminated signs. On the city's streets only wooden and metal signs were permitted. No neon or transparent plastic was allowed. Levels and methods of lighting vary from culture to culture, and what is considered a dramatic necessity in the United States may be a violation of tradition elsewhere.[44]

So, not only have the best technologies not always triumphed in the market, the meanings given to new technologies often prove to be unexpected and nonutilitarian. Economics alone does not explain the amount of electricity used by refrigerator owners or the popularity, in America, of spectacular displays. From their inception, technologies have symbolic meanings and nonutilitarian attractions.

PREDICTIONS AS NARRATIVES

A technology is not merely a system of machines with certain functions; rather, it is an expression of a social world. Electricity, the telephone, the radio, television, the computer, and the Internet are not implacable forces moving through history, but social processes that vary from one time period to another and from one culture to another. In the United States these technologies were not "things" that came from outside society and had an "impact"; rather, each was an internal development shaped by its social context. No technology is a thing in isolation. Each is an open-ended set of problems and possibilities.

Each technology is an extension of human lives: someone makes it, someone owns it, some oppose it, many use it, and all interpret it. And given the multiplicity of actors involved, the interpretations of technology are diverse. Prediction, forecasting, and projection are by no means the only forms of interpretation. What is the larger structure of discourse that contains these narratives? In *Narratives and Spaces* I have argued that while in theory Americans can choose to understand technology using a large variety of narratives, in practice they usually have understood them through just six.[45] None of these six narratives is inherently true or false, and different people may insert the same invention into quite different narrative forms.

American Technological Narratives

Utopian
1. Natural. Technologies are natural outgrowths of society.
2. Ameliorative. New machines improve everyday life.
3. Transformative. New machines reshape social reality, for example, collapsing space or speeding up time.

Dystopian
4. Hegemonic. A minority uses technologies to gain/maintain control over others.
5. Apocalyptic. New technologies are agents of doom.
6. Satiric. New machines unexpectedly make life worse or lead to the reverse of expected outcomes.

"Natural" narratives treat machines as outgrowths of society that come ready-to-hand when needed. Such stories take technology for granted as background, and assume that necessity will automatically mother any invention required.[46] The other two utopian narratives have been the focus of this essay, since inventors and innovators themselves are almost always found espousing such stories. Both *forecasts* and *projections* commonly appear as part of ameliorative stories about the diffusion or improvement of already existing machines. The ameliorative position, for instance, emphasizes the positive social benefits that computers can have in education and commerce. Lynn Spigel's essay in this volume is concerned with this category, as she examines the ameliorative expectations attached to the portable television in the 1960s. *Predictions* about inventions can also be ameliorative, but they are more likely to appear in narratives of radical transformation. Claims that the Internet was the most important human invention since the discovery of fire would fall into this category.

Scenarios of domination, doom, and disaster are just as important as the rosy prognostications of inventors, marketers, and public relations departments. Dystopian predictions about negative transformations are also evident in several contributions. They are examined in Langdon Winner's exploration of the failed utopian promises of earlier communication technologies. Finally, the satiric narratives of technology are not predictive but retrospective, not utopian but ironic. Edward Tenner's *Why Things Bite Back* is an excellent example of such a satiric work, tracing what he calls "the revenge of unintended consequences."[47] Among his many examples, he notes that computers are usually expected to improve office efficiency. But in practice, people spend enormous time adjusting to continual new versions of software and they suffer eye strain, back problems, tendonitis, and other forms of cumulative trauma disorder.[48] The present article represents another form of the satiric narrative. Inventors and other experts fail as often as they succeed when making technological predictions about what new inventions may be possible. And once an invention exists and innovations refine it, engineers and entrepreneurs find it hard to forecast either the sales or applications. Ultimately, the accuracy of technological prediction is unpredictable.

NOTES

1. James M. Utterback, *Mastering the Dynamics of Innovation* (Boston: Harvard Business School, 1994), 193.

2. There are many examples of machines becoming much more popular after designers re-create them. See Jeffrey Meikle, *Twentieth Century Limited: Industrial Design in America, 1925–1939* (Philadelphia: Temple University Press, 1979).

3. CNN Evening News, European edition, October 12, 1998.

4. On how corporations exhibited themselves at fairs, see Roland Marchand, *Creating the Corporate Soul: The Rise of Public Relations and Corporate Imagery in American Big Business* (Berkeley: University of California Press, 1998), 249–311.

5. David E. Nye, *Electrifying America: Social Meanings of a New Technology* (Cambridge, Mass.: MIT Press, 1990).

6. George Wise, *Technological Prediction, 1890–1940* (Ph.D. diss., Boston University, 1976).

7. Intel tells this story on its Web page. "In 1965, Gordon Moore was preparing a speech and made a memorable observation. When he started to graph data about the growth in memory chip performance, he realized there was a striking trend. Each new chip contained roughly twice as much capacity as its predecessor, and each chip was released within 18–24 months of the previous chip. If this trend continued, he reasoned, computing power would rise exponentially over relatively brief periods of time. Moore's observation, now known as Moore's Law, described a trend that has continued and is still remarkably accurate. It is the basis for many planners' performance forecasts. In 26 years the number of transistors on a chip has increased more than 3,200 times, from 2,300 on the 4004 in 1971 to 7.5 million on the Pentium(R) II processor." Retrieved October 20, 1998, <http://web.jf.intel.com/intel/museum/25anniv/Hof/moore.htm>.

8. This discussion began in the 1950s. See A. H. Raskin, "Pattern for Tomorrow's Industry?" *New York Times Magazine*, December 18, 1955, 17. Kurt Vonnegut's *Player Piano* (New York: Avon Books, 1952) is a fictional exploration of these possibilities. For a general discussion, see Juliet Schor, *The Overworked American: The Unexpected Decline of Leisure* (New York: Basic Books, 1991), 4–5, *passim*. For a pessimistic assessment, see Eric Hoffer, *New York Times Magazine*, October 24, 1965. Reprinted in Wilbert E. Moore, *Technology and Social Change* (Chicago: Quadrangle Books, 1972), 66.

9. Paul Ehrlich, *The Population Bomb* (New York: Ballantine Books, 1968).

10. In 1902, when there were only a few thousand automobiles in the country, Americans took 4.8 billion trolley trips and made one billion transfers. See Nye, *Electrifying America*, 96.

11. See Joseph Corn, *America's Romance with Aviation, 1900–1950* (New York: Oxford University Press, 1983). For an advertisement from the 1930s showing a "typical" family in a small plane over the Midwest, see Marchand, *Creating the Corporate Soul*, 348. On the perception of flight as sublime, see David E. Nye, *American Technological Sublime* (Cambridge, Mass.: MIT Press, 1994), 201–3.

12. Cited in Spencer R. Weart, *Nuclear Fear: A History* (Cambridge, Mass.: Harvard University Press, 1988), 166.

13. Utterback, *Mastering the Dynamics of Innovation*.

14. However, the growth in overall energy use was still 50 percent in the 1970s. For discussion, see David E. Nye, *Consuming Power: A Social History of American Energies* (Cambridge, Mass.: MIT Press, 1998), 217–48.

15. John Allen Paulos, *A Mathematician Reads the Newspaper* (New York: Basic Books, 1995), 98. For a critique of Toffler and Naisbitt, see Howard P. Segal, *Future Imperfect: The Mixed Blessings of Technology in America* (Amherst: University of Massachusetts Press, 1994), 165–78.

16. Utterback, *Mastering the Dynamics of Innovation*, 195.

17. The term *technological momentum* comes from Thomas P. Hughes, and applies to any technology that achieves a standard design that is widely adopted.

18. Another example of the same sort of paralysis within a leading firm would be how Xerox failed to exploit its own development of the Windows program.

19. Menahem Blonheim, *News Over the Wires: The Telegraph and the Flow of Public Information in America, 1844–1897* (Cambridge, Mass.: Harvard University Press, 1994), 31; Paul Israel, *From Machine Shop to Industrial Laboratory: Telegraphy and the Changing Context of American Invention, 1830–1920* (Baltimore: Johns Hopkins University Press, 1992), 39.

20. Admittedly, the case of the telephone is complex, as Western Union hired Thomas Edison to create another version of the telephone, which he succeeded in doing. W. Berhard Carlson, "Entrepreneurship in the Early Development of the Telephone: How did William Orton and Gardiner Hubbard Conceptualize this New Technology?" *Business and Economic History* 23 (Winter 1994): 161–92. Carlson develops these ideas further in "Taking on the World: Bell, Edison, and the Diffusion of the Telephone in the 1870s" conference paper, "Prometheus Wired," October 8, 1998.

21. On the discovery itself, see Robert A. Rosenberg et al., *Menlo Park: The Early Years, April 1876-December 1877, The Papers of Thomas A. Edison,* vol. 3 (Baltimore: Johns Hopkins University Press, 1995), 660–74.

22. This was a formal document signed by Edison and his two principal assistants Charles Batchelor and John Kruesi. Ibid., 686.

23. I am indebted to Leo Marx for this anecdote, which stems from the mid-1970s, when he had recently taken up a post at MIT's program in Science, Technology and Society. Subsequently, Langdon Winner confirmed it.

24. Yet another example would be cable television, which was around on a small and local scale for roughly two decades without attracting much interest. I thank Eric Guthey for drawing my attention to this example.

25. I discuss marketing of electricity in the United States in *Electrifying America*. Often street railways had their own power stations, and competed with the central stations until at least the second decade of the twentieth century. Urban utilities, led by Samuel Insull in Chicago, won over their business through differential rate making. Factory electrification began in the 1860s with security systems based on telegraph technology, expanded to include lighting in the 1880s, and gradually moved toward electric power in the 1890s. However, the real growth in electrified factory power only came after 1900, once the war between alternating and direct current had been sorted out and reliable motors had been on the market long enough to prove their superiority. The next market was the home, which was an institution in transition well before electricity entered the domestic scene. Finally, General Electric and Westinghouse vigorously pursued the farm market in the early part of the century, but utilities lagged behind, until prompted by New Deal competition.

26. Likewise, utilities operated appliance stores and ran campaigns designed to build the electrical load. See Thomas P. Hughes, *Networks of Power: Electrification in Western Society, 1880–1930* (Baltimore: Johns Hopkins University Press, 1983), 223–24.

27. See Bob Schwabach, "Home Users Lead the Way in Growth of Video Mail," Universal Press Syndicate, story carried in *Minneapolis Star Tribune*, November 5, 1998, D2.

28. George Eastman figured out something similar in the 1890s: there was more money to be made selling film and processing than in selling cameras. Utterback, *Mastering the Dynamics of Innovation*, 175–76.

29. When the first transatlantic telephone service came on line in the 1920s, a call cost $5 a minute, and this was when $5 a day was a good salary. As with electricity, the basic cost of service declined after technical improvements and economies of scale.

30. This fact was recognized early. See Barry Boehm, "Software and its Impact: A Quantitative Assessment," *Datamation* 19, no. 5 (May 1973): 48–59.

31. Photographs document two of these, General Electric Photographic Archives, at the Hall of History in Schenectady, New York. Negatives 506119 (toilet seat) and 281181 (sprinkler).

32. See Michael A. Cusumano et al., "Strategic Maneuvering and Mass-Market Dynamics: The Triumph of VHS over Beta," *Business History Review* 66 (Spring 1992): 51–94.

33. Utterback, *Mastering the Dynamics of Innovation*, 28.

34. For a brief summary of how RCA refused to adopt FM and hindered its diffusion in the 1930s and 1940s, see Thomas P. Hughes, *American Genesis: A Century of Invention and Technological Enthusiasm* (New York: Viking-Penguin, 1989), 146–50.

35. In that prototypical American town, Muncie, Indiana, district heating served more than 400 customers in the central business district during the 1920s. By the late 1920s the utility had 13,000 feet of pipe, serving 425 customers. Yet this business gradually declined and was abandoned in the 1960s due to interlinked economic and technological factors that encouraged new power plant construction far from potential steam customers. The most important technological change was the availability, after around 1895, of alternating current that could be transmitted much farther than direct current, making possible larger, more efficient, (and consequently fewer) generating plants. The ease of long-distance transmission allowed utilities to build on inexpensive land outside the central business district, a strategy that also overcame public objection to smoke pollution. The farther power plants moved from the center, the less economic sense it made to sell steam heat. Frank Smikel, "Last Steam to Hiss Through Downtown Lines Next Tuesday," *Muncie Star*, May 26, 1966. History, Growth, and Development of the Indiana General Service Company, n.d., c. 1935. Copy in author's possession.

36. See Matthew Josephson, *Edison, a Biography* (New York: McGraw Hill, 1959), 318–22.

37. Daniel J. Czitrom, *Media and the American Mind* (Chapel Hill, N.C.: University of North Carolina Press, 1982), 68–72.

38. Another example from Muncie, Indiana, makes the same point. The inter-

urban trolley cars sometimes made a point of getting a little ahead of schedule, so that they had time to stop on a bridge over a stream, drop an electrified wire into the water, and electrocute enough fish for dinner.

39. Bruce Hackett and Loren Lotsenhiser, "The Unity of Self and Object," *Western Folklore* 54 (1985): 317–24.

40. Ibid., 323.

41. See Shoshana Zuboff, *In the Age of the Smart Machine: The Future of Work and Power* (New York: Basic Books, 1988).

42. *General Electric Review* 1 (November 1903), 17.

43. Nye, *Electrifying America*, 60.

44. Ibid., 49–50.

45. David E. Nye, *Narratives and Spaces: Technology and the Construction of American Culture* (New York: Columbia University Press, 1998), 179–89.

46. As should be evident from the argument presented here, many historical examples suggest problems with this view. I will mention only one, the failure, after a full century of hard work, to create a lightweight car battery that can quickly be recharged. Electric automobiles have been held back by this problem. Edison could not solve it.

47. Edward Tenner, *Why Things Bite Back* (New York: Vintage, 1996).

48. Ibid., 220–23.

John Perry Barlow

9 The Future of Prediction

Anyone who predicts the weather around here is either a newcomer or a fool.
—Old Wyoming saying

It is useful to remember, as Niels Bohr once observed, that prediction is extremely difficult, especially about the future. It is probably also useful to remember that Niels Bohr was a man who realized that time flowed backward and forward and that only consciousness made it appear otherwise. Nevertheless, he was clearly on to something important.

Of course, there is a lot of money in predicting the future even when you know you are wrong. More important, the best way to invent the future is to predict it—if you can get enough people to believe your prediction, that is. I have some desired futures that I would like to predict so persuasively that they will come to pass. I have been doing so for years and can even point to some success in this regard. Nevertheless I am not a futurist, despite being commonly accused of such audacity. I am a presentist. I predict the present. And indeed, predicting the present is not an entirely useless enterprise, since most people are very busy predicting the past.

For instance, Wendy Grossman writes in this volume that in the future, the Internet may allow us to choose our governments through a citizenship broker, no matter where we live. In a sense, that future is already here—though, as usual, it's unevenly distributed. I once addressed the International Chamber of Commerce in Paris, which was considering the question of how to define international transactions in a borderless environment, and what nation-state terms of contracts both parties would agree to use as the binding system. Here is an international body that has already reached the conclusion that you can pick your own government, depending on whose rules you want to go by.

I'm wary of trying to predict the future for many reasons, some of them arising from chastening personal experience. Years ago, I believed that the Internet would permit me to leave the cattle business—a proposition I knew was doomed since most of my competitors didn't have to make a living at it—while leaving my body in my little cowtown of Pinedale, Wyoming. I could let my mind roam the planet to make a living. Instead, however, my mind stays located at barlow@eff.org while my body roams the planet and makes a living.

This is because people, once they start to communicate virtually, desire to ascend the spectrum of human bandwidth and communicate in a much more broad spectrum way—that is, as directly as their growing relationship calls them to do. There is no substitute for being there and there never will be. But I didn't know this at the time, and my naive ideas about how I was going to design my own life turned out to be ironically false. Hence, I have learned to be modest about trying to predict how other people's lives are going to turn out.

Nevertheless, I *will* predict this—that, on the basis of what it has done to me, the Internet is going to do for jet fuel what the personal computer did for paper. (You may recall that absolutely everyone knew that the personal computer was going to eliminate the use of paper, which so far anyway, it manifestly has not done.) I look around at the people I know who are most wired and I see that they are also the people who move their personal flesh around most. A few years ago, I randomly encountered Nicholas Negroponte, Alvin Toffler, and George Gilder in the same hotel lobby, all of us speaking at different conferences in the same town. These four very wired guys immediately started arguing about which of us had the most frequent flier miles. This is because we all knew that text, transmitted asymmetrically, carried our message less far less effectively than interactive presence, compete with body language, intonation, and collaboration with the audience.

I also am getting old enough now so that I can remember futures that didn't come to pass. I went to the 1961 Seattle World's Fair and saw there a vision of Seattle in the Year 2000, where the big deal was that you would be able to drive to Portland at 240 mph. At the time, transportation was everything. Getting the flesh around was the deal. Telecommunications seemed less significant. The only interesting thing I saw on telecommunications at the 1961 World's Fair was an AT&T video phone from which you could call someone in the next booth. Ironically, that technology is about at the same level now as it was then. It's a technology of the future. And it probably always will be the technology of the future.

There was certainly nothing about the Seattle World's Fair to indicate that the future of Seattle—indeed of the world—would be dominated now by a young, nerdy guy who was making something that consisted entirely of magnetically stored ones and zeros. Nobody had such a wild imagination as that. Certainly I didn't. On the other hand, I did tend to believe (like many others) that by the time we got to the year 2000, we would have reached a point where the machines would be doing most of the work and that human beings would be out talking philosophy, probably in plastic togas. This was a *Popular Science* magazine vision of the future, robotic slaves doing most of the manufacturing and farming.

The weird thing is, I would submit that this prediction actually has come true—and hardly anyone has noticed. It is often the case that, by the time once-giddy dreams become reality, everyone takes them for granted. In any event, it is certainly true that if you live in an industrial economy, you are probably not making your living with the sort of activities thought to be work when I was young. Chances are, you're not earning your living by producing anything you can touch. You're almost certainly not directly involved in the material production of subsistence, shelter, or clothing. You are probably engaged in a somewhat less enjoyable version of sitting around and talking philosophy.

I spend my time and collect my frequent flier miles going around and talking to everyone from interior designers to banking marketers about what are essentially philosophical principles. I am paid to speculate airily in matters of ethics, culture, politics, and economic theory and so are many others these days. We may spend a couple of days in exceptionally pleasant environments—groves if you will, sometimes they're literally groves, even if owned by Ritz-Carlton—talking philosophy. In other words, we may have reached that *Popular Science* future, yet haven't noticed it. Indeed, we keep ourselves very busy trying not to notice it because we are desperately terrified of actually having as much leisure time as we potentially do.

Of course, there are also plenty of people out there talking philosophy who are *not* getting paid. Every street corner in this city has a couple of them. They're called homeless people. We've bifurcated ourselves into those who get paid to do it and those who don't and we still haven't figured out an economic model that would see to everybody somehow reaping the benefit of all this work that is now being done by machines.

We are, of course, in a transitional period between the old industrial model and the new information economy. We cling to the models of the past—managing offices as though they were factories, paying people for time rather than results, trying to homogenize the behavior of the work-force—even though all of these practices are inimical to the real creativity that is the base resource of an information economy. We fail to recognize the value of leisure, which the Greeks regarded as the apex of human activity, because we can't figure out a good way to pay people not to work in the conventional sense. It may be that part of the reason we aren't adapting to the conditions of the present is that we still think those conditions lie in the future. Eyes fixed on the horizon, we are blind to what already surrounds us.

By the same token, we often give our predictions too little time to come true. If they're not immediately realized, we think of them as bunk, despite the likelihood of their accuracy in the much longer run. I have often heard the early and giddy predictions for telegraphy and telephony cited as evidence that similar carryings-on over the Internet are foolish. However, if you think of those nineteenth-century telecommunication predictions as applying to *the present*, they don't seem quite so silly.

I believe that the invention of telegraphy—that is, the first ability to manifest oneself instantaneously over great distance—established a continuous chain of developments of which the Internet is the most recent manifestation. I consider the sum of this series of events to be the most important technological development since the capture of fire. What God really wrought when Samuel Morse tapped out that famous question in 1847 was the first step in creating a planetary nervous system. In my opinion, it is not out of the question that every synapse on this planet will one day be wired directly and continuously into every other synapse on this planet. And that would be such a big deal as to be essentially "hype-proof." Anything you could say about such a global ecosystem of Mind would be an understatement.

Still, connecting every individual nervous system into one vast matrix is likely to take a rather long time. After more than 150 years, it's still only gathering energy. Even with regard to the Internet, we may be in such an early phase of development that we don't really know what it is yet. We may be in the same condition Bell was in when he thought that the telephone was a broadcast device or when Marconi thought that the radio was a one-to-one medium. We have in our grasp tools that are not yet known to us, that we will use in ways that are entirely unpredictable—as was the World Wide Web—and yet not so unpredictable—as was electronic mail.

Generally, as these tools come into use, our sense of having them disappears. We tend not to think of clothing or shelter as technological manifestations, but they surely are. Indeed, it seems to me that when people talk about technology, especially the Neo-Luddites that I run across in academic circles, I find that they're almost referring to tools that were invented after they were twenty-five. They're not talking about their car. They're not talking about their shoes. They're certainly not talking about language, which they use prolifically and which is a form of technology. They're just talking about the technologies that were invented after their minds gelled, or, in some cases, calcified—the ones that make them afraid. Most dystopian views are produced by people who have forgotten how to dance with the future. Dancing with the future is the responsibility of anybody who wants to live well in these confusing times. Dancing with the future requires both a humility and an optimism in one's projections of it. It requires as well the ability to discard one's cherished visions as they demonstrate themselves to be dreams, along with enough patience to await their eventual fruition.

It's important to recognize that when a new technology bursts forth on the scene, some will become immediately overexcited. There will always those "reverse coal mine canaries" like me, who immediately start jumping up and down and going on about how great the air is in here all of a sudden. "Utopia Now!" we're likely to declare. It's well to be somewhat skeptical of the likes of us. On the other hand, by the time our predictions come true, which they often do, they seem such a commonplace that nobody bothers to congratulate our prescience. I made a number of statements about the rapid expansion and ubiquity of the Internet back in the late 1980s that were sniggered at by all who heard them. Now that almost every billboard in America has "www" someplace on it, no one's apologizing for their earlier derision.

Paul Saffo, at the Institute of the Future, has a very useful notion called "macromyopia." By this, he means that the first predictions about a socially transforming technology are usually inflated, while the long-term effects are usually deflated. He claims that it takes about thirty years for anything really new to arise from an invention, because that's how long it takes for enough of the old and wary to die. There are several things that I think we can count on and death is certainly one of them. Ironically, that's an encouraging perspective for anybody who's fighting for a vision, especially if she or he is under twenty-five. Take heart, Young Pioneers, someday we'll be dead and you'll still be alive.

In addition to the death of gray and phobic multitudes, there are several other trends that we can almost certainly count on to have enormous effects on the foreseeable future. One of them is Moore's Law. Gordon Moore predicted in 1977 that processor speed would double every eighteen months for as long as his mind could project. I don't know if anybody really understands why, but through the combined efforts—one could say, belief systems—of hundreds of thousands, perhaps millions of people, this has turned out to be true. In fact, it now *has* to be true, since the entire computer industry and a good deal of the world economy depend on it continuing to hold. In other words, it may be true because we insist that it be so, an example of inventing the future by predicting it. From it arises the very real possibility that shortly every lamp and door knob and toaster in the world will have a super computer embedded in it that will constantly exchange data with every other lamp and door knob and toaster. I don't know what all these appliances are going to be saying to one another, but they are certainly going to create a more interactive environment than the one we live in. Our very surroundings will seem alive with information. That is one reasonable prediction.

Then there is the explosion of the Net itself. One of the reasons that I tied my future to the Internet back in 1986 (when it was still well below most other people's radar) was that I could see it had been growing exponentially ever since it was switched on in 1969. There was no reason not to think it would continue to do so, which meant that by the mid-1990s, it would be a Very Big Deal (as might anyone who knew a lot about it).

Exponential growth curves are another basis for macromyopia. Phenomena that expand by doubling at regular intervals grow slowly until they suddenly stay under the radar for a long time and then they burst into view rather dramatically. There is the great and certainly apocryphal story about the emperor of China who wanted to reward the fellow who invented chess by giving him whatever he wanted. The fellow who invented chess said put a grain of rice on the first square, two on the second, four on the third, and so on. The emperor of China agreed with this reward, not realizing that continuing this series to the thirty-sixth square it would require more rice than had ever been produced. That's how an exponential growth curve works.

The Internet has been growing in this same fashion. If it continues to do so, we might reach a point sometime around 2010 when every man, woman, and child on the planet Earth will have access to it. Now I don't think that's actually going to happen, but on the basis of having spent a lot of the last couple of years in the Southern Hemisphere, I would say that it's going to come closer to happening than practically everyone in the North believes. I believe that those parts of the world that we in the North have tended to redline from the age of the Internet are actually going to come online with extraordinary rapidity.

In fact, they are already doing so, and doing so with a profound understanding this sort of environment. I believe they have particular capacity to "get it" based on the fact that they are accustomed to living in horizontally networked societies and are thus far better equipped to understand horizontally networked economies and organizations. Moreover, their cultural resistance to industrialization, so long an apparent liability, will now become an asset. They will not be burdened by the habits of mind—the inappropriate notions of property, boundary-clarity, time-obsession—that will inhibit the transformation of Northern economies. I believe the Southern Hemisphere will do very well in the twenty-first century. That's a prediction. Of course, I could be wrong. This is only how the future world looks through the narrow aperture of my crystal ball.

I am well aware that, as we attempt to divine the future, we are like the blind men and the elephant, each defining it on the basis of our extremely limited experiences and cultural filters. We can see only what we are prepared to see. To make matters trickier, there are six billion of us, each with his or her own unique perceptions. And the elephant is not only immense, it shape-shifts constantly, often in response to our descriptions of it. As I say, we build the future from the architecture of our expectations. We create the future we believe we deserve.

This worries me because I don't think we give ourselves enough credit. Indeed, many of us, especially in academic circles, seem personally threatened by optimism, especially in regard to the potential of the Internet to promote positive social change. There are several reasons for this. For one thing, many middle-aged academics were Marxists in their youth and there is nothing that irritates a disillusioned utopian more than someone whose utopia has not yet failed. Academics also suspect Internet boosters like me because they incorrectly assume that the Internet is a medium and therefore prey to the excesses and depredations wrought by previous media once they became the tools of power. They think of the Internet as being like television, easily captured by same corporate and governmental powers that have misused it throughout its history.

But the Internet is not a medium. It is an environment and, furthermore, it is an environment that can expand almost infinitely to assume all the shapes of human imagination. Unlike television or any of the other previous media, the information pathways of the Internet require neither wealth, nor privilege, nor force to inhabit. Freedom of the press no longer belongs only to those who own one. The first order of revolutionary business is no longer seizing the radio station. And even though the usual godless suspects are pouring billions into the World Wide Web, they are losing most of those billions and the vast majority of Web pages remain noncommercial.

Granted, the new boss, whether Microsoft or America Online, seems no great improvement over the Time Warners of the world, but the longevity of the new Titans seems greatly abbreviated. The short history of the software business is already a graveyard of the once-invincible. In general, size appears increasingly to be a liability. In fact, the Fortune 500 has lost thirteen million employees in the past decade within the United States and the fastest growing employer by far is called "self." This is a fact of the present, not the future, that needs to be reckoned with.

For these reasons, and many others, I don't find my optimism about the potential benefits of the Internet to be flagging. Nor am I particularly persuaded by my fellow humanists who are convinced that this self-amplifying explosion of digital technology is going to further diminish the human spirit. Even though I suspect the development of a global nervous system may alter what it is to be human more than any previous technological manifestation, it seems apparent to me that nothing changes what it is to be human very much.

My mother died recently at ninety-three. She spent the first quarter of her life living in frontier conditions in Wyoming where the fastest way to get information around was a galloping horse. By the time she died, she was sending me e-mail. She lived through the entire spectrum of technological explosions in communication and transportation that populated the history of this last century, and yet on the day she died, she was still telling stories in which technology was invisible. While technology might have provided the medium, the message was always human. Her stories were about the same things that Chaucer told stories about, that Shakespeare told stories about, that I tell stories about on a good day. These are stories about what human beings do, what we keep in our hearts, where we are led by their weaknesses—in other words, they are about the ancient battle between the Seven Deadly Sins and the Three Graces. There remains, underlying all this technological change, human behavior.

Even though I believe that our advances in telecommunications are creating a great Mind that will combine all of our minds, I don't believe that individual human personalities will be subsumed into this vast organism. There is already evidence to support this contention, since it seems to me that the "Metamind" has been actively thinking for a long time. Its thoughts are called technology, culture, and language. It is the environment in which these immaterial life forms live. This can happen in ways that are not particularly comprehensible to us—in the same way that we exist in a way that is not particularly comprehensible to the mitochondria that still populate our cells and behave in the ways that they did when they were one-celled critters free-floating in the primordial soup. Nature layers its advances each on top of the previous ones. It's very important to recognize that each layer in this philogenetic accumulation goes on being pretty much the same. At the base of the human genome is blue-green slime genome. It's still doing what it's been doing for billions of years. And like blue-green slime, human beings will likely go on being human for a long time.

But, at the same time, something else is evolving into existence. Unlike previous editions, it is not simply an upgrade on the most complex life form but is rather something very different from anything that has existed on this planet before. It is made from all our minds, and right now we tend to call it the Internet. That's why I'm going to stick to my belief that the Internet is the most important development since the capture of fire. I think this is a profound event in human history because of its ability to make something that is more than human, even as we remain essentially unchanged.

Stewart Brand likes to say that if we are going to become as gods, we should get good at it. Personally, I don't expect us to become any more god-like than we've ever been, but I do expect us to become, together, a God. A new God upon the earth. But in saying that, I may be predicting the present again. Perhaps that new God is already here and only growing perceptible as it forms more completely. Perhaps it's already making its own great and lonely predictions. I hope it assumes a long future for itself and all its human parts.

WENDY M. GROSSMAN

10   Penguins, Predictions, and Technological Optimism

A Skeptic's View

Prediction is extremely difficult. Especially about the future.
—Niels Bohr[1]

PEOPLE IN the technology world are always looking ahead: the future, the new, and whatever's next are their business. Current discussions of technology, like those of the past, are preoccupied with predicting the future, pinning hopes on particular beliefs about how certain new technologies will become indispensable throughout the world. However, there are a lot of problems with trying to predict the future impact of a new technology. There is always the temptation to go for strong claims that are sensational or terrifying, ones that grab attention and headlines. Yet the fact is that even proven experts get it wrong.

The now out-of-print book *The Experts Speak*, by Christopher Cerf and Victor S. Navasky, includes the often-quoted statement in the 1950s by then IBM chairman Thomas J. Watson that he foresaw a world market for only about a dozen computers.[2] More recently, in 1990, supreme computer salesman Michael Dell told a leading British computer magazine that he didn't know if Windows would be successful, or if any operating system would be able to replace DOS because of its huge installed user base.[3] Seeing experts get it wrong is a lot of fun if you have a malicious turn of mind. If you do, you fit right in on the Net.

Predictions depend on the present for their essential character: we are better at thinking up tiny, incremental changes to the world constrained by today's limitations than at imagining radical change. Even someone as far-seeing as computer scientist Vannevar Bush, when he fantasized about the Memex in his well-known 1945 essay "As We May Think," imagined a tiny, head-mounted camera would capture images of the world around the wearer, but assumed it would be taking still pictures because video hadn't been invented yet.[4] Bush also foresaw a very good likeness of the

186

World Wide Web as a worldwide library of interconnected information. However, he didn't foresee computer storage or networking, so his Memex was a physical desk belonging to an individual researcher, which would store its own copy of this Web-like information base—on microfilm. If we lived in the late 1990s as they were depicted in the science fiction novels of the 1950s, we'd each have multiple robots serving us, but there would be only one giant computer, perhaps stationed on the Moon or another planet. Edison imagined that the telephone would be used to broadcast music, and that the phonograph would be used for dictating office memos (an example of using a phonograph this way showed up in the 1948 movie *Unfaithfully Yours*, in a scene in which Rex Harrison also demonstrated that user manuals have always been awful). In 1927, the American Newspaper Publishers Association said, "Fortunately, direct advertising by radio is well nigh an impossibility."[5]

A lot of the hopes we have for technology come, of course, from its inventors and its early adopters—the people who are most enthusiastic but possibly least unbiased. The promises these people make for technology is rarely the reality. We are promised voice recognition so our computers can listen to us and interpret what we say intelligently. Instead, we get voice menus.

My own perspective on this kind of thing is a little unusual. I spend most of my time writing about technology, particularly the Internet, for a variety of publications. As a sideline, however, I am also co-editor of a British magazine I founded in 1987 called *The Skeptic*, which is dedicated to the scientific examination of paranormal claims. Critical thinking is one of the values *The Skeptic* espouses. Since I started writing about technology, I have been startled frequently by the number of technology writers who have been burned over and over again by bug-ridden software from incomplete beta versions of a new operating system software that never quite delivers what it promises, and yet retain enough giddy hopefulness that this time will be different. I like to think of those of us who write about computers for specialist magazines as an endangered species, and not just because the new operating system software just ate all the partially finished articles on our hard drives. According to one British journalist, at one time there were three refrigerator magazines in the United Kingdom, each of which ran features about the best way of arranging food and managing the temperature controls. It is worth noting that in 2000–2001, many computer magazines closed due to the combination of the dot-com bust, the stock market downturn, and the post-September 11 loss of advertising.

This means that we have to assume that fifty or one hundred years in the future everything we've been saying here is going to look just as silly—or irrelevant. The only person who ever had much success in the line of prediction was Nostradamus, and his predictions depend for their success on later interpretation. They are simply vague enough that anything can be read into them afterward by determined believers.[6]

Skepticism about the paranormal turns out to be good training for covering technology and listening to Internet hype. Any skeptic spends a lot of time listening to people make unsustainable claims about how their dreams predict the future, or how they have exposed a giant government cover-up of alien visitations to the planet (a cover-up that somehow always leaves them able to appear on TV and radio and publish books and magazines). It's important to be careful when arguing against the likelihood of these claims, not only because of the intensity with which people often cherish these beliefs, but also because science requires that one always bear in mind the principle that they may turn out to be right after proper investigation. These experiences require the ability to listen tolerantly, which is a useful skill if you want to spend a lot of time on the Net, particularly Usenet.

Yet, of all contemporary claims, there has been more hype and silly things said about the future and impact of the Internet than probably just about any other invention we've ever had. Sillier, because we have the experience of past inventions to draw on, and yet we seem to have learned nothing. This can be thought of as the penguin syndrome, that is, at least according to myth, penguins forget everything they know every time they molt. Even if it's not true of penguins, it's a great metaphor for our relationship with technology: every time something new is invented, we seem to forget everything we know about everything that's gone before. We start all over again with the same wide-eyed hopes, dreams, fears, and hallucinations. We always hope that new technology will make us better people, which is as logical as hoping that buying a new personal digital assistant or laptop will make us write the Great American Novel, when the truth is that nothing is stopping us from writing it on that old typewriter, or with a quill pen. It is more likely that we will stay the same, and that as the technology becomes more pervasive it will more and more reflect what we already know as "real life" in all its variety.

Even so, the notion that the Net is going to change the world in a way that no other technology ever has is pervasive, even though we generally have the same hopes for it that we've had for every other technology. And many of these statements can be found on the Net itself. For instance, French technology consultant and former minister (under Mitterrand) Jacques Attali states: "The impact of information technology will be even more radical than the harnessing of steam and electricity in the 19th century. Rather it will be more akin to the discovery of fire by early ancestors, since it will prepare the way for a revolutionary leap into a new age that will profoundly transform human culture."[7]

In a 1995 *Wired* article, Web developer Mark Surman summed up the hype disseminated by Net pioneers:

> They believe that their technology—what has been called the information highway—will redeem society. They believe they're living through [a] "once every 500 years revolution." (Keegan p. 40) The ubiquitous talk of digital revolution which fills newspapers and TV programs echoes the hopefulness that drove cable activists in the 1970s. . . . But the techno-revolutionary ante has also been upped since the 1970s. Bigger and broader revolutionary visions are needed to convince people of the momentous changes that are going on. In the first issue of *Wired*, publisher Louis Rossetto related the Digital Revolution to " . . . social changes so profound their only parallel is probably the discovery of fire." (*Wired* 1.1, p.10.) In typical *Wired* style, Rossetto had to prove that his revolution was bigger, better and cooler than anyone else's.[8]

The "discovery of fire" analogy, as stated by Attali and Rossetto, is apparently the meme of the new millennium. "Cognitive dissident" John Perry Barlow claims the analogy was originally his; when criticized for it, Barlow speaks grandiloquently of the possibility that one day soon every human brain will be directly wired to every other, a possibility that not everyone may welcome, given the things inside some of the brains out there.

If the Internet really is the biggest thing since the discovery of fire, then it deserves to have the biggest hype since then, too. But is the Internet really on a par with a technology that enabled us to keep warm, cook food so it wouldn't poison us, help keep predators at bay, and allow us to defy the seasons and the daily schedule of night and day? What about electricity, which gave us a new version of all that which didn't burn down our homes periodically and made possible the creation of many generations of insomniac geeks? Or the birth control pill, which gave women personal control over their fertility and spawned a sexual revolution? What about the Industrial Revolution? The development of reliable clocks? Or public hygiene: if you were living in a cholera-infested village, would you rather have an Internet connection or clean water?

Let's take another example: on November 25, 1997, Nicholas Negroponte, who runs MIT's Media Lab, one of the leading academic research labs, told the European IT Conference in Brussels that the Internet will bring world peace by breaking down world borders. Twenty years from now, he predicted, kids will not know what nationalism is because they will be so used to being able to find out about other countries at the click of a mouse. As I have written elsewhere, if simply giving kids information made that kind of difference, we'd have long since recruited encyclopedia salesmen into the diplomatic corps.[9] Kids have long been able (and, in social studies classes, required) to look up other countries at the turn of an encyclopedia page, and this practice seems to have made no significant contribution to world peace.

If Negroponte had said that kids wouldn't know what nationalism was because every day they shared daily conversation and interaction with people from foreign countries—as people do on Usenet—he'd have had a slightly better case. But only very slightly: one does not have to look far on Usenet to find rampant nationalism and vicious jingoistic hatred. Probably most of us had foreign pen pals when we were in school, and there are many other things that have made the world appear to be a smaller and more intimate place: television, cheap travel. Many more things, however, remind us daily of our nationalism: the Olympics, the human instinct for groupings, and, especially, language. Yet, having access to other languages does not automatically create mutual understanding. Here we could remember Douglas Adams's simultaneously translating Babel fish, which by giving everyone instant understanding of everything said to them in any language caused more and bloodier wars than anything in the history of the universe.[10] He was joking, but we laugh because we know it's true.

Furthermore, Negroponte was talking about the essentially passive medium of the Web, rather than the interactive discussions and chats, the two-way many-to-many communication most of us think of as the unique feature of the Net as a medium and its true future. We could compare Negroponte's comment to this statement: "What can be more likely to effect [peace] than a constant and complete intercourse between all nations and individuals in the world?"

This quote is not about today's Internet, but about the invention of the telegraph. It comes from the British ambassador in 1858, and is cited in Tom Standage's *The Victorian Internet*.[11] As Standage writes,

> As one writer put it in 1878, the telegraph "gave races of men in various far-separated climes a sense of unity. In a very remarkable degree the telegraph confederated human sympathies and elevated the conception of human brotherhood. By it the peoples of the world were made to stand

closer together." The rapid distribution of news was thought to promote universal peace, truthfulness, and mutual understanding. In order to understand your fellow men, you really couldn't have too much news.[12]

Of course, Bill and Monica might care to argue with that.

The similarity between the advent of the telegraph and the development of the Internet is striking. There were romances among telegraphers online, there were weddings performed over telegraph connections. People complained about information overload, and there was a lot of fuss and regulation about secret codes, used to protect the content of messages from prying eyes and to shorten the messages so they'd cost less to send. In the end, it's arguable that the telegraph was a much greater revolution than today's Internet is. Before its invention, news took six to eight weeks to arrive by boat from distant parts of the globe. Before today's e-mail, we still had telephones and TV to bring us instant news.

It could also be argued that what connects us globally isn't the Internet but television—another technology that people imagined would be educational and democratizing in its infancy despite its rapid growth into a medium that it has always been fashionable for intellectuals to despise. CNN, which diplomats at the Virtual Diplomacy conference in 1997 described as the single biggest change in their working lives, hasn't brought world peace, even though it's watched by every leader. It has, however, changed the nature of diplomacy a good deal, in ways that are going to become increasingly familiar to us as the Internet penetrates farther and farther. Former State Department spokeswoman Margaret Tutwiler explained at that conference, for example, the difficulties of drafting a statement knowing that it would be seen by not only the American troops the State Department might want to inspire, but also by the folks back home and the leader of the foreign army. During the 1991 Gulf War, the wide penetration of CNN meant that it was no longer possible to create different presentations for those different audiences, to whom one might want to give completely different messages. The Internet may give us untrammeled access to all sorts of information that would have been restricted in earlier ages, but it's arguable that CNN and, before it, the telegraph gave us a taste for it.

In the long run, citing examples of earlier technologies and the hype and hopes that accompanied them is unlikely to make a dent in today's hype about the Internet. No amount of debunking causes the claims to be modified.[13] In skeptical circles, this is known as the "ratchet effect," a phrase coined by British TV producer Karl Sabbagh in 1985.[14] It's an effect often seen on the Net. Whatever the person's belief is—immortality, ghosts, astrology—if confirming evidence comes in that supports the belief, the belief winds tighter. If contradictory evidence comes in, no loosening of the belief is observed: there is no effect. On the Net, this phenomenon means that material is recycled endlessly, no matter how often it's critiqued, fueled in part by the endless supply of newcomers who believe they've stumbled upon information no one's ever seen before. One example is the newsgroup *rec.aviation.military*, where the theory that the TWA 800 crash was caused by a hit by a "friendly" missile originated; although the theory has been conclusively demolished many times by experts in the field, parts of this newsgroup simply will not let it drop. Another is the newsgroup *comp.software.year-2000*, which is (in part) home to a group of people who believed that the year 2000 computer problem would bring the end of the world as we know it (TEOTWAWKI), who would not accept that there was any chance that remedial efforts might succeed (which they did).[15] When I wrote an article for *Scientific American* about these beliefs and suggested that chances were that civilization would survive, the editors got a storm of e-mailed protests, one of which called me a "dizzy broad," a characterization I would never have predicted would be applied to me.

The ratchet effect is relevant, because in that same 1997 speech Negroponte repeated a favorite prediction of his—there will be one billion people using the Internet by the year 2000, half in developing countries—that had already been comprehensively debunked more two years earlier by San Francisco reporter and author David Kline, who pointed out in a column for *HotWired* in 1996 that in 1995 there were only 750 to 800 million phone lines in the world.[16] Even in the United States, where take-up of the Net is highest, Nielsen Media reported in September 1997 that only 40 percent of households had a computer, and only 22 percent had access (loosely defined) to the Internet. Nonetheless, Negroponte additionally claimed (two months later) that 85 percent of American kids have a computer at home. When Negroponte is queried about figures like this, his standard answer is, "If I'm wrong, it's only for ten minutes," a rather cavalier response for the leader of an academic lab. More recently and more realistically, Vinton Cerf, the co-inventor of the TCP/IP protocols that make the Internet work and a vice-president at MCI Worldcom, predicted the turn of the millennium would see 300 million Internet users.[17]

Half of those users are not in developing countries. Today, even in a place like Crete, which is, after all, part of western Europe, no one outside the business community and a few expatriates has a computer. Well, that's not quite true: a friend living in a remote mountain village that scrapes by on subsistence farming using methods that are tens of thousands of years old tells me that one of his neighbors does have a computer. That's what he calls the remote control for his TV set.

Could the Net foster international peace and brotherhood? The Net that most of us know is a fomenting stew of incompatible beliefs, cultures, and opinions, where the first thing you do when you disagree with someone is to electronically bash them senseless with a barrage of abuse. This seems to be a law of computer-mediated communication wherever it takes place—on Usenet, in the material posted on Web sites, on electronic mailing lists, even within internal corporate electronic discussion areas.[18] The Internet as I know it is a place where campaigners against abortion put up a Web site called The Nuremberg Files that publicizes and solicits the personal information and pictures of every doctor performing abortions in the United States and marks whether they're working, wounded, or dead, stopping only just short of encouraging the dead part—not only the doctors, but their relatives and assistants.[19] In defense of the Net, its other side is the heart-warming stories of rescue and support, such as the outpouring of letters, meals, and donations to help a San Francisco family wage a seven-year losing struggle against their son's leukemia, or the help eighty doctors worldwide gave in diagnosing and treating a comatose Chinese cello student suffering from thallium poisoning after they saw a newsgroup posting from concerned friends.

Yet for every story like that, there's the virulent racism, homophobia, and sexism displayed daily in the Net's public areas. It is not such a terrible thing that we know that people are thinking repulsive things or what those things are—the clean, banal, sanitized world presented by a company like Disney is in many ways worse because it is such a lie. However, the capacity computer-mediated communication has to polarize viewpoints and to allow people to state their views far more strongly than they probably would in person is going to take us a long way from the kind of tolerance and understanding hoped for by the early Net pioneers. These were people who, imbued with 1960s idealism, viewed the virgin snow of the untouched Net and envisioned it as a new world they could make in their own image. Not surprisingly, a lot of other people saw the same virgin snow and thought they, too, could remake the world in an image of their choosing. To some extent, this is what the hype is about: people hoping yet again that new technology will reinvent the world according to their own ideals.

Negroponte's belief that we live in the twilight of the nation-state is not uncommon. John Perry Barlow, for example, has said a number of times that on the Net everything is local and everything is global—but nothing is national. Former Citicorp chairman Walter Wriston carefully argued this case in his 1992 book *The Twilight of Sovereignty*, and plenty of others have come along to agree with him since.[20] In a 1995 interview British liberal leader Paddy Ashdown spoke of the difficulty of bringing multinationals under democratic control, and accepted it as a given that no single nation can now control its own economy. In the December 1997 *Atlantic Monthly*, author Robert D. Kaplan argued that the future holds an undemocratic division into the major multinational corporations, who currently have fifty-one of the world's one hundred largest economies, and many of whom, he goes on to say, already deliberately compose management teams of representatives from different countries so that the company itself will have a seamless global culture.[21] This pattern is repeated in many other areas. Nongovernmental organizations offer aid of all kinds in troubled areas of the world, and across the Net groups come together according to interest, not nationality. Anyone who has traveled knows that increasingly every place looks the same: every TV has its CNN, every town has its McDonald's.

If these trends lead to a non-national future, they mean that we will have to become adept at the art of balancing divided loyalties. To some extent, we do this already, for example, when the demands of the company we work for conflict with the needs of our families. But things are likely to be a lot more complex in the future. I live in the section of London known as Kew, but I spend more time every day talking to people on the WELL, most of them in San Francisco, than I do talking to my immediate neighbors, with whom I have less in common. If the WELL and Kew went to war (unlikely as that seems), it would be a difficult choice. Often, in the short history of the Net, when a decision is made that affects the Net by policy makers, businesses, or politicians who do not themselves spend much time online, many people seem to experience the impact of those decisions as a sort of declaration of war. The passage of the 1996 Communications Decency Act is a good example: people on the Net, even Americans, simply did not see it as an attempt, however deluded, by "our" government, however deluded, to protect and help us.

The antitrust case brought by the Department of Justice against Microsoft seems to have been experienced by many of its participants as a war, certainly at least by some of Microsoft's employees. This case may be the way of the future: a world in which the multinational company you work for collides with the government whose citizenship you claim. The Internet and its successors are and will be the technologies that make it possible to support a unified multinational structure for a single organization; symbiotically, the existence of global multinational corporations is one factor pushing the further development of those networks. Who predicted the dominance of multinationals when the telegraph and the telephone were invented?

One interesting possibility for the future of nationality is suggested by the efforts of the British and U.S. governments to electronify the delivery of services such as welfare benefits and social security checks. Part of this sort of initiative, at least in Britain, is supposed to involve giving us as taxpayers the kind of service we're used to as customers—24/7 access, fast response, a lack of red tape (at least until voice-operated menu systems become more widespread). But the difference between being customers and being taxpayers is that as taxpayers we have no choice of supplier. Why not? Given Internet access, it should be entirely possible to go to a citizenship broker, lay out the details of our personal situation, and get advice as to which government would be the most advantageous to adopt in terms of medical benefits, pension rights, welfare entitlement, even passport prices. The lawyer Duncan Frissell used to talk about the Net's making it possible for someone to become an expatriate without leaving home, and it seems like a perfectly reasonable possibility. Or, you might agree to allow your employer to lease or buy your citizenship rights outright in return for lifetime employment.

Having considered such possibilities, and having scorned the whole idea of predictions, I feel that I ought to stick my neck out and make some, if only so future generations can look back and make fun of me.

1. There will never be such a thing as a single Net.

There will always be many Nets that take on the characteristics of their users. I've been online for more than ten years and have spent as much time as anyone surveying the online landscape. Even so, there are millions of Web sites I've never visited, and there are vast areas of the Net that I know nothing about, like Peacenet, GreenNet, most MUDs (multi-user dungeons), and most of Internet Relay Chat (IRC). These are vast unmapped territories for me. I have no doubt there are many more connections being made daily that I have no idea about. Similarly, there won't be a single Net in a technological sense either: a few years ago everyone talked about things as though the Web was going to be the single interface. It is, at least for now, the single most important interface and the one that has fueled the mass adoption of the Net by both individuals and businesses. But the earlier technology is still there, and it doesn't have to be just old-timers who use IRC, Telnet, Gopher, and FTP (file transfer protocol) via older, text-based interfaces. Even within the confines of the Web, the Net is not a single entity but in turn an analog of a store, bar, library, or video arcade. For example, since 1999, Napster, Gnutella, and their offspring have created peer-to-peer file-sharing networks that have changed how people think about using the Net. Today, it looks as though the future of the Internet is likely to be at least in part in such applications (despite their current stigmatization as vehicles for unauthorized copying), which take advantage of the many-to-many characteristic of the medium.[22]

2. For a lot of people the Net will make little or no difference for the foreseeable future.

For instance, the big difference recently in that subsistence farming Cretan village is the advent of electricity in the past thirty years that drove the last donkeys out of olive oil production. Access will be a challenge in Greece, where 50 percent of the population is concentrated in a single city and the rest is scattered across more than 7,000 islands (though newer technologies such as ultra-wideband wireless may make this possible). Even in the United States, it's easy to confuse Net access and its ability to speed up communications—and replace limited book references with the apparently limitless library on the World Wide Web—with fundamental change. As the Net stands today, the benefits are available primarily to those who can read fluently and have a computer at home.

3. The Net will be invisible for a lot of people.

It will be embedded in household appliances, telephones, or clothing. The period in which computers are the only way to access the Net is likely to be short, in the grand scheme of things. Having said that, though, I believe that the people who will get the best advantage from the Net will always be the people who use computers and can program them to do what they want, unless the Net becomes so tightly controlled that this becomes impossible.

4. For many people, including a large percentage of today's kids, the Net will be an essentially passive medium except for games.

Many kids use the Web and exchange e-mail; they may even have Web pages and accounts on the chat software system ICQ. But they don't necessarily make the kind of great, imaginative strides or the active demands that the net.prophets were predicting only a few years ago. It's perfectly possible that the number of people who use things like Usenet newsgroups, online conferences, IRC, and the role-playing games known as MUDs will forever remain a small percentage of overall Net users consisting of those who enjoy reading and writing online and communicate well by that medium. After all, public-access television exists in most localities in the United States, and even so only a relatively small percentage of the population actually want to get out there and make TV shows. A lot of belief in the Net as an active medium has come from people who hate television—and the fact is, they're a fairly small minority of overall society.

It's a shame to say that the Net will be largely passive, because the unique feature of the Net as a medium is its potential for two-way, many-to-many communication, and its ability to connect people who otherwise would not have known of each other's existence. But for many people, even kids— perhaps especially kids, once parents are convinced the Net is a dangerous place for them to play—the Net is a way to contact people they already know and look up reference material. One answer to this is community bulletin boards; as Langdon Winner and Steve Cisler have said, the best online communities are an extension of real-life communities, because the essential nature of a community is to impose obligations on its members and require them to deal with people they don't like. Systems like London's CIX and San Francisco's the WELL derive a lot of their cohesiveness from the fact that many of the participants meet in real life at parties and professional gatherings, not just in the context of the systems themselves.

A great danger of the Net is that the longer people are online the more they filter out anyone or anything they disagree with, becoming so blinkered that they ultimately believe everyone thinks the way they do. At the same time, traveling online to places where one's closest friends, family, spouses, and employers don't go gives the Net the same feeling of escape as a vacation in some exotic locale: people are free to reinvent themselves temporarily, to experiment, and to behave badly without the fear of real-life consequences.

5. It will take a lot of vigilance to protect the public spaces of the Net from threats such as tightly controlled corporate ownership, regulation by governments, and less well understood threats like content ratings, which sound harmless but could provide the infrastructure and justification for control.

But the ace in the hole in this scenario is that the technology that predates the Web and forms the basis of services like Usenet still works, and as the setting up of the *alt* hierarchy on Usenet showed, it would be possible to start all over again by hooking a few computers together to exchange news.[23] In a world where the Web and the other mainstream public faces of the Net became tightly controlled, this could be extremely important.[24]

If it sounds impossible that the wild and diverse Net we know today could become a corporate oligopoly owned by, say, Microsoft, Disney, and Time-Warner, bear in mind Robert McChesney's statistics about early radio: "An AT&T survey of US broadcasting in 1926 determined that approximately one-half of US stations were operated to generate publicity for the owner's primary enterprise, while one-third were operated by nonprofit groups for eleemosynary [charitable] purposes. Only 4.3 percent of US stations were characterized as being 'commercial broadcasters,' while a mere one-quarter of US stations permitted the public to purchase airtime for its own use."[25] The pattern those figures represent is more like today's Web than it's comfortable to think about. Radio, which in the 1920s was expected to be a great democratizing medium (also like today's Web), is now almost entirely commercially controlled.

This is actually one area where some of the Internet technologies that preceded the Web may come into their own. It's currently fashionable to dismiss Usenet as a wasteland of noise and spam or to regard it simply as a vast unreliable but searchable database via Deja News, but Usenet is in reality the town square of the Internet. Usenet got started by three guys as a "poor man's ARPAnet": they wrote some software to copy UNIX files from one computer to another over telephone lines, and got started trading news articles. Usenet is important if only because if all of the rest of the Net falls into a few corporate hands Usenet could be restarted without reference to the commercial Net. No one owns Usenet, and this makes it vital at a time when so much of the rest of the Net is being squabbled over by governments, major multinational corporations, and other interests.

6. It will take constant vigilance to make sure that history does not attribute the invention of the Internet to Bill Gates.
Already, a certain amount of the publicity material coming out of Microsoft's PR agencies gives this impression, along with the notion that Gates invented BASIC. Those of us who admire the work of Net pioneers like Vint Cerf, the late Jon Postel, and others need to make sure their contributions to history don't get lost.

7. My final prediction is less a prediction than an observation: it is not a binary world, as net pioneer Bill Washburn likes to say.
There are more choices than utopia or dystopia. We argue about the Net and its issues in those terms: censorship or freedom of speech, free cryp-

tography or not, settlement or cooperative carriage of Net traffic, public or private. But in our nonbinary world there are not only two possibilities, one of which wears a white hat and the other of which wears a black hat, and which can stage a shoot-out on live TV. The technology can support diversity, and can support multiple possibilities. Narrowing the possibilities to two makes for easy news production, but it involves throwing out plenty of viable alternatives that might coexist comfortably as choices. As we continue to push this new technology to realize the hopes and dreams we've always had, we should also remember the popular saying: Insanity is keeping on doing the same thing and expecting different results.

NOTES

1. This quote is generally attributed to Niels Bohr, though occasionally to Yogi Berra. See <http://www.larry.denenberg.com/predictions.html> for a more or less complete list. Accessed January 2004.

2. Christopher Cerf and Victor S. Navasky, *The Experts Speak: The Definitive Compendium of Authoritative Misinformation* (New York: Pantheon Books, 1984).

3. Wendy M. Grossman, ed., *Remembering the Future: Interviews from Personal Computer World* (London: Springer Verlag, 1997), 96.

4. Vannevar Bush, "As We May Think," *The Atlantic* (July 1945): <http://www.theatlantic.com/atlantic/atlweb/flashbks/computer/bushf.html>. Functional as of December 2, 2003.

5. Robert McChesney, *Telecommunications, Mass Media, and Democracy: The Battle for the Control of US Broadcasting 1928–1935* (New York: Oxford University Press, 1993).

6. James Randi, *The Mask of Nostradamus* (Buffalo, N.Y.: Prometheus, 1993).

7. Jacques Attali, *Millennium: Winners and Losers in the Coming World Order* (New York: Times Books, 1992). Quoted in Lecture #3: The Digital Revolution, <http://milproj.ummu.umich.edu/version2/classes/highered/lecture3/lec3part01.html>. Accessed November 1998.

8. Mark Surman, "Wired Words: Utopia, Revolution, and the History of Electronic Highways," <http://gea01.pangea.org/inet96/e2/e2_1.htm>. Accessed November 1998. Also given as a talk at INET 96, third annual conference of ISOC (Internet Society).

9. Wendy M. Grossman, "Why the Net Won't Deliver Peace," *Daily Telegraph,* December 9, 1997, 10. Online at <http://www.telegraph.co.uk>.

10. Douglas Adams, *The Hitchhiker's Guide to the Galaxy* (New York: Harmony Books, 1979).

11. Tom Standage, *The Victorian Internet* (New York: Berkley Books, 1998), 90.

12. Ibid., 163.

13. This is true in the paranormal world no matter how extravagantly comprehensive the disproof. In the Internet world, the stock market crash did sober the financial community for a while, but the conviction that the Internet will change everything persists.

14. Karl Sabbagh, in a talk at the London conference of the Committee for Scientific Investigation of Claims of the Paranormal.

15. See Wendy M. Grossman, "The End of the World as We Know It," *Scientific American* (October 1998).

16. David, Kline. "Stupid Net Tricks," *HotWired*, June 3, 1996: <http://www.hotwired.com/market/96/23/index1a.html>. Functional as of December 2, 2003.

17. According to Nua Internet surveys, by June 2000 the best guess was there were 332.73 million online users worldwide (<http://www.nua.ie/surveys/how_many_online/index.html>). User estimates are notoriously variable. By 2002, NUA had estimates of 544.2 million (February 2002) and 323.7 million (April), with the United States more or less static between December 2000 and January 2002 at roughly 165 million (Nielsen Media), or about 57 percent of the U.S. population.

18. See, for example, Sara Kiesler and Lee Sproull, *Connections: New Ways of Working in the Networked Organization* (Cambridge, Mass.: MIT Press, 1992). In 2002, a new Web initiative sought to turn webcams on the women arriving at clinics for abortions.

19. The Web site was at <http://www.christiangallery.com/atrocity/>. In early 1999, the site's owners were fined $10 million and ordered to take the site down. It was almost immediately mirrored elsewhere on the Net.

20. Walter B. Wriston, *The Twilight of Sovereignty* (New York: Scribner and Sons, 1992).

21. In 2002, it became easy to see what Paddy Ashdown was talking about, as it became public knowledge that some of the largest U.S. corporations were avoiding paying taxes by incorporating in Bermuda. The series of corporate scandals that began with Enron and included Worldcom's filing for Chapter 11 bankruptcy protection, after it became evident that the company had falsified its profits, made it even clearer.

22. The growth of peer-to-peer (P2P) networks and file sharing have tended to reinforce this view, especially as the bigger, public P2P networks have found themselves under attack from copyright holders. Everywhere, small groups use P2P techniques to share material among themselves and trusted friends.

23. Wendy M. Grossman, *net.wars* (New York: New York University Press, 1998).

24. In his 2001 book, *The Future of Ideas*, Lawrence Lessig tackles just this issue, arguing that changes to the Internet's infrastructure to guarantee oligopolistic corporate control are in fact under way, and noting that under some of the laws proposed during 2001–2, peer-to-peer networking and Usenet could be eliminated as potential checks and balances. Lawrence Lessig, *The Future of Ideas: The Fate of the Commons in a Connected World* (New York: Random House, 2001).

25. McChesney, *Telecommunications, Mass Media, and Democracy*, 15.

PETER LYMAN

11 Information Superhighways, Virtual Communities, and Digital Libraries

Information Society Metaphors as Political Rhetoric

INFORMATION POLICY discussions are often conducted in the language of futuristic technical codes, whether that of lawyers debating the shape of new intellectual property regimes to govern digital information or that of computer scientists designing the information architectures through which digital communications will flow. Yet this technical discourse about the shape of the information society is framed in turn by visions of the future that use metaphors taken from the past—information superhighways, virtual communities, and digital libraries. Just as the automobile was first called a horseless carriage, we are now in a transitional phase in which we interpret the future of the Internet by using the language of the past—highways, communities, and libraries.

Superhighways and *libraries* were among the most successful twentieth-century public-sector innovations. Thus when used as metaphors they help us think about how digital technologies should perform similar functions, namely transportation and information management. The term *community* was used by Max Weber to contrast the *Gemeinschaft* of feudal villages with the impersonality of modern institutions, and, in this tradition, is still an important critical concept because of the feeling that the growth of markets and technology has diminished the quality of social life. The point, however, is not to criticize the use of metaphor in political discourse—indeed, poetic thinking is among our most important political resources—but to suggest that the subject might deserve better poetry. This project, then, is to explore information society metaphors, to see how well they function as heuristics for thinking about the relationship between technology and social policy. What do they illuminate, and what do they conceal?

Setting aside the contested question about whether the information society is something new or not,[1] metaphors about it are essentially political because the techniques of law and computer science are reshaping our economic and social institutions. New intellectual property regimes determine how information will be created and consumed, thereby redefining the boundaries between the public domain and private property.[2] Terms like the *knowledge economy* suggest that the laws governing information and knowledge will shape the distribution of wealth and power. If so, all of the traditional questions about economic and social justice surrounding industrial capital will now apply to control of information and knowledge. How should property and wealth—information and knowledge—be distributed? What are the characteristics of economic power in the form of intellectual capital? How should the public interest in access to information for the purposes of education and political participation be balanced with the economic progress that may derive from treating information as private property? Each of the information society metaphors tacitly answers these questions, but each also conceals discussion of them as what they are, questions of justice.

Similarly, the techniques of computer science are legislating the context and form of social relations at work, in the polity, and of everyday life in an information society. Computers not only process symbols, they instantiate social relations in the material form of hardware and software. For this reason Bruno Latour describes computer hardware as "society made durable," and Steve Woolgar describes computer design as "programming the user."[3] Each phrase alerts us to the way that technology has a political dimension in legislating behavior. "Because information is an integral part of all human activity," says Manuel Castells, "all processes of our individual and collective existence are directly shaped (although certainly not determined by) the new technological medium."[4] The engineering of social relationships through computer technology therefore raises a second kind of question about justice, one concerning the quality of everyday life in a world in which social relations are computer-mediated. What is the impact of computer-mediated work on the family, on political participation, and on the presence or absence of social capital to support public life? Answers to these questions are implicit in information society metaphors.

To revise the question in the light of these premises, then, what do the information superhighway, virtual community, and digital library metaphors teach us about the principles of justice governing an information society, and what do they fail to teach us?

The Information Superhighway: A Metaphor about Transportation

Microsoft advertisements invoked the information superhighway metaphor when they asked, "Where do you want to go today?" The information superhighway is a powerful idea, for it frames computer networks as revolutionary new means of *transportation*. As social theory reminds us, transportation technologies control the scope of control of organizations, including the state, markets, and corporations. Thus the global scope of the information superhighway may become a world historic innovation in economic and political organization.

The metaphor suggests a parallel between the Internet and the Interstate highway system, providing a model for the proper relation between the state and the economy. The Interstate highway system was a public works program to build an infrastructure to carry interstate commerce, promoting national wealth and security. By extension, the information superhighway metaphor tacitly defines the relationship between government and private industry for the Internet economy. The government's most important role, the metaphor suggests, is to build infrastructure (superhighways, Internets) as a public good to promote economic growth. Moreover, if the Internet is defined as a transportation technology, it follows that information, the commodity that is being transported at light speed around the globe, should be treated as a new kind of property, deserving to be protected by the same kind of laws as other kinds of economic commodities.

The idea of an information superhighway was the symbol of the Clinton administration's National Information Infrastructure (NII), replacing the National Research and Education Network (NREN) policy. Discussions of research and education tend to be framed by the digital library metaphor, because they concern the creation and use of information, but discussions of markets use the information highway metaphor. NREN, as an education and research initiative, was located in the Department of Education, but the NII, as a policy to build and regulate a transportation system, was located in the Department of Commerce, which has the responsibility for regulating interstate commerce. Here metaphor may be seen to be directing politics.

If we accept the frame of the information superhighway metaphor, it follows that the government's role in the information economy is to build network infrastructures—especially tax incentives, laws, regulatory rules, and treaties—but to leave invention and innovation to the private sector. In 1998 the Digital Millennium Copyright Act (DMCA) extended federal copyright law to protect digital information, but without the fair use provisions that allow education special rights to use printed information. Now a second stage is being enacted, the revision of section 2B of the Uniform Commercial Code (UCC), a national model for state laws governing commercial transactions. UCC 2B would allow digital information to be regulated under contract law like any other commodity, without the First Amendment and fair use complications of copyright. Here the power of language to answer the question of jurisdiction is illustrated. Transportation metaphors treat information as a commodity, governed by contract law; virtual communities treat information as a form of speech, protected by the First Amendment; and digital libraries would treat information like print, governed by copyright law.

The DMCA. The DMCA extended copyright concepts to include digital signals, including three dimensions that reveal the use and limits of the transportation metaphor.

First, the concept of the right to copy, the copyright concept so useful in regulating print, has been extended to include the transmission of signals. This created a "transmission right," which defined digital transmissions as a form of copying that must be legitimated by permission or payment. This is, of course, a fiction—transmissions do not copy, they transport—but it is a highly useful fiction, one of many that make social life possible. The argument could have been made using the transportation metaphor, but the language of copyright creates an appearance of continuity in the law, suggesting that this change is evolutionary (although it is not).

But digital signals are not like printed copies. Copyright regulation takes advantage of the specific characteristics of print technology: printing presses make copies of physical commodities, which are then distributed. These distinctions are not easily applied to digital networks, where there are no physical commodities, and copying and distribution are indistinguishable. Nor does the economics of digital copyright make sense. Commodities are scarce because my consumption of them deprives you of their use; ownership of them is easily protected because they are physical things; and they are transparent in that the buyers know about their utility before purchase. Economists have names for each of these characteristics of commodities: rivalry, excludability, and transparency.[5] None is necessarily a characteristic of information.

Therefore, and second, in order to make signals *behave* like commodities, the DMCA encourages the use of techniques such as encryption to encase information into commodity-like forms, and it prohibits the development or use of technologies to break through these technical protections. This is an important change in the nature of copyright, reflecting the problems posed by the ease of copying and transmission on digital networks. Copyright is ultimately an ex post facto protection, in that it is always possible to make and distribute copies, at least until a legal complaint is filed. This flexibility allows for fair use, the permitted use of copying for educational purposes, whereas encryption prevents use absolutely.

And third, the NII White Paper proposed a program of moral education—"Just say no to copying!"—to instill a reverence for intellectual property as a fundamental part of literacy at the earliest stages of education. Here the DMCA goes beyond the transportation metaphor to recognize that in some respects information is also part of communication and culture. While information may have economic value, it is also inherently a medium of cultural discourse and behavior that cannot be entirely regulated by laws, and hence must be protected by cultural means.

These three strategies were intended to provide a legal infrastructure for the development of a digital economy, within a classic liberal market strategy. However, advantages of claiming that the DMCA was simply an evolution of copyright law were soon outweighed by the costs, for copyright makes explicit allowances for the public good that the entertainment and publishing lobby could not tolerate. The information superhighway metaphor came to the rescue, in the form of UCC 2B.

The Contract Option. While copyright law protects the *expression* of ideas as private property, it also sometimes treats them as a public good. The First Sale Doctrine allows libraries to circulate books and journals and fair use allows for limited copying for educational purposes as long as markets are not harmed. And provisions related to the First Amendment allow copying of brief sections in order to conduct debates about the value of the ideas contained within. The contract regime in the revision to UCC 2B contains a revolutionary model for the management of information, namely licensing, or rent. Information itself is never to be sold, rather its use is rented, and the license defines the terms and conditions of use. The contract need not contain special consideration for public goods like education, although that could be negotiated for a price. Since commercial codes are the business of the states, the UCC 2B concepts are being implemented by state legislatures, while copyright policy will continue to be the federal framework for information management. What is interesting is that copyright and contract are not entirely compatible strategies for treating information as a commodity, suggesting friction may develop between state and federal jurisdictions.

As we shall see, the virtual community and digital library metaphors raise fundamental questions about the information superhighway, but even within its frame very important questions of justice arise, including three of particular interest.

Equality. Universal service has been the principle of justice underlying information policy since the 1934 Telecommunications Act, which subsidized access to local telephone service as a public good. By extension, the information superhighway metaphor asks the government to ensure that everyone has *access* to the Internet through special subsidies for educational institutions like schools and libraries, but access to information property on the network is to be a market exchange between buyer and seller.[6] Although universal access may subsidize access, information commodities are sold on a fee-for-service basis. Ultimately, then, information commodities will be distributed on the basis of wealth, creating a new kind of inequality that may be particularly pernicious in a society in which information itself may be a source of wealth. The public library was the political response to this problem in an industrial society. But the information superhighway metaphor is silent about libraries, suspicious of fair use, which the NII White Paper describes as an unfair subsidy paid for by a tax on publishers, and of the first sale doctrine, for sale of information is to be replaced by information rents.

Privacy. Unlike other forms of reading, the use of networked information is always, in principle, under surveillance. As a consequence, information about personal use of information is perhaps the first genuinely new kind of commodity in the digital marketplace. In response, the European Union (EU) has issued a Privacy Directive defining personal digital information as the inalienable property of the individual. American policy, in contrast, relies upon industry self-regulation, and accuses the EU of restraint of trade. Thus the information highway metaphor has constructed the issue of information privacy as a trade dispute with Europe, rather than a political issue about the commercialization of private information or privacy.[7]

Economic growth. The information superhighway metaphor protects the property rights of the corporations that dominated industrial society, but it is not clear that it serves the public interest in innovation and economic growth. Is digital information really a commodity that resembles print or manufactured goods? Manuel Castells describes information as a kind of raw material that is continuously refined by technology, each cycle of use adding value, and suggests that the idea of "information flows" might replace the idea of information commodities.[8] If Castells is right, the fluid nature of information in cyberspace is its essence, and if so, intellectual property protections (such as encryption) may well create economic disadvantage by constricting information flows.

In sum, the information superhighway metaphor is useful in treating the transportation of commodities as a policy framework, but taken alone, it focuses attention narrowly on market development. As a policy for digital markets it offers universal service as a theory of justice, but does not clarify the classic questions of economic inequality. And, by focusing solely on markets, it does not address issues of public good. As Newton Minow has asked, what is the Internet equivalent of the part of the radio telecommunications spectrum that is reserved for public interest broadcasting?

The Virtual Community: A Metaphor about Communication

Technology predictions are rarely accurate, thus in retrospect it is not surprising that the vision of the Internet as an information superhighway missed the most important network innovation, the World Wide Web. Yet it was inevitable that the emergence of the Web could not be predicted by NII's industrial policy because, in Brian Kahin's words, it implies "a paradigm shift from circuits to tiny packets of information as the organizing unit of telecommunications."[9] The NII was based on an industrial model of a distribution technology for mass-produced products, whereas the Web is a participatory technology organized around the collective production of knowledge. In other words, the information revolution is about *communication*, not an infrastructure for transportation.

The virtual community metaphor describes the new modes of communication and organization emerging on the Internet. The term *virtual community* refers to an unanticipated social cohesion that occurs on the Internet, even among people who have never met face to face, a cohesion based on exchanging gifts of information as a medium for social collaboration. In this sense the word *community* is apt, even when applied to technology-mediated communication, for a sense of community is often based on gift exchange.

This idea of a network-mediated community was first used to describe the many ways the Net served as a medium for the exchange of gifts of information—the chat groups, lists, electronic mail, and later, Web pages—that unexpectedly began to build a sense of intimacy and belonging.[10] Electronic communications are in some ways spontaneous and intimate, like speech. Because the Net is largely a written medium, the conversation of virtual communities creates archives of written information, giving groups a sense of history and identity. In sum, the virtual community metaphor is a way of envisioning a new kind of public space, using a nonmarket theory of justice based upon cooperative gift exchange.

The idea of a *virtual* community is enticing, but perplexing, in a world in which technology is often associated with increasing routinization and a sense of loss of social capital.[11] Electronic communication seems to create a risk-free environment that encourages spontaneous conversation, particularly when conducted anonymously.[12] Thus the Web might well be described as a gift exchange economy, one within which millions of authors have collaboratively created the largest text ever written for the sake of developing a sense of community.[13] From this beginning, distinctive new kinds of virtual social groups are emerging, strongest when face-to-face social relationships are complemented by virtual extensions, but possible even without them.[14] Indeed, some of the most important kinds of communities can exist only virtually because their members are socially isolated, such as disabled senior citizens, gay and lesbian teenagers, people with extremely rare diseases, peoples in diaspora, and social movements whose members are geographically dispersed, such as Greenpeace.[15]

Thus the idea of virtual community opposes the transportation metaphor's construction of information as a market commodity with an understanding of information exchange as a collaborative activity. This critique is important, for it reveals the ambiguity at the heart of any concept of intellectual property—ideas themselves cannot be property, they are an activity of human intelligence, not manufactured things. Copyright law is clear about this, treating the *expression* of ideas as property, "expression" referring to the specific economic value that is added to an idea by a particular formulation or presentation of an idea. "Intellectual property" is a useful, perhaps an essential fiction, like the fictions that land, labor, and money are commodities.[16] But the great power of the virtual community metaphor is to point out that information often originates in gift cultures, such as educational and research communities. Perhaps it might even be argued that markets are ultimately dependent upon communities that treat information as gifts, such as libraries, families, and research teams. If so, perhaps there is a public interest in nurturing intellectual communities.

But beyond exploring new modes of communication, the idea of virtual community contains an argument that cooperative institutions can be built in cyberspace that are alternatives to the market vision of the information superhighway. Manuel Castells describes the "network enterprise" as a malleable organization that manages global information flows to produce wealth, and Walter Powell writes about network organizations as a new third dimension of organization, one that is neither market nor hierarchy.[17] Bernard Lietaer, a Belgian banker, in a planning paper for the European Community argues that money can no longer be treated as a commodity; it is now a global information flow beyond the fiscal control of national banks. Therefore, Lietaer argues that we must study the new kinds of barter and gift exchange economies to discover the beginning of entirely new modes of nonmarket exchange organized without money.[18]

Thus the idea of virtual community has an empirical basis in the beginnings of new kinds of social relations based upon gift exchange in cyberspace, but like every information metaphor, its rhetorical power is derived from a theory of justice. A gift is given to establish or renew a social relationship, not primarily for economic advantage, although there may be secondary economic advantage to membership in social networks. Even today, a sense of community is marked by gift giving—within the family, among friends, in the academic community, and as a form of social capital in civil society. Nor does the concept of the gift exclude self-interest, for in giving away intellectual property on the Web, one expects to receive information of equal or greater value in exchange, or perhaps social status in the community.[19]

There are two important instances of the Internet as a gift economy with the potential to sustain cooperative social life, each with important consequences for the idea of intellectual property. First, some argue that authorship in cyberspace is communal, not individual, changing the foundation of the natural rights theory of intellectual property. And second, there are significant experiments, such as Linux, that test the proposition that software can be created by networked organizations and the intellectual property produced might be without copyright or contract protection.

The Future of the Author. There is a specific finding about virtual community that may challenge the foundation of intellectual property in the natural right theory, the idea that an author in creating an original expression of an idea creates an exclusive property right. It is startling to discover that in cyberspace the idea of the author is evolving into the idea of a *community of practice*.[20] The idea of communities of practice, often professional groups whose solidarity comes from shared work in research and learning rather than a shared sense of place, has become the most important analytic tool in analyzing knowledge management in the corporation, replacing the idea of the individual genius or author. Wallace Powell describes a biotechnology paper that was published with 133 authors, from a number of corporations and countries.[21] If the idea of the author changes, everything else about intellectual property must change. Perhaps it is not so surprising that an idea made to justify seventeenth-century property law may not fit the information culture of the twenty-first century. In some respects, then, the idea of virtual community is an attempt to describe this new information culture, even while it is still in the early stages of formation.

Open Software as Gift Exchange. In a world in which the protection of commercial software has become the highest priority of intellectual property law, Linux stands as a counter-example, a Unix operating system for personal computers built by a virtual community of programmers. Linus Torvalds created Linux by organizing a division of programming tasks that was assigned to a vast number of volunteer programmers around the world, then placed in the public domain and peer-reviewed by hackers. Eric S. Raymond, one of these programmers, calls this the "bazaar style" of software building, in which code placed on the network is subject to peer review and revision by other programmers, in contrast to commercial software that is built "cathedral style" by hierarchical corporations.[22] Linux (and other software in the public domain) is protected by a form of copyright called GPL, the General Public License, sometimes called "open software" or "copyleft," which allows for free use by individuals but is intended to prevent economic enclosure by corporations. Linux is becoming the standard software among Third World nations that do not wish the information age to be subject to technical domination by Western corporations.

The great virtues of the virtual community metaphor, then, are two. First, it reminds us that ideas are not commodities, although they may usefully be treated as commodities in some contexts, because they are primarily the content of social and cultural communication. *Information* and *information content* are terms that signify the economic value of digital copyright in legal discourse, but these terms are empty of empirical content because we know so little about the social contexts within which networked information has value. In this sense the virtual community metaphor restores social context to the concept of information by focusing on the communities that create and consume information. And second, the virtual community metaphor suggests that the information superhighway metaphor has focused too narrowly upon the market, for the uses of a new technology for collaborative communication in the family, in education, in civil society, and in political life may be as, or more, important. But there are also problems with the virtual community metaphor, interesting problems.

First, what does the word *community* mean in this technological context? The rhetorical force of the virtual community metaphor is important in the political arena because it raises questions about the relationship between markets and society. Virtual communities have been romanticized in the press, but social science has not yet been able to describe and analyze these new social phenomena. In part this is because information technology is evolving so rapidly, in part because the social consequences of technological innovations develop slowly and in discontinuous stages.

Second, the problem with the gift economy on the Internet is the lack of structure and quality of the information in the public domain. The commodification of information is not entirely a bad thing; the great virtue of the information superhighway concept is that it creates incentives for investment in standards and quality.

It follows, third, that the idea of virtual community does not adequately understand the symbiosis between the market and communities, by ignoring the subsidies that make the Internet possible. The origin of scientific journals was in the exchange of letters among scientists in the seventeenth century, perhaps an early kind of community of practice; out of this developed the markets that support high-quality commercial scientific journals that support today's global scientific community.[23] Can this symbiosis between markets and communities be re-created in the digital realm, in the space between information superhighway and virtual community metaphors?

THE DIGITAL LIBRARY:
A METAPHOR ABOUT THE PUBLIC DOMAIN

The digital library metaphor suggests that the public library of the twentieth century should serve as a model for a new kind of public domain in cyberspace, one that could mediate between the needs of markets and communities. The information superhighway metaphor often goes too far, as in some UCC 2B discussions in which every information use in any social context ought to require a payment. The virtual community metaphor often goes too far, as in the claim that "information wants to be free." In industrial society the public library successfully managed the boundary between markets and communities. Libraries buy information in the marketplace and subsidize its free use by specific communities, within the limits defined by the fair use doctrine.

The digital library metaphor raises interesting problems of scale. How does the print library provide a useful model for digital collections with a global scope and potentially encompassing all digital information? Who is the user—is it the individual consumer of information, or some vision of a virtual community? And what does the user need—the freedom to search all information, or a high-quality selection of relevant information? As a consequence the digital library metaphor has two major variants, with computer scientists tending to focus upon the problem of information retrieval by individual users, and librarians emphasizing the relationship between well-ordered selected collections and user communities.

The computer science option might be called the cyberspace digital library. Cyberspace could be described as the name of a libertarian utopia, a place where individual choice is optimized by technology. The term *cyberspace* probably originated in William Gibson's science fiction novel *Neuromancer*, and is often used precisely because it does not imply a sense of place or limits, like the terms *outer space* or *mathematical space*. Cyberspace connotes that one is free of constraints in searching for information, reflecting the tacit libertarian politics of computer science, in which institutional constraints on individual research are overcome by technology. This is reflected in the research and development practices of computer science, in which there is virtually no investigation of the social contexts of technology or the needs and cultures of users.

The library metaphor, in contrast, addresses the need for *information management*, the selection and organization of information for practical use— one might say, to enable information to be turned into knowledge by a given community or organization. In this sense, a library is an *authoritative* collection of information, reflecting the information needs and use of its users, documenting its history and supporting its future evolution.

But the need to re-create this kind of information management in cyberspace is opposed by the libertarian values instantiated in the design of information technology. The digital library, as defined by computer scientists, is to include all information in a searchable form—this is the vision behind search engine design—rather than a select or authoritative sample, for any quality filter limits the options of the searcher. In the techno-libertarian view, both publishers and libraries exercise illegitimate authority in the name of quality control, because they impose limits upon the possibility of the individual finding, using, and reusing information. If that authority were ever justified, in the techno-libertarian view, it was because of the physical constraints of place and budget, but there are no limits to the size or scope of a digital library.

Because they are *places*, library collections reflect the specific educational needs of the community that uses them. And, in turn, the idea of a public domain is founded in the kind of sense of place that institutions like the library create. Mary Ryan describes the growth of the public domain in American cities at the turn of the twentieth century as the creation of public places that were safe for immigrants from farms and boats.[24] These places included libraries, museums, public parks and voluntary associations—such as the YMCA and YWCA, Elks or Rotary—hospitals, and so forth. But throughout the twentieth century, commercial spaces have replaced such public places, starting with the department store and evolving into the mall. With the creation of commercial spaces that provide substitute forms of sociability, political subsidies supporting public places are increasingly seen as illegitimate.

And now the Internet seems to suggest the possibility of a new kind of public place. It is striking that in 2002 a U.S. District Court found the Children's Internet Protection Act (CIPA) to be unconstitutional on these grounds. CIPA required libraries receiving federal funds to use filters on networked computers to prohibit access to pornography, and was unconstitutional *because the Internet is a public forum,* hence the free speech requirement of the First Amendment was paramount:[25] "Regulation of speech in streets, sidewalks, and parks is subject to the highest scrutiny not simply by virtue of history and tradition, but also because the speech-facilitating character of sidewalks and parks makes them distinctly deserving of First Amendment protection. Many of these same speech-promoting features of the traditional public form appear in public libraries' provision of Internet access." The emergence of virtual communities suggests that it is possible to design a new sense of place—a kind of public domain like a library—within cyberspace. Implicit in the quote above, perhaps, is an analogy between the printing press and the Internet, not as technologies but as media for building political communities.

While the information highway is designed for the use of consumers, and the virtual community is designed for participation in communities, the digital library is emerging first as an information management technology for organizations. It is the corporation that has first felt the centrifugal force of information technology, and is the first to turn to information management to create a sense of virtual organization. Japanese information management theory offers the concept of *Ba,* the equivalent of our term "a sense of place," to extend the sense of place derived from geography and architecture to include cyberspace.[26] *Ba* might reside in a physical place (such as a library), or in a virtual place (such as a computer network), or in a cultural or intellectual place (such as that given by shared ideals or cultures), or, most likely, in some combination of all of these kinds of places. In Japanese management theory the presence of such a sense of place is the precondition for the creative life of any social group, hence its design is the ultimate creative act.

As a theory of justice, the digital library metaphor is focused upon the social functions of the library as a public information resource capable of sustaining a shared sense of public life in a world increasingly divided between the private world of the family and the market.[27] Digital libraries must protect copyright, but at times intellectual property must be treated as a public good to provide for equality of opportunity in a society in which access to information and education will be a fundamental right. Fair use gave education a special status in copyright law, and the Constitution suggests that innovation, or in the language of the eighteenth century, "progress in the sciences and useful arts," is also a public good. That said, it is not entirely clear that libraries will be allowed to perform their boundary maintenance function in an information age. Digital libraries have not inherited the legal status given to print libraries, and in fact have become an occasion for the revaluation of rights such as fair use, as the UCC 2B movement illustrates. Thus the digital library metaphor has encountered some important problems that remain unsolved.

Who Pays? One of the fundamental purposes of the digital library metaphor is to defend the legitimacy of subsidized public goods. The UCC 2B discussions have focused upon fee-for-service information access, reflecting the current emphasis upon market mechanisms rather than public subsidies. To this end micro-payment technologies have been developed to charge for Internet information on the telephone bill model, but thus far the public is resisting the pay-to-read concept. At the other end of the spectrum, the information superhighway concept engenders hostility toward the idea of public subsidies for information.

Is Information Manageable? Libraries not only collect and preserve information, they organize it. But the variety and volume of information goes far beyond the ability of current technology to control. More and more information is being produced, far beyond the financial capacity of a library to collect. More information was produced between 1999 and 2002 than has been created in all previous human history, far beyond the financial capacity of a library to collect.[28] And if it is collected, can it be managed? A recent article in *Science* magazine pointed out that no two commercial search engines present the same findings when given the same instructions.[29]

The value of the digital library metaphor is the reminder that market economies and gift exchange economies are symbiotic, not opposites, but pragmatic laws are the precondition for institutions like libraries that can manage the boundary between private property and public goods. Granted, this may be difficult when regulating the flow of information on a global information network, in which no one nation has sufficient jurisdiction to enforce its laws. This has thrown intellectual property discussions into treaty negotiations, the least democratic of all the policy-making processes under the U.S. Constitution.

CONCLUSION

Just as the automobile was first called a "horseless carriage," we are now in a transitional phase in which we interpret the future of the Net using the language of the past. Information superhighways, virtual communities, and digital libraries are metaphors within which an indirect dialogue about questions of economic and social justice in an information society is occurring. Each has strengths and weaknesses as a metaphor, but fundamentally, discussions of economic and social justice should not be indirect. How can we find a language to talk about the Internet as an innovation?

The Italian philosopher Giambattista Vico once argued that history changes when "barbarian poets" create new languages and paradigms that have the power to generate new cultures and institutions. Inevitably, one generation's poetry becomes the next generation's cliché as old metaphors are used to conceal partisan interests, and thus begins the need to find new barbarian poets. Barbarian poets, by definition, come from outside authoritative institutions; thus, perhaps it would be useful to listen to the language of those working in cyberspace to find the new images that can take us farther than the noble but tired industrial-society metaphors that we now use. Where will the new poetry be found?

It is curious that we have evolved a popular language for digital technology—the *Net*, the *Web*, and the *computer*—but not for the new social arrangements that are occurring among those who use these technical things. We have only the awkward term *user*, a word that places technique at the center, and even contains a hint of dependence upon or subordination to technology. The special power of the virtual community metaphor is that, however vague, it leads us back to the way the Net is changing work, communication, and social relationships. Sociologist Karen A. Cerulo argues that information technologies extend the process of innovation begun by industrial technologies, observing that, "Like the railroad and the telegraph, the new technologies have redefined space, place and time. In doing so, technology has provided us with new sites of empirical experience and it has re-configured the complex ties that bind the social and cognitive worlds."[30] We must turn to these new sites of empirical experience to find our poets, and to discover what an information society might be.

NOTES

Note: If Web sites cited in this essay are no longer accessible, an archival copy may be found in the Internet Archive at The Wayback Machine, <www.archive.org>.

1. Frank Webster, in *Theories of the Information Society* (New York: Routledge, 1995), argues that the idea of an information society is already implicit in most theories of industrial capitalism. See also James R. Beniger, *The Control Revolution: Technological and Economic Origins of the Information Society* (Cambridge, Mass.: Harvard University Press, 1986). Manuel Castells, *The Rise of the Network Society* (Oxford: Blackwell, 1996) argues the case that digital networks are creating new social forms.

2. Yochai Benkler, "Intellectual Property and the Organization of Information Production" (October 1999) at <http://www.law.nyu/benklery/IP&Organization. pdf>. Published in the *International Review of Law and Economics* 22 (2002).

3. Steve Woolgar, "Configuring the User: The Case of Usability Trials," in *A Sociology of Monsters: Essays on Power, Technology and Domination* (New York: Routledge, 1991). In the same volume, see also Bruno Latour, "Technology is Society Made Durable," 103–31.

4. Castells, *The Rise of the Network Society*, 61. See also Manuel Castells, *The Power of Identity*, (Oxford: Blackwell, 1997), 5–67.

5. J. Bradford DeLong and A. Michael Froomkin, "Speculative Microeconomics for Tomorrow's Economy" at <http://www.j-bradford-delong.net/movable_type/ 2003_archives/000164.html>. Accessed on November 19, 2003.

6. See <http://www.fcc.gov/ccb/universal_service/welcome.html> for a review of NII policy on universal access, and <http://tap.epn.org/cme/ushmpg. html> for a report on the political struggles about funding universal access through the e-rate, particularly "Deepening the Digital Divide: The War on Universal Service."

7. See Peter P. Swire and Robert E. Litan, *None of Your Business: World Data Flows, Electronic Commerce and the European Privacy Directive* (Washington, D.C.: Brookings Institution Press, 1998).

8. Castells, *The Rise of Network Society*, 61–62.

9. Brian Kahin, "Beyond the National Information Infrastructure Initiative: Technology-Informed Policy and Policy-Enabling Technology," in *Investing in Innovation*, ed. Lewis M. Branscomb and James Keller (Cambridge, Mass.: MIT Press, 1998).

10. See Howard Rheingold, *The Virtual Community: Homesteading on the Electronic Frontier* (New York: HarperCollins, 1994).

11. See Robert Putnam, "The Strange Disappearance of Civic America," *The American Prospect* 24 (Winter 1996): 34–48. See also Anita Blanchard and Tom Horan, "Virtual Communities and Social Capital," *Social Science Computer Review* 16, no. 3 (Fall 1998): 293–307.

12. See Sherry Turkle, *Life on the Screen: Identity in the Age of the Internet* (New York: Simon & Schuster, 1997).

13. See Peter Lyman and Brewster Kahle, "Archiving Digital Cultural Artifacts," *D-lib* (July–August 1998) <http://www.dlib.org/dlib/july98/07lyman.html/>. Accessed November 19, 2003.

14. See Julian Dibble, "A Rape in Cyberspace: How an Evil Clown, a Haitian Trickster Spirit, Two Wizards, and a Cast of Dozens Turned a Database into a Society," in *Internet Dreams: Archetypes, Myths and Metaphors*, ed. Mark Stefik (Cambridge, Mass.: MIT Press, 1996), 293–316.

15. On diaspora, see Daniel Miller and Don Slater, *The Internet: An Ethnographic Approach* (New York: New York University Press, 2000). On the elderly, see Mary S. Furlong, "An Electronic Community for Older Adults: The SeniorNet Network," *Journal of Communication* 39 (1989): 145–53. On community networks, see Mary E. Virnoche and Gary T. Marx, " 'Only Connect'—E.M. Forster in an Age of Electronic Communication: Computer-Mediated Association and Community Networks," *Sociological Inquiry* 67, no. 1 (1997): 85–100.

16. Karl Polanyi, *The Great Transformation* (Boston: Beacon Press 1957).

17. Walter W. Powell, "Neither Market nor Hierarchy: Network Forms of Organization," *Research in Organizational Behavior* 12 (1990): 295–336.

18. Bernard Lietaer, *The Social Impact of Electronic Money: A Challenge to the European Union?* A Report to the European Commission's Forward Studies Unit (1998). See also John Hagel III and Arthur G. Armstrong, *NetGain: Expanding Markets Through Virtual Communities* (Boston: Harvard Business School Press, 1997).

19. Barry Wellman and Milena Gulia, "Net Surfers Don't Ride Alone: Virtual Community as Community," in *Networks in the Global Village*, ed. Barry Wellman (Boulder, Colo.: Westview Press, 1999), 331–67.

20. Jean Lave and Etienne Wenger, *Situated Learning: Legitimate Peripheral Participation* (Cambridge: Cambridge University Press, 1991), 94–99. See also Bernardo A. Huberman and Tad Hogg, "Communities of Practice: Performance and Evolution," *Computational and Mathematical Organization Theory* 73 (1995): 3–74.

21. Walter W. Powell, "Learning from Collaboration: Knowledge and Networks in the Biotechnology and Pharmaceutical Industries," *California Management Review* 40, no. 3 (1998): 228–40; see also Mario Biagioli, "The Instability of Authorship: Credit and Responsibility in Contemporary Biomedicine," *FASEB Journal* 12 (1998): 3–4.

22. Eric S. Raymond, "The Cathedral and the Bazaar," published on the Web at <http://www.catb.org/~esr/writings/cathedral-bazaar/cathedral-bazaar/>. Accessed November 19, 2003.

23. John Seeley Brown and Paul Duguid, *The Social Life of Information* (Boston: Harvard Business School Press, 2000).

24. Mary Ryan, *Civic Wars: Democracy and Public Life in the American City During the Nineteenth Century* (Berkeley: University of California Press, 1997).

25. See *American Library Association v. U.S., Civil Actions* 2001–1303 and 2001–1322. Available at <http://www.paed.uscourts.gov>. Accessed January 2004. Note that the U.S. Supreme Court reversed this opinion on June 23, 2003. See also Lawrence Lessig, *Code: and Other Laws of Cyberspace* (New York: Basic Books, 1999).

26. Ikujiro Nonaka and Noboru Konno, "The Concept of 'Ba': Building a Foundation for Knowledge Creation," *California Management Review* 40, no. 3 (Spring 1998): 40–54.

27. See Christine L. Borgman, Social Aspects of Digital Libraries, Final Report to the National Science Foundation, November 1996, <http://www.gslis.ucla.edu/research/dl/index.html>. Accessed November 19, 2003; and Peter Lyman, "Designing Libraries to Be Learning Communities: Towards an Ecology of Places for Learning," in *Information Landscapes for a Learning Society: Networking and the Future of Libraries* (London: Library Association Publishing 1999), 75–87.

28. Peter Lyman and Hal Varian, "How Much Information 2003?" at <http://www.sims.berkeley.edu/how-much-info-2003>. Accessed November 19, 2003.

29. Steve Lawrence and C. Lee Giles, "Searching the World Wide Web," *Science* 280 (April 3, 1998): 98–100.

30. Karen A. Cerulo, "Reframing Sociological Concepts for a Brave New (Virtual?) World," *Sociological Inquiry* 67 (1997): 48–58.

Douglas Thomas

12 Rethinking the Cyberbody

Hackers, Viruses, and Cultural Anxiety

Technology, traditionally, has been a subject of great debate concerning our hopes, dreams, fears, and anxieties. In particular, the personal computer (PC) has had a remarkable effect on our culture. Perhaps no other invention has spread so quickly or produced such a staggering gap between haves and have-nots. As computer technology becomes ubiquitous, it outstrips our ability to understand it, and as a result we find ourselves in a state of anxiety not only about the PC, but in relation to technology more generally. One of the sites of this state of cultural anxiety is the figure of the hacker or virus writer, who occupies a precarious space between the physical and virtual worlds and is often an object for the displacement of fears about virtual space. Positioned as a bodiless figure able to roam the world of cyberspace with impunity and with great effect, the hacker/virus writer is seen as being capable of fantastic deeds precisely because he or she is free of the physical constraints of the real world. It is that sense of the body that merits careful exploration as both the site of broader cultural concern as well as the site of discourse about both hackers and computer viruses.

Anxiety about technology and the body preexists the computer (most recently in the discourse about television and addiction), but reaches its zenith with discussion of virtual reality and the literal disappearance of the body. This anxiety can be located in the movement from the physical to the virtual. The idea of technology as a threat to the body is a long-standing trope of technological dystopian thought, dating back at least as far as Mary Shelley's *Frankenstein*, and probably well before. The fear of the virtual as well had already been established in connection with television viewing for two decades. Television, like most forms of technically mediated communication, can be considered a virtual medium. In TV's early development, a great deal of anxiety was centered on the fear that the medium of television would either sap one's strength, addle one's brain, or decimate one's critical reasoning abilities, turning viewers into couch potatoes or producing a generation of juvenile delinquents. In short, the television was seen as capable of altering or disabling the physical through participation in the virtual. The introduction of the video game, and later the PC, met similar criticisms. The virtual came to represent, as a manifestation of anxiety about the technological, a threat to the body.

The transformation into virtual reality threatens the body at the most basic level by making the body disappear. Virtual worlds are worlds without physical presence and, accordingly, they are worlds without bodies. The idea of the virtual, then, produces a new kind of anxiety, one that is an outgrowth of early concerns about technology and the body. This new anxiety is marked by a concern about how the virtual world returns to affect the physical one. In the first case the virtual is marked by a disappearance of the body. The second case, the return to the physical, is marked by the fear produced by the virtual in the physical world. In other words, the threat that the virtual poses to the physical is akin to the threat a ghost or specter poses to the living. A virtual presence is a threat to the living precisely in terms of its incorporeal existence. The virtual haunts the physical world. It is, quite literally, a dead presence, a spirit.

Not surprisingly, in the underground of computer culture we find the most likely targets for such anxiety, the bodies to whom fear and expectation can be attached through images in popular culture, the news media, and the legal system. In what follows, I examine the manner in which cultural anxieties are played out in terms of two distinct elements of underground computer culture: hackers and viruses. Both anxieties are dealt with or contained through a system of regulation and what is being regulated or controlled is not the threat of the hacker or virus itself, but rather the state of anxiety that surrounds those objects as sites of displacement.

Hackers, Addiction, and Technology: Rethinking the Cyberbody

One of the most readily identifiable figures in the discourse of technology is the hacker. Seen as an expert with computers or a hi-tech wizard, the hacker is regarded as being capable of extraordinary feats with computers and computer networks. Hackers are thought to be a primary threat to the computers and networks that they inhabit because in a virtual form, hackers are nearly impossible to regulate.

Regulation occurs, through law enforcement and the courts, by creating a corporeal subject who can be monitored. As a result, criminality is defined solely in terms of identity and the ability or inability to match that identity to a corporeal presence. Like ghosts that haunt and terrorize the living, hackers who maintain a virtual existence remain beyond the grasp of the law and in so doing are able to elude the gaze of state surveillance. The criminalization of virtual identity has become the goal of law enforcement and is now the primary locus of discussion about the threat of hackers and cyberspace to society. As law enforcement describes it, the loss of the body to virtual identity not only serves to make the body of the hacker disappear, but it also makes the hacker legally *unaccountable,* providing an identity through which the hacker can inflict violence on bodies (or even on the social body as with the threat of espionage) with impunity.

The body is the locus of criminality and deviance, as well as punishment, justice, and correction. It is identifiable, definable, and confinable. For the hacker, however, the body is also the site of access or the point of connection between the two worlds. Taking up the mantle of cyberpunk science fiction, hacking envisions a world without bodies, in which hackers exist, first and foremost, as virtual beings. Such an incorporeal nature is generally thought of as a technical invention, perhaps best described by William Gibson in his envisioning of cyberspace in his 1984 novel, *Neuromancer.*[1] In *Neuromancer,* Gibson tells the story of Case, a computer cowboy, who, after stealing from his employer, was neurologically damaged so that his body could no longer interface with the computer matrix as form of punishment or payback. Describing the protagonist's now defunct relationship to the technological, Gibson writes: "For Case, who'd lived for the bodiless exultation of cyberspace, it was the Fall. In the bars he'd frequented as a cowboy hotshot, the elite stance involved a certain relaxed contempt for the flesh. The body was meat. Case fell into a prison of his own flesh."[2] The primary vision of hacking, then, is founded in the hacker's reliance upon the technological. The infliction of such punishment is not confined, however, to the world of the future. In the everyday world of hacking and "computer crime," the elimination of the technological is the greatest threat the hacker faces, and, not unlike Case's employers, judges are fond of proscribing penalties for hackers that include forbidding them to access technology such as telephones, computers, or modems.[3] The modern judicial system attempts to produce legally the equivalent of Case's neurological damage.

The 1988 arrest, trial, and conviction of hacker Kevin Mitnick for breaking into the phone company's COSMOS system (the computer system that controls phone service), provides a striking parallel to Gibson's character Case. During the trial, the judge sharply restricted his telephone access, allowing Mitnick to only call those numbers that had been approved by the court.[4] After being found guilty (and serving five years' prison time), Mitnick was diagnosed by the courts as "compulsive." When he was released, Mitnick was prohibited from touching computers. A short time after, when it was determined that he could control his behavior, Mitnick was allowed to use computers again, and even look for employment in computer-related fields, but was still not allowed to use a modem.[5] Even more striking are the conditions of probation for Kevin Poulsen, another Los Angeles hacker, convicted of fraud for using his computer to fix radio call-in contests (among other things). He was given the following "special conditions" of supervision for probation:

> You shall not obtain or possess any driver's license, social security number, birth certificate, passport or any other form of identification without the prior approval of the probation officer and further, you shall not use for any purpose or in any manner, any name other than your legal true name; you shall not obtain or possess any computer or computer related equipment or programs without the permission and approval of the probation officer; and you shall not seek or maintain employment that allows you access to computer equipment without prior approval of the probation officer.[6]

Poulsen writes, "It got even more interesting when I was released. When I reported to my P.O., he explained to me that, not only could I not use any computer, with or without a modem, but that I couldn't be in the same room as a computer. I had to look for a job with an employer that had no computer equipment on the premises. 'Oh, and by the way, don't forget that you have to pay $65,000.00 in restitution in the next three years.' "[7]

Characterizations of compulsive behavior were not only employed by the courts. The label of addiction was used by Mitnick's lawyers in an effort to get a reduced sentence. Upon Mitnick's arrest in 1988, his "lawyer convinced the judge that Mr. Mitnick's problem was similar to a drug or gambling addiction."[8] After his release, Mitnick was sentenced to six months in a halfway house, complete with a twelve-step program for drug and alcohol offenders.

The notion of addiction, particularly in Mitnick's case, is specifically located in terms of the body. As Katie Hafner and John Markoff describe him in their book *Cyberpunk*, Mitnick was "plump and bespeckled," "the kind of kid who would be picked last for the school team," "his pear-shaped body was so irregular that any pair of blue jeans would be an imperfect fit."[9] In almost all media accounts, his body is described as the *cause* of his addiction. Harriet Rossetto, his counselor from his halfway house in

Los Angeles, attributes his addiction to computers to the fact that "he is an overweight computer nerd, but when he is behind a keyboard he feels omnipotent."[10] Even Markoff, a staff writer for the *New York Times* who followed Mitnick's story for a number of years, characterized an almost involuntary relationship between technology and Mitnick's body. "During the treatment program," Markoff writes, "Mr. Mitnick was prohibited from touching a computer or modem. He began exercising regularly and lost more than 100 pounds."[11] Markoff and others seem to suggest that it is the physical connection to technology itself that perverts and deforms the body. Joshua Quittner, writing for *Time,* reports the connection in precisely the same way: "As a condition of his release from jail in 1990, he was ordered not to touch a computer or modem. By June of 1992 he was working for a private eye, doing surveillance and research, and had dropped 100 lbs."[12] The connection between Mitnick's not touching computers and modems and his weight loss is presented as mini-narrative in and of itself, a story that suggests both a causal connection between his lack of access to technology and his weight as well as the broader suggestion that technology is, itself, somehow harmful to the body. While the first connection is obvious on the face of things, the second is a bit more elusive.

Hacking, according to the judicial system, is akin to "substance abuse" (the actual term deployed by Mariana Pfaelzer, the sentencing judge for U.S. District Court in Mitnick's case). The judge's decision was aided by the arguments of Mitnick's attorney, who stated "that his client's computer behavior was something over which his client had little control, not unlike the compulsion to take drugs, drink alcohol or shoplift."[13]

What is interesting about this case is how it reveals the manner in which the law and the structures of punishment remain blind to the social dimensions of technology. In Mitnick's sentence, the computer is viewed as an object that is essentially negative in character. It is not a value-neutral tool, one that can be used beneficially or maliciously. It is seen not as a substance, but as a dangerous substance, likened to drugs and alcohol. The shift is subtle but important, and betrays an underlying anxiety and hostility toward technology. It is also, most likely, the reason why the plea was successful.

The equation of technology with drug addiction is a powerful one. It is also the means by which technology is attached to the body and out of which is constructed the activity of hacking not as a malicious or even intentional activity, but rather as an obsessive disorder resulting from physical contact with a particular object. Mitnick's "treatment" consists of not "touching" a computer or modem, suggesting that it is the physical contact with technology, rather than the actual usage of it, that produces the addiction. Again, the body, particularly its physicality, plays a crucial role in the construction of the hacker. Technology itself is written as a drug and the hacker is written as an addict. Yet, as Mike Godwin of the Electronic Frontier Foundation puts it, "The great ones are all obsessed, which is what it's about."[14]

In the discourse surrounding hacking and the body, the most interesting definitions of computer crime are to be found in the nomenclature used to describe hackers during actual investigations and "manhunts." The tracking of hackers is a discourse so thoroughly gendered, that it is literally impossible to separate the characterizations of the hunter and his prey from traditional masculine stereotypes. The two enact a drama of the hunter and the hunted—a contest of wills, where one will emerge victorious and one will be defeated. The hunter (often another computer expert working for law enforcement) tracks the hacker, we are led to believe, using only his wits, cunning, and instinct. It is an act that reduces each to their most primitive, masculine roles. Just as the hunter relies on his instincts to bring in his quarry, the hunted survives on his abilities to escape detection and foil the hunter's efforts. The discourse surrounding the hunt leads us to believe that the contest is decided, fundamentally, by who has the better instincts or who is the better man.

It is during these "hunts" that characterizations of the cyberbody take on heightened importance and emphasis. This way of describing hackers in terms of computer crime during these periods of pursuit deploys a well-embedded narrative that fosters clear perceptions of who the hacker is and what threat she or he poses. It is commonly framed in the basic "cops and robbers" vernacular, where the hacker is often described in criminal, but nonviolent terms. Those who pursue him are often characterized as "sleuths," "trackers," or "hunters." The hacker is a "cyberthief" or, for high drama, a "master cyberthief," and the pursuit invokes the language of the hunt ("tracking," "snaring," "tracing," or "retracing"). Often this narrative will feature hackers as "fugitives" who "elude" and repeatedly, they will be described (once apprehended) as being "caught in their own web." In some cases, hackers are even given honorific titles, such as "Prince of Hackers" or "Break In Artist."

What is the most compelling about this discourse is the manner in which the metaphors of the hunt are enacted. The hunt is not, as one might immediately suspect, a strategy of depersonalization—the hacker is not reduced to some animal form that is tracked, hunted, and captured or killed. In fact, the discourse of the hacker is less about the hunted and more about the hunter. As we read about the hunt, we uncover two dynamics. First, the drama of the hunt itself, which always seems to hold a particular narrative fascination, and second, the narrative of the hunter himself or herself, who, in order to catch his or her prey must learn to think like him or her. Part of our fascination is with the act of repetition, which we live out vicariously, through the hunt. We watch as the hunter learns to think like the hunted and it is through *that* process that information about the hacker's motives, intentions, and worldview is disclosed.

Accordingly, the hunt is always about thinking the thoughts of the other. If the hunter is to succeed, he or she must understand the hunted better than the hunted understands them. As a result, the hunt begins to exist in a world of its own, a world that possesses a gamelike quality. Markoff, after helping to get Mitnick arrested, explains his reaction to seeing him actually being sent to jail: "It felt odd to me. It was as if it had all been a game, and all of a sudden the game was over and everybody realized this is the real world."[15] The sense of "real worldness" can be traced to the moment when federal agents knocked on Kevin Mitnick's door and placed him under arrest. The hunt lost its gamelike quality the moment a body was made present.

In this sense, we must understand the hunt as a hunt for the body. In the case of Mitnick, everything that was needed to make the arrest and prosecute the case was already known, documented, and recorded, yet Mitnick's body had not yet been found. Given the manner in which Mitnick's body figures into the narrative of his relationship to technology, it shouldn't be surprising that his "Wanted" poster reads, under the heading "Miscellaneous Information"—"Subject suffers from a weight problem and may have experienced weight gain or weight loss."[16]

Hackers, however, are not the only denizens of the underground who are confronted by anxieties about the body. As networks have become increasingly infected and affected by computer viruses and worms, the language of technology has begun to deploy biological metaphors in an effort to combat computer viruses.

FROM TECHNOLOGY TO BIOLOGY: WORMS, VIRUSES, AND MEDICAL PERCEPTION

Five years, almost to the day, after Adleman and Cohen had defined computer viruses in November 1983, Robert Morris, a graduate student in computer science at Cornell and the son of Bob Morris, a well-known computer security expert for the NSA, would unleash what would be called the "Internet Worm," a program that clogged the Internet so severely that it was considered crippled for a period of days. Morris's program was the first instance of a massive, network-wide infection.

The program, released on the ARPANET, spread throughout the then budding university, corporate, and government research networks. As Peter Denning describes it, the program "expropriated the resources of each invaded computer to generate replicas of itself on other computers, but did no apparent damage. Within hours, it had spread to several thousand computers attached to the worldwide Research Internet."[17] As the program spread throughout the network, it would tie up computing resources and eventually cause machines to grind to a halt. Along the way the program would exploit known security holes and attempt to crack users' passwords. Denning notes, "computers infested with the worm were soon laboring under a huge load of programs" and "attempts to kill these programs were ineffective: new copies would appear from Internet connections as fast as old copies were deleted. Many systems had to be shut down and the security loopholes closed before they could be restarted on the network without reinfestation."[18] As to whether the rapid spread of the program was intentional, accidental, or the product of sloppy coding was the subject of much speculation. One thing was clear, however, Morris's worm program was unlike anything that the computer community had seen before. PC viruses attacked stand-alone computers and most likely were transferred by infected floppy disks or through shared software. One of the primary issues that concerned computer security experts was that Morris's program had been unleashed in a networked environment. This virus was built to travel through a network. The Morris worm was different because it did not rely on a user running a program. It moved on its own, replicating quickly and spreading not only through the computer system, but also to any computer connected to that system on the network. The program was similar to what two Xerox PARC researchers, John Shoch and Jon Hupp, had described in a 1982 article—the first computer worm, a program that moved across the computer network under its own power, in Shoch and Hupp's example, performing useful functions.[19]

After Morris's Internet "attack," the computer community had considerable debate about what to call the program, a "worm" or a "virus"? After a series of debates, the term *worm* won out. The debate hinged on how one defined the program. In terms of the code itself, the worm was significantly different from how viruses were programmed, making it a distinct type of program. In terms of the effects of the program, it looked much more similar to a computer virus than it did to any previously programmed worms. The analysis that centered on the program itself was more persuasive and, as a result, the worm nomenclature stuck.

This moment of definition marked an important point in the history of computer viruses, as it set the standard by which all viruses would be defined and ultimately discussed. Not surprisingly, the history of discourses about computer infection parallels the discourse of diseases in the eighteenth century identified by Michel Foucault.[20] As Foucault argues, the discourse of diseases took on a new form in the eighteenth century with the creation of a system of medical perception where doctors identified disease by watching the effects on the body and categorizing diseases accordingly. Like diseases, computer viruses have spawned a vocabulary that is constructed primarily around their effects (symptoms) rather than their design or nature. Spafford, for example, lists a number of programs that are "self-reproducing or malicious," but are generally considered as distinct from viruses. These include "back doors," "trapdoors," "logic bombs," "worms," "Trojan horses," "bacteria," "rabbits," and "liveware."[21] Such definitional machinations mirror precisely the evolution of disease that Foucault identified in the eighteenth century. Viruses have, however, an added difficulty: it is impossible to define a computer virus in such a way that it is distinct from all other types of computer programs.[22] The inability to separate viruses from other types of programs presents a problem similar to the science of pathology. Just as beneficial and harmful bacteria are both bacteria, computer viruses are programs much as any other. The only way to distinguish the helpful from the harmful is by their effects, and judging by effect assumes a "rational order" that exists outside of the program itself. In the case of biology that order is health, which is only able to be defined by an absence of disease.

Viruses as well, by the very inability to define or classify them independently, produce an entire structure or "rational order" from which they are systematically excluded, the idea of a "clean network." As a result, an entire discourse springs up out of the *inability* to define a computer virus. Computer viruses, like diseases, become defined by analogy. They are *like* other programs that are different from what is accepted as "useful" or "normal" in computer programming. Computer viruses are unlike "normal" programs because they are *like* other dangerous programs, which are also different from what is considered useful or proper. In Foucault's terms, the distance that separates one "dangerous" program from another "can be measured only by the *degree* of their *resemblance*," without reference to their histories or the logics that create and sustain them.[23] The computer virus cannot be distinguished from other types of programming by its very definition. Instead, it is differentiated from programming by being *like* several other types of programs that are also to be excluded from the essential nature of programming, primarily because of the effects they produce.

In this moment of separation of viruses from other types of programs, what appears to be revealed is two "natures" of the computer. On one side is the "rational order" of technology, maintained by a narrative of progress, linearity, and order. On the other side is that which is excluded from the rational order, that which is noise or blockage in that linear narrative progression, those things which, like disease, interfere with the rational order. From that moment of difference is abstracted a second order or rationality that defines what is to be excluded. Viruses and other "self-replicating" or "malicious" programs are endowed with their own sense of order or purpose, constructed in opposition to the rationality of the master narrative.

A related problem in defining viruses is their rapid rate of change and polymorphism. In order to stay ahead of antivirus software such as scanners and inoculation programs, virus writers rely on constant change and development, here the concept of polymorphism, the idea that a virus can take many different shapes or forms, not just one. The viruses are, themselves, "self-mutating," capable of changing their appearance and digital signatures to become undetectable. Change, then, is not only a tool for virus writers, but also a concept that is encoded into the very structure of the virus itself.

This idea of change makes it nearly impossible to define viruses in such a way that they are clearly delineated from other types of useful programs. Instead, viruses are defined more commonly by the effect they have on the user's machine. More properly called "malware" (for *mal*icious soft*ware*), these programs are designed to cause harm to a user's computer. While these programs make up the minority of the computer viruses written, they have the highest visibility and inspire the greatest fear. As a result, they have come to represent the entire family of programs that more properly bear the name *virus*.

DISSECTING THE INTERNET WORM:
VIRUS CULTURE AND MEDICAL PERCEPTION

That computer viruses are often tied to their biological counterparts should come as no surprise. In a culture that often privileges simulation over reality, computer viruses are one of the few objects that have direct, profound, and immediate effects on the world. They are a reminder of the connection between the virtual and the real. But they also make plain, in often dramatic ways, the degree to which our culture has grown to rely on computers in nearly every context of human activity and interaction.

Morris's worm marked an important moment in the history of computer viruses because of the discourse it spawned. In particular, the Internet worm put into play the discourse of medial perception, whereby debates ensued not only over what to call the Morris program, but more generally how to analyze and respond to future infections. In short, what was being decided was the direction that the discourse would take as well as the ways in which we would perceive computer viruses.

One of the primary responses to Morris's Internet worm came from researchers at MIT. In order to understand the worm, John Rochlis and Mark Eichin (two of the MIT researchers who worked on the project) literally engaged in medical perception, treating it as a disease that needed to be understood through dissection. As they would describe it, "Our group at MIT wound up decompiling the virus and discovering its inner details."[24] The connection to medical perception was made explicit both in their media releases and in the title of the paper they published in the *Communications of the ACM*, "With a Microscope and Tweezers." Donn Seeley, a University of Utah professor, performed a similar dissection on one of the worm's key algorithms.[25] Like Foucault's notion of "medical perception," the idea of the medical gaze being the primary means of diagnosis for disease, these computer scientists relied on watching what the program did and recording and analyzing its effects.

The idea of a "postmortem" analysis of the Internet worm firmly established the medical gaze as the primary epistemological frame of reference for the study of computer viruses. Just as Foucault had documented a shift in medical perception with the ability to open up corpses, the analysis of viral infection deployed precisely the same techniques and logics of "pathological anatomy." In Foucault's terminology, the institution of pathological anatomy was to become medicine's "most vital expression and its deepest reason."[26] The analysis of the Internet worm had three main approaches:

an analysis of its structure, a chronicle of its spread, and a detailing of its algorithms.[27] Regardless of the decision as to whether or not to call Morris's program a worm or a virus, the means by which the program was apprehended and neutralized firmly entrenched medical perception and pathological anatomy as the means by which the program would be understood. The "host," a term that has meaning in both biological and computer science, is infected by a disease.

Since the eighteenth century, Foucault reminds us, disease has been subject to the medical gaze when it invades the body and medical perception becomes the science of measuring the effects of the disease upon the body in order to identify and classify that disease by its effect. Corporeal objects provided a space for invention and refinement of the medical gaze. The body was, in Foucault's terms, "the concrete space of perception."[28] While the discourse (both technical and popular) that followed Morris's Internet worm incident invoked corporeal metaphors, the connection between the body and computer networks had already been developed a year earlier by Charles Cresson Wood. Wood argued that computer security necessitated a "new way of thinking" and "new reference models. Just as military advances were inspired by animals (birds inspired airplanes, bats inspired radar)," he argued, "the human body's immune system can inspire new advances in systems security."[29] The references that Wood suggests specifically are "vaccinations," "white blood cells," "antigens," "free radicals," "inflamation and fever," and "acquired immuno-deficiency syndrome (AIDS)."[30] Such suggestions document a whole-scale epistemological shift from a broader discourse of biology (which included evolution as well as disease) to a system of medical perception. In Wood's terms, "the human body can provide a wealth of security-relevant ideas."[31]

Wood's connection between the body and computer security was intended to complement what he saw as a paradigm shift occurring in contemporary thinking about technology. That shift positioned viruses within a biological discourse similar to Adleman and Cohen's understanding of networks, biology, and evolution. Wood himself argues that "a systems security analogy to the human body's immune system is fully compatible with the now-underway paradigm shift from the information age to the age in which we holistically regard the planet earth and its subsystems as intricately linked webs of technologies and systems . . . the futuristic view of the world as one integrated organism."[32] Wood's analogy introduced a model that would be developed in a number of different directions in the years that followed.

The transformation of the computer into a body was made explicit in a series of connections put forward by ACM President Bryan Kocher in his President's Letter, published in the *Communications of the ACM* under the title "A Hygiene Lesson."[33] The letter was a response to the incidents surrounding Morris's 1988 Internet worm. The Internet worm, rather than being about evolution, technology, or ethics, was about what Kocher called an "electronic epidemic." Kocher calls for a particular kind of medical perception in the analysis of and protection against computer viruses. "I believe," he wrote, "that after many years of fruitless admonitions by the NSA, a way has finally been found to focus serious attention on system security, i.e. hygiene."[34] Kocher compares the spread of Morris's Internet worm to the spread of cholera in Calcutta and, later, in Britain. The lesson, he argues, is that "just as in human society, hygiene is critical in preventing the spread of disease in computer systems. Preventing disease requires setting and maintaining high standards of sanitation throughout society, from simple personal precautions (like washing your hands or not letting anyone know your password), to large investments (like water and sewage treatment plants or reliably tested and certified secure systems)."[35] Kocher's message received a mixed response, with a large number of computer scientists maintaining that the issue was an ethical one, resisting the descriptions of "disease," "infection," and public health scares. Those, however, would be the terms that would capture both the media's attention and the public imagination. As Kocher concluded, "We must heed the public health warnings from NSA, practice personal systems hygiene, adhere to sanitary standards, and support the development of secure systems to keep the germs out."[36]

As some (notably Gene Spafford) had predicted, there are dangers with "coopting terms from another discipline to describe phenomena within our own (computing). The original definitions may be much more complex that we originally imagine, and attempts to maintain and justify the analogies may require a considerable effort."[37] Spafford's concerns recognized the problem only in terms of the computer science community itself. The broader anxiety about viruses would be realized as the discourse about viruses became an issue of public concern.

MEDICAL PERCEPTION AS SOCIAL CONTROL

Cast as a public health threat, viruses sparked two discourses of social control. The first was a discourse that vacillated between arguments in favor of stiff legal penalties and one advocating a more normative solution through the establishment of "a stronger and more effective ethical code among computer professionals" and "better internal policies."[38] In the late 1980s and early 1990s, however, these remedies were seen as irrelevant for the simple reason that viruses were not judged to be "a sufficiently serious threat to the public welfare," even in the wake of the Morris Internet worm.[39] The second discourse, which emerged from the Morris Internet worm debates, treated viruses not as legal or moral issues, but as biological and medical ones.

Historically, the discourse of hygiene has had a number of functions. Its primary function, however, is as a means of social control. Indeed, the very concept of the "police," Foucault argues, originated in part with enforcement of "general rules of hygiene" and in the eighteenth century, as the health of the population became increasingly important to the economic well-being, there emerged a "more general form of a 'medical police.' "[40] The role of the medical establishment, born out of responses to the epidemics of disease and plagues of the seventeenth and eighteenth centuries, developed into a "program of hygiene," which entailed "a certain number of authoritarian medical interventions and controls."[41] Specifically, Foucault argues, "the needs of hygiene demand an authoritarian medical intervention in what are regarded as the privileged breeding grounds of disease."[42]

This second discourse of hygiene, which focuses on disease, contamination, and public health, transcends questions of legality or morality. Biological infections neither obey the law nor do they respond to or violate moral or normative codes. What they do provide, however, is a justification and warrant for extreme measures, particularly in relation to "sanitation." Those sanitary practices are located in two distinct domains. First, in the machines themselves, which Kocher had described in terms of hygiene. The solution, at least in part, rests in changing the conditions that allow the disease to grow unchecked. "The UNIX epidemic," he argued, "is like any other epidemic disease. It won't go away until the conditions that allow it to flourish are changed to prevent further infection."[43] Kocher's comments were met with a flurry of criticisms, mainly aimed at Kocher's failure to hold the virus's author responsible. As Thomas Narten and Gene Spafford argued, for example, "computer viruses are created by persons deliberately circumventing known safeguards and actively seeking to spread infection."[44]

The separate discourses of the legal/normative and the biological appear to be in opposition, particularly around the question of agency and responsibility. They meet, however, in the discourse of hygiene. The discourse of hygiene allows the virus writer to be seen as both legally and morally responsible for biological infection. Typical of such descriptions is Jan Hruska's characterization of virus writers (whom she labels as "hackers") as "people analogous to drug addicts. They need their 'fix' and cannot leave the machine alone. Like addicts they seek novelty and new experiences. Writing a virus gives them this, but unlike addicts who get immediate relief after a fix, they are not usually present when the virus triggers and releases the payload."[45] The metaphors of drugs and addition (a primary public health concern in the early 1990s) is further developed by Hruska in his discussion of what he calls "freaks." Freaks, Hruska writes, are "an irresponsible subgroup of hackers, in the same way that while some drug addicts remain reasonably responsible (and use sterile needles), others (psychopaths) become irresponsible (and share needles). Freaks have serious social adjustment problems and often bear general, unspecified grudges against society. They have no sense of responsibility or remorse about what they do, and are prepared to exploit others in order to achieve their aims."[46] While such claims are wildly hyperbolic, they are effective as a rhetorical strategy. The connection between drug use and viral infection (particularly hepatitis and AIDS) from unclean or shared needles is further documentation of virus culture as a public health threat. It is a threat without specified agency. Although IV drug users are at great risk from infection, it is wrong to say that they *desire* infection. The public health threat is not found in their desire, agency, or intention, but in their lack of hygiene.

Hygiene is transformed in Hruska's description into a lack of moral agency. The virus writer occupies the position of the psychopath, without moral or ethical conscience. The virus writer is seen as unable or incapable of distinguishing between good and evil and between right and wrong and this lack of moral agency poses a dire threat to the public. As Hruska concludes, "The mentality of the freak virus writer is not unlike that of a person who leaves a poisoned jar of baby-food on a supermarket shelf. He delivers his potion, leaves and is untraced, and in his absence the victim falls."[47]

In contrast to these descriptions of the virus programmer as a stealthy murderer, virus writers themselves see computers and the program that run on them from an entirely different vantage point. Rather than a discourse of hygiene, virus writers have invoked a number of other discourses to justify their activities, including politics, free expression, the history of programming, and broader discourses of art and style. Their programs are often coded and named to reflect broader social concerns and often feature direct political messages. They see viruses as the means by which to challenge the meaning of technology, computers, computer culture, and programming.

The emergence of computer viruses in popular culture was coincident with an evolving discourse of AIDS, which had risen to the level of a public health epidemic. In this context, the discourses of infection, contamination, and hygiene had already been mobilized in public debate with dramatic effect and provided an immediate and highly charged language for understanding computer viruses.

Unlike other types of infection, AIDS was constructed in the popular imagination as a kind of smart virus. As Marita Sturken argues, the discourse of AIDS disrupted the conventional narratives of infection in part because AIDS was endowed with agency and intentionality, and seen as "learning" how to mutate in response to the body's immune system.[48] AIDS, Sturken argues, transformed the nature of viral infection in the popular imagination: "A virus is not 'alive,' according to science, yet neither is it dead; it can be killed. It is a 'bundle' of genes, an incohesive tangle. It 'contains instructions' but apparently did not write them itself. It is 'pure information,' yet information that acquires meaning only when in contact with cells."[49] Just as computer science has co-opted the discourse of biology, biological science turns to information sciences for its metaphors. AIDS was defined as different because it learns, propagates, and mutates, properties that were well understood and easily modeled in self-replicating computer code and computer models and simulations.

While the body is the site of discourse for AIDS, the larger social body and networks are the space in which the discourse of computer viruses is localized. In the wake of the 1988 worm for example, Peter Denning would write: "Certainly the vivid imagery of worms and viruses has enabled many outsiders to appreciate the subtlety and danger of attacks on computers attached to open networks. It has increased public appreciation of the dependence of important segments of the economy, aerospace systems, and defense networks on computers and telecommunications. Networks of computers have joined other critical networks that underpin our society—water, gas, electricity, telephones, air traffic control, banking, to name a few."[50] This sentiment would be picked up on by the press, the media, and the popular imagination.

Until the release of Morris's Internet worm, the concept of a computer virus was abstract, limited, and contained. Viruses were occasional programs that spawned a few variants each year. For example, in 1988, prior to

Morris's Internet worm, there were eleven known viruses for the IBM PC. In the year after the worm, that number nearly doubled (to twenty-one) and in the next few years that followed, the number grew rapidly doubling, roughly, every ten months. Even so, the number of virus programs still numbered in the low hundreds until Microsoft released a version of the Word word-processing program that had a built-in macro function. The macro function allowed users to embed commands inside Microsoft Word documents, giving near complete control over file access, creation, and deletion to the Word program. In doing so, Microsoft created a new virus delivery system that made it possible to transmit viruses through text documents (rather than as executable code). It also allowed viruses to be created without any knowledge of assembly language or computer programming. Macros were their own high-level language, easily understood and quickly apprehended by even computer neophytes. It was a language that was designed to be simple to utilize.

The release of Microsoft Word would turn out to be the most significant event in virus production. By 1994, the year of Word's release, the number of viruses were in excess of 5,000, nearly all of the new additions took advantage of the Word macro function.[51] The trend continued throughout the 1990s. In 1998, the number of known viruses in the wild was in excess of 18,000.[52] By April 1999, roughly one year later, McAfee and Associates reported 40,000 known viruses.[53]

The very idea of a virus connotes illness, sickness, and even death. Interestingly, however, the majority of computer viruses don't cause significant damage. In a 1996 survey, viruses were found to be the "most common type of security breach," with half of the companies surveyed reporting "virus incidents," however, only 5 percent of those incidents were described as having a "serious or significant impact."[54] What surveys routinely show is that industry spends huge sums of money protecting against virus attacks and attributes large losses to virus infection (usually first on the list of "sources of financial loss" for organizations reporting virus infections), but that a very small number of actual "attacks" account for most of the damage. Even recent reports of the top ten viruses reported on the Internet find that only one carries any payload at all.

Most viruses, instead, fall into the category of what could be considered "pranks," a longtime mainstay of both the mainstream and underground computer communities. Those pranks take on a heightened importance and danger in the context of a networked environment where it is difficult or even impossible to predict their effects. As Denning argued, "these software 'pranks' are very serious; they are spreading faster than they are being stopped, and even the least harmful of viruses could be life-threatening. For example, in the context of a hospital life-support system, a virus that 'simply' stops a computer and displays a message until a key is pressed, could be fatal."[55] The transformation of the computer virus from harmless prank to dangerous contaminant marks the moment at which it became possible to conceive of virus programming as criminal conduct.

Conclusion

Anxiety is a state that manifests itself around an "expectation," whereby we find, according to Freud, a "general apprehensiveness, a kind of freely floating anxiety which is ready to attach itself to any idea that is in any way suitable, which influences judgment, selects what is to be expected, and lies in wait for any opportunity that will allow it to justify itself."[56] In other words, anxiety is related to a sense of the unknown and uncertainty. This particular form of anxiety—what Freud called "expectant anxiety"—clearly manifests itself around technology. Such anxiety is different from what we commonly think of as a phobia. With computer technology, people are not necessarily afraid of the machines themselves. What they fear is the future created by technology—they "foresee the most frightful of all possibilities, interpret every chance event as a premonition of evil and exploit every uncertainty in a bad sense."[57]

The anxiety over technology, as an expectant anxiety aimed at the future, calls into question almost every aspect of daily human interaction. Accordingly, such anxiety calls forth the process of displacement, whereby the anxiety over something important can be rethought and managed in relation to something unimportant. The process of displacement occurs through allusion. In such an act, the object onto which anxiety is displaced is "easily intelligible" (unlike allusions in dreams, for example) and the "substitute must be related in its subject-matter to the genuine thing it stands for."[58] In the discourse surrounding hackers and viruses, the main site of displacement is the body itself in response to the challenge that technology poses to corporeality, to the structure of the law, and to the structure of society, more generally.

As the examples of Mitnick's pursuit and capture and Morris's Internet worm illustrate, concerns about technology serve as a site of displacement for broader cultural concerns, particularly in terms of the body. In the case of hackers, the fear of the loss of the body animates a hunt to find their corporeal substance. With viruses, the anxiety over disease, illness, and infection creates a warrant for measures of social control. In both cases, technology produces and is produced by large forces of cultural anxiety that allow those fears to be displaced in the popular imagination onto the tropes of technology that dominate the underground landscape: hackers' bodies and computer viruses.

NOTES

1. Interestingly, *cyberspace* is a term that emerged from cyberpunk literature in the early 1980s, and was popularized by John Perry Barlow (one of the inventors of the WELL). Bruce Sterling attributes the popularization of Gibson's terminology to Barlow's usage of it, claiming that it was the term "as Barlow employed it, [that] struck a useful chord, and this concept of cyberspace was picked up by *Time, Scientific American*, computer police, hackers, and even constitutional scholars." See Bruce Sterling's *The Hacker Crackdown: Law and Disorder on the Electronic Frontier* (New York: Bantam, 1992), 236.

2. William Gibson, *Neuromancer* (New York: Ace Books, 1984), 6.

3. While there are documented cases of hackers engaging in serious computer crime, more often, the efforts of law enforcement are aimed at cracking down on fairly innocuous behavior. For an instance of the former, see Clifford Stoll, *The Cuckoo's Egg: Tracking a Spy through the Maze of Computer Espionage* (New York: Pocket Books, 1989). For an analysis of the latter, see Sterling's *The Hacker Crackdown*.

4. Katie Hafner and John Markoff, *Cyberpunk: Outlaws and Hackers on the Computer Frontier* (New York: Simon & Schuster, 1991), 342.

5. Ibid., 343.

6. Letter from Marc J. Stein, U.S. Probation Officer, to Kevin Lee Poulsen, May 22, 1996.

7. Kevin Poulsen, "Many Happy Returns," <http://www.kevinpoulsen.com>. Accessed December 1998.

8. John Markoff, "Cyberspace's Most Wanted: Hacker Eludes FBI Pursuit," *New York Times*, July 4, 1994, 1.

9. Hafner and Markoff, *Cyberpunk*, 26.

10. Markoff, "Cyberspace's Most Wanted," 1.

11. Ibid.

12. Joshua Quittner, "Kevin Mitnick's Digital Obsession," *Time*, February 27, 1995.

13. Hafner and Markoff, *Cyberpunk*, 343.

14. Mike Godwin, quoted in Douglas Fine, "Why is Kevin Lee Poulsen Really in Jail?" Posting to the WELL, 1995. Accessed December 2003.

15. John Markoff, interview, January 19, 1995.

16. U.S. Marshals Service, NCIC entry number NIC/W721460021.

17. Peter Denning, "The Internet Worm," *American Scientist* (March–April, 1989), 126.

18. Ibid.

19. John Shoch and Jon Hupp, "The 'Worm' Programs—Early Experiments with Distributed Computing," *Communications of the ACM* 25, no. 3 (March 1982): 172–80.

20. Foucault's insights regarding surveillance and the relationship between technology and the body are extensive. However, examining those lines of thought is beyond the scope of this essay. These themes, as well as other elements of Foucault's thought, are further discussed in relation to hacker culture in Douglas Thomas, *Hacker Culture* (Minneapolis: University of Minnesota Press, 2002).

21. Eugene Spafford, "Computer Viruses," in *Internet Besieged: Countering Cyberspace Scofflaws*, ed. Dorothy Denning and Peter Denning (New York: ACM Press, 1998), 75–78.

22. Since the inception of the term in 1983, attempts to define computer viruses in plain language as a distinct category of computer program have failed. Only by defining them in terms of sets in the language of mathematics can computer viruses be seen as distinct entities and then only in relation to other sets of programs.

23. Michel Foucault, *Birth of the Clinic*, trans. A. M. Sheridan (New York: Vintage Books, 1973), 6.

24. Mark W. Eichin and John A. Rochlis, "With a Microscope and Tweezers: The Worm from MIT's Perspective," *Communications of the ACM* 32, no. 6 (1989): 689.

25. Donn Seeley, "Password Cracking: A Game of Wits," *Communications of the ACM* 32, no. 6 (1989): 700–703.

26. Foucault, *Birth of the Clinic*, 124.

27. Spafford, Eichin and Rochlis, and Seeley, respectively.

28. Foucault, *Birth of the Clinic*, 9.

29. Charles Cresson Wood, "The Human Immune System as an Information Systems Security Reference Model," *Computers & Security*, 6 (1987): 512–13.

30. Ibid., 513–16.

31. Ibid., 516.

32. Ibid.

33. Bryan Kocher, "A Hygiene Lesson," *Communications of the ACM* 32, no. 1 (January 1989): 3.

34. Ibid.

35. Ibid., 3, 6.

36. Ibid., 6.

37. Eugene Spafford, "The Internet Worm Incident," in *Rogue Programs: Viruses, Worms, and Trojan Horses*, ed. Lance J. Hoffman (New York: Van Nostrand Reinhold, 1990), 206.

38. Pamela Samuelson, "Can Hackers Be Sued for Damages Caused by Computer Viruses?" *Communications of the ACM* 32, no. 6 (1989): 668.

39. Michael Gemignani, "Viruses and Criminal Law," *Communications of the ACM* 32, no. 6 (1989): 671.

40. Michel Foucault, "The Politics of Health in the Eighteenth Century," in *The Foucault Reader*, ed. Paul Rabinow (New York: Pantheon, 1984), 278.

41. Ibid., 282.

42. Ibid., 283.

43. Kocher, "A Hygiene Lesson," 3.

44. Thomas Narten and Eugene Spafford, "ACM Forum," *Communications of the ACM*, 32, no. 6 (1989): 674.

45. Jan Hruska, *Computer Viruses and Anti-Virus Warfare*, 2nd rev. ed. (New York: Ellis Horwood, 1992), 64.

46. Ibid.

47. Ibid., 65.

48. Marita Sturken, *Tangled Memories: The Vietnam War, The AIDS Epidemic and the Politics of Remembering* (Berkeley: University of California Press, 1997), 245.

49. Ibid.

50. Denning, "The Internet Worm," 128.

51. VIRUS-L FAQ, section F1. <http://webworlds.co.uk/dharley/anti-virus/vlfaq200.txt>. Accessed December 1998.

52. *Dr. Solomon's Anti-Virus Deluxe*, Edition 1.1, April 1998.

53. McAfee Virus Information Center, <http://vil.mcafee.com/villib/alpha.asp>, April 11, 1999.

54. The Information Security Breaches Survey 1996, DTI, ICL, UK ITSEC, NCC. Cited in Dorothy E. Denning, "Cyberspace Attacks and Countermeasures," in *Internet Besieged: Countering Cyberspace Scofflaws*, ed. Dorothy Denning and Peter Denning (New York: ACM Press, 1998,) 39.

55. VIRUS-L FAQ.

56. Sigmund Freud, *Introductory Lectures on Psychoanalysis* (New York: W. W. Norton, 1966), 494.

57. Ibid., 494–95.

58. Ibid., 214.

Carolyn Marvin

13 Peaceable Kingdoms and New Information Technologies

Prospects for the Nation-State

How WILL global communications technologies transform the nation-state? Could they threaten its existence as the linchpin of the international system? Those who ponder new technologies gathering steam in the early twenty-first century and the ponderously creaky social formation called the nation-state disagree about the likely outcome of the collision between them. Some prophets have imagined an end to two centuries of nation-state tribalism and armed conflict. Other visions sketch powerful nation-states hemorrhaging sovereignty from onslaughts by predatory supercapitalism. Dramatic fantasies of doom and salvation have always accompanied shifts in communications technology. They are less informative about the likely character of the future than about important strains in the social structure of societies experiencing technological change.[1]

Social distance changes when technological innovation raises or lowers customary communicative barriers. Writing, telegraphy, and telephony all have transformed social distance in this fashion. Today we are witness to the restless and continuing reorganization of local, intermediate, and global social distances by the Internet, cell phones, instant messaging, tape cassettes, compact disks, digital imagery, and more on the way. It would be surprising if major shifts in how humans communicate with one another had no important implications for social structure. At the level of lived existence, social structure is visibly anchored by conventions of proper social distance in face-to-face exchanges between persons of similar or different statuses. Related conventions govern mediated interaction. Such rules govern public and private boundaries and generate procedures for establishing trust in role encounters. The most visible shifts in communication technology rearrange familiar social distances and imperil this carefully calibrated social trust. Because they are both unsettling and exciting, such rearrangements are a prominent theme of popular culture, which faithfully registers popular desires and fears that emerge from them.

It would be hard to conclude from inspecting contemporary popular culture that the fate of nations *as nations* hangs in the balance of new communications technologies from the perspective of most citizens, however. According to popular discourse, new communications technologies affect morality, and not for the better. Likewise affected are civility and various kinds of authority, including parental authority, many forms of professional authority, and the private authority citizens have over information about their own lives. But the stability of the nation-state seems secure in popular imagination. (This is a different matter than the fate of particular nation-states, which always hangs in the balance.) Popular assessments do not guarantee that drastic political consequences do not lie ahead. They do mean that popular identification with nation-state belonging is an especially stable feature of modern social and personal identity.

Communicatively speaking, nation-states descend from eighteenth-century newspapers, nineteenth-century telegraphy, and twentieth-century broadcasting. Measured against the history of other significant communications technologies, digital technologies thus seem destined for large political consequences, popular assessments notwithstanding. Discussion on this point is necessarily speculative, and humility is definitely in order for any effort to discern through a glass darkly the long-term consequences of technological change. Still, with no thought that nation-state forms are eternal or inevitable, it is far from obvious that the nation-state will be a front-line casualty of new forms of global communications. Nation-states are likely to weather the transformations of digital technology for a long time to come.

How shifts in communications set in motion transforming cultural shifts has always preoccupied theorists of the grand sweep, for whom print offers the prototype example. One of the best known, Elizabeth Eisenstein, argues that the cultural episode we call the Renaissance flowed directly from the diffusion of printing.[2] She also gives print a propelling role in two powerful ideologies of Western modernity, early modern science and Protestantism. For Harold Innis, the transformative power of printing is a function of the dramatic expansion it made possible in cultural memory, and in its exponential enlargement of the transmission and distribution of information. Computing likewise vastly amplifies cultural memory (the dimension Innis calls "time-binding")[3] and transmission and distribution in real time (which Innis calls "space-binding"). For Innis, communication technologies that bind both space and time in new ways, as printing did and computing now does, foster geographically large, politically centralized forms of empire. The United States is this kind of empire.

Benedict Anderson ties his grand argument about print to felt solidarity more than to increases in mechanical capacity. He argues that the emergence of nation-states in the eighteenth and nineteenth centuries was the direct outcome of the diffusion through print of nationalist sentiment. Shared written vernaculars linked colonial bureaucratic elites in "imagined communities" that nourished new-nation sensibilities. Anderson sees modern nations as communities of strangers imagining one another as comrades through shared texts that provide the affective bonds of nationhood.[4] If, in fact, community boundaries are as malleable as printed imaginings of them are fluid and abundant, global communities are possible because global texts may be distributed with little effort. But there is a gap in Anderson's formulation between the moral sentiments people have and the claim that these convictions arise automatically from the existence of an appropriate vehicle along which they may travel.

Nation-states are not simply well-coordinated daydreams of language and information. They are communities of moral obligation whose members' bodies are committed to mutual common defense. Such commitments include sacrifices willingly undertaken by citizens and acquiescence to the state's willingness to compel citizen sacrifice through conscription and other means. Where popular readiness for sacrifice is lacking, visible state compulsion will imperil national unity and purpose. The Vietnam War provides the living memory example for the United States. Mere diffusion of information and propaganda proved unable to persuade a large enough majority of citizens that North Vietnam posed a threat to American national security. Where lives and not only words are at stake, more than mere textual imagination of new political forms is needed to create or sustain the affective glue of enduring group cohesion. By the same logic, there is a missing piece in most assessments of the role digital technologies will have in the larger political transformations we might expect them to facilitate.

WHAT IS ESSENTIAL TO COLLECTIVE IDENTITY?

To resolve this issue we must consider the nation as the locus of collective identity for its citizens. Among all the overlapping communities of identity to which modern persons belong, why does the rhetoric of sweeping technological change focus especially on *nations*? Eric Hobsbawm puts the puzzle this way:

It [the nation-state] is, in Benedict Anderson's useful phrase, an "imag-ined community," and no doubt this can be made to fill the emotional void left by the retreat or disintegration, or the unavailability of real human communities and networks, but the question still remains why, having lost real communities, people should wish to imagine this particular type of replacement.[5]

If we could say why nation-states constitute the core group of belonging in modernity, as Liah Greenfeld and other theorists of nationalism insist they do, we might better understand the cohesive dynamics of contemporary communities and better predict the likely rearrangements of time and space that digital technologies will encourage.[6]

Hobsbawm has no doubt that there exists a *real* human community, even if humans have somehow contrived to lose it. How this could happen is not a trivial question, but I take Hobsbawm to be asserting a foundational mode for human society. He perhaps implies that "real" communities are organized around face-to-face interaction, which makes possible the au-thentic connections upon which "real" communities depend. At the very least, more bodies cannot be made without such interaction![7] I believe the same applies to collective action for solving the most difficult tasks of sur-vival, and propose that what makes nations the key source of political iden-tity for modern people is that national communities are the most potent bloodletters, the most visible users of bodies in the contemporary world. To paraphrase Weber's description of the state, sovereignty at its most basic is having legitimate killing authority.[8] Citizenship is a relation of submission to such killing authority.

Without bodies, society is impossible, to be more concrete about it. The more removed from immediate bodily presence the community of belong-ing is from those who must be persuaded to belong to it, the more dramatic must be the means of overcoming the gap that mediated forms open up between belonging as a moral relationship and intimacy as an experien-tial condition. Where members have personal experience of all other mem-bers in small-scale societies, there is no gap between belonging and inti-macy. Where connections are attenuated by distance and mediated through texts—in the sprawling industrialized nations where readers of this essay are likely to live—ties of compelling psychological and social power must be generated in the absence of physically intimate bonds that unite mem-bers of face-to-face communities.

How to bind the loyalties of the foot soldiers who must be enlisted to project nation-state power abroad and ensure domestic tranquility at home—and the loyalties of the families that offer them? It is no accident that Clausewitzian total war was invented and theorized contemporaneously with the rise of the nation-state. Carl von Clausewitz (1780–1831) was a Prussian officer and veteran of German and Russian campaigns against both the French Revolutionary Army and Napoleon in the regimental system that antedates modern nation-state military organization. Regimental armies were invented by absolutist rulers seeking an end to the structural instabilities of feudalism. In that system rulers were required to reward noble princes with land for fighting men and services rendered. Through strategic alliances and the acquisition of ever more territory, ambitious feudal lords might contrive to topple the rulers they served only to become vulnerable themselves in an endless, exhausting cycle of bloodshed and conquest.[9]

Regiments, or standing armies, changed this. Skills in the strategic command of men at war were transferred from an aristocratic class of princes to a bureaucratized officer corps forbidden to acquire territorial holdings. In exchange for fighting services, men at arms were housed and maintained permanently at the ready by the sovereign power. By this means a ruler with a body of dedicated landless fighting men at his disposal no longer faced the nobility as a rival military power.[10] The nobility was brought into court, a waning decorative testament to a dying social system. Standing armies required two innovations. Royal taxation of a merchant bourgeoisie anxious to have peace for the sake of commercial enterprise solved the economic problem of sustaining permanent armed bodies of landless men. And cultivation among the citizenry of a willingness to make any sacrifice at all in the service of the nation, an ethic of total war, provided both justification and engine for social and psychological unity.

Clausewitzian theories of war were conceived within the assumptions of emerging centralized states. Lawful bearers of arms bound to surrender their lives to authority on demand were distinguished from irregular soldiers outside disciplined authority. Our image of total war is masses of men standing in rows, slaughtering and being slaughtered, perhaps for hours at a time. Such wars of attrition became the blood sacrifice rituals of nation-states partly because they aroused emotions of religious intensity and force. The ritual lesson of total war is that Durkheimian sentiments of solidarity manifest as nationalism can be generated where—but more to the point, only if—blood sacrifice is great enough to trump competing ties of kinship, ethnicity, class, and religion that threaten it. Large numbers of casualties unify the community by equalizing the sacrifices of citizens. A large sacrifice guarantees that blood, the most magical of bodily substances, sooner or later touches everyone in the group. Soldiers are touched directly. All who are connected to them by kinship or close affiliation are indirectly touched. The greater the number of soldiers sacrificed (short of a sacrifice too great for the group to sustain itself, which possibility is used to wring ever greater dedication from those who are called), the more demanding and personal is the shared ordeal of every member of the community in sending them, and the larger the community that may be thus unified. Where men have lost what Hobsbawm calls a "real" community, only conditions this severe can generate a shared bond equivalent in moral strength to those long associated with face-to-face social intimacy.

Compared to one knit together by blood rituals, can such solidarity be generated in the famously imagined Andersonian textual community? Events experienced in one's own skin provide the deepest forms of emotional life available to humans. Textual experience is derivative by definition.[11] Though Anderson never systematically considers the content of national texts, these contribute to solidarity largely by cementing bodily sacrifice to nationalism. The specific examples of national texts Anderson puts forward are of exactly this kind, though he fails to notice that the crucial mechanism of connection is sacrifice rather than print, which provides a necessary means of distribution but not the engine of motivation. And though shared texts disseminate and amplify knowledge of sacrificial bodies, texts simply as texts cannot create the compelling feelings of responsibility we call patriotic obligation and guilt. In rituals of national solidarity, texts play a supporting liturgical role. There is no substitute for real blood shed by striving and suffering bodies in producing the conviction of shared national kinship.

The limiting size of political communities, therefore, is not only how much physical territory can be coordinated and integrated through systems of transportation and communication, nor even the number of people that can be kept in line by force. The size of political communities is limited by the size of a population *for which it is possible to enlist men's deepest moral sympathies through body-to-body ties*. The farther-reaching the links of movement and message, the more citizens are bound to be physical and moral strangers to one another. The more citizens are strangers, the more dramatic and compelling—the more *violent*—must be the rituals that elicit their willingness to sacrifice despite (and frequently in defiance of) family, religion, and other body-based affiliations that compete for moral supremacy and have the capacity to derail or destroy national purpose. Texts play a critical role in recalling past national sacrifice. But without real bodies to back them, as gold backs currency, and without periodically renewed ritual offerings of those bodies that constitute the real treasure of the community, enduring groups can neither maintain themselves or address serious threats to their existence.

All this sounds strangely primitive in an era when textual authority is plainly powerful. In the modern West, it might be said that all bodies are disciplined with respect to literacy. Some are disciplined in its use, others are disciplined to keep away from it. Social distinctions based in literate practice separate those who use and expend their bodies in physical work from those with relative discretion to preserve and protect their physical bodies from labor and hardship. Those with access to literate currencies learn to conceal their bodies in the production and manipulation of literate signs through costly stratagems of self-control. It is the privilege of the pre-served body to remain concealed within and protected by the practices and products of literacy. Compared to the less socially esteemed body, which remains relatively more visible and unprotected, suppression of the body is the condition of literate achievement.[12]

Those whose cultural power depends on controlling the production and reception of texts make up the textual classes. Those who depend on the labor of their bodies, who cannot conceal themselves behind texts, comprise the bodily classes. In Western history the agonistic play of texts against bodies was propelled decisively forward by the Reformation, a deep and sustained attack on traditional body-based forms of ritual magic in the name of textual authority.[13] For the performative magic of bodies, manifest in the transmutation of bread and wine, curing the sick, and even baptism, the sixteenth-century Reformation substituted an equally magical commitment to textual authority and practice, manifest as correct scriptural belief. Now focused on the system of secular constitutional law, reverence for literate authority still undergirds the system for conferring and distributing social resources and prestige in modern industrialized societies.[14]

Textual communities do not engage in blood fighting. They leave this task to the body classes. In textual communities, intellectuals are front men. Stereotypically not in control of their own bodies, ridiculed as asexual, powerless to command other bodies, intellectuals legitimize textuality to the bodily classes. Existing at the sufferance of more powerful (textual) elites than they, they are charged to idealize textual sensibilities as noble, ethereal, and morally exalted. The body class learns its subordinate social place from these textual class missionaries. Through rituals of cultural deference, body class members are schooled not to notice that the true power of the textual class consists of controlling and disposing of the bodies of nontextual classes.

Electronically mediated communications are simply the most contemporary form of textualized messages. Like texts that have preceded them, digital texts are abstracted from the bodies that produce and receive them. Like these texts, they are endlessly duplicated and effortlessly distributed. Even digital prophets who expect nation-states to recede as residues of a primitive past, replaced by text-based digital communities, are historically familiar. The vision of a universal textual language that links metropolitan cultures while effacing traditional rural populations recalls Enlightenment elites who offered this dream to liberal cosmopolites of eighteenth-century Europe. Internationalism, observes Tom Nairn, has always been the ideology of metropole intelligentsia, not rural peasantry or the countryside.[15]

Literate elites benefit first and disproportionately from new textual technologies. They reinforce their elite positions by absorbing and dominating these technologies. They imagine the extension and triumph of their technology over all others. They have a stake in ignoring the sacrifice of nonelite bodies to support their dominant position. In industrialized countries, this sacrifice is exacted especially from police and soldiers whose bodies guarantee the safety of textual elites through forcible expulsion of illegal immigrants, and from the poor who lack textual skills for amassing cultural capital in the struggle for status. These dispossessed fight back with their bodies—and mostly lose.

VISIONS OF THE GOOD STATE

In fairness, the vision of a universal culture is not limited to the textual class. If societies may be broadly classed as dominated by textual or bodily elites, there are instances enough of the latter. With the instructive exception of Nazism, bodily elites have not been dominant in the modern West. In recent history, Khmer Rouge nationalists forced urban-educated elites into the countryside to labor for Pol Pot's body-dominated ruling cadres. The Taliban of Afghanistan visited draconian spectacles of punishment on those who failed to comply with the strict bodily observances mandated by their own brand of Islam. Mao's Great Leap forward was launched in the name of a utopia of the body and the political subordination of the textual classes. The brutality of bodily regimes is more visible than that of textual regimes, their injustices more easily recognized and denounced from outside. Falling behind in a society dominated by textual elites has a more hidden profile since less literate and nonliterate groups lack means and skill to call effective outside attention to the economic and physical violence visited on them. The chains of social and economic dependence are also longer in textualized regimes than in regimes of the body. Elaborated, textually mediated connections between power-holders and those at the mercy of power are not only less visible, the less participants know one another, but arguably more difficult to intervene in as well.

Those who foresee a decline in nation-state sovereignty do not argue that nation-states are too big or too small or otherwise unable to provide physical protection and sustenance to their citizens. After 200 years it is clear that the administrative and political form of the nation-state offers a stable foundation for productive societies. Prophets of nationalism's demise claim that digital technologies portend a centrifugal denationalizing power of irresistible force. This is a surprising claim if we consider that other distance- and time-annihilating communications technologies—telegraphy, radio, and television—have expanded rather than contracted the power of nation-states.

Prophets of denationalization like Jean-Marie Guéhenno and Francis Fukuyama argue that the digital "despatialization" of the world spells the "end of politics" and the nation-state as the most prominent of political structures.[16] Just as Daniel Bell once proclaimed that information age technologies portended the "end of ideology," Francis Fukuyama has claimed that history, conventionally understood as dramas of nation-state strife, is at an end.[17] His version of technological transformation proposes a Hegelian progression from nationalism to liberal democracy, a view also advanced by early twentieth-century thinkers such as Durkheim in France and Dewey in the United States.[18] A less sanguine stages-of-history argument is offered by theorists who take to heart Marx's admonition that the existence of nation-states has long permitted capitalists to divert workers from their true class interests. These critics hope for the end of what Fukuyama labels the thymic aspects of nationalism—chauvinism, ethnocentrism, racism, fascism, and militarism. Thus John Lukacs observes that the struggle of the twentieth century was not a struggle of classes but nations.

What could replace the tottering nation-state? Benjamin Barber, Wilson Dizard, and Walter B. Wriston predict that increasing economic interdependence across political borders will prevail over political interests that fuel armed conflict.[19] The European Union (EU) offers a hopeful model for proponents of this view. It is also an ambiguous one since its success rests on the political stability of its nation-state members. A successful EU would not resemble a new political form so much as a superstate of those now comprising it. Still, Samuel Huntington has warned that commercial contacts are a dubious thread on which to hang hopes for peace.[20] No nations were more economically interdependent than Germany and France in August 1914, or the Germans and the Soviets in June 1941.[21] Commerce is as likely to inform people about their differences as their commonalities. One of the lessons of the antebellum U.S. Post Office was that mail from Northern abolitionists inflamed Southern resentment toward the North wherever it circulated. Increased communication may as easily sharpen conflict as promote harmony.

The debate over America Online's policy of removing individual subscribers and messages that "harass, threaten, embarrass, or do anything else to another member that is unwarranted" offers a quick snapshot of the issues that surround digitally communicated conflict. The issue here is instructive because it represents no great challenge to nation-state peace and security. It simply offers a window on the quotidian comings and goings of social exchange in the cyberage.[22] By excluding the rude, America Online hopes to minimize conflict and provide an atmosphere of civility for millions of subscribers. The unmourned victim of this policy is open democratic communication in which conflict is no less likely than harmony to manifest itself. If America Online's goal is not democratic access for the rude and civil alike, but eliminating uncivil disagreement, powerful compulsory restraints must be applied. These will always serve the most entrenched notions of the status quo. The tactics of pacification never eliminate force. They simply disguise it. America Online itself exists only so long as a nation-state able to exercise force is willing to defend it. All nation-states, even the most democratic, are supported by violence, even when they have learned to hide it behind layers of distracting text.

Invent the printing press, Thomas Carlyle is supposed to have said in an early version of the optimism that drives utopian prophets of globalization, and democracy is inevitable. Apparently not. The printing press has been as useful to entrenched totalitarian states as to model democracies. If electronic communications were inherently democratizing, we could depend on "technologies of freedom" simply to wear down the hierarchies that frustrate democracy.[23] But technological form provides no democratic guarantees. Global communications systems often require expressly undemocratic centralizing infrastructures in order to stay up and running. If global electronic communications could further democracy, would this be a gain for world peace? James Lee Ray asserts that liberal democracies have never attacked one another by force of arms.[24] He also acknowledges that democracies have not been reluctant to initiate war against nondemocracies or to colonize vulnerable peoples. Having divested themselves of colonial empires in the twentieth century, the most powerful among them project force geopolitically through client states caught in webs of dependence that constantly threaten escalating conflicts.[25] The notion that citizens linked by new forms of communication will have no motivation to fuel the passions of nationalism simply disregards the history of nation-state violence by democracies and nondemocracies alike.

I hasten to acknowledge that the arguments put forward here apply to textual, or explicitly re-presentational, technologies. Were forms of virtual interaction to become genuinely indistinguishable from face-to-face encounters, all bets are off. I am prepared to believe that body re-forming technologies might present genuine alternatives to the body-based moral communities of nation-states. In fanciful visions from teleportation to human cloning, they constitute the limiting case for the present analysis.

THE POLITICS OF THE BODY

However secure their political form for the near term, nation-states do face significant challenges in an era of globalized computing. The perception that bodies are increasingly detached from "real" human communities offers a vantage point from which groups whose livelihoods are directly threatened, and whose cultural and social authority is greatly reduced by digital technologies will interpret their situation and consider their options. They include workers who provide personal services (e.g., travel agents, financial consultants, real-estate brokers, messengers, traveling salesmen, private-practice physicians) that can be offered more efficiently and extensively by new technologies, or whose consumers can be cream-skimmed by electronically based providers. They include educators, librarians, and other petty bourgeois members of the textual class whose professional authority is eroded by networked databases and automated retrieval systems. They include body class workers in domestic manufacturing whose living standards have declined along with these industries. They include those who lack basic literacy skills, and are able to command only the most menial of jobs in the digital economy.

Those who experience the erosion of bodily authority as a loss of social power experience it as the destruction of morality, civility, authority, and autonomy. At home and abroad, such groups may be expected to resort to rituals of restoring the purified body to power. In the United States a presidential impeachment focused around the sexually scandalous (and lying, finger-pointing) body was consistent with such anxiety. So are moral panics about sex and violence; health issues such as smoking and irradiated food; and perceived assaults on the family such as gay marriage, abortion, and priestly pedophilia. The politics of the body is registered in increased resistance to immigration and other expressions of tribal resistance to impure bodies. It predicts ever greater hostility from those who, lacking textual skills, find themselves on the wrong side of the global and national economy. Nor should we be surprised to see enhanced punishments (more prisons incarcerating more bodies and lesser crimes punished with penalties that display the stigmatized body to the community) for bodily crimes from murder to prostitution. We can expect the rhetoric of alarm eventually to embrace computing itself as a threat to the nation-state (the Taliban, for example, forbade computing on the grounds that monitors could receive forbidden images). Such expressions already haunt the political discourse of marginalized body-class groups who fear conspiracies by international textual elites such as the United Nations and the Trilateral Commission.

That the modern technologically integrated state will strike with special vengeance against body-based challenges is also clear. Terrorism is the obvious case. Consider also domestic hate crimes, which increase penalties for violent assaults motivated by prejudice against bodies that are symbolically privileged in the current political climate—minorities, women, gays. Such penalties demonstrate to members of the body class, the primary perpetrators of bias crimes, that angry efforts at retribution for the raw deal they perceive themselves to have from a society that disdains the bodies they offer will be dealt with more severely than text-based injustices. Red-lining, employment discrimination, and corporate consolidation are deeds on paper that eliminate jobs, pensions, and health care. For those without recourse to the textual machinery of expensive litigation or relatively protected textual-class employment, these deprivations result in lost life opportunities. Textual class crimes may be less visibly brutal than hate crimes but are no less determinative of the life courses of their victims, and the number of their victims is significantly greater. Thus do the social sorting mechanisms of a textual society deflect and devalue the body class and keep it under control, not least by keeping its members divided against themselves.

CONCLUSION

Nation-states are the form that human tribes take in a technological world. Though digital technology may support and re-present blood sacrifice to citizens as print and broadcasting have done before it, the existence of nation-states requires forms of blood commitment by citizens for which, finally, there is no substitute. Texts give central authorities far-reaching power to monitor bodies at a distance. Such coordination has been among the chief contributions of computing technology to nation-state power. But if texts, including digital texts, provide the means, they cannot provide the distinctive glue of group loyalty. To replace the nation-state with alternative moral communities will require new rituals of sacrifice and fertility able to compete with nation-state war in emotional scale and power. Such rituals are not impossible to imagine; they could well make total wars of attrition look limited and civilized. They should give us great pause. If nation-states turn out not to be adequate suppliers of sacrificial ritual demand, what new levels of ferocity and brutality might be necessary to command the dedicated loyalties of more extended communities of strangers?

Not that brutality has ever been partial to particular political forms. Lynching, clan warfare, domestic violence, and slavery are all robust genres in the familiar record of man's inhumanity, and none requires nation-states for their expression. They remind us that enduring communities at every level organize violence, like sex, to promote their own survival. The collective tension that surrounds violence does not arise, in the first instance, from its destructiveness to individuals, but from the knowledge that energies so powerful can destroy the very communities they are deployed to sustain. This powerful combination of creativity and destruction is part of violence's religiously compelling aura. Whatever new computing technologies offer in the way of challenges and opportunities for the nation-state will be faithfully manifest in the fortunes and misfortunes, advances and retreats, rewards and punishments of the interface between bodily violence and increased textual coordination and control. To chart the most disruptive consequences of the digital revolution, follow the bodies.

NOTES

Acknowledgments: The author acknowledges with thanks discussion of a number of ideas in this essay at the "Place and Identity in an Age of Technologically Regulated Movement" workshop sponsored by the National Center for Geographic Information and Analysis Varenius Project to Advance Geographic Information Science, October 8–10, 1998, Santa Barbara, California.

1. See Carolyn Marvin, *When Old Technologies Were New: Thinking about Communication in the Late Nineteenth Century* (New York: Oxford University Press, 1988).

2. Elizabeth Eisenstein, *The Printing Press as an Agent of Change: Communications and Cultural Transformations in Early-modern Europe*, vols. 1 and 2 (Cambridge: Cambridge University Press, 1979).

3. Harold A. Innis, *Empire and Communications* (Toronto: University of Toronto Press, 1972) and *The Bias of Communication* (Toronto: University of Toronto Press, 1951).

4. Benedict Anderson, *Imagined Communities: Reflections on the Origin and Spread of Nationalism*, rev. ed. (London: Verso, 1991). A similar perspective is shared by Ernest Gellner, *Nations and Nationalism* (Ithaca, N.Y.: Cornell University Press, 1983).

5. E. J. Hobsbawm, *Nations and Nationalism Since 1780: Programme, Myth, Reality* (Cambridge: Cambridge University Press, 1990), 46.

6. Liah Greenfeld, *Nationalism: Five Roads to Modernity* (Cambridge, Mass.: Harvard University Press, 1992), 18.

7. Even this is no longer certain, but on the scale that replenishes national populations, reproduction will continue to be a face-to-face activity for the foreseeable future.

8. For an extended analysis of nationalism and patriotism as civil religion, see Carolyn Marvin and David W. Ingle, *Blood Sacrifice and the Nation: Totem Rituals and the American Flag* (Cambridge: Cambridge University Press, 1999).

9. The classic discussion of this transformation is Norbert Elias, *The Civilising Process: The History of Manners and State Formation and Civilization*, trans. Edemund Jephcott (1939; Cambridge, Mass.: Basil Blackwell, 1982).

10. See John Keegan, *The History of Warfare* (New York: Alfred A. Knopf, 1993).

11. By "text" I refer throughout to mass-mediated messages, both printed writing and printed images.

12. See Carolyn Marvin, "The Body of the Text: Literacy's Corporeal Constant," *Quarterly Journal of Speech* 80, no. 2 (May 1994): 129–49.

13. See Peter Burke, "The Repudiation of Ritual in Early Modern Europe," in *The Historical Anthropology of Early Modern Italy: Essays on Perception and Communication* (Cambridge: Cambridge University Press, 1983), 223–38.

14. European regimental armies, the priestly classes of the new body-based religion of nationalism, were organized over the course of the sixteenth and seventeenth centuries, just as ritual claims on the body by traditional Christianity were weakening.

15. Tom Nairn, *Faces of Nationalism: Janus Revisited* (London: Verso, 1997).

16. Jean-Marie Guéhenno, *The End of the Nation-State*, trans. Victoria Elliott (Minneapolis: University of Minnesota Press, 1993).

17. Daniel Bell, *The Coming of Post-Industrial Society: A Venture in Social Forecasting* (New York: Basic Books, 1973).

18. Francis Fukuyama, *The End of History and the Last Man* (New York: Avon Books, 1992).

19. Benjamin R. Barber, *Jihad Vs. McWorld: How Globalism and Tribalism are Reshaping the World* (New York: Ballantine Books, 1995, 1996); Walter B. Wriston, *The Twilight of Sovereignty: How the Information Revolution is Transforming Our World* (New York: Scribners, 1992).

20. Samuel P. Huntington, *The Clash of Civilizations and the Remaking of World Order* (New York: Simon & Schuster, 1996).

21. Edward Luttwak, *Turbo-Capitalism: Winners and Losers in the Global Economy* (New York: HarperCollins, 1999).

22. Amy Harmon, "Worries About Big Brother at America Online," *New York Times*, January 31, 1991, section 1, 20.

23. Ithiel de Sola Pool, *Technologies of Freedom* (Cambridge, Mass.: Harvard University Press, 1984).

24. James Lee Ray, *Democracy and International Conflict: An Evaluation of the Democratic Peace Proposition* (Columbia: University of South Carolina Press, 1995).

25. John J. Mearsheimer, "Here We Go Again," *New York Times*, May 17, 1998, section 4.

LARRY GROSS

14 Somewhere There's a Place for Us

Sexual Minorities and the Internet

NEW MEDIA create opportunities for the formation of new communities, and the Internet is no exception. In contrast to most other modern media, the Internet offers opportunities for individual engagement as both senders and receivers, permitting the coalescing of interest-based networks spanning vast distances. The potential for friendship and group formation provided by the Internet is particularly valuable for members of self-identified minorities who are scattered and often besieged in their home surroundings. A brief tour of the Web will reveal countless sites devoted to specialized interests that draw like-minded participants across national and international boundaries. Notable among the interests served by this (so far) uniquely egalitarian and open medium of communication are those represented by sexual minorities.

Sexual minorities differ from traditional minorities in several significant respects. In many ways we have more in common with fringe political, religious, or ideological groups. Like other social groups defined by forbidden thoughts or deeds, we are rarely born into minority communities or families in which parents or siblings share our minority status. Rather, lesbians and gay men are a self-identifying minority, and rarely recognize or announce our status before adolescence. Up until that point, society simply presumes us to be heterosexual and treats us as such. Like unwitting spies, then, we spend our formative years tucked away in the homes of people who assume we are like them, who school us in traditions that will ultimately exclude us, and who teach us, quite often, to despise the people we will become. Little wonder, then, that at the hour of sexual awakening gay and lesbian youth often feel they are alone in the world, with no sense that they belong to a people or to a past, with no public heroes to call their own.

ALONE IN THE LIVING ROOM

Tamar Liebes and Elihu Katz returned from their travels accompanying *Dallas* into living rooms around the world with the conclusion that "viewing

255

escapist programs is not as escapist as it seems. In fact, viewers typically use television fiction as a forum for discussing their own lives."[1] But, when Liebes and Katz go on to argue that, therefore, "the best place to begin [cultivating critical ability] is at home with familiar television programs" (155), they fail to connect with the experience of those whose families might not welcome the opportunity to discuss, or even to acknowledge, their lives. Particularly for lesbian and gay adolescents, home is not necessarily a haven in a heartless world.

In the summer of 1992 the daytime TV serial *One Life To Live* (OLTL) began what was to be the longest and most complex television narrative ever to deal with a lesbian or gay character. Billy Douglas is a high school student who had recently moved to Llanview (the fictional small town outside Philadelphia where OLTL takes place) and become a star athlete and class president. When Billy confides, first to his best friends and then to his minister, that he is gay, he sets off a series of plot twists that differ from the usual soap opera complications in that they expose homophobia and AIDS-phobia among the residents of Llanview and thus offer the characters—and the audience—an opportunity to address topics that daytime serials, along with the rest of U.S. mass media, have generally preferred to ignore.

The plot line featuring Billy Douglas was the dominant thread of OLTL from July through early September 1992. Billy Douglas was played by a young actor named Ryan Phillippe, in his first professional role, and he received an unusually large amount of mail even for a good-looking young soap opera actor. Even more unusual was the fact that so many of the hundreds of letters he received during the months that he appeared on OLTL came from young men, most of whom identified themselves as gay—in one interview Phillippe reported getting 2,000 letters, adding that "a good 45 percent . . . [were] from homosexual teenagers."[2]

Many of the young gay men—and several of the older men—wrote that they were particularly moved by and grateful for Ryan's sensitive portrayal of an experience much like their own, being isolated and vulnerable in a society that would prefer not to know they existed. While it is not difficult to imagine that an African American, Asian American, or Latino actor would get letters from teenagers who identify with and appreciate their representation of an under-represented group on the public media stage, it is inconceivable that they would receive letters like the following:

August 31, 1992

Dear Ryan,

First of all, I want to thank you for the courage you have shown playing the part of a homosexual teenager. Especially in this day and age when discrimination and violence against gays is on the rise.

As you act on *One Life to Live* as a gay teenager, I also act. I act as a straight, normal twenty one year old. It has become routine to act like the perfect son or brother. *You are the first person I have ever told and may be the last, that I am gay.* I don't think I will ever be able to tell anyone the truth. Had not your portrayal and this storyline of a gay teen hit me so deeply, I probably would not be telling you. Your character is so realistic and you do such a great job portraying how gay teens really feel.

Recently, I saw phone numbers for gay youth in *Soap Opera Weekly* magazine. For those who are troubled about their sexuality. I honestly don't feel I have enough courage to call any of these places. For some reason, I think somehow, someone will find out. If my family or friends find out, I'm afraid they wouldn't look at me the same or would never love me as much as they do now.

I feel that way because of things I hear my family say about homosexuals. Until recently, I would laugh at jokes about gays or would pretend to dislike the way they were. I cannot and will not do that anymore. Now I just stay silent and try to ignore things that are said about gays and even AIDS itself. I overheard my father say that faggots started AIDS and normal people like Magic Johnson have to suffer for what gays have done. Well, do you think I could ever tell him that I am one of those who he thinks have caused normal people to suffer and die from AIDS. It's something I could never foresee.

I know this is just your job and I'm sorry for throwing all of my problems at you like this. I certainly don't expect you to solve any of them but it feels good just to tell someone . . . Thank you for your time. [emphasis added][3]

How should we think about, understand the nature of the relationships these writers feel that they have with Ryan Phillippe, an actor they have seen in a single role and, possibly, in TV and magazine interviews; or is it with Billy Douglas, the troubled but courageous gay teenager, who reminds them of themselves? Why do these writers, both isolated and fearful gay teens and adults haunted by memories of unhappy childhoods, feel that a young actor (known to be straight) portraying a confused and troubled youth is an appropriate target for their confessions, their overtures, and their pleas for help?

Back in the 1950s, when Donald Horton and Richard Wohl first labeled the phenomenon of parasocial interaction, within a psychiatric framework, they defined such responses as pathological only when they are a "substitute for autonomous social participation, when [they proceed] in absolute defiance of objective reality."[4] Joli Jensen summarized their view: "These extreme forms of fandom, they claim, are mostly characteristic of the socially isolated, the socially inept, the aged and invalid, the timid and rejected. For these and similarly deprived groups, para-social interaction is an attempt by the socially excluded (and thus psychologically needy) to compensate for the absence of 'authentic' relationships in their lives."[5]

Apparently in the 1990s many teenagers and even adults confronting the choice between the stifling agony of the closet and the possibility—even certainty—of familial and societal rejection were living in pathological circumstances and did not have the option of authentic relationships with anyone who could help them deal with their emotional crises. Thus an inexperienced but sincere young heterosexual actor found himself playing not only role model but also confessor and phantom friend to people in great pain and need.

A Place for Us

In recent years new options have emerged that offer isolated members of a minority the opportunity to reach out to and communicate with like-minded fellows: scattered cable-TV and radio programs that are available to those lucky enough to live within their range,[6] and for those with access to cyberspace, the Internet, and the World Wide Web. Currently there are online forums, bulletin boards, home-page sites, and online "zines" addressed to lesbian and gay readers. These include, to give two relevant examples, a weekly listing of television programs with lesbian/gay-related content, and the Oasis, a Web site dedicated to providing information and contacts for lesbian and gay teenagers.[7] These technological innovations permit the construction of virtual public spaces that can be life—or at least, sanity—saving refuges for many who have reason to feel they are living in enemy territory.

"Does anyone else feel like you're the only gay guy on the planet, or at least in Arlington, Texas?" When seventeen-year-old Ryan Matthew posted that question on AOL in 1995, he received more than 100 supportive e-mail messages.[8] Similar accounts abound, not only in the United States but in many other parts of the world. University of Haifa researcher Lilach Nir interviewed Israeli gay teenagers who participate in online discussions unavailable to them in their "real" environments of smaller cities, rural villages, and kibbutzim.[9]

The popularity of the Internet for gay men and lesbians isn't limited to teenagers. According to the Associated Press, "It's the unspoken secret of the online world that gay men and lesbians are among the most avid, loyal and plentiful commercial users of the Internet. On any given evening, one-third of all the member-created chat rooms on America Online are devoted to gay topics."[10] As described by Tom Reilly, the Internet executive who created Planet Out as the "gay global village of cyberspace[,] . . . Gays and lesbians don't have a high level of ownership of mainstream media properties. The internet is the first medium where we can have equal footing with the big players."[11]

While one of the clichés of computer-mediated communication is that one can hide one's true identity, so "that nobody knows you're 15 and live in Montana and are gay,"[12] it is also true, as Nir's informants told her, that in their Internet Relay Chat (IRC) conversations they "are unmasking the covers they are forced to wear in their straight daily lives."[13] The opportunities for deceptive (as well as truthful) self-presentation on the Internet have featured in the alarms raised in response to the Internet's potential to disseminate that most volatile of media substances, sexually explicit words and images.

OLD AND NEW TRAPS FOR THE YOUNG

The Internet is only the latest in a stream of communications technologies that have appeared since the invention of photography in the mid-nineteenth century (or, since Gutenberg). In instance after instance, as a new technology arrives on the scene it can safely be predicted that among its earliest users will be churches spreading the Christian gospel and the creators and purveyors of explicit sexual imagery. Those with the strongest, if not necessarily the purest, motives will be the first to explore the possibilities inherent in each medium to capture words and images and to convey them to those hungering for their messages. In the case of pornography—if not the Gospels—sexual images and stories have generally been officially condemned while privately enjoyed. They also have offered channels for the vicarious expression and satisfaction of minority interests that are difficult, embarrassing, and occasionally illegal to indulge in reality. For lesbians and gay men, whose sexuality is officially denied and erased, pornography often provides a vital message: "For isolated gays porn can be an important means of saying 'other gays exist.' "[14]

Lesbian writer Dorothy Allison recalls her first encounter with "hard-core" paperbacks she found under her parents' mattress when she was a child:

> What the books did contribute was a word—the word Lesbian. When she finally appeared . . . I knew her immediately . . . When she pulled the frightened girl close after thirty pages, I got damp all down my legs. That's what it was, and I wasn't the only one even if none had turned up in the neighborhood yet. Details aside, the desire matched up. She wanted women; I wanted my girlfriends. The word was Lesbian. After that, I started looking for it.[15]

The pornography Dorothy Allison found was (most likely) written by and for straight men, who have always appreciated a bit of lesbian spice in their erotic menu, an appetizer before the main course. For gay men, how-ever, heterosexual pornography has never been a welcoming venue. Still, as Thomas Waugh has documented, gay men have long created, collected, and enjoyed their own pornography.[16] However, only in recent decades has it become possible for most gay youth and adults to enter and explore this narrow channel of imagery created of, for, and by this minority.

John Burger has written an account of gay male video pornography that illustrates several ways "these videos serve as history texts of the gay male experience": "These videos . . . are important documents not only of the all-gay environment, real or invented, but of the gay male psyche which so desperately envisions such spaces where they can be free from the so-cial oppressions encountered daily . . . If we must be marginalized, let us at least create enjoyable spaces on the fringe—whether in imaginary repre-sentations or in reality, like the bathhouses."[17]

The existence of this minority channel is seen as a threat by those who guard the ramparts of the sexual reservation. The visible presence of les-bian or gay (or any unconventional) sexuality poses a serious threat: it un-dermines the unquestioned normalcy of the status quo, and opens up the possibility of making choices that people might never have otherwise con-sidered could be made. In fact, of course, all explicit sexual imagery has been controversial whenever it threatens to spill out of a narrow channel designed to reach elite (male) audiences.

The fight to keep sexuality invisible (especially in its "deviant" forms) is part of an ancient battle waged by the forces of established order against the subversive potential of powerful images and the wayward impulses they might inspire in the vulnerable. The vulnerable, it is important to recognize, are rarely if ever the holders of established power themselves, but rather those over whom that power is held: children, women, and "lower classes" of all sorts.[18] Note that this is the typical order in which the argument is couched: children are the model group of vulnerable charges to be protected, guided, and educated—controlled. Women and the "lower classes" (the poor, the uneducated) are often cast in the mold that previously set the form for dealing with children.

Traditionally, the only acceptable storytellers outside the family were those certified by religious institutions. Schools, also originally religious, gradually forced a new group of specialists between children and the world they grow up into. The arrival of mass media of communications fundamentally altered the situation: children were increasingly open to influences that parents, priests, and teachers could not monitor or control. Beginning with the widespread availability of printed materials to the literate, increasing with the invention of media less dependent on literacy (graphic reproduction technologies, photography, movies, radio, and even the telephone), and culminating with television's omnipresence and, newly sweeping over the horizon, the Internet, children have become more and more independent consumers of mass-produced stories.

But, as I've noted, children are only one source of concern. Popular media have consistently raised the specter of unrest and misbehavior among the "lower orders." Whether the suspect and controversial media are newspapers, novels, and theater, as in the nineteenth century, or movies, radio, comic books, television, and now the Internet, in the twenty-first, concern tends to focus on the possibilities of disruption that threaten established norms of belief, behavior, and morality.

The feared power of images—verbal or, even more powerfully, visual— seems to reside in the representation of precisely those behaviors and options that the holders of power wish to deny to those they control, protect, and fear. To draw upon the language so beloved of Senator Jesse Helms, such images "promote, condone, or encourage" forbidden behavior.

For reasons that extend beyond the scope of this essay, images of violence have remained ubiquitously available although they have been repeatedly denounced by moral authorities and endlessly studied by media researchers. Images of sexual behavior, in contrast, have been the targets of more effective attack and their availability has been generally hedged around with legal proscriptions. While parents, preachers, and politicians have criticized violence in the movies, comic books, and television, they have succeeded in criminalizing many explicit sexual images and have prosecuted those who produce or distribute and even, on occasion, those who consume them (however, the government-mandated "V-chip" for U.S. television—and in Canada—has had little effect on television offerings).

The legal term for prohibited sexual representations (in words or images) is *obscenity* and its most influential definition in Western law comes from Victorian England's Lord Chief Justice Cockburn, who ruled in 1868 (*Regina v. Hicklin*) that, "the test of obscenity is this: whether the tendency of the matter charged as obscenity is to deprave and corrupt those whose minds are open to such immoral influences, and into whose hands a publication of this sort may fall."[19] Just a few years later, in the United States, Anthony Comstock successfully lobbied for the passage of *An Act for the Suppression of Trade in, and Circulation of, Obscene Literature and Articles of Immoral Use,* which President Grant signed in 1873 and which was widely referred to as the Comstock Law.

Comstock came to be a symbol of America's fear of uncontrolled sexuality, just as his unique position as Special Agent of the U.S. Post Office for over forty years made him its moral policeman. In his writing and in his crusades against immorality Comstock articulated a widespread obsession with the ubiquitous *Traps for the Young* (the title of his 1883 work) that lay in wait. "Newspapers, 'half-dime' novels, advertisements, theaters, saloons, lotteries, pool halls, postcards, photographs, even painting and sculpture—wherever the poor child turned, in Comstock's nightmarish America, something lurked, ready to debauch him."[20] As Walter Kendrick insightfully notes, Comstock's chief dread was the universal distribution of information:

> The prospect called up nightmarish images of a world without structure, where all barriers had been breached and all differences leveled. It was appropriate that sex should become the focus of such nightmares, since long before the modern threat arose, sex already stood for loss of control and the scattering of substance. Comstock found in the postal system a perfect metaphor for this ancient terror: spread throughout the country, indiscriminately accessible, public and private at once, the postal system had (odd as it may sound) something sexy about it. Left unpoliced, sex bred chaos; uninspected, the mails might do the same.[21]

Sandboxes and Mailboxes

If Comstock were still alive he would be even more terrified of the Internet, as it far exceeds the postal system in speed (to put it mildly) and in its potential to reach those he considered susceptible to the traps laid for the young.

Take fifteen-year-old Daniel Montgomery, for example. In June 1995, the Seattle papers reported that the teenager had been "lured" away from home by a stranger, but not someone "casing his neighborhood or hanging around outside his high school."[22] "Instead, the mysterious character known to the Montgomerys only as 'Damien Star' was lurking in a place that proved much more ominous: cyberspace." The encounter took place in a "gay chat room" on America Online—"it was there that the man apparently enticed Daniel Montgomery with secret promises" to run away from home and join him in San Francisco. Daniel's father believed his son was the victim of "an organized attempt by adults to recruit boys like Daniel." The vice principal of his school told the paper that "we've certainly had runaways before . . . but holy cow, this makes you sick." The police were sympathetic but not alarmed: "If a child is listed as a runaway, what we do is take a runaway report . . . We don't go and actively seek them out."

Within a few days, however, it seemed that things were not quite as Comstockian as earlier reports had suggested. Daniel's father was identified with the religious right, and acknowledged that "there [were] issues between him and the teenager," presumably because "Daniel may have been sexually confused."[23] More important, it turned out that Damien Starr wasn't the pseudonym of a dirty old man who was infiltrating the Internet to lure innocent teenagers into a life of depravity. Damien Starr is the real name of a San Francisco teenager who met Daniel Montgomery in a gay America Online chat room and apparently responded sympathetically to accounts of his difficulties with his parents.

The unmasking of Damien Starr did nothing to allay the fears of those who see in the Internet a threat to the innocent and vulnerable. The week after Daniel Montgomery returned home to his parents the U.S. Senate voted to impose heavy fines and prison terms on those who distribute sexually explicit material over computer networks:

> Voting 84–16 in a session rife with lurid talk about child pornography and on-line descriptions of bestiality, advocates of tough regulation easily overwhelmed objections from a handful of lawmakers who said the measure would violate constitutional rights to free speech and threaten

the growth of computer networks. "Take a look at this disgusting material, pictures which were copied for free off the Internet only this week," said Sen. Jim Exon, D-Neb., the measure's chief sponsor, as he brandished a big blue binder with a bright red label: "Caution."[24]

Senator Exon, like his predecessors back to Comstock, presented his role as protecting children, not as restricting expression. "I'm not trying to be a super censor. The first thing I was concerned with was kids being able to pull up pornography on their machines."[25] Special Agent Comstock was present in more than spirit, however, as the U.S. Congress moved toward the inclusion of Senator Exon's Communications Decency Act (CDA) as part of the omnibus Telecommunications Reform Act signed by President Clinton on February 8, 1996. The CDA revived the provisions of the 1873 Comstock Act prohibiting mailing of abortion-related materials across state lines, which are still on the books, though essentially nullified by *Roe v. Wade*, and added them to the prohibition against making available to minors online materials that "in context, depicts or describes in terms patently offensive as measured by contemporary community standards, sexual or excretory activities or organs." The CDA was the target of an immediate lawsuit filed by the ACLU in the name of a group of plaintiffs that included Planned Parenthood, Critical Path AIDS Project, and an online publisher of writings by lesbian and gay teenagers.

In June 1996 a three-judge federal district court panel struck down the CDA. Judge Stewart Dalzell wrote that "the Internet may fairly be regarded as a never-ending worldwide conversation. The Government may not, through the CDA, interrupt that conversation. As the most participatory form of mass speech yet developed, the Internet deserves the highest protection from government intrusion" (*ACLU v. Reno*). The following year the U.S. Supreme Court voted 7 to 2 to affirm the lower court's decision, explicitly resisting the politically popular appeal of child protection rhetoric: "Regardless of the strength of the government's interest [in protecting children], the level of discourse reaching a mailbox simply cannot be limited to that which would be suitable for a sandbox."[26]

Comstock's heirs are not easily discouraged, however, in their zeal to protect children from sexuality. In October 1998, the U.S. Congress passed a more narrowly drawn version of the CDA, the Child Online Protection Act (COPA), which President Clinton opposed, but signed, relying on the courts to protect citizens from the legislative and executive branches. In the debate over COPA in the House Commerce Committee, Representative (now Speaker) Dennis Hastert articulated the familiar cry: "Even though our children may be at home with the doors locked that doesn't mean that they are safe. We must continue to be proactive in warding off pedophiles and other creeps who want to take advantage of our children. It's not infringing on our liberties, it's about protecting our kids."

COPA was immediately challenged by the ACLU and seventeen plaintiffs, many of them lesbian and gay bookstores, publications, organizations, writers, and Internet activists. As PlanetOut founder Tom Reilly testified in Federal Court in January 1999, "Many people find just being gay to be 'harmful to minors,' . . . We operate a community of interest, rather than a community of geography, but based on our community standards no information on our site is offensive in any way."[27]

The drafters of COPA attempted to narrow its focus, thus hoping to avoid the fate of CDA, and they targeted commercial sites by requiring that they obtain credit card information before admitting users to so-called adult sites. The plaintiffs argue that these restrictions impose an economic hardship and barrier for both providers and users, and that they also constitute a chilling effect that will lead providers to self-censorship. On June 22, 2000, the Third Circuit Court of Appeals unanimously upheld a lower court's injunction against COPA, citing serious constitutional flaws. The Supreme Court heard arguments on COPA and sent it back to the Appeals Court which, in March 2003, again rejected it. While it is reasonable to expect that COPA will ultimately suffer the same constitutional fate as the CDA, the forces of censorship opened a new front through the imposition of measures involving Internet filtering software.

CYBERSPACE PATROLS

Having lost the battle of the CDA, congressional censors turned to a technological fix akin to the V-chip mandated for inclusion in future TV sets: the requirement that Internet "filtering software" be used by schools and libraries that receive federal funds for Internet access, in order to block material deemed inappropriate for children. The introduction of the Internet School Filtering Act in the spring of 1998 opened a door much wider than that of the local school and public library, however, as commercial providers have rushed to offer parents a variety of filtering services. In the words of Joan Garry, executive director of the Gay and Lesbian Alliance Against Defamation (GLAAD), "we had gone from the frying pan of active censorship [the CDA] into the fire of censorship by passive omission."[28]

Commercial filtering software works by blocking access to sites based on keywords presumed to signal sexual content, and this often includes the very words *gay, lesbian, homosexual,* or even *sexual orientation.* Parents— or schools and libraries—that install such filtering software thus prevent teenagers (and adults, in many instances) from gaining access to support groups, informational sites, and even the Association of Gay Square Dance Clubs. As a representative of CyberSitter put it, "I wouldn't even care to debate the issue if gay and lesbian issues are suitable for teenagers . . . We filter anything that has to do with sex. Sexual orientation [is about sex] by virtue of the fact that it has sex in the name." Thus, sites offering safer sex information are routinely excluded by many filtering programs (along with sites focused on breast cancer). Some filter providers, such as SurfWatch and CyberPatrol, promised to permit access to informational, educational, and support sites, but GLAAD and its allies remain concerned about the implementation of these commitments in deciding on specific instances and keywords.

Even when filtering programs do not automatically exclude sites that address lesbian and gay people and concerns, they pose other dangers to gay teenagers. NetNanny, CyberSitter, and SafeSearch, among others, allow parents to set their own exclusionary criteria, and they make suggestions that some might find questionable. The president of Solid Oak, the provider of CyberSitter software, cited the National Organization for Women's Web site as a target: "The NOW site has a bunch of lesbian stuff on it, and our users don't want it." CyberSitter was at the time the filter recommended by the ultra-right Focus on the Family organization.

The filtering technology has another worrisome feature: an "audit trail" that allows parents (or librarians and school administrators) to trace which sites and newsgroups their children (or other users) have tried to access. As GLAAD points out, this auditing feature is particularly dangerous to youth, if it leads to the accidental disclosure of their sexual orientation before they are ready. As a sixteen-year-old lesbian put it,

> Living in a small town in South Carolina makes it almost an impossibility to be open about sexuality. Both emotional and physical safety is in the hands of those who are not primarily known for their open-mindedness and understanding. Through e-mail, I've created a support system for myself of different gay/lesbian listservs, and through people I could not have otherwise contacted. Coming to terms with my sexuality would have been so much harder if I had been alone. I owe a debt of gratitude to the people I've met, and who have supported me—the people who told me I was not "evil," or "immoral," or "sick" after these very things were drummed into my head. At 16, I am content with myself.[29]

Although the Internet School Filtering Act, signed by Clinton in December 1999, was immediately halted by a court injunction, this was not the first skirmish on this new legal battlefield. In November 1998, a federal court in Virginia struck down the use of filtering software by the Loudon County public library on the grounds that such filters violate adult patron's First Amendment rights. But, as usual, the forces of censorship are crusading to protect children from the dangers of sexually explicit materials. In January 1999, a plaintiff in Livermore, California, accused the public library of violating the constitutional rights of her twelve-year-old son, because he was able to access and download sexually graphic pictures from a library Internet terminal.[30] "Children have a right to be free from infliction of pain," stated the plaintiff's lawyer, although he didn't explain the precise form of pain inflicted when twelve year-old Brandon P. downloaded "color images of semi-nude and nude women" on a disk he had brought to the library, and "proceeded to use a computer at a relative's house to print out the images . . . [and] allowed one or more minors to view certain of the images . . . Brandon P. did this activity approximately 10 times."[31]

Seventeen-year-old Virginia represented the kind of success story that should make any proponent of Internet access proud. Before going online she suffered from "a bout of clinical depression that had been with me since middle school, a condition that left me vulnerable to causing myself injury, marring that pretty skin, and thinking about committing suicide." Reading articles at the Oasis Web site "was like a lifeline for me . . . Nowhere else could I read about people who were experiencing everything I was, and not feel like a freak for being able to relate to them . . . Now I'm the one getting e-mail from people, and now I'm the one trying to help other people get a glimpse of what it's like, of how to cope and how it really happens."[32]

The battle over unfiltered access to Internet sites brought a second victory to the opponents of censorship when the Court of Appeals for the Third Circuit struck down the CIPA in June 2001. The court, while sympathetic to the goal of "protecting children," ruled that the technology blocks so much unobjectionable material that it falls afoul of the First Amendment.[33] The issue will undoubtedly end up in the lap of the Supreme Court, and even if the forces of freedom prevail, as they did with the CDA, Comstock's heirs will continue their campaigns to search out and destroy technological traps for the young. If the cybernannies win the battle, teenagers like Virginia may be cut off from the lifeline represented by resources such as Oasis, left feeling like the desperate sixteen-year-old who wrote soap opera actor Ryan Phillippe, " Ryan, the only person in this world I can relate to is your character Billy Douglas on *One Life to Live*. Ryan, I'm so scared. I don't know what to do and I'm afraid of what I might do. You, God, and I are the only ones that know! Ryan, please help!"

NOTES

1. Tamar Liebes and Elihu Katz, *The Export of Meaning: Cross-Cultural Readings of "Dallas"* (New York: Oxford University Press, 1990), 154.

2. M. Scott Mallinger, "I'm Not a Homosexual, But I Play One on TV," *Au Courant* (Philadelphia) 11, no. 19 (March 22, 1993): 14.

3. Larry Gross, "You're the First Person I've Ever Told: Letters to a Fictional Gay Teen," in *Taking Liberties: Gay Male Essays on Politics, Culture, and Art*, ed. Michael Bronski (New York: Kasak Books, 1996), 369–86.

4. Donald Horton and Richard Wohl, "Mass Communication and Para-Social Interaction: Observation on Intimacy at a Distance," *Psychiatry*, 19, no. 3 (1956): 200.

5. Joli Jensen, "Fandom as Pathology: The Consequences of Characterization," in *The Adoring Audience: Fan Culture and Popular Media*, ed. Lisa Lewis (New York: Routledge, 1992), 9–29.

6. Los Angeles radio producer Greg Gordon, recalling his experience as a teenager ("I thought I was the only one"), "found a way to reach into the closets and countrysides where gays are painfully isolated: gay radio. He started *This Way Out*, a weekly half-hour show of news and commentary that now airs on 70 radio stations in six countries . . . Those who tune in are often older gays in rural areas or young people who feel they can't talk to their parents or teachers about being gay." Deb Price, "Friendly Voices: Gay Radio Eases Isolation," *Detroit News*, March 4, 1993.

7. See Steve Silberman, "We're Teen, We're Queer, and We've Got E-Mail," *Wired* (December 1994), 1–3; and Jeff Walsh, "Logging On, Coming Out," *The Advocate*, October 18, 1994, 6.

8. Trip Gabriel, "Some On-Line Discoveries Give Gay Youths a Path to Themselves," *New York Times*, July 2, 1995, 1.

9. Lilach Nir, "A Site of Their Own: Gay Teenagers' Involvement Patterns in IRC and Newsgroups," paper presented to the International Communication Association's 48th Annual Meeting, Jerusalem, 1998.

10. Associated Press, "Gay and Lesbian Net Surfers: A Dream Market in an On-line World," June 24, 1996.

11. Peter Lewis, "Planet Out's Gay Services on Virtual Horizon," *New York Times*, August 21, 1995, D3.

12. Gabriel, "Some On-Line Discoveries Give Gay Youths a Path to Themselves."

13. Nir, "A Site of Their Own," 11.

14. Kobena Mercer and Isaac Julien, "True Confessions," in *Black: Representations of Masculinity in Contemporary American Art*, ed. Thelma Golden (New York: Harry Abrams, 1994) 195.

15. Dorothy Allison, "A Personal History of Lesbian Porn," in *Skin: Talking About Sex, Class, and Literature* (Ithaca, N.Y.: Firebrand Books, 1994), 187.

16. Thomas Waugh, *Hard to Imagine: Gay Male Eroticism in Film and Photography from Their Beginnings to Stonewall* (New York: Columbia University Press, 1996).

17. John Burger, *One-Handed Histories: The Eroto-Politics of Gay Male Video Pornography* (New York: Harrington Park Press, 1995).

18. Sociologists and communications researchers will recognize this as the "third person" effect described by Philip Davison; others might recognize this as an argument against the arts first made by Plato in the *Republic*.

19. Walter Kendrick, *The Secret Museum: Pornography in Modern Culture* (New York: Viking, 1987), 121.

20. Ibid., 138.

21. Ibid., 144–45.

22. Susan Byrnes, "Parents Suspect Cyberspace 'Kidnap,' " *Seattle Times*, June 2, 1995.

23. Elizabeth Weise, "Cyberspace Runaway," *Associated Press*, June 5, 1995; and "Cyberspace Suspect Also a Teen," *Associated Press*, June 7, 1995.

24. Edmund Andrews, "On-line porn may be illegal," *New York Times*, June 15, 1995.

25. Edmund Andrews, "Panel Backs Smut Ban on Internet," *New York Times*, March 24, 1995.

26. Quoted in Philip Jenkins, *Moral Panic: Changing Concepts of the Child Molester in Modern America* (New Haven: Yale University Press, 1998), 213.

27. *Yahoo News* (January 22, 1999).

28. GLAAD, "Access Denied: An Impact of Internet Filtering Software on the Gay and Lesbian Community," 1997, <http://www.glaad.org/publications/archive_detail.php?id=103&>. Accessed November 2003.

29. Ibid.

30. Matt Richtel, "City Seeks Dismissal of Library Filtering Case," *New York Times*, January 14, 1999.

31. From the complaint: <http://www.filteringfacts.org/liv-comp.htm>. Accessed March 1999.

32. Andy Oram, "When You're Blocked Online, Where Can You Go?" Channel Q News Desk, December 9, 1997.

33. John Schwartz, "Court Overturns Law Mandating Internet Filters for Public Libraries," *New York Times*, June 1, 2002.

SARAH BANET-WEISER

15 Surfin' the Net

Children, Parental Obsolescence, and Citizenship

ON APRIL 20, 1999, two young high school boys, Dylan Klebold and Eric Harris, went to Columbine High School in the upper-middle class suburb of Littleton, Colorado, and proceeded to shoot twelve students, one teacher, and themselves. Occurring shortly after several other school shootings across the United States, this event became the catalyst for a number of cultural and political debates about American laws, guns, and childhood itself. Predictably, a mass-mediated and widely public debate ensued over the benefits and disadvantages of gun control, with politicians and spokespersons on both sides of the issue using the Columbine tragedy as a platform from which to launch specific agendas. The shooting also inspired a widespread public lamentation over the state of America's children and the escalating amount of violence committed on schools and playgrounds. As the Colorado shootings were just one of many adolescent shootings around the country committed exclusively by boys, the topic of teens and violence became another element in the increasingly public debates about the crisis of masculinity in the United States. Cultural discourse around the shootings also had a racial dimension. Not only was one of the students shot and killed because he was black, but the discourse surrounding this incident encouraged a shocked dismay that was felt around the country in part because the two shooters, both upper-middle-class white boys who lived in a primarily white suburb, were seen as exceptional compared to children of color for whom violence is dominantly understood as a way of life.

Yet, there was also another debate that circulated around the cultural habits, tastes, and activities of the two young men involved in the shooting. After the killing, it was suggested that the two students were members of a school gang called the "Trenchcoat Mafia." Apparently, the gang primarily conducted its activities in and around the Internet, which was constructed in sensational terms in the media as the place that evidently provided not only instructions on how to make homemade pipe bombs, but also plugged these two smart yet "impressionable" youngsters into the vast, dark wasteland of the Net. This wasteland was framed by the media as a space populated by angst-ridden teens who were apt to wear gothic clothing styles, listen to heavy metal and industrial type music such as Marilyn Manson, and play horribly violent and technologically realistic computer games. This interaction with technology—and specifically the Internet— was seen as a crucial element in the cultural downfall of America's youth. In fact, according to the *Washington Post*, "82 percent of Americans cite the Internet as a potential cause for the [Colorado] shootings."[1] The Colorado shootings reinvigorated a public debate over the fate of American children, but with a specific twist: the fate that American culture faced was not about innocent children, but rather kids who are computer-savvy and sophisticated in their use of computer technologies, most specifically the Internet.

While new technologies and the Internet have been widely recognized by corporate culture and politicians as offering enormous potential in terms of democracy, tolerance, and most important, commerce, the "dark side" of technologies such as the Internet is often understood in terms of the influence and control it seemingly has over children. The fear and anxiety that preoccupies adults regarding the interaction of children with the Internet is discursively constructed in two primary ways. First, there is a cultural fear and shame regarding the exposure of pornography and other sexually inappropriate material on the Internet. The fear is both about children unwittingly encountering "cyberporn" and "cybersmut" (which label is used clearly depends on who is using it) on the Internet, and about children being lured by pedophiles who are believed to frequent cyberspace. The second central discourse that characterizes the interaction children have with technology is perhaps more deep-seated, and certainly is more subtle. It concerns the threat and anxiety generated by the superior skills and knowledge children are gaining regarding the use of technology. This set of skills not only renders adults potentially useless as guardians, but also limits the amount of control parents have over the kinds of information their children are receiving.

The adult fear over children encountering pornography or other inappropriate material on the Internet is clearly the one that garners the most public and political attention. The contents of pornographic Web sites are continually represented by the media as yet another laundry list of the evils of technology, as simultaneously the contents of these sites are fetishized and ironically become legitimated through media scrutiny. Pornographic sites on the Internet are indeed numerous, but are not nearly as common as the media purports them to be. Rather, pornographic Web sites themselves are constantly on display within the media, attracting public attention and encouraging a kind of voyeurism that vilifies pornography even as it makes it a central exhibition. Consider, for example, the political debate over the Communication Decency Act of 1996, an act that had virtually been voted down by Congress even before it came up for debate because of its obvious First Amendment offenses. The act, which was designed to extend regulations written to govern the dial-a-porn industry into the computer networks, proposed to outlaw obscene material on the Internet and to impose fines and prison terms on anyone who knowingly makes "indecent" material available to children under the age of eighteen.[2] Introduced by Senators Exon and Coats, it was initially predicted that the measure would be a sure failure because of the various ways in which it violated free speech. Yet when Senator Exon arrived in the Senate with downloaded pornographic pictures from the Internet, it was surprisingly passed, apparently because of the "incontrovertible" truth that the text and images offered.[3]

The debate over the Communications Decency Act tapped into a well-maintained ideology about childhood, one that situates childhood and sexuality as two necessarily separate realms. Childhood has been culturally understood as a precious artifact to be protected from the world of sexuality, despite the increasing presence of objectified children in advertisements, and the use of sexualized little girls and boys as means to spark public debate (JonBenet Ramsey and even Britney Spears are good examples of this). As James Kincaid documents in his work on eroticism and childhood, various discourses have produced the category "erotic child," and then encouraged culture to invest this category with meaning. Using examples from popular culture, Kincaid argues that many images of the child "are public spectacles of child eroticism, an eroticism that can be flaunted and also screened, exploited and denied, enjoyed and cast off, made central and made criminal."[4]

The idea that connections between children and sexuality are both "made central and made criminal" frames the debate around children and technology, where political interventions made around technology, such as the Communication Decency Act, invoke children as discursive means to figure sexuality centrally and to simultaneously pathologize it. Indeed, discourses of sexuality are largely understood as part of what Lynn Spigel calls "adult secrets," inappropriate ideas that it is believed children, through the world of technology and outside of parental control, can potentially access and learn.[5] The notion that the world is full of secrets that should only be divulged to adults who are mature and responsible enough to handle them relies upon a set of assumptions concerning the invention of modern childhood. The belief that children and sexuality are necessarily separate cultural discourses—that, indeed, children should be specifically *protected from* sexuality—is intricately tied to the cultural definition of the innocent child.

THE INNOCENT CHILD AND SEXUALITY

Perhaps the most significant factor fueling adult fears concerning children and technology revolves around the notion that children are by nature innocent, and that somehow this innocence is threatened, and perhaps even destroyed, through interaction with technology. The abstract figure of the innocent child has enormous symbolic value in America's cultural, political, and economic history, and is often used to invoke and fuel political battles over the fate of America's future. As cultural scholar Henry Jenkins has noted, in the wake of the Communications Decency Act, news magazines such as *Time* and *Newsweek* often reproduced the innocent child visually, where the child "appear[s] as a hypnotized young face awash in the eerie glow of the computer terminal on the cover of *Time*, rendering arguments about the First Amendment beside the point"[6] (Figure 15.1). In the case of the murder of six-year-old JonBenet Ramsey, the relentless media coverage of the crime was, and continues to be, accompanied by highly stylized images of a heavily made-up, deeply feminized and sexualized "innocent." During the numerous schoolyard shootings in the United States in the past five years, it was a commonly used media tactic to broadcast the baby photographs of the shooters, as examples of children who have "gone bad" due to a variety of speculated factors.[7] In the last several years, most stories about America's youth are written and broadcast with a simultaneously perplexed and sober tone about "what went wrong," with the implicit (and often explicit) message that there is something outside of human life that is to blame for the horrific tragedies that seem to be plaguing America's schools and playgrounds. The media representations of children in the United States are predominantly framed by this discourse of lost innocence, and countless public debates occur over not only how to regain innocence, but also where to name what destroyed it in the first place. For obvious reasons, legislators, educators, and parents often identify the media as the culprit, and for just as obvious reasons, the media itself goes to great expense to focus the blame elsewhere: bad parenting, poverty, gun access, and so on. Recently, however, the blame has been more squarely placed on

Figure 15.1 *Time Magazine*, May 10, 1999. Photo by Raymon Gendreau/Tony Stone Images. © Time Inc./Time Life Pictures/Getty Images.

technology, where the increasing use of the Internet, chat rooms, and violent video games by children has resulted in a widespread cultural fear about the new techno-child. The history of the innocent child provides some insights to understanding and situating the fear and anxiety that frames current discourses of children and technology. The debate regarding children and technology revolves around a variety of factors, but much of it concerns adult control. Specifically, the debate about children and technology bears the legacy of the history of adult intervention around children's relationship with sexuality and consumerism.

Many scholars have persuasively argued that the current understanding of childhood is in fact a cultural invention, a product of a variety of social, political, and economic discourses. Philippe Ariès, Michel Foucault, James Kincaid, Viviana Zelizer and others have historicized the contemporary construction of childhood as a means to pry open the status of our investment in particular notions of childhood innocence. An account of the historical evolution of childhood is crucial to both denaturalize and challenge the universalism of current conceptions of childhood. In other words, it is the notion that childhood innocence is both "natural" (that is, basic to all human nature) and "universal" that continues to legitimate the cultural and economic status of the innocent child. In this sense, as Jenkins points out, the cultural construction of the innocent child is a crucial element in the cementing of not only "official" politics such as public policy decisions, governmental regulatory practices, and child labor laws, but it also is necessary for justifying racial and sexual hierarchies, for determining what can be considered culture and what cannot, and for situating adult identity in the world.[8]

The mutual dependency between constructions of childhood and adult identity is certainly not a new phenomenon. Ariès, in his book *Centuries of Childhood*, states that the purposeful use of the child to solidify adult identities comes into play only at the moment where childhood itself is created. The creation of a separate category of identity called "childhood" marks a clear line between the world of the adult and that of the child, a division that in eras previous to the seventeenth century was much less differentiated. Ariès historicizes the modern construction of childhood by tracing its developments throughout various historical and political eras, and argues that the boundaries between adults and children in the seventeenth century were created through cultural understandings of sexuality, morality, and pedagogy. Specifically, Ariès focuses on the difference in cultural discourses about sexuality because children were "assumed to be closer to the body, less inhibited, and thus unlikely to be corrupted by adult knowledge."[9] In other words, in the seventeenth century, because children were believed to be "unaware or indifferent" to sex, sexual jokes, gestures, and references *ceased to have meaning for children*—they lost their significance as sexual, and were therefore not thought to be corrupting forces.

Another reason that sexuality in the seventeenth century took on meaning only for adults (or for children who reached the age of puberty) is, according to Ariès, that innocence itself was a concept not associated with children, a startling fact given the complete collapse of childhood and innocence that characterizes life since the nineteenth century.[10] Throughout the seventeenth century the concept of innocence became gradually connected to expectations of childhood through such discourses as pedagogy and newly enforced moral codes, resulting in a cultural opposition between innocent children and sexuality.[11]

Michel Foucault similarly discusses the various ways in which sexual discourse shifted in Europe in the seventeenth and eighteenth centuries. Foucault argues that in the eighteenth century, sex itself became a matter of "administration," both a concept and an act that was policed and regulated through public discourses.[12] Similar to Ariès, Foucault argues that sex became a matter of utmost importance during this historical moment; it was not the case that sex had no meaning for children, or that there were no discussions about sex and sexuality. Rather, a new discourse was created around sexuality and children that explicitly focused on this relationship, a discourse that relied upon assumptions of "appropriate knowledges" and "innocence." Children were at the center of this "new regime of discourses" about sex, and as Foucault argues, sex was discussed in relationship to children as a way to create a new subjectivity of childhood itself:

> What this actually entailed, throughout this whole secular campaign that mobilized the adult world around the sex of children, was using these tenuous pleasures as a prop, constituting them as secrets (that is, forcing them into hiding so as to make possible their discovery), tracing them back to their source, tracking them from their origins to their effects, searching out everything that might cause them or simply enable them to exist.[13]

Children's relationship with sexuality thus became the central definition of childhood, where sexuality was increasingly a matter of regulation and surveillance. Kincaid, in his discussion of the "erotic child," argues that this identity category is produced in what he refers to as "cultural factories," or the systems of meaning that characterize culture. These factories "tell us what 'the child' is, and also what 'the erotic' *is* . . . for the last two hundred years or so, they have confused us, have failed to distinguish the two categories, have allowed them to dangerously overlap."[14] Foucault argues that this kind of "confusion" about the connections between eroticism and childhood is precisely that which constitutes childhood as an identity characterized by surveillance, forbidden desires, danger, and a need for protection. The discourses of childhood and sexuality are intimately intertwined; these discourses function as a device that separates children and adults into two different realms, even as they perform to define each identity—that of an adult and a child—as mutually constitutive.

THE CHILD AS CONSUMER

Thus, the figure of the erotic child is purposefully used to maintain particular assumptions and standards about both adulthood and childhood. Another social realm that children have historically been protected from is industrial capitalism. Children have been seen as too innocent to be corrupted by the crass processes of capitalism, too precious to be connected in any way with the distribution and production of capital. According to dominant ideologies, the purity of children is threatened by the vulgar determination of economics; children are not revered for their monetary value, but rather for their sentimental and emotional value.

This construction of the sentimentalized child is part of a larger cultural discourse about modern notions of progress and consumerism. In fact, economist Viviana Zelizer argues that childhood "is actually an invention that accompanied other modern inventions that promised rational progress and innovation."[15] In the late nineteenth and early twentieth centuries in Western cultures, children were employed as laborers, and their labor was understood as crucial for contributing to a family's income. The practice of employing children revolved around an understanding of children themselves as not only useful for the family, but also a crucial element in a capitalist system. Contributing to a family's income was a particular role for children, a role that Zelizer argues was crucially understood in obligatory terms: children worked in order to "begin to pay back their keep" in their families.

The consideration of children as useful changed in late eighteenth- and early nineteenth-century U.S. society, when laws were developed that eventually prohibited the employment of children. These legal changes relied upon a particular understanding of childhood as rationale for implementing a shift in the age requirements for labor. Zelizer argues that during this historical moment, children, newly seen as corruptible by social forces, began to be protected from the economic world of labor. Children themselves were understood as explicitly noncommercial. This process of shifting the social value of children, motivated in large part by changing labor laws so as to prohibit children from working for wages outside the home, encouraged what Zelizer calls "the sacralization of children," a process whereby adults invest children, and childhood, with sentimental or religious meaning.[16]

Child labor reform was central to the sacralization of children, and child labor reformers positioned children in a new light, where instead of being seen as individuals who could secure the future of their parents, they were seen as worthy of their parents' sacrifice. Thus, in the late nineteenth century, the cultural roles of the parent and child were reversed so that parents should be obligated to offer protection from the harsh realities of an adult, working world. This obligation was extended to the protection of an idealized concept of the "future." As Zelizer argues, according to reformers, "true parental love could only exist if the child was defined exclusively as an object of sentiment and not as an agent of production."[17]

This notion of the parental obligation to the child, rather than the other way around, is important for a contemporary discussion of technology and children. For, the construction of childhood was also a newly organized construction of adulthood; adults were given a new role as parents, providers, and protectors, just as children were given a new role as objects of sentiment. This conceptualization of these roles holds true to contemporary politics, where the child, and childhood, is understood as a sentimental object, something or someone in which to invest hopes and desires about a better world, a more innocent politics, a more productive future.[18] The "true parental love" insisted upon by the reformers, is writ large on a national stage, where the "true love" that a nation holds for its children takes the form of protecting the innocent.

Yet, the cultural and political insistence that children be protected from the world of commerce in the nineteenth century as laborers clearly did not extend to the new construction of children as domestic *consumers*. In fact, the domestic realm became one of the largest targeted markets for consumer products during the early twentieth century.[19] As middle-class children and their mothers were securely nestled in their domestic worlds, away from the harsh realities of the working world, marketers sought new ways to commercialize this space, and to portray the domestic sphere as in constant need of new products.[20]

Central to creating domestic space as a lucrative commercial avenue was what Stephen Kline calls the "commercialization of childhood." Throughout the Industrial Revolution, as factories were producing more and more goods, marketers pursued children as a profitable new market: "The Victorian awakening to the preciousness of childhood helped ensure that children's goods would expand along with other markets. Culturally, childhood was increasingly characterized by specific behavioral traits and products. The increasingly vivid image of a separate domain of childhood became standard in both the late Victorian arts and product appeals."[21] Thus, the sacralization of childhood that Zelizer details separated children from the production end of capitalism, but in so doing, situated them squarely within the consumer world. Children, precisely because of their presumed innocence, were newly understood as in need of proper guidance and motivation—a cultural construction of which toy and game companies, children's clothing manufacturers, and educational resources took full advantage. Toys and games (and later, new technologies such as radio and television) were marketed as crucial to a child's development; as the industrialized world made room for and then encouraged the necessity of leisure time, "parents were increasingly approached with a widening range of consumer goods for children's leisure."[22] Products designed specifically for children were marketed as key to maintaining innocence and purity—through leisure time, ideally spent at home with one's mother—while at the same time providing for a proper education. The cultural expectations of a child's innocence and new discourses on the value of appropriate education translated, according to Ellen Seiter, "into various product claims, such as toys create happiness; toys teach skills; toys bring parents and children close together; toys keep children busy; toys inspire activity."[23] Toys and other consumer products were marketed not only as new goods for children's leisure, but also as specific tools in morally and intellectually guiding a child. No longer connected to the commercial world as producers, sacralized and sentimentalized children were targeted as a new niche in the world of consumers at the beginning of the twentieth century.

The history of the commercialization of childhood must be taken into account when examining the various ways in which children interact in the contemporary world of technology. Parents in the early twentieth century were encouraged to demonstrate their love for their children through the purchase of particular consumer goods, and this theme of "parental love" continues to be at the heart of public discourse over the relationship of children with media and technology. The various ways in which this relationship is forged is often expressed as the love a parent has for a child—a love that is clearly not disingenuous, but is perhaps more accurately articulated as a particular kind of protection. As Ellen Seiter, Heather Hendershot, and others have argued, there were obviously efforts on the part of corporations and marketers to ensure that the rhetoric of advertising to children did not emphasize a commercial relationship with the child, but rather how companies and corporations can assist in loving children properly through the use of products.[24]

In the contemporary world, children and childhood are increasingly understood in marketing terms. As Jyotsna Kapur states, "Children—that is, preteens—have emerged as the fastest growing market segment based on the premise that the earlier they are hooked on brand names, the longer they will stay with a particular product."[25] Yet at the same time as the children's market continues to grow, and as children are becoming consumers at very early ages through the interaction with television, peers, schools, and the like, the notion that children are by nature innocent remains ideologically intact. According to the discourses of consumer society, the fact that contemporary children are savvy consumers does not, apparently, threaten their inherent innocence. Yet, the American public is constantly bombarded with messages about the loss of this innocence. If culturally sexuality is hidden from children, and children are enthusiastically encouraged to become sophisticated consumers, who, or what, then is the culprit in this loss of innocence? Historically and presently, the blame is often placed on technology and the media.

CHILDREN AND TECHNOLOGY

The development of communication technologies, and their cultural acceptance, has consistently involved adult expectations of children. The processes described in this essay concerning the construction of the innocent child, protected from sexuality and the production of capital, feature centrally in the public discourse framing the advent of new communication technologies. The threat of new technologies for parents is, at first glance, fairly obvious: systems of communication that disseminate information, such as television and the Internet, jeopardize the "original" source of information for children, their parents. As Seiter states, "Mass media targeted at children have shortened the period of exclusively parental influence over children. A distinctive, peer-oriented consumer culture now intervenes in the relationship of parents and children, and that intervention begins for many children as early as two years of age."[26] This perceived loss of parental control manifests itself in systems of surveillance and restraint over children's interaction with technology, ranging from governmental legislation to policy decisions to new technologies created precisely for this purpose, such as the V-Chip. These interventions can be read as what Kapur calls "a reinstatement of parental authority," a means of wrestling control from the overwhelming influence of technology.[27] Recent media reports on the potential pitfalls and evils of new information technologies often frame the issue of regaining parental control as newly significant in the age of the Internet. However, it is clear that the current debate waged in public discourse and the media about children's interaction with technology has its legacy within other, earlier forms of media, especially television.

Lynn Spigel persuasively demonstrates the role of the child in the emergence of the television in mid-century American domestic society. For both men and women, children were considered the key to establishing and maintaining social power. For middle-class white women, this meant encouraging a strong mother-child bond that afforded women a new type of empowerment (even as it ever more vigorously contained women in the domestic sphere), because mothers were culturally positioned as necessary to a safe and productive future. For men of the same socioeconomic class, in the postwar period of industrialization and increasing numbers of white-collar jobs, fathers were encouraged to turn to their children as a way to renegotiate their identities and their authority in a context separate from the alienating work world.[28] As Spigel points out, central for both of these endeavors was the notion "that children were innocent creatures who needed guidance into a world that they would help transform."[29] Children were therefore understood as both "innocents and arbiters of progress" for future society. Despite the child's apparent role in the "future," this vision was imagined and conceptualized by adults (more specifically, by parents). Children were the key to transforming society, but only with the proper and moral guidance of adult culture.

This is a key difference from the way in which the future is envisioned in twenty-first-century U.S. culture, when the advent of new technologies and the increasing power of the Internet have encouraged white, middle-class adults to feel anxiety and insecurity over the shape that a transformed world will take. Presently, adults may feel less empowered to envision and determine the future world. This, then, is at the heart of the contemporary fear and anxiety over the relationship of children with technology: children *are* transforming the world, but crucially through means and methods that are unfamiliar to many adults.

But for postwar America, child development, and concurrently, the development of the concept of childhood itself, was something that was easily grasped and understood by an emerging class of experts in this field.[30] This turn to experts for assistance in negotiating the unfamiliar world of media and technology resulted in a cultural discourse that emphasized not simply parental guardianship, but also an adult obligation to mediate the information coming from new technologies. This duty on the part of adults took the form of exercising control over television, leading to various public debates about the nature and the longevity of its effects. The television was often described as something completely beyond one's control, and was considered a direct threat to the unity of the family.[31] The notion that technology could somehow threaten the coherence of the family unit sparked public questions about the nature of parental authority, with an implicit message that only a reassertion of parental authority could prevent some of the harmful, apparently inevitable, effects for a child who regularly engaged in watching television.

Indeed, public discourse around the effects of television found "evidence"—in the form of recalcitrant children, troubles at school, and other "problems" of adolescence—that television led to increased aggression, passivity, or addiction. Television was also seen as the culprit in a new category of identity that focused on children's interaction with technology: juvenile delinquency. Juvenile delinquency, in 1950s U.S. society, was understood as the predictable result if children were exposed to the "adult secrets" contained within the television screen, secrets that revolved around sexuality, crime, and rebellion. As Spigel argues, television was identified as the perpetrator in producing bad children, leading to a new motivation for parents to reassert control and authority over technology, a technology that was understood as retaining autonomous control over those who engaged with it.[32] These earlier anxieties over children and television viewing resonate with the apprehensions of the late twentieth/early twenty-first century, which identify the Internet, video games, and other new technologies as equally to blame in producing bad children. In both historical moments, the public and private anxieties that surround the interaction of children with technology can be understood as efforts to maintain a division between adults and children.[33]

The notions that children should be protected from adult sexuality and productive labor, made into "objects of sentiment," and properly guided through the complicated morass of technology continue to be central themes in cultural debates around children and technology. This by no means implies that somehow the love and protective emotions adults feel for children are the products of a conspiracy, or indeed are false in any way. It means simply that protection is not a naturalized symbolic gesture; it is enacted according to the particular cultural and economic conditions of a society in a given historical moment.[34] This history of the various efforts and discursive strategies exercised in order to control and regulate childhood is crucial for understanding the regulatory strategies of childhood in contemporary U.S. society. The imagined progressive future so prevalent in American ideology has depended, at least in part, upon an adult ability (and not children's) to control that imagined future.

CURRENT PRACTICES: GUIDING CHILDREN ON THE INTERNET

In the contemporary U.S. climate, the maintenance of this symbolic future requires cultural interventions specific to new forms of technology. The relationship of children and media culture, and the larger social context in which this relationship is forged, is one that is constantly debated and reshaped in the popular press and in public discourse. And, the fear and anxiety generated by children becoming skilled users of the Internet may have elements that are genuinely legitimate.[35] It is true, for example, that pornographic Web sites are relatively accessible to the skilled—or not-so-skilled—web surfer, and it is also true that much of this pornographic material might be considered appropriate only for adults. However, as Marsha Kinder asserts, it is not that children's interactions with technology should be dismissed as harmless, but rather, how is it that that interaction is perceived—through what set of assumptions?[36] Or according to whose standards, or values?

Currently, although the fear conjured up by children using the Internet may take place in a new technological realm, the way in which it is organized and marketed relies on conventional tactics. Rather than attempting to theorize the apparently unique capabilities of the Internet to corrupt children, it makes more sense to query *why* it is that this particular anxiety—one that revolves around children, technology, and sexuality—takes hold with such force in American culture when it does. One important reason is, of course, economic: the promise of e-commerce has certainly found a market in the culture of fear that surrounds children using technology in the proliferation of blocking and filtering software available that enables parents to have more control over accessible information. Sociologist Barry Glassner argues that a "culture of fear" in contemporary American culture has been legitimated because of the immense profit to be made off adult insecurities. Those who are economically savvy enough to capitalize on the culture of fear are skilled in tapping "into our moral insecurities and [supplying] us with symbolic substitutes."[37] This sentiment clearly applies to the increasing number of manufacturers who sell software to block and filter inappropriate material for children. The companies who design the software are bald-faced in their strategies to appeal to parental insecurity; the rhetoric used to market blocking software draws on conventional conceptual frameworks in order to not only capitalize on but also to constantly re-create parental fear and hysteria.

For example, a quick glance at the list of blocking software clearly illustrates this rhetorical strategy: Bo Dietl's One Tough Computer COP; ChatNANNY; CyberPatrol; CyberSnoop; CyberSitter; Disk Tracy.com; Gulliver's Guardian; KidControl; and MoM, to name only a few. These software devices purposefully name themselves in order to invoke security and control even as they perpetuate fear and anxiety—names such as cops, nannies, patrols, guardians, snoops, and detectives create a discourse based on predictable notions of protection, but also rely upon the implication that there is a need for secret and covert action on the part of parents. In other words, parents need to subversively control and monitor their children in order to protect them—to let them out of your sight on the Internet is framed as an insidious form of parental neglect at best, and child abuse at worst. Using these products, of course, not only protects your child, but also allows parents to feel secure about their role as protectors. Another example illustrates this point: the online store for the software filtering organization Net Nanny cites, "Net Nanny filtering software for your PC protects children from the worst of the Internet and provides peace of mind when using your PC." Net Nanny continues to warn parents: "We encourage all parents to become Internet-savvy. The more you know about the Internet, the easier it will be to protect your family from its potential pitfalls. Knowledge is power!"[38] The rhetorical strategy used here clearly recalls Foucauldian theories of power and surveillance: the software company urges parents to find out all information about their children's interaction on the Internet, but in a way that insists upon voyeurism and clandestine activity. The "knowledge is power" mantra invokes a panopticon-like structure of information where parents, not children, are not only able but expected to negotiate the "pitfalls" of the technology.

Another filtering software company, CyberSitter, is even more unabashed about the need for furtive parental activity: "Working *secretly* in the background, CYBERsitter analyzes all internet activity. Whenever it detects activity the parent has elected to restrict, it takes over and blocks the activity before it takes place. If desired, CYBERsitter will maintain a complete history of all Internet activity, including attempts to access blocked material."[39] Evidently, CYBERsitter is capable of an even more overtly Orwellian surveillance; this software "blocks activity before it takes place," suggesting that it is capable of detecting not only restricted behavior, but restricted thoughts about that behavior. Of course, each of these software companies offers this kind of security at a price, and as with all other computer software, the blocking and filtering technologies become rapidly obsolete, so there is always a need for an upgrade. One of the reasons why this kind of paranoia is so profitable is not only because companies are capitalizing on a situation defined in terms of fear and insecurity, but also because of the ever-changing technological structure of the Internet itself. The organization of the Internet creates the instability, while simultaneously its configuration provides opportunities—by way of requiring updated software—to restore order.

The software companies that produce surveillance technology may provide yet another facet of this debate, but they do not necessarily function to alter its terms. Clearly, some of these interventions are significant as efforts to organize the complicated technology of the Internet, but my question is not why these interventions exist in the first place. Rather, my interest lies in why they exist *in the way they do* in contemporary culture. The blocking and filtering software emphatically tells parents to set up rigid boundaries around the kinds of information to which their children have potential access, but like the policy regulations that structure children's television, these boundaries are being drawn around a relatively simple premise of parental fear. And again, it is not only the fear that parents hold regarding their children gaining access to "adult secrets" such as pornography. It is also, and perhaps more important, a fear that doesn't necessarily concern the child at all, but rather parents themselves: the fear that the increasing expertise children are demonstrating in their use of technology renders parental guidance ineffective if not obsolete. And if adult guidance is no longer needed to navigate the complex ways of the Internet, the implication is that parental guidance in other areas—moral, intellectual—is also threatened.

The Fear of Parental Obsolescence

A 1998 MCI television advertisement promising the utopian potential of the Internet features a medley of faces—young, old, black, white—who claim with much conviction that the Internet brings with it the notion that "there is no race," "there is no age," "there are no genders," and "there are no infirmities." The ad ends with the textual question, "Is this utopia? No, it is the Internet." The promise of the Internet is rhetorically framed in the negative: this technology has the capability to obliterate all those messy categories of identity that so determine us in cultural and social life. Not unexpectedly, the ad does not include the idea that the Internet may also assure that "there are no parents." Yet the commercial clearly promises that the Internet is the key to freeing ourselves from those bounds of control set up by social life—age, race, gender, infirmity. And while the ad features many children, it does not raise the possibility that the Internet also may also offer a new space in which to carve out a contemporary, child-defined youth identity. The MCI ad reaffirms the naturalized and universalized separation between adults and children, and does not acknowledge that this relationship, like other categories of identity, is similarly structured by control.

Of course, the omission of the parent-child relationship in the MCI ad is predictable, for it is precisely that relationship that has been rendered precarious by the technology of the Internet. The cultural rhetoric that frames the technology of the Internet continually stresses the possibilities that this technology offers for reimagining the future of the nation. However, unlike earlier technologies, such as the radio and television, the structure of the Internet changes the terms through which the interaction of children and technology is understood. Simply put, children can negotiate the space of the Internet without the help and guidance of adults. For all the benefits of the new social and cultural spaces of the Internet that are lauded by MCI and other media corporations, there is an equally forceful downside to this new space: adults are not necessarily running the show. The possibility that the Internet might breathe new life into the cultural politics and ideals of the nation is one that is at best half-heartedly explored, both by the media and by Internet users, because this new space potentially supersedes the moral guidance of parents. The Internet is ominous precisely because of the different ways that adults *and* children conceptualize the space of the Internet, and because of the ways children have begun to occupy that space.

The Internet is proving to be important for the negotiation of identities for children; a *Newsweek* cover story on "Tweens," children ages eight to fourteen, calls the "on-screen universe" an "obsession" for kids, and brings in a noted scholar to offer tips to parents about the apparently dismaying notion that "whether it's Pokemon or Harry Potter or Quake III, tweens seem inextricably drawn to mastering complicated worlds with Byzantine rules or becoming experts on obscure topics."[40] The idea that children, through the use and mastery of technologies such as the Internet, can become specific kinds of experts, or perhaps can merely understand "complicated worlds with Byzantine rules" forces parents to reexamine the reliance of their children on adult guidance. Thus, like the cultural debate that surrounded the teenager and the potential for juvenile delinquency in the 1950s, the enthusiasm for the Internet by current "Tweens" has adults fearful that children are growing up too fast.

That adults have particular anxieties about the tastes, habits, and practices of the younger generation is certainly nothing new, but the relationship of children with technology in the twenty-first century does contain a different salience than this relationship in other eras. Specifically, as Jenkins focused on when called before Congress to testify about "selling violence to our children," adults are afraid of children, afraid of new technologies, and most important, afraid of the usage by and reaction of children to digital media and new technologies.[41] Adolescence is already widely understood as a confusing, liminal stage of life—indeed, as a truly alien stage of life, and the wide use of the Internet by teenagers merely adds to this social construction. This has functioned to reconstruct twenty-first-century childhood as a mystifying and frightening state of affairs: innocent, yet sophisticated; impressionable, yet world weary and desensitized.

It is important to note that current cultural debates surrounding children's use of the Internet focus on the perception that technology has somehow *created* this confusing and unfamiliar definition of childhood. The debate rarely centers on the ways in which use of technology can be empowering—not just in terms of technological skill, but more important, in terms of the conditions of possibility the Internet may offer. If children are using the Internet to construct independence and discrete identities, the debate surrounding the use of technology needs to recognize the positive aspects of this. Larry Gross, in his essay in this volume, notes the various resources available on the Internet to gay and lesbian users, and argues that "these technological innovations permit the construction of virtual public spaces that can be life—or at least, sanity—saving refuges for many who have reason to feel they are living in enemy territory."[42] The idea that the Internet can provide "a place for us," for those individuals who are ostracized from mainstream society and their families because of their identity, is an important—and indeed, as Gross argues, crucial—function of technology. The Internet, as with other technologies, can and does "contribute to children's growing understanding of themselves as gendered, raced, socially connected members of a network of linked communities, and to their emerging perception of their own position and potential empowerment within a changing global public sphere."[43] Technology can provide a particular kind of community, or a sense of belonging, that may otherwise be absent in one's social and cultural life. Perhaps focusing on this element of children's use of technology—the potential for empowerment, or for a kind of citizenship—rather than centering on adult anxieties about their role in the lives of children, may reactivate the debate about children and technology in a more productive way.

A significant part of an adult conception of citizenship in the United States is the sense of membership in a national, imagined community. As Benedict Anderson theorized in his classic work, *Imagined Communities*, this sense of membership in Western society has been forged in part by technologies and media: "print capitalism" and the advent of the newspaper in Western cultures allowed citizens to feel connected with others in a way that constructed a national, even if imagined, community.[44] But children, because of their status as nonadults and thus nonpolitical, are usually left out of this dynamic. However, as both new technologies such as the Internet and older forms of technology such as television demonstrate, children can and do use technology as a means to establish community and a sense of belonging; in short, the Internet is one cultural space through which children can forge a sense of national identity.

Jon Katz, writing in *Wired*, begins his essay with a blunt statement about the relationship between children and technology:

> Children are at the epicenter of the information revolution, ground zero of the digital world. They helped build it, and they understand it as well or better than anyone. Not only is the digital world making the young more sophisticated, altering their ideas of what culture and literacy are, it is connecting them to one another, providing them with a new sense of political self. Children in the digital age are neither unseen nor unheard;

in fact, they are seen and heard more than ever. They occupy a new kind of cultural space. They're citizens of a new order, founders of the Digital Nation.[45]

Katz emphasizes the idea that this newly organized "citizenship" of children can emerge precisely because the measures of parental control over children are precarious within the world of technology. Through the Internet, argues Katz, children can "reach past the suffocating boundaries of social convention," and thwart age-old parental mottos such as "children should be seen and not heard." Moreover, children, through their interaction with technology, can "occupy a new cultural space," a space in which a new child's definition of national identity can be formulated.

Katz's vision is clearly utopian—it is not evident, for example, that the Internet, given its conventional trajectory toward commercialism and traditional formulations of information dissemination, will in fact realize a "new order" of the "Digital Nation." At the same time, the world of the Internet *is* different from other technologies in its emphasis on personal interaction and engagement. It is a place where, as Gross argues, those with marginalized identities can "find a home" in a much more effective and rapid way than, say, television. It is also a place where the imagined community of a nation can connect in ways that were previously impossible, simply given geographic, economic, and political barriers.

And it is a place where children are constructing a sense of community that is not only *about* them, but defined and determined *by* them. This, finally, is one of the most significant influences of new technologies such as the Internet on the cultural constructions of childhood: the Internet is a social and political space where children can potentially move out from under parental and authoritative control. While there are considerable efforts to regain that control through governmental policy decisions, new innovations in software, and mass-mediated warnings to parents about the evils of the Internet, the ever-changing nature of the Internet often circumvents these efforts. Perhaps it is time to rethink what these forms of protection are accomplishing. It is not the desire to protect children from what is obviously a difficult and often dangerous world to navigate that is problematic. Rather, it is our assumptions about who and what children are, and what they themselves may be capable of producing, that need to be redefined or newly conceived. As Katz argues, banning access to those "dangerous" pitfalls of the Internet through filtering software does not truly protect children, but merely restricts entry to an ever-changing, potentially productive space: "Rather than preparing kids for the world they'll have to live in . . . parents insist on preparing them for a world that no longer exists."[46]

The Internet is not utopia. The social, political, and economic factors of identity that categorize and often stigmatize human beings are not magically erased simply by joining a chat room. However, more and more frequently children are finding that interaction with technologies such as the Internet gives them a definition of culture and belonging that exists outside of adult standards and assumptions. Katz insists that in contemporary times, "children have the chance to reinvent communications, culture, and community."[47] Unlike Katz, I am not as confident that offering this chance will directly result in a major reinvention of our sense of culture and community. But it is apparent that new technologies such as the Internet present us with an opportunity. This opportunity allows both children and adults to imagine new conditions of possibility for defining childhood, community, and national identity.

NOTES

1. This statistic is cited in an online e-mail essay from Henry Jenkins, "Prof. Jenkins Goes to Washington" May 8, 1999. <http://www.mit.edu/21fms/www/faculty/henry3/profjenkins.html>. Accessed December 2003.

2. Philip Elmer-Dewitt, "On a Screen Near You: CyberPorn," *Time* (July 3, 1995).

3. Barry Glassner, *The Culture of Fear: Why Americans are Afraid of the Wrong Things* (New York: Basic Books, 1999). See also Elmer-Dewitt, "On a Screen Near You."

4. James Kincaid, "Producing Erotic Children," in *The Children's Culture Reader*, ed. Henry Jenkins (New York: New York University Press, 1998), 247.

5. Lynn Spigel, "Seducing the Innocent: Childhood and Television in Postwar America," in *The Children's Culture Reader*, ed. Henry Jenkins (New York: New York University Press, 1998), and *Make Room for TV: Television and the Family Ideal in Postwar America* (Chicago: University of Chicago Press, 1992).

6. Henry Jenkins, "Introduction," in *The Children's Culture Reader*, ed. Henry Jenkins (New York: New York University Press, 1998), 9.

7. Seen on *World News Tonight*, with Peter Jennings, American Broadcast Company, April 22, 1999; various local news stations picked up this same story and strategy.

8. Jenkins, "Introduction," in *The Children's Culture Reader*, 15.

9. Philippe Ariès, "From Immodesty to Innocence" in *The Children's Culture Reader* (New York: New York University Press, 1998), 16. For a more detailed study of the construction of childhood during this time period, see Ariès, *Centuries of Childhood: A Social History of Family Life*, trans. Robert Baldick (New York: Vintage, 1962).

10. Ibid., 46.

11. Ibid.

12. Michel Foucault, *The History of Sexuality: An Introduction* (New York: Vintage, 1978), 24–25.

13. Ibid., 42.

14. Kincaid, "Producing Erotic Children," 247. Emphasis in original.

15. Viviana Zelizer, *Pricing the Priceless Child: The Changing Social Value of Children,* (Princeton, N.J.: Princeton University Press, 1985), 59.

16. Ibid.

17. Ibid., 72.

18. See Jenkins, "Introduction," in *The Children's Culture Reader,* for a more detailed analysis of this.

19. For a more detailed analysis, see Ellen Seiter, *Sold Separately: Children and Parents in Consumer Culture* (New Brunswick, N.J.: Rutgers University Press, 1993); and Spigel, *Make Room for TV.*

20. Obviously, not all children and their mothers were nestled securely in a domestic space. Marketers at this time were directly influential in the creation of a cultural ideal of the home, where mothers remained with their children and guided them—morally, intellectually, spiritually. The commercialization of childhood that occurs at this time is part of this ideology. See Spigel, "Seducing the Innocent," for further discussion.

21. Stephen Kline, "The Making of Children's Culture," in *The Children's Culture Reader,* ed. Henry Jenkins (New York: New York University Press, 1998), 102.

22. Seiter, *Sold Separately,* 52.

23. Ibid., 54.

24. For more on this, see Heather Hendershot, *Saturday Morning Censors: Television Regulation before the V-Chip* (Durham, N.C.: Duke University Press, 1998); Seiter, *Sold Separately*; and Stephen Kline, *Out of the Garden: Toys and Children's Culture in the Age of TV Marketing* (London: Verso, 1993).

25. Jyotsna Kapur, "Out of Control: Television and the Transformation of Childhood in Late Capitalism," in *Kids' Media Culture,* ed. Marsha Kinder (Durham, N.C.: Duke University Press, 1999), 125.

26. Seiter, *Sold Separately,* 9.

27. Kapur, "Out of Control," 125.

28. Spigel, "Seducing the Innocent," 112.

29. Ibid., 113.

30. Ibid., 113–14.

31. For a more detailed discussion of this, see Spigel, *Make Room for TV,* especially Chapter 2.

32. Spigel, "Seducing the Innocent."

33. Ibid.

34. See Spigel, *Make Room for TV,* and Seiter, *Sold Separately.*

35. Kinder, "Kids' Media Culture: An Introduction," in *Kids' Media Culture,* 3.

36. Ibid.

37. Glassner, *The Culture of Fear,* xxviii.

38. NetNanny Web site, url: <http://www.netnanny.com/>, March 2000.

39. CYBERSitter Web site, url: <http://www.cybersitter.com/>, March 2000, emphasis in the original.

40. Barbara Kantrowitz and Pat Wingert, "The Truth About Tweens," *Newsweek* (October 18, 1999), 72.

41. Jenkins, "Professor Jenkins Goes to Washington."

42. Larry Gross, "Somewhere There's a Place for Us: Sexual Minorities and the Internet," in this volume.

43. Kinder, "Kids' Media Culture," 19.

44. Benedict Anderson, *Imagined Communities: Reflections on the Origins and Spread of Nationalism* (London: Verso, 1983).

45. Jon Katz, "The Rights of Kids in a Digital Age," *Wired* (July 1996), accessed online at *Wired* archives, archive 4:07. Accessed July 6, 2000.

46. Ibid.

47. Ibid.

Katie Hafner

16   When the Virtual Isn't Enough

One Saturday early in August 1998, I called my father, Everett, for our usual weekend chat. We talked about his life, my life, his work, my work, our family. I told him a joke, and we both laughed. He had bread in the oven he needed to tend to. We said good-bye. The next night my sister called. She sounded out of breath, but really she was having trouble forming the words to tell me that the small plane my father had been flying that afternoon had crashed. He and the passenger, Neil Hammer, a photographer who had gone with him to take aerial photographs, had both died. A few hours later I flew across the country to Williamsburg, Massachusetts, a town of 2,500 people in the Berkshire foothills.

By the time I arrived, a shrine had been erected in front of the library, on a board normally reserved for announcing readings. It read: "We Love You Everett and Neil." I hadn't met Neil, but I soon learned that he was a gifted photographer who lived with his wife, Tamara, a few houses up the street from my father. His photographs were in the bank, the library, people's living rooms. Williamsburg residents started bringing flowers from their gardens to place next to the sign. Over the next few days, the buckets and vases multiplied. People not only left them there but returned to straighten them out and freshen the water. Everywhere I went, I felt not just my own shock and grief but the shock and grief of an entire town. Five days after the accident, 200 people, perhaps even more, walked up the hill to the town cemetery to attend Neil's graveside funeral. A month later, at a gathering at my father's house following his memorial service, women from the church materialized, like angels out of nowhere, to serve food and clean up.

The week I spent in Williamsburg just after the crash was a blur. But what did stay in sharp focus was the face and voice of each person who came to the door, or stopped me on the street, to tell me they had known my father. They knew his comings and goings, his eccentricities. They had been to his house for dinner and heard his stories, his endless repertoire of jokes, his theories. They knew when he had visitors, and when he was out of town. They knew that he was growing tomatoes, and that he worried they wouldn't ripen before the frost. They had argued with him at town meetings, and read his letters to the local paper.

I had been to Williamsburg, a beautiful and unspoiled slice of historic New England, many times since my father had moved there nearly twenty years ago to escape the busier pace of Amherst and Northampton, which are close by. But I had had little interest in knowing the town itself, or the people who lived there. Now I didn't want to leave. Being near the people who knew my father kept me warm. Even if they hadn't known him well, they had seen him in his everyday life. They watched him grow old. In some ways, they knew him better than I did. When I did leave, although I stayed in touch with many of these same people by e-mail and telephone from northern California, I felt too far away and wanted to return.

The plane crash wasn't the only tragedy in Williamsburg that summer. An elderly woman was killed in a car accident, her husband badly hurt. The three-year-old daughter of a woman who worked in the bank drowned. "It just seemed so relentless," said Lisa Wenner, the director of the Williamsburg library. "It seemed like nothing good was going to happen, only bad things." Professional grief counselors came to town and held sessions at the church.

My experience in Williamsburg gave me a sense of community in a particular and visceral way that allowed me to consider the idea of community in new ways. For several years, I have studied and written about virtual communities, that is, communities that exist prmarily online, and I had felt in many ways that these provided important and often vital experiences of community for their participants. Yet, seeing the hole these deaths left in the heart of Williamsburg shook my faith in virtual communities.

An online community, of course, is one that consists solely of words on a screen. Its members needn't meet one another face to face to form strong bonds. In fact, many never do meet one another. Still, with just words typed on a computer screen, they share their lives, their fears, their personal crises. And that brings them close. It could be argued that there is a lot less at stake in a virtual community than in a real one. If you are unhappy in a real place, you have to physically pick up and move. If you don't like what's happening in a virtual community, on the other, you can just log off. Yet, for many people, participation in these communities is crucial to their daily lives.

An online community can take the form of a mailing list on, say, the topic of rare coins, or a Web site with real-time chat to discuss the New York Knicks. They have sprung up everywhere in the past few years, catering to every possible special interest. For instance, eBay and iVillage distinguished themselves as online communities. It is difficult to say what makes some online communities succeed where others do not. Both eBay and iVillage managed to tap into a certain audience with a certain set of interests, which can be crucial to an online community's success. Virtual communities have proven invaluable for people with physical disabilities, and people who are geographically isolated. Stories abound of online communities giving people a regained sense of belonging to something, somewhere.

At the same time, the word *community* has itself been elevated—some might say corrupted—in the world of online business. Executives at America Online, with its multimillion-user base, at Amazon.com, and countless other, smaller online venues, have all tried to divine the magic of community, which, in a business sense of the word, is now synonymous with keeping people tied to a Web site. The longer people stick around, the more likely they are to click on ads.

However, there are online communities that defy the status of the Web as a site of commerce. Perhaps the most famous online community is the WELL, a conferencing system in Sausalito, California, now owned by Salon.com, that was set up in the mid-1980s as a social experiment. The intense connectedness fostered by the WELL is extraordinary by any standards. The WELL has been admired and studied as a model for online communities. In the course of writing a history of the WELL in the late 1990s, I saw people grieve for their fellow members when they died and marshal support in an emergency.[1] I saw intense commitment to the community. I watched online flirtations turn into real-life marriages. I saw emotions flare and barbs fly.

The WELL started in 1985 as a VAX computer and a rack of modems in a ramshackle set of offices in Sausalito. Although in principle the WELL had made a conspicuous attempt to be accessible to anyone with a modem, in reality, by attracting a certain kind of person—smart and left-leaning without being self-consciously PC, it has always been something of a club. For the most part, the WELL is composed largely of people around the same age—baby boomers in their late thirties and early forties, most of them male, many of whom hold postgraduate degrees. They had come of age in the 1960s. In the process, the WELL had become one of those cultural phenomena that spring up now and again, a salon of creative and thoughtful and articulate people who are interested in one another's stories in a self-absorbed, cabalistic way.

Howard Rheingold, a Bay Area writer who is also the author of *Virtual Communities*, lurked for a while at first. Recalls Rheingold, "One of my earliest shocking experiences on the WELL was to find that people in the Whole Earth conference were discussing a book I had written. And one person offered a negative opinion. I immediately got the idea that the WELL consisted of this tight little cabal of Whole Earth types." His first post was a description of tarantula sex to the sexuality conference. The response was enthusiastic. He was accepted. And he was hooked. Rheingold started a conference called Mind, a spinoff of his writings on how the mind works. "The WELL took over my life," he says. "It's this territory where you know your behavior is somehow obsessive and taboo in the protestant sense, that you should be working, that there's something sick and dehumanized about spending time doing this, but you also know that it's sociable, and you're doing it together. That was the unholy attraction of it."

It took a particular type of person to feel at ease with the medium. Facility with language helped. Fast typists had an edge. And when the personality matched the particular quirks of online living, it was something to behold. A good number of those who thrived as members of the online world, for instance, were hopeless outcasts in the real world. Perhaps they were self-conscious about their looks, or acutely shy, when it came to face-to-face interactions. But put them in front of a computer and, liberated from the constraints of their physical appearance, they blossomed. Years later, people recalled their first post on the WELL much as they recalled the first time they heard about the Beatles.

There was an art to posting. The best posts were neither long-winded nor so brief as to be cryptic. One unofficial rule was to keep posts to twenty-two lines, or no more than a screenful. The reasoning was this: it's rude to make people pay to read unnecessary verbiage, and there are very few ideas that you can't get across in a screenful of information. And if you can't, well then you're not really trying very hard. It wasn't unlike writing office memos, or postcards. "Either you had that kind of instinct or you didn't," says Jon Carroll, a San Francisco newspaper columnist who did. And for every post to a lively discussion, there were probably half a dozen other related e-mail discussions swirling around it. The WELL established its own rhythm. Soon enough, people had become predictable in the times they were online.

For many members of the WELL, just logging on at 4:00 A.M. to see who else wasn't getting any sleep could be a comfort. Of course, everyone knew that <smiles> and <hugs> weren't going to replace the real thing. At the same time, just being on the WELL, talking with people they might or might not consider befriending in any other context, was its own seduction. They may not get to see what anyone else was wearing or hear what their voices sounded like, but in a way, absent of those trappings, the isolated prose revealed something still more intimate. In this way, the WELL was a harbinger, really, of similar concerns and wrangles that would arise on the Net over time—debates over the appropriate uses of electronic networks and virtual dialogues, over free speech, privacy, and the dangers of anonymity.

For a lot of people, five or six hours a day online was as good as their social life got. If the wired world was a response to the breakdown of physical community, then this wasn't such a bad place to be. Many of these were mobile, urban people for whom going down to the general store to gossip wasn't an option. The WELL was the best, or most plausible, shot they had at community. Others might have turned to the WELL precisely because they could avoid real-life encounters that way; they were people for whom the offer of real-life community might not seem so attractive. These were people who might be too shy to strike up a conversation with the bank teller. And for a lot of people on the WELL, being there was as much a suspension of reality as watching a good movie, or being engrossed in a novel.

When Ramon Sender Barayon, a San Francisco writer and musician, logged on to the WELL for the first time, it reminded him of places he'd been to—the Open Land communes in the 1960s. "The tribal need is one our culture doesn't recognize," he says. "It's antithetical to our value structure somehow. Capitalism wants each of us to live in our own little cubicle, consuming as much as possible. The WELL took that need for tribe and said, 'Hey let's see what happens if we become a disembodied tribe at core.' The Farm graduates helped it along, but also it was an innate ingredient, a fortuitous gathering of energies."

And what role did the physical play? One of the most cohering rituals surrounding the WELL was the monthly WELL office party. The first party happened in September 1986, when a few WELL regulars decided to have a party. It was a Friday afternoon, and around the end of the day people just started showing up at the Sausalito office. Even a few people who preferred to avoid social scenes showed up. For many people well known to each other online, this was the first time they had met in the flesh, and it was a strange, unsettling experience. Most everyone there found that the shapely personalities projected electronically bore scant resemblance to the people who showed up at the party in the flesh. By and large, they were what Stewart Brand, one of the WELL's founders, once described as "a portly keyboarding group," perhaps not completely at peace with their bodies, or themselves, or each other. Some of those people, upon arriving at the WELL office, headed straight to a computer and logged on. The earliest WELL parties couldn't sustain enough social energy to last more than a couple of hours. A smaller group often repaired to a nearby Chinese restaurant at the end of the gathering. Yet soon the parties were a monthly tradition.

Those physical meetings proved invaluable in contributing to the closeness people felt when online. In fact, as Brand had predicted, there was something about having people meet each other in physical space that intensified their closeness on the WELL. It was the fact of face-to-face contact, not even so much the quality of it, that made the difference.

In my research into the WELL, I focused on one WELL member, Tom Mandel, who had been one of the most visible members of the club—perhaps even the quintessential member. Mandel was born in Chicago in 1945, and adopted as an infant by well-to-do department store owners. When he was five, his father sold his share in the business and moved to Honolulu to open a stamp shop. After a stint in the Marine Corps, and Vietnam, Tom graduated from the University of Hawaii with one of the nation's first degrees in futurism. For most of his professional career he worked at SRI in Menlo Park as a futurist or, as he put it, a professional forecaster, or scenarist. One WELL regular who met Mandel a few times once described him as "easy on the eyes." Another once suggested a cross between Jeremy Irons—mustachioed, dark, and slender-faced—and Glenn Gould—temperamental and eclectic. Not only was Mandel widely read, but he read carefully. It gained him respect on the WELL. On a "good keyboard," as Mandel put it, he could type more than 100 words a minute.

Mandel was a creature of contradiction. His bachelor's condo in Mountain View was so slovenly that even his friends couldn't bear to visit. Yet he often dressed for work in finely pressed suits, made by Armani and Zegna, custom-tailored to his small frame. He was wire-thin, an unlikely athlete. Yet while growing up in Hawaii he had been an avid surfer. He could be a rigidly demanding and self-disciplined intellectual, yet he indulged a compulsive and hedonistic streak. He smoked two packs of Benson & Hedges Ultra lights a day—a real-life habit that would have put off many a WELL user—and had a fondness for Lagavulin, a pricey single-malt whisky. And he spent much of his time online, yet had close real-life friends who didn't know it.

From the moment he first logged on to the WELL, as simply <mandel>, he posted voluminously. He started topics about anything, it seemed, that popped into his head: "Have you ever saved someone's life?" (Mandel had, in a heroic plunge into a river to pull someone from a submerged vehicle).

"Best and worst memories of the sixties." "Great Operas on CD." In the drugs conference, he once started a topic called "Sex on acid." Mandel's more or less continuous presence on the WELL made him something of an ever-present force. He provoked, bullied, jeered, one-lined, and pontificated his way around the WELL. But he was seldom just plain offensive. His challenges were often friendly, making him more like a sparring partner than a true adversary. When Gail Williams once posted in the Environment conference that every blade of grass is sacred, he shot back, "Now you'll never run for public office." He could be irksome, to be sure, but people on the WELL respected him and even liked him. He had a keen sense of humor, and he was actually very kind, in a cranky sort of way. Those who were able to see beneath the crust appreciated him.

Like others on the WELL, Mandel revealed pieces of himself but by no means everything. He told stories of his adoptive father, his childhood in Honolulu, his time in the Marines, and his generally poor health. He had once been stricken by a tuberculosis-like illness, and then there was the back surgery that laid him up for weeks and brought him to the WELL. He spent a lot of time in the Health conference complaining about this sore throat or that head cold. Still, for all the time Mandel spent online, the biggest drama in his life revolved around something very physical: Maria Syndicus, the love of his life. Maria was also a WELL regular, and her login was Nana. The two had met in 1984, when Mandel interviewed her for a job in his department. When Nana began her new job, her office was next to his, and they began dating each other discreetly. For the most part, they didn't advertise their attachment to other WELL members, although everyone figured it out quickly enough. Privately, they sent each other dozens of e-mail messages and instant messages every day.

Nana's and Mandel's desks faced each other on opposite sides of the office wall. When Nana heard the white noise of Mandel's modem as it connected with Sausalito, followed by furious typing, she logged on too. If something especially interesting was happening, one of them banged on the wall. It went on that way for years. But the relationship was a tempestuous one from the start. When their stormiest breakup occurred, Mandel began to stalk Nana electronically, following her every move on the WELL. Then he began to attack her publicly, in the WELL's different forums.

Here was an example, in sharpest relief, of the WELL as a place where anyone could act out in ways they simply didn't in real life. Mandel wasn't sidestepping reality so much as augmenting it. On the WELL he was uncontained. He was expressing anger and pain and everything else he could not express to Nana's face. The rest of the WELL community, of course, followed the turn of events like bloodhounds, feeding on the few known facts that could be summarized in bullets: Tom and Nana broke up. Nana took up with another person on the WELL and ignored Tom. Mandel started showing up in any conference where Nana was and harrassing her. He was told by some members to stop. Instead of stopping, he escalated his attacks.

From those threadbare snippets of information about Mandel and Nana, the WELL community pieced together a breathtaking array of perspectives, intepretations, and judgments. Everyone was ready to supply explanations for the unaccountable behavior of the principals. Blanks in the narrative were filled in with rich imagination. The entire affair was becoming everyone's personal Rorschach blot, onto which they projected their own set of feelings. The reaction to Mandel and Nana became a window into the medium's ability to magnify and embellish. Nana once joked that if something didn't happen on the WELL, it didn't happen. To those on the WELL, immersed in life online, the WELL didn't mirror reality. It was reality.

Of course, none of this was much different from half a dozen socialites gossiping on the telephone about their own closed, self-referential sphere. But in this case, the medium was text. Not since the days when people corresponded daily by letter had text carried such freight in quotidian life. The WELL returned text-based communications to a prominent role in the lives of its users. And the text generated on the WELL often led to familial-like disputes that ended up really hurting people's feelings. Cliff Figallo, who helped to run the WELL for years, once commented that the WELL was like a group household where people put one another under the karmic microscope day after day. In the process, not only does the group discover that nobody's perfect, but everybody is willing to point out what's wrong with the others. It's a strange kind of intimacy—at once public and solitary in a way that almost no other environment affords. It is someone sitting at a computer in the dead of night, in their underwear, in the quiet and isolation of their own room, typing for all the world to see, with none of the intimidating aspects of the simple, sobering fact of another person's presence.

But the fact remained that this community probably would not have thrived solely in virtual space. The WELL defied current notions about virtual community in that it wasn't one—entirely. Problems that arose online got worked out offline, and vice-versa. The login prompt was the membrane through which people passed back and forth. In this way, it fostered what Sherry Turkle would call the "multiple and fluid" self. Mandel was, according to Turkle's model, the perfect postmodern human being. Online experiences, she writes in her book, *Life on the Screen: Identity in the Age of the Internet*, help people develop a sense of the psychological makeup that allows multiplicity and flexibility.[2] The WELL gave Mandel the ability to alter and modify his identity, to fragment himself in ways he couldn't have done nearly so easily without the medium. Those who regularly spend time online, on the boundary between the real and the virtual, fall into what Turkle calls the "crucible of contradictory experience": "Some are tempted to think of life in cyberspace as insignificant, as escape or meaningless diversion. It is not. Our experiences there are serious play. We belittle them at our risk."[3]

After some time, in a turn of events that suprised no one, Mandel and Nana reconciled. Then, in late 1994, Mandel got sick.

People on the WELL have likened hearing the news of Mandel's lung cancer with living in a large rambling boarding house and having something god-awful happen in a remote room. You feel its reverberation and, before long, word spreads and even if you spend all your time in the Parenting or Books or Genx conference, you find yourself heading straight to the Health conference, where Mandel, whose path you may or may not have ever crossed, has just announced that he has lung cancer.

To the WELL community, Mandel had presented the news dispassionately, almost serenely, as if he were reporting the five o'clock traffic. But offline, his friends got a different picture. When he telephoned a friend of many years, Ian Tilbury, to tell him, Mandel was shattered and desperate. He was equally desperate and frightened when he spoke with Nana.

Mandel's cancer, it turned out, was inoperable. This news, too, he reported a short time later with surprising calm. The more he was at home, the more he was online. The next few months were a steady march of status reports, pep talks, and beams. In March 1995, Mandel and Nana announced plans to marry within a few weeks. Mandel was still posting elsewhere on the WELL—in current events, about the Republican Congress, and the fiftieth anniversary of V-J day. He was still picking fights with a few of his nemeses.

Five months after his diagnosis, the illness was evident even online. Mandel prided himself in his impeccable posts, free of typos and spelling errors. Now he was beginning to slur. Every once in a while, a slip of the fingers could be seen. And he admitted, for the first time, that he might not be up to the task of staying on the WELL much longer. On April 5, 1995, he died listening to Beethoven's *Ninth Symphony*.

By the time I finished reporting and writing the story of the WELL, although I had never laid eyes on Tom Mandel, I felt I knew him. And in the process of working on the WELL piece, I had, very nearly, accepted virtual communities as reasonable approximations of the real thing.

But my experience in Williamsburg, in the aftermath of my father's death was proof to me that the two are not interchangeable, that physical communities are very much alive and their importance endures. People still want a sense of place, a sense of belonging, in a physical way. They still want to go off to the library and see who else might be there. They still want to gossip about the marital troubles of those nasty neighbors they never liked anyway. They want their new car to be seen by everyone else in town. They want the everyday, unspoken rewards that come with seniority and the privilege of preaching to newcomers.

Where virtual communities are by definition intentional there's a lovely haphazard quality to the way the people in a place like Williamsburg came to live there. They did not choose their fellow townspeople, necessarily, but something drew each of them to the town. In daily interchanges over time, a fondness and trust have developed.

This raises the question of how it is that people really come to know each other. Because they are based on words alone, virtual communities like the WELL have a lot to do with how people think about one another intellectually. In places like Williamsburg, there's a kind of nonverbal knowing that evolves from seeing and interacting with someone over time—at the Post Office, the library, the grocery store, the local dump, or the Lunch Box restaurant, where locals often eat. "There's something about actually seeing people and experiencing whatever it is they're carrying with them that gives you a sense of how they're feeling that day," says Lisa Wenner.

As in many small towns, people in Williamsburg know each other's business. They know whose children have perfect teeth. They know who bought a new car. They know who's sick. When romances become entangled, they are discussed one on one, not in groups. In the case of my father, the one difference between virtual and real that made all the difference, to me at least, was his voice. It had a deep yet mellow timbre and it conveyed pretty much all that he was: erudite and filled with good humor. His jokes, in particular, famous among family, friends, aquaintances, and near-strangers, had to be told with a certain rhythm and intonation. He spent many years perfecting the art of his joke telling. And people loved them. More, however, they loved his ability to tell them. If he had tapped those same jokes out on a computer screen, naked and soundless, void of his gestures and the glimmer in his eyes, they'd have fallen flat.

And when bad things happen in Williamsburg, the whole town feels it.

"You're more vulnerable," said John Merritt, a Williamsburg native. When my father died, people helped in ways that no one could have done online. They came to the door and delivered their sympathetic words in person. They brought cakes over. They had me to their houses for dinner. One generous neighbor volunteered to go to the airport where my father's car was still parked and retrieve it, an errand I could not bring myself to do.

At times, controversy—a protracted and bitter debate over proposed zoning reform, for instance—has cleaved the town. Anger can fester, but for the most part, once an issue has been decided, people move on. "I can disagree terribly with someone on one issue, and then work with them as a team on something else," said Heidi Johnson LeBaron, a Williamsburg resident. And physical details matter. When the town lost power after a large truck knocked over a utility pole, the local newspaper reported that it happened as the driver was leaving the parking lot of the Lunch Box, where he bought a cup of coffee. As it turned out, he didn't buy the coffee at the Lunch Box. He parked in the Lunch Box parking lot and bought the coffee at the Cumberland Farms next door.

Williamsburg residents, incensed that the Lunch Box had been misrepresented, were quick to set the record straight. "I got a half a dozen calls on that," said Frederick Reiken, the reporter for the *Gazette* who covered the incident. "People are so aware of the pulse of the town that when you get a completely irrelevant detail wrong, people get upset. The message was, 'Be more careful with your facts. This is our town.'" The newspaper printed a correction. Although many people in Williamsburg remain resolutely off the Net, others say they now have the best of both worlds. They use the Net for e-mail and research, and to stay connected in their various fields. Lisa Wenner, for instance, subscribes to a mailing list for librarians in western Massachusetts. It's not that the town residents are against the Net per se. They simply do not need an online community because they have their own.

But for the most part, having the real thing eliminates the need for a virtual equivalent. "Virtual communities are risk free," said Fred Goodhue, a social studies teacher who chairs the board of selectmen, "because you can always back out anonymously."

People in Williamsburg told me that my father had grown more involved in town politics in his last years. I found evidence of this while seated at his computer one day after the accident, trying to figure out what he had been working on. I stumbled across a lengthy, painstakingly written document that was his own attempt to draft a new zoning bylaw for the town. I can't ask him, but I'm guessing that for some reason, before the accident, my father had been thinking about what I was now pondering. On his nightstand lay a copy of *Wired* magazine with my article about the WELL in it. I vaguely remembered having sent it to him when it appeared in 1997, but didn't recall having talked to him about the subject of physical and virtual communities.

And on his desk next to the computer was a piece of his familiar green stationery. On it, in his small, unmistakable handwriting, was a quotation from the city planner and social critic Lewis Mumford: "Democracy, in any active sense, begins and ends in communities small enough for their numbers to meet face to face."

NOTES

Acknowledgments: Portions of this essay first appeared in the *New York Times* ("In Real Life's Shadows, Virtual Life Can Pale," *New York Times* [August 26, 1999], 10) and the May 1997 issue of *Wired* magazine.

1. Katie Hafner, "The Epic Saga of the Well," *Wired* (May 1997).

2. Sherry Turkle, *Life on the Screen: Identity in the Age of the Internet* (New York: Simon & Schuster, 1995).

3. Ibid., 268–69.

RICHARD CHABRÁN AND ROMELIA SALINAS

17   Place Matters
Journeys through Global and Local Spaces

Borders are set up to define the places that are safe and unsafe, to distinguish us from them. A border is a dividing line, a narrow strip along a steep edge. A borderland is a vague and undetermined place created by the emotional residue of an unnatural boundary. It is in a constant state of transition. The prohibited and the forbidden are its inhabitants. —Gloria Anzaldúa, *Borderlands*[1]

The view of place advocated here, where localities can in a sense be present in one another, both inside and outside at the same time, is a view which stresses the construction of specificity through interrelations rather than through the imposition of boundaries and the counter position of one identity against another. —Doreen Massey, *Space, Place, and Gender*[2]

IN THE image on the next page by digital artist Alma Lopez (Figure 17.1), a young girl sits with her eyes blindfolded by a red, white, and blue bandana branded with *187*, the California anti-immigrant measure. This places her at the end of twentieth-century California, though she is surrounded by images of past, present, imagined, and lived spaces. At her feet is an historical map of the Americas bordered by an image of the Virgin of Guadalupe, the patron saint of the Americas, with the words *Manifest Destiny*, and a more contemporary map, with the words *English Only* faintly visible. This map in turn fades into recent Los Angeles high-rises, signifying L.A.'s participation in today's global economy. A bright blue sky provides the background for the image and evokes, perhaps, hope. It is not hard to imagine a point in time when the young girl will throw off the blindfold as an act of resistance and affirmation. Technology is manifested in map-making, in remnants of old and new architecture, in writing, and in the very construction of the image. Alma Lopez's contrapuntal image illustrates the multiple determinations and contingencies of space and place in Los Angeles similar to those produced in cyberspace.[3]

305

Figure 17.1 *187* by Alma Lopez © 1998. Reprinted with permission from the artist. (Special thanks to Melissa and Leticia Lopez.) <http://home.earthlink.net/~almalopez/digital/1848/187.html>.

PONDERING PLACE

Place is one of the most taken-for-granted terms in our vocabulary. Traditionally it has signified a location, a space or site. It has often been tied to a physical or geographic space but can be used to identify a social location, as in a class location, or an existential space.[4] Some theorists have questioned the continuing importance of physical or geographical place in the current digital era. We provide an opposing view, which articulates *space* as constitutive of formative processes that are open and contradictory, and we reserve the term *place* to signify the contingent result of these formative and contradictory processes. We explore ways in which people are making space as the practice of place in an emerging digital society. This view of social space allows us to consider how digital productions are conditioned and regulated by cultural practices in the analog world. We use Stuart Hall's notion of a "circuit of culture" as a means of exploring how gender, race, and class constitute social space, and the practices that both constitute and limit digital social space in Latino communities.

The emergence of digital technologies at this moment is characterized by great fluidity. In order to capture this fluidity we have chosen to describe our narrative as a journey. The metaphor of travel allows us to explore issues of history, globalization, gender, identity, and the public sphere in our search for a social version of space and place.[5] Each stop on our journey highlights a particular theoretical point and demonstrates how Latinas/Latinos occupy a number of strategic sites that have been ignored in the cyberspace literature. Our identities as a Chicana and Chicano-Riqueño mark our travel narrative in the spaces/places we visit, as well as the manner in which we read and construct our narrative. In framing our narrative as a journey through and in between spaces and places we conceptualize cyberspace as an extension of existing places and spaces rather than a self-contained ether.

Toward Articulating the Conditions of Digital Practice

> We will socialize in digital neighborhoods in which physical space will be irrelevant and time will play a different role.
> —Nicolas Negroponte, *Being Digital*[6]

The first part of our journey traverses the United States, stopping at various universities known as high-tech in some cases and high-theory in others. It is a journey that most often takes us to analog libraries where we read analog books but also find valuable resources on the Internet. Through these readings we attempt to recover the role of the *social* in the production of cyberspace.

Through our reading we find that the beginning of the twenty-first century has been characterized by epistemological crisis, rapid expansion of global economies, and the unparalleled rise of communication technologies.

While the emergence of global economies has received much attention, the new modes of digital communications, spaces, and places have become arenas of great debate.[7] Utopian visions, such as Nicolas Negroponte's *Being Digital*, perceive social space in a fashion that emphasizes the *tele* and marginalizes *communication*.[8] His construction of a utopian vision of a digital world where all our human needs would be provided seems to necessitate a denial of physical space. His digital world is under development in Cambridge at the world-renowned Massachusetts Institute of Technology (MIT) Media Lab. On the other side of the United States in the Department of Communication at the University of California at San Diego, a campus known for its scientific endeavors, Dan Schiller publishes *Digital Capitalism*, a Marxist dystopian view of the emerging digital economy. In his narrative, digital communication remains at the instrumental level rather than being acknowledged as constitutive of social formations.[9] Schiller provides us with a detailed, pessimistic view of the digital economy where there is little hope for a different future. In our view, Schiller is led to this position because his economistic view does not allow for the moment of culture and agency.

And while MIT is known for its work in technology development it is also the place where Sherry Turkle conceptualized digital cultural productions as forms of simulacra.[10] In *Life on the Screen* she suggests, "The objects on the screen have no simple physical referent. In this sense, life on the screen is without origins and foundation. It is a place where signs taken for reality may substitute for the real. Its aesthetic has to do with manipulation and recombination."[11]

Her narrative seems to ignore the material production base of the communication infrastructure, leading her to suggest that physical place does not matter. History and the forces that enable and promote technologies, forces that in our time emerge from specific geographic spaces and places, are obscured in her narrative. While Turkle is not alone in proclaiming that physical place is irrelevant in the age of the Internet, her use of postmodernism is novel. She uses Fredric Jameson's essay "Postmodernism, or the Cultural Logic of Late Capitalism," to demonstrate how subjects are fragmented, fluid, and decentered.[12] She describes postmodernism's fascination with play, a term she uses to name her fascination with simulation. Unlike Turkle, Jameson places postmodernism within an historical frame that foregrounds its relationship with late capitalism. None of these positions acknowledges the deeply social basis of communication, which we feel is central to any consideration of space and place. For this we need to travel across the Atlantic Ocean to England, where Raymond Williams's and Stuart Hall's articulation of "cultural materialism" and "circuit of culture," respectively, provide alternative means for framing digital communication and production.

We find that Raymond Williams was always concerned with the conditions that promote and limit cultural practices and the extent that these practices and conditions promote and/or limit democratic spaces.[13] In *Keywords* he reminds us that the term *technology* has a long history; originally referring to a systematic study of the arts, during the nineteenth century it was associated with the culture and society debate, then becoming specialized to refer to the industrial arts and ultimately with economics.[14] In discussing the transition from oral traditions to writing cultures, Williams notes that "the technology of writing is not only the series of inventions—a script, an alphabet, and materials for its production—which initiate the process, but the mode of distribution of the work thus produced—this mode of distribution is itself not only technical—but depends on a wider technology, primarily determined by social relations, in which the ability to read, which is part of the substance of distribution, is itself produced."[15] In a related discussion on television, Williams suggests that the means of communication always precede popular uses of technology: "It is especially a characteristic of the communication systems that *all were foreseen—not in utopian but in technical ways—before the crucial components of the developed systems had been discovered and refined.*"[16]

Williams's concern for the development of democratic cultures led to his theory of cultural materialism, which focuses on identifying the conditions of cultural practices rather than identifying the components of such practices. He cautions us that focusing on the components often results in analyzing cultural texts as autonomous objects. His insistence on viewing cultural practices as variable and changing led him to articulate the concepts of the dominant, the residual, and the emergent as a way of describing the different moments of this cultural process.[17] He further stipulates that the residual and the emergent can be alternative or oppositional to the dominant. Finally, he notes that the dominant continually seeks to incorporate oppositional practices.[18] Williams notes that the means of communication are always a means of production. By means of communications he includes both direct and indirect communications. Direct forms of communication include physical speech and nonverbal communication. Indirect forms of communication include writing, drama, radio, television, cable, and, more recently, digital forms. Indirect forms include technological devices used to capture, store, manipulate, and transmit information. These devices are manufactured, hence socially produced, within a specific historical period, inscribed by specific social relations, and have a finite technical capacity.[19] Regardless of form, communication is always social, produced, and reproduced. While Williams's theory of cultural materialism is useful at the general level, we find Stuart Hall's theoretical work offers strategies for applying these perspectives to how cultural products are produced and consumed.

Hall describes the communication process as a "complex structure in dominance that is produced and sustained through the articulation of linked but distinctive moments—production, circulation, distribution/consumption, reproduction."[20] Each moment contains its organization and practices. Hall's articulation of the "circuit of culture" focuses on both the economic and the symbolic aspects of communication and cultural production. The circuit of culture describes processes and practices that are fluid and subject to change and political contestation. These readings lead us to consider digital practices as an *array of practices* that are part of a circuit of culture but first it is important to elaborate our use of space and place.

Re-Presenting the Production of Space, Place, Gender, and Race

Our journey takes us not only to universities but also to high schools and community-based organizations across the United States. Our journey includes different forms of communication, such as lectures, workshops, informal talks, and of course discussions in cyberspace. In our journey we note contested conceptions of time, space, and place, which prompt us to consider a more explicit spatialized dimension of the circuit of culture. On our journey through libraries we notice that place serves as a background in literally all Latino texts and is constituted in a number of ways. Yet until recently, place and space had remained largely untheorized in Latino texts.

Carlos Vélez-Ibáñez, in *Border Vision*, cautions us that his spatialized ethnography "is not about place, as such, but rather an attempt to piece together the history and understand the processes by which human beings with their own ideology moved into the U.S. Southwest and created a sense of cultural place and to try to understand the attempts by others to define or deny that cultural place by building fences of various sorts."[21] For Vélez-Ibáñez, cultural constructions of place are best understood as cultural processes, which are shaped by various practices and discourses and the power relations that underlay them.

Rosaura Sanchez in *Telling Identities*, a rich analysis of nineteenth-century Mexican women's autobiography, argues that "social spaces could be said to have a generative capacity." For Sanchez, the importance of studying the configuration of social spaces lies in the promise of discovering the social formation that gave rise to a particular social practice.[22] In a similar reading, José David Saldívar, in *Border Matters*, notes the "profound interaction of space and history, geography and psychology, nationhood and imperialism." He defines space "not just as a 'setting' but as a formative presence."[23] Many of these readings have been informed by the writings of Henri Lefebvre's *The Production of Social Space*, which is an unrelenting call for the rearticulation of social space. Lefebvre's concept of social space is made up of three major concepts: spatial practice, representations of space, and spaces of representation.[24] Lefebvre sees social space made of the interaction between perceived, conceived, and lived space. In *Postmodern Geographies*, Edward Soja, drawing heavily from Lefebvre's work, discusses the limits of using physical space as an "epistemological foundation upon which to analyse the concrete and subjective meaning of human spatiality." He notes that while "space in itself may be primordially given, . . . the organization, and the meaning of space is a product of social translation, transformation, and experience."[25] For Soja, people participate in the social construction of spatialities and are therefore spatial beings.

Linda McDowell and Doreen Massey offer a re-presentation of the notion of place. McDowell argues that socio-spatial practices define places and these practices result in overlapping and intersecting places with multiple and changing boundaries, constituted by social relations of power and exclusion.[26] Massey maintains that localities are produced by the intersections of global processes that lead to "a momentary coexistence of trajectories, a configuration of a multiplicity of histories all in the process of being made."[27]

In our journey we find that the majority of theoretical discussions of spatiality deal with either space or place with limited attention on the relationship between these terms. An exception to this trend is Michel de Certeau, who defines place as a structure through which the dominant order uses its power to organize and control society and space as constructed by people through the practice of living.[28] This articulation of place is somewhat narrower than the theoretical perspectives already discussed since it does not allow for the possibility that places can be constructed outside of the dominant realm. However, in an important theoretical move, John Fiske expands de Certeau's conception of space to include alternative and oppositional practices.[29]

We are led to ask how the new digital economy has altered our conceptions of space and place. Manuel Castells, a student of Lefebvre, argues in the *Information Society* that "the historical emergence of the *space of flows*, [is] superseding the meaning of *the spaces of places*."[30] By this Castells acknowledges that corporations are no longer dependent on the same historical locations for production and distribution. His remarks are extended in *The Rise of the Network Society* where he states, using concepts borrowed from telematics, that "space is the material support of time-sharing social practices."[31] While both of Castells's most recent books explore the role of new digital economies in the restructuring of contemporary society, it can be argued that he has conflated both conceived space and lived space into perceived space. As a consequence, it could be argued that he obscures the role of history and agency in people's construction of space and place. Yet that would belie the rest of his argument in his trilogy and his subsequent work the *Internet Galaxy*.[32] We would like to offer the following slight revision. *In the current global era the rearticulation of space can be characterized by a variety of different forms of flows that alter, shape, and are shaped by the relative importance of different places.*

In our journey we note that a major feature of digital technologies is how they drastically reduce the amount of time it takes to accomplish extremely complex tasks. We also observe that digital technologies serve as a bridge to link people so they can communicate across great distances. We find that some have mistakenly misread this reduction in time and distance as signifying that space and place no longer matter.[33] Saskia Sassen contests the dominant view by arguing that firms are both information-based and place-bound.[34] Sassen describes the rise of electronic space as being associated with global cities and value chains, centrality, and cybersegmentation that lead to the following major new conditions:

> The growing digitization and globalization of leading economic sectors has further contributed to the hyper-concentration of resources, infrastructure, and central functions, with global cities as one strategic site in the new global economic network [and] the growing economic importance of electronic space has furthered global alliances and massive concentrations of capital and corporate power the above have contributed to new forms of segmentation in electronic space.[35]

She goes on to argue that while "electronic space is easily read as a purely technological event and in that sense as self contained and neutral—electronic space is inscribed, and to some extent shaped, by power, concentration, and contestation, as well as by openness and decentralization."[36] Sassen's articulation of electronic or digital space is close to Lefebvre's notion of perceived space but it can be seen as moving toward the conceived and lived level.

As we view the notes from our journey we see that digital spaces and places are perceived, conceived, and lived. They are constituted and embedded with social, historical, cultural, political, and economic relations and thus are full of contradictions. They are not pregiven nor do they constitute any kind of totality. While they include dominant practices, they also include alternative and oppositional practices. As such they are potential sites for social change. As in other types of social practice, alternative and oppositional spatial practices often arise from the popular. It is therefore crucial that we turn our attention to describing an array of digital practices. We can thus look at how people are making space as the practice of place in an emerging digital society.

ARTICULATING THE INTERNET AS A DIVERSE ARRAY OF COMMUNICATIVE PRACTICES AND RESIDUAL SOCIAL SPACES

> Bits will be borderless, stored and manipulated with absolutely no respect to geopolitical boundaries. —Nicolas Negroponte, Being Digital[37]

In order to interrogate the aspects of place within the Internet it is necessary to view the Internet as a site for a set of diverse practices rather than a unitary practice. A technological focus, sometimes referred to as telematics, of the Internet allows us to spatialize it within a global economy. The Internet is often defined as a computer network of networks that are tied together using various telecommunication mediums such as copper wire, twisted pairs, fiber optic, cable, and various types of wireless forms. The analog form of the Internet is made possible through various physical devices, such as computers, digital assistants, cameras, and so on, which are manufactured in the global economy.

Revisiting Saskia Sassen helps us situate the relationship of the manufactured products by locating them as outcomes of the digital economy within a process of globalization. She remarks, "alongside the well-documented spatial dispersal of economic activity have appeared new forms of territorial centralization of top-level management and control operations." She identifies the role of global cities as strategic sites where the centralization of management and control operations take place. She demonstrates that "even the most advanced information industries have a work process—that is, a complex of workers, machines, and buildings that are more *placebound* than the imagery of the information economy suggests."[38] Moreover Sassen notes that there is a "need to distinguish between the capacity for global transmission/communication and the material conditions that make this possible."[39]

Discussions on our journey concerning the use of the Internet often treat it as if it was a unitary practice when in fact it can be considered an array of distinct communication practices that are commonly referred to as applications or protocols. These protocols include but are not limited to e-mail, electronic lists, chat groups, Multi User Domains (MUDs), gophers, and Web sites. Each application makes possible a distinct communication practice. E-mail and electronic lists are asynchronous forms of communication while chat can be synchronous (real time). MUDs encourage the construction of texts or images that represent people, places, things, while Web sites share several characteristics with written texts.

We view these constructions as texts that are encoded by race, class, and gender, as well as space and place. We gather these constructions from our travels in the field as librarians, producers of Internet content, and developers of a community-computing center. Our journey also takes us to libraries where we read historical texts and attempt to capture traditional notions of place in cyberspace. This journey to the past reminds us that many practices we consider novel today have been preceded by older technological practices. We find it essential to highlight the connections of history to current practices. Moreover our journey of historical places and practices brings to the fore how many of the metaphors we use to describe digital practices are products of earlier residual discourses.

James O'Donnell relays the importance of seeing the relationship between oral, print, and digital forms of communication rather than considering that one form supplanted the other. He argues that the idea of a virtual library was already present in ancient Alexandria, claiming that hyperlinks are forms of indexes, concordances, and headers, which exist with printed materials.[40] This allows us to see that much of what is claimed as new can be considered residual cultural practices.

In traveling to the so-called New World, we observe that while Mesoamerican iconography predated the arrival of Spaniards, many of the best-known codices were created at the behest of Spanish missionaries. Our readings inform us that these codices were produced utilizing indigenous plants taken from the local area and that the majority of these codices, taken from Mesoamerica to Europe, are named after the places in which they came to reside. Such an example is the *Florentine Codex*, written by several indigenous inhabitants in collaboration with Fray Bernardino de Sahagún. This bilingual edition, in Nahuatl and Spanish with some of the Nahuatl not translated into Spanish, suggests that not all of the content was accessible to the Spaniards. Completed in 1577, its value as an imperial cultural artifact is demonstrated by the fact that Phillip II gave the codex as a wedding gift to Francis the First and Bianca Capello in 1579. It now resides in the Biblioteca Medicea Laurenziana in Florence, Italy. Print facsimiles of the codices were created and made available to libraries.[41] Today part of this codex is being digitized and integrated into the curriculum of various university courses.[42] Our journey reveals that diverse technologies facilitate the migration of hybrid indigenous and colonial texts into different spaces and places. As such we see them as part of an ongoing historical struggle for space and place between peoples in the Old and New Worlds.

GLOBALIZATION IN LOCAL PLACES

> Place is central to the multiple circuits through which the economy is constituted . . . hypermobility needs to be produced, serviced, and maintained, and this requires places and workers.
> —Saskia Sassen, "Foreword," *Latino Metropolis*[43]

On our journey we notice that many recent discussions conceptualize the Internet and associated technologies as principally telecommunications phenomena without recognizing the underlying socioeconomic forces that have propelled their development. The underlying motives and technologies for developing the Internet were defense-related (tactical) and only later was it considered a means of facilitating the flow of human and social capital. Thus any discussion of place must recognize the basic economic forces and specific places that develop the technologies that help manufacture the hardware with which the Internet is built. The role of Third World people as part of the labor force that produces computer chips is often erased in contemporary discussions of new technologies. We find it is necessary to re-present them.

The Silicon Valley in California is a principal site for the production of digital technology. Manuel Pastor and Marta Lopez Garza report that in 1990 Anglos represented 62 percent of the labor force in Santa Clara County but were 76 percent of the executives and managers, while Latinos were only 16 percent of the labor force but 36 percent of the machine operators.[44] Similarly, Hossfeld finds that the majority of machine workers in the Silicon Valley are immigrant women.[45] The current debate concerning a digital divide obscures the role of immigrants within the production of digital technologies. In our journey we find immigrants and ethnic minorities are present within the global economy often working in the production of digital products. The current emphasis on the founders of digital technologies, such as Bill Gates, also shifts focus away from the workers who manufacture these technologies. Indeed, Sassen notes that one aspect of globalization is that certain sectors of the economy such as finance are overvalorized while other aspects, such as labor or production, are devalorized. She notes that "this devalorization of growing sectors of the economy has been embedded in a massive demographic transition towards a growing presence of women, African Americans, and Third World immigrants in the urban workforce."[46]

On our journey we find that the presence of Latinos in the global economy has also been the focus of the Inter University Consortium for Latino Research (IUP). In 1995, we journey to work with IUP faculty and librarians to promote the use of the Internet by providing training and technical support, and assisting them in constructing a Web site. IUP is a consortium of Chicano, Puerto Rican, Cuban, and Dominican research centers in the United States. These centers are located in Boston, New York, Austin, Los Angeles, Tucson, Tempe, and Miami. Their locations are significant because they represent places where various Latino subgroups reside. Those in the Southwest have higher concentrations of Mexicans, while those in New York have higher concentrations of Puerto Ricans and Dominicans. We find that a significant part of IUP's activities are formulated and implemented by working groups that include representation from the various centers. Our explorations of IUP's history reveal that the use of the new technologies as an important delivery system has not gone unnoticed in the Latino community. In 1988, IUP held a conference at the Rockefeller Bellagio Conference facility in Italy on Latinos in a global society. This IUP conference recognizes Latinos as cultural actors who are entering into the development of a global society and the discourses that are being developed around these global movements. Their deliberations detailed both how Latinos are a critical part of manufacturing as witnessed by their presence in maquiladoras (border industries), and how Latinos are becoming part of global policy discussions, especially within the Americas. In a video by Susan Zeig entitled *Latinos in a Global Society*, Latinos articulate the potential benefits of technology as a means to facilitate communication. Consider the following remark by Luis Falcon: "One of the ways that globalization has affected not only Puerto Ricans but Latinos in general in the United States is because of the reduction of borders, the reduction of barriers, for example, the advances in communications, the ability to remain in touch with the *country where people are coming from*" (our emphasis). In this excerpt we have Luis Falcon, a Puerto Rican professor from Rutgers University, speaking at the Bellagio conference at a villa in northern Italy about how new technologies are serving as vehicles to communicate with the folks back home. This discussion was captured in the above noted video, then digitized as part of the IUP Web presence and published in the proceedings, *Borderless Borders*.[47] This example illustrates the movement and migration of both people and products within a global economy and recognizes Latinos as social actors, struggling for space and a place in an ever-changing global world.

Identifying and Representing Divides

Our journey also identifies access, literacy, and relevant content as the major issues concerning Latinas/Latinos in cyberspace. We find that the term *digital divide* is the current popular metaphor representing the lack of equity within telecommunications. Keith Fulton, from the National Urban League, states that "in a very rapid way, the term 'digital divide' began to emerge as a leading phrase for describing a range of disparities between those who enjoy the benefits of information and communications technology and those who do not."[48]

The metaphor of the information superhighway provides an opportunity for Chicano comic Lalo Alcaraz to recall the destructive role that building highways through communities have played[49] (Figure 17.2). The history of the development of highways reveals a practice of building them through the heart of local Latino communities. If a demographic map of Los Angeles is overlaid with a freeway map it will illustrate how freeways have divided, hence destroyed and disempowered a traditional Mexican community in East Los Angeles.[50] Now with the development of computers and the new era of telecommunications, Alcaraz suggests that a new kind of highway, the information superhighway, is bypassing the Latino

Figure 17.2 *Traditional Highway/Super Information Highway*, by Lalo Alcaraz. <http://clnet.ucla.edu/buttons/highway.gif>. © 2003 Lalo Alcaraz. First appeared in *L.A. Weekly*. Reprinted with permission from the artist.

community. For Alcaraz, the information superhighway is not being built through Latino communities; on the contrary it is circumventing the community because the telecommunications industry and governing institutions do not deem the Latino community as a potential market, a place that matters. Yet, these contested decisions of where to build the infrastructure that provides access to the Internet demonstrates precisely that place does matter. Alcaraz's caricature captures the idea of electronic redlining and the symbolic creation of a digital divide.

While Lalo Alcaraz discusses one aspect of access to new technologies symbolically, Blanco Gordo coins the term *enhanced access* to expand the discourse of the digital divide. She cautions us that as we consider such items as computer ownership and Internet access, which tend to focus on consumption, that we need to refocus on the conditions under which people can use high technologies to become producers.[51] This has led us to reconsider Sassens's term *cybersegmentation* as a better way of describing what is popularly known as the digital divide.[52] We reformulate cybersegmentation as *the inequalities that exist with regard to the material capacity, acquired skills, and differential use of digital technologies.*

We find that many emerging technologies are built upon an existing communication infrastructure—in this case, the telephone system. Many assume that Americans have home phone access, but numerous studies document that there is still a significant divide among racial groups' access to telephones.[53] We also find that the principal means of connecting to the Internet or other online services is via the telephone. While cable, DSL, and/or wireless systems may become more popular in the future, their ability to reach the unreached Latino populations remains only a promise that will face the same obstacles as telephone service.

Beginning in 1994, we read several reports produced by the Clinton administration, under the leadership of Larry Irving, the assistant secretary of the National Telecommunications Information and Administration (NTIA), which seek to move beyond tracking telephone diffusion to collecting data on modem and computer use and ownership.[54] They do so because they believe that "while a standard telephone line can be an individual's pathway to the riches of the Information Age, a personal computer and modem are rapidly becoming the keys to the vault"[55] (Figure 17.3).

In 1994, *Falling Through the Net* reported that 27.1 percent of the Anglo population had access to computers compared to 12.3 percent of the Latino population. By 2001, 70.7 percent of the Anglo population owned computers compared to 48.8 percent of Latinos. Despite the falling price of computers the gap between the Anglo population and Latinos widened from 14.8 to 21.9 percentage points. An even bleaker picture becomes clear when we examine access to the Internet. In 1997, 21.2 percent of Anglo households had access to the Internet compared to 8.7 percent of Latinos. By 2001, Anglo households online access rose to 59.9 percent while Latino online access rose to only 31.6 percent. The technology gap grew from 12.5 percentage points to 28.

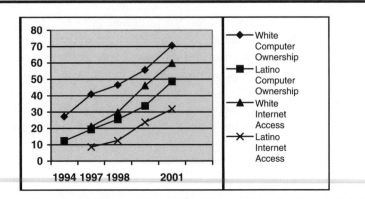

Figure 17.3 *White and Latino Computer Ownership and Internet Access* by Richard Chabrán, based on data in *Falling Through the Net* series and *A Nation Online*. Note: In *A Nation Online*, computer use rather than computer ownership was measured.

Technological disparities in the area of telephone access, computer ownership, and online access are critical issues that need to be addressed if we are to speak about emergent technologies as tools for creating an equitable and truly democratic society. Toward the end of our journey the Bush administration dismisses any notion of a digital divide.[56] These sobering household statistics demonstrate, in yet another way, how place matters.

CULTURAL REGULATION: CONSTRUCTING PORTALS

In our journey we have witnessed the explosion of the World Wide Web as a site for cultural production. We see the development of a variety of strategies for locating relevant information. An interrogation of these strategies discloses their relationship to various social formations. Search engines and directories, such as Yahoo, Lycos, and HotBot, have substantive affiliations with major corporations. The role of advertising within these sites is central even as they may help us find various resources; of less notice is their emerging role as portals to the Internet, through which they are positioning themselves as future information gatekeepers.[57] We ask ourselves, Will such portals also serve as "censoring agents?" Will the "agents," "cookies," and "bots" they utilize be used to invade the privacy of at-risk individuals such as undocumented workers? Will sites have to pay to be included in these portals?[58] Can these portals reflect the intellectual process that is present in the development of specific cultural sites?

During our journey we build Chicano/LatinoNet (CLNet), a University of California project now located at the University of California at Los Angeles campus.[59] It is part of the Chicano/Latino Electronic Network (CLEN), which also includes the UC Linguistic Minority Research Institute (LMRINet) that focuses on linguistic minorities. CLNet assists LMRI in managing various electronic lists and in training activities. As founders of CLNet, and as librarians, we use the metaphor of a library as a means for identifying, selecting, and organizing digital information. In the 1960s, Octavio Romano suggested that if aliens came from outer space and visited libraries they would conclude that Mexican Americans were a people without a history.[60] We recall that Chicano Studies libraries were developed across the United States as a strategy for supporting emerging Chicano Studies teaching and research initiatives. Their development responded to the failure of many libraries to collect and make available material on the Chicano experience. The lessons of that earlier encounter with traditional libraries set the stage not only for the development of many fine ethnic collections but also provided the springboard for the development of a host of research tools, such as the *Chicano Database*.[61] The fundamental goal of all of these initiatives was the identification, selection, and inclusion of a corpus of work largely excluded in American libraries.[62] During the late 1960s and early 1970s the Chicano and Civil Rights movement produced a plethora of materials that took the forms of newsletters, newspapers, flyers, manifestos, and the like. At the time many libraries discarded or did not attempt to collect those materials, because they were not considered research quality. Chicano Studies libraries worked hard to identify, collect, and organize that material. Today such materials are considered valuable, primary source research material by many elite institutions. Ironically, the Chicano Studies library is now becoming an endangered species as these libraries are being incorporated into more traditional collections. CLNet's development was tied to this history and serves in a similar role as a Chicano Studies library in cyberspace.

During this journey it has commonly been asserted that anyone can have a presence on the Internet. On January 1, 1994, in response to NAFTA and hundreds of years of oppression, the indigenous people from the state of Chiapas, Mexico, led by Commander Marcos, took control of four cities and declared war with Mexico. Although their struggle was remote and isolated, it gained international attention as information was disseminated worldwide through faxes, e-mails, and other computerized networks. This set in motion a wave of solidarity and support for an army of the poor who identified themselves as "Zapatistas" after the Mexican Revolution hero, Emiliano Zapata.[63] The early use of the Internet by the Zapatista movement in south-central Mexico provides support for the view of digital practices as a liberating force.[64] However, this view is tempered by the reality of the cybersegmentation we documented earlier. This vision of the Internet's revolutionary potential is also tempered by the acknowledgment of the massive developments of Intranets being constructed by business. In fact much of the publicly developed technology of the Internet is now being used to support private resources.[65] The sheer volume and relatively open access to the Internet leaves many calling for various ways of managing Internet resources. Many complain about the quality and reliability of the information. Others respond that rather than attempting any kind of censorship we need to promote critical literacy, the ability to not only critically read the word but also, as Paulo Freire noted, to read the world.[66]

In constructing CLNet we take the position that librarians and scholars must work together in the identification, selection, organization, creation of Internet material, and promotion of critical literacy and technological fluency. Our goal is an opening up of the selective tradition to include Latina/os and other marginalized groups. The first critical task is to continue the building of space/places (physical and digital) that contain the voices of all peoples. Another goal is the promotion of critical literacy in all places and spaces. By critical literacy we include being able "to recognize when information is needed and have the ability to locate, evaluate and use effectively the needed information."[67] It also means the "ability to use today's computer applications and apply information technology immediately; . . . understand basic principles & ideas of computers, networks, and information, which underpin technology; and . . . possess the intellectual capabilities to apply information technology in complex and sustained situations."[68] Critical literacy must go beyond skills, toward a practice that promotes how to read the word but also how to read digital and analog places in the world.[69] Search engines and other related Internet developments must be viewed as supplementary to this process. It was tragic to see that a draft of the American Library Association's "The Role of Libraries in the Networked World" was cast in technological rather than people terms, and did not include literacy. REFORMA, the National Association to Promote Library and Information Services to Latinos and the

Spanish-Speaking, worked together with ALA to remedy this situation.[70] The voices that come from these places powerfully matter.

TRADITIONAL PLACES IN VIRTUAL SPACES

> The role for us, then, was to assume, once again, the unpleasant but necessary role of cultural invaders, techno-pirates, and coyotes (smugglers). And then, just like multiculturalism was declared dead as soon as we began to share the paycheck, now as we venture into the virtual varrio for the first time some asshole at MIT declares it dead.
> —Guillermo Gómez-Peña, "The Virtual Barrio @ The Other Frontier"[71]

The next stop on our journey reproduces a traditional place in a virtual setting. The Virtual Varrio Web site re-creates a traditional Chicano barrio[72] (Figure 17.4). This digital place invites users to stroll down Varrio streets and visit one of its many locations, such as the local Roach Motel, the local Taco Stand, or the Cyber Cholo Chat Room. Each of these virtual spaces serves multiple functions. On the one hand they seek to reinscribe positive value to terms that are commonly used to disparage the Chicano community. For example, within the dominant society the presence of roaches represents filth and uncleanness. Oscar Acosta's *Revolt of the Cockroach People* counters this assumption by illustrating that cockroaches symbolize not only poverty but also a species that cannot be stomped out.[73] The taco stand is represented as Taco Bell, which symbolizes the incorporation and commodification of Mexican food within the United States. The Chicano community that Alcaraz depicts is not pure but hybrid and contradictory. These images create a sense of familiarity for Latinos on the Web. This virtual site can also be seen as a contestation to what Sharon Zukin has named "landscapes of power."[74]

The Virtual Varrio utilizes satire to communicate its position on issues relevant to the Latino community. For instance, the Pocho Palace, a virtual theater, features movie productions expressing satirical views on social and political issues that negatively impact the Latino community. One of its features is *Dia de la Independencia*, a parody of the movie *Independence Day*. In the context of today's anti-immigrant political climate, Alcaraz mocks anti-immigration messages by using animated images of flying sombreros invading planet Earth. This production contains an audio clip capturing and ridiculing the opinions expressed in the Save Our State Initiative that led to the passing of California's anti-immigrant Proposition 187.

Figure 17.4 *Virtual Barrio* by Lalo Alcaraz. © 2003 Lalo Alcaraz, first appeared in *L.A. Weekly.* <www.pocho.com/varrio.html> accessed October 1998. Reprinted with permission from the artist.

> This is not a test. I repeat this is not a test. Attention citizens and legal residents only, this is a national emergency. Planet USA has been invaded by alien beings. Their aim is to take over our planet's natural resources, our bodies and our jobs. These dangerous aliens refuse to learn our official language; their customs are strange, and, other worldly . . . They have superior family values. They work harder than we do. Save your selves. SOS. Save our State. SOS. Save our State. SOS. SOS. SOS . . .

This satiric public announcement broadcasts the invasion of "our" world by aliens, exposing the xenophobic and racist fears behind Proposition 187.

Virtual Varrio is a response to the racial and social marginalization of the Latino community. The historical realities of political exclusion, economic exploitation, and media misrepresentation all play a role in shaping the construction and content of this site. Although it is a new place created to express and disseminate an alternative discourse, it is nevertheless a place tied to a history, culture, and community.

CONSTRUCTION OF SELF: MULTIPLE IDENTITIES

When we began to dialogue with artists working with new technologies, we were perplexed by the fact that when referring to cyberspace or the Net, they spoke of a politically neutral/raceless/genderless/classless "territory" which provided us all with "equal access" and unlimited possibilities of participation, interaction and belonging. Their enthusiastic rhetoric reminded us of both a sanitized version of the pioneer and cowboy mentalities of the Old West . . . The unquestioned lingua franca was of course English, the official language of international communications;, the vocabulary utilized in these discussions was hyperspecialized and depoliticized; and if Chicanos and Mexicans didn't participate enough in the Net, it was solely because of lack of information or interest (not money or access), or again because they were "culturally unfit."
—Guillermo Gómez-Peña, "The Virtual Barrio @ The Other Frontier"[75]

Our journey raises critical questions concerning the representation of identity on the Internet. The Internet is referred to as a space where participants are equal regardless of race, age, class, or gender. Although on the surface this discourse seems to have found a solution to society's inequalities and discrimination, it also calls for an examination of the ramifications of moving such an agenda forward. Is this discourse in essence creating a digital platform for assimilation? Certainly a culture is being created in cyberspace that calls for participants to interact according to what is perceived as proper netiquette. Mark Warscharer recalls the popular saying that "nobody on the Internet knows that you're not a dog, nor can they easily determine if you're black or white, male or female, gay or straight or rich or poor. But they can immediately notice what language and dialect you are using"—and that language is usually English.[76] In 2002, OCLC found that 72 percent of the public Web sites in the world were in English.[77] Non-English Web sites usually have an English version and international electronic mailing lists usually communicate in English. Clearly a dominant culture exists on the Internet and for participants to become part of that network they must function within that culture's essential goal of assimilation. Anatoly Voronov, director of the Russian Internet service provider Glasnet, states:

It is just incredible when I hear people talking about how open the Web is. It is the ultimate act of intellectual colonialism. The product comes from America so we either must adapt to English or stop using it. That is the right of any business. But if you are talking about a technology that is supposed to open the world to hundreds of millions of people you are joking. This just makes the world into new sorts of haves and have nots.[78]

However, there are always those who choose to create alternative cultures, cultures that are tied to physical realties and places. We find Anne Balsamo's discussion of the body as particularly instructive, especially as she describes the social construction of the body: "as a *product*, it is the material embodiment of ethnic, racial, and gender identities, . . . personal identity, of beauty, of health . . . As a *process*, it is a way of knowing and marking the world, as well as a way of knowing and marking a 'self.'"[79] She goes onto offer the phrase "technologies of the gendered body" as a way of describing such interactions between bodies and technologies. Gender, in this schema, is both a determining cultural condition and a social consequence of technological deployment.[80]

The geographer Linda McDowell argues that people and places are gendered and constituted by sets of social relations that cut across spatial scales but are not always visible unless you look at specific localities.[81] The Web site for Glass Houses provides a tour of American neo-colonialism from a Mexican American woman's perspective[82] (Figure 17.5). Jacalyn Lopez Garcia describes her Web site as a desire to create a voice for the "modern" Chicana living in the suburbs. Using the floor plan of her home she provides a metaphor to explore a variety of themes associated with daily living: fears, ritual, traditions, opportunity, and desires.[83] Blending various formats and technological media such as photographs, music, art, digital images as well as oral traditions, she explores issues of culture, identity, and history, documenting and preserving her story for her children and community.[84] She tells her story of struggle in the land of opportunity and the privileges bestowed on her for being born fair-skinned and light-haired in this society. Each room represents a part of her identity. She places her history in the living room, relating her mother's experience of deportation after being reported by a "hateful" neighbor as well as other experiences of growing up. In her closet, her secrets are kept, including how she learned about racism, a silent topic in her family. The family room houses her culture, where she examines issues of language, folklore, and family. On the second floor we find her exploration of identity. Here she shares her dilemma of what it means to be a Chicana. As she would cross the Mexican border she would proudly declare that she was American to the Border Patrol but in California people would ask her, "What are you?" and she would reply "Mexican." In the bedroom she hides her fears, the fear that her children will also experience the pain of "otherness." The vanity provides a mirror of self-portraits where she expresses herself artistically.

Figure 17.5 *Glass Houses* by Jacalyn Lopez Garcia. Reprinted with permission from the artist. <http://www.cmp.ucr.edu/students/GlassHouses/>.

The creation of this site is shaped by Lopez Garcia's experiences of growing up in the United States as a Chicana, adhering to the pressure of assimilation, and coming to the realization of the consequences of leaving behind a culture. This site raises various issues that are left unresolved but provide a record of how race, class, and gender play a role in the construction of community identity even in cyberspace. While Lopez Garcia seeks to tell a story about identity and gender, people who partake in electronic lists create community by participating in conversations.

Building Virtual Communities

My collaborator Roberto Sifuentes and I bullied over selves into the Net . . .
Then we started sending a series of "techno placas" in Spanglish.
—Guillermo Gómez-Peña, The Virtual Barrio @ The Other Frontier"[85]

In our journey we seek to develop a digital dialogue among people with similar interests utilizing electronic lists. An electronic mailing list, often called a listserv, provides a forum for ongoing communication among people with common interests. CLEN sponsors a number of mailing lists on issues related to Chicano/Latino Studies and/or language minority education. *Mujer-L*, a CLEN list, seeks to provide an electronic forum to discuss, present, distribute, and create information dealing with Chicanas and/or Latinas as well as to build an international network among those who share an interest in Chicana-Latina issues. *Mujer-L* also seeks to establish the presence of the Chicana and Latina on the Internet. It has come to play many different roles over the course of time. For example, Chicanas who find themselves working or studying in places distant from their homes turn to *Mujer-L* as a place to find cultural comfort, to dialogue without having to explain cultural sayings or beliefs, to feel a sense of community. *Mujer-L* develops into a virtual community where issues of identity, literature, education, racism, and the like can be shared and explored. It also functions as a mentoring forum for Chicana graduate students and faculty as they share experiences and resources. *Mujer-L* is an example of how mailing lists are used to create spaces in cyberspace that are tied to actual places and cultures.

EMERGING PUBLIC SPHERES: CRITICAL SPACES

> The social is spatially constructed too, and that makes a difference . . . society is necessarily constructed spatially—the spatial organization of society—makes a difference to how it works.
> —Doreen Massey, *Space, Place, and Gender*[86]

Perhaps our most profound insight on our journey is the need to develop geographic places that could promote new public spheres. As several critics have noted, the creation of a new democratic space will take more than bits and bytes but new forms and spaces where we can educate a critical citizenry. Sassen notes that "we need to dissect the economic of globalization to understand whether a new transnational politics can be centered in the new transnational economic geography . . . dissecting the economics of place in a global economy allows us to recover non-corporate components of economic globalization and to inquire about the possibility of a new type of transnational politics, a politics of those who lack power but now have 'presence.' "[87] Similarly Raymond Rocco reminds us a new public sphere will need to be a space that rethinks citizenship in a manner that acknowledges and benefits all of the members of our changing local communities. He argues for broadening the way we think about civic society:

> sites of mediation are the spaces of everyday life, in which individuals and groups engage and encounter the norms, boundaries, customs, networks that define institutional relationships, and then experience the effects of economic and political policies. Schools, churches, the workplace, parks are all sites in which the activities of everyday life are carried out and the effects of the practices of power are experienced—in which the boundaries set by privilege, status, and access are encountered as limits of action. But they are also the sites of association, in which individuals and groups establish a wide variety of relatively stable networks of activity that not only sustain their survival, identity, and sense of worth, but also serve as the basis for the development of practices and activities that are concerned with the direction of community and collective life—with the constitution of a "public sphere."[88]

So what are these new spaces? The *Falling Through the Net* report cited earlier suggests that schools, public libraries and community centers play an important role in addressing the digital divide.[89] Community technology centers have the potential to become key sites for the promotion of the kind of public sphere articulated by Rocco. However, while they constitute new public places they have not received or been eligible for much public funding.[90] They can serve as the site to develop what Anthony Wilhelm has called antecedent resources that include the promotion of reading, writing, and critical uses of digital technology that can advance economic well-being and civic participation.[91] Blanca Gordo argues that community technology centers should concentrate on providing what she has termed "enhanced access," which "is about production of knowledge rather than simple consumption of information. It is a combination of technical and including social skills needed to compete in a flexible and contingent labor force. In this way, technology can be viewed as an enabling and productive tool, an information resource, and vehicle for communication."[92]

We would like to end our journey by describing our participation in the creation of an alternative space and place—the UCR Community Digital Initiative (CDI). CDI is one of eleven sites in the Computer in Our Future (CIOF) Program that is part of a larger Work and Health Initiative. CIOF represents a unique attempt to develop a community technology center. Essential aspects of the CIOF model are a physical computer center and a virtual learning center, located in a community that offers open access to residents, educational and training programs, links to employment services, and a nascent effort to engage local communities in policies that would support community computing.[93]

CDI established a community-computing center in the heart of a predominately Latino and African American community in the east side of Riverside, California. Its physical location is at the Cesar Chavez Community Center in the Bobby Bonds Sports Park complex. The center was named after the Mexican American labor leader and the park complex was named after an African American baseball star. CDI targets youth and in partnership with local community-based organizations and institutions, it provides computer and information literacy training to a sector of society that might not otherwise have access.

We have heard and read the statistics of unequal access to technology for low-income minority communities, but at CDI we actually met the individuals that represent those numbers. We have witnessed the impact that centers, such as CDI, may have not only on levels of technological fluency and critical literacy but in building a lived space that promotes a sense of self-empowerment. CDI offers a space that is different than library or schools because we are not constrained by the same limitations that exist in many public institutions. We strive to teach our youth how to empower themselves and their local communities by providing them a lived space where they can use technology to create different types of projects to express themselves. We encourage them to explore methods of self- and community documentation through technology. Outcomes of such projects have resulted in the creation of personal Web pages that create a virtual representation of their lives and communities. These products and expressions have a clear connection to who they are and where they live. The rendition of William Blake's *The Ancient of Days* demonstrates how a Chicana youth appropriated, feminized, and updated this classic (Figure 17.6). CDI has provided a forum for people who otherwise would not have the means for contributing content to the information world of the World Wide Web.

We end this travel narrative by suggesting that fluidity and change will remain as markers of the twenty-first century. We are certain that while cyberspace will grow place will continue to matter. Our travel narrative reveals the ongoing struggle of Latinos to develop or open up spaces and places where they can survive and thrive. This struggle will take place at all key junctures of social space in the circuits of culture. In this century we will need to give our attention to not only developing an infrastructure that includes low-income Latino communities but also developing relevant digital collections and tools and promoting critical literacy and technological

Figure 17.6 *Rendition of William Blake The Ancient of Days, 1794* by Clarissa Duran
<http://www.clnet.ucla.edu/cdi/clarissa.html>. Reprinted with permission from the
artist.

fluency. We will also need to consider new technologies as an array of digital practices. Our future discourses as well as material constructions will be better prepared for tomorrow if they take note of today's analog people. We agree with Albert Fong, a colleague from CompuMentor, who says "that place better matter for if it does not those who wish to control us have already won a crucial battle by separating people from their history."

NOTES

Acknowledgments: The authors would like to thank Marita Sturken, Sharon Ann Lemelle Chabrán, Jose M. Prado, and Frank Bonilla for their close reading of this essay. We would also like to thank Raymond Rocco for his theoretical insights and suggestions concerning space and the public sphere.

1. Gloria Anzaldúa, *Borderlands: A New Mestiza* (San Francisco: Spinsters/Aunte Lute, 1987), 3.

2. Doreen Massey, *Space, Place, and Gender* (Minneapolis: University of Minnesota Press, 1994), 7.

3. Alma Lopez studied under Judy Baca at the SPARC Digital Lab in Santa Monica, California. A Web site of her work is available at <http://www.alma.lopez.net>. While it would be easy to label this work as pastische, it does include unmistakable historical references. Rather, we can think of it as contrapuntal, a term used by Edward Said in *Culture and Imperialism*, in which he notes "a contrapuntal reading must take into account both process, that of imperialism and that of resistance." *Culture and Imperialism* (New York: Alfred Knopf, 1993), 66.

4. Carlos Castaneda, *The Teachings of Don Juan: A Yaqui Way of Knowledge* (New York: Ballantine, 1970).

5. We have attempted to situate our use of theory in specific contexts to avoid the totalizing tendencies named in Edward Said's "Traveling Theory," in *The World, the Text and the Critic*, (Cambridge, Mass.: Harvard University Press, 1983), 241–42. Rather than universal truths we seek to articulate what Donna Haraway and later Patricia Hill Collins described as "situated knowledges." See Donna Haraway, "Situated Knowledges," in *Simians, Cyborgs, and Women: The Reinvention of Nature* (New York: Routledge, 1991), 183–201. See also Patricia Hill Collins, *Black Feminist Thought: Knowledge, Consciousness, and the Politics of Empowerment* (New York: HarperCollins, 1990), 233–35; and Rosa Linda Fregoso and Angie Chabram, "Chicana/o Cultural Representations: Reframing Alternative Critical Discourses," *Cultural Studies* 4, no. 3 (October 1990): 203–12.

6. Nicolas Negroponte, *Being Digital* (New York: Knopf, 1995), 7.

7. See especially the work of Saskia Sassen, *Globalization and Its Discontents: Essays on the New Mobility of People and Money* (New York: New Press, 1998).

8. Negroponte, *Being Digital*. Negroponte's analogy of bits as the DNA of information is an excellent example of the lack of the social in his utopian vision. He states that everything can be reduced and represented by bits.

9. Dan Schiller, *Digital Capitalism: Networking the Global Market System* (Cambridge, Mass.: MIT Press, 1999). Schiller now teaches at University of Illinois, Champaign-Urbana.

10. Sherry Turkle, *Life on the Screen: Identity in the Age of the Internet* (New York: Touchstone, 1995), 29–73. See Jean Baudrillard, *Simulations* (New York: Semiotext(s), 1983). Anne Balsamo notes that Baudrillard's discourse "remains within the logic of the image and the disembodied." See *Technologies of the Gendered Body: Reading Cyborg Women* (Durham, N.C.: Duke University Press, 1999), 197.

11. Turkle, *Life on the Screen*, 47. Turkle's work has been immensely important for suggesting new ways to think about how the Internet has altered communication. Our critique only wants to make sure we consider life beyond the screen. See also Mark Poster, *The Mode of Information; Poststructualism and Social Context* (Chicago: University of Chicago Press, 1990).

12. Fredric Jameson, "Postmodernism or the Cultural Logic of Late Capitalism," *New Left Review*, 146 (July–August, 1984): 53–92.

13. While arguing for Williams' continuing relevance, we concur with various critiques that have noted his lack of attention to the roles of imperialism, gender, and race. See, for example, Kuan-Hsing Chen, "Cultural Studies and the Politics of Internationalization, An Interview with Stuart Hall," in *Stuart Hall: Critical Dialogues in Cultural Studies*, ed. David Morley and Kuan-Hsing Chen (New York: Routledge, 1996), 394; Said, *Culture and Imperialism*, 14; and Paul Gilroy, *The Black Atlantic: Modernity and Double Consciousness* (Cambridge, Mass.: Harvard University Press, 1993), 10–14.

14. Raymond Williams, *Keywords: A Vocabulary of Culture and Society*, rev. ed. (New York: Oxford University Press, 1983), 315–16.

15. Raymond Williams, *The Sociology of Culture* (New York: Schocken, 1982), 108.

16. Raymond Williams, *Television: Technology and Cultural Form* (New York: Schocken, 1975), 19. Our emphasis.

17. The dominant is composed of "a central system of practices, meanings, and values—which are organized and lived" by those in power. The dominant is represented as *the* tradition, when it is rather a *selective* tradition, which recognizes certain practices and marginalizes and/or excludes others. The residual is composed of "experiences, meanings, and values, which cannot be verified or cannot be expressed in terms of the dominant culture, [but which] are nevertheless lived and on the basis of the residue—cultural as well as social—of some previous social formation." By emergent, Williams refers to "new meanings, new practices, and new significances and experiences." Williams, "Base and Superstructure in Marxist Cultural Theory," in *Problems in Materialism and Culture* (London: Verso, 1980), 38–41.

18. Ibid., 41.

19. See Schiller, *Digital Capitalism*.

20. Stuart Hall, "Encoding/Decoding," in *The Cultural Studies Reader*, ed. Simon During (New York: Routledge, 1993), 91.

21. Carlos Vélez-Ibáñez, *Border Visions: Mexican Cultures of the Southwestern United States* (Tucson: University of Arizona Press, 1996), 4.

22. Rosaura Sanchez, *Telling Identities: The Californio Testimonies* (Minneapolis: University of Minnesota Press, 1995), 45.

23. José David Saldívar, *Border Matters: Remapping American Cultural Studies* (Berkeley: University of California Press, 1997), 79. See also Raul Homero Villa, *Barrio Logos: Space and Place in Urban Chicano Literature and Culture* (Austin: University of Texas Press, 2000), 16; and Devon Pena, ed., *Chicano Culture, Ecology, Politics: Subversive Kin* (Tucson: University of Arizona Press, 1998), 11.

24. Henri Lefebvre, *The Production of Space* (Malden, Mass.: Blackwell, 1991).

25. Edward Soja, *Postmodern Geographies: The Reassertion of Space in Critical Social Theory* (New York: Verso, 1989), 79–80. See also his *Thirdspace: Journeys to Los Angeles and Other Real-and-Imagined Places* (Malden, Mass.: Blackwell, 1996).

26. Linda McDowell, *Gender, Identity and Place: Understanding Feminist Geographies* (Minneapolis: University of Minnesota Press, 1999), 4. See also Paul C. Adams, Steven Hoelscher, and Karen E. Till, *Textures of Place: Exploring Humanist Geographies* (Minneapolis: University of Minnesota Press, 2001); and Derek Gregory, *Geographical Imaginations* (Cambridge, Mass.: Blackwell, 1994), xxv.

27. Doreen Massey, "Traveling Thoughts," in *Without Guarantees: In Honour of Stuart Hall*, ed. Paul Gilroy, Lawrence Grossberg, and Angela McRobbie (New York: Verso, 2000), 229.

28. Michel de Certeau *The Practice of Everyday Life* (Berkeley: University of California Press, 1984).

29. John Fiske, "The Culture of Everyday Life," in *Cultural Studies*, eds. Lawrence Grossberg, Cary Nelson, and Paula Treichler (New York: Routledge, 1920), 160. See also Pierre Bourdieu, *Outline of a Theory of Practice* (Cambridge: Cambridge University Press, 1977).

30. Manuel Castells, *The Information City: Information Technology, Economic Restructuring, and the Urban-Regional Process* (Malden, Mass.: Blackwell, 1989), 348, our emphasis.

31. Manuel Castells, *The Rise of the Networked Society* (Malden, Mass.: Blackwell, 1996), 411.

32. Manuel Castells, *The Internet Galaxy: Reflections on the Internet, Business, and Society* (New York: Oxford University Press, 2001).

33. Paul C. Adams, Steven Hoelscher, and Karen E. Till also note that "time-space compression and technological simulations work together to *disguise* casual connections, while scientific theories increasingly involve uncertainty, indeterminacy, relativity, subjectivity, and chaos." See *Textures of Place*, and Gregory, *Geographical Imaginations*, xxv, our emphasis.

34. Saskia Sassen, "Analytic Borderlands: Race, Gender and Representation in the New City," in *Re-Presenting the City: Ethnicity, Capital and Culture in the 21st Century Metropolis*, ed. Anthony King (New York: New York University Press, 1996), 196.

35. Saskia Sassen, "Electronic Space and Power," *Journal of Urban Technology* 4, no. 1 (1997): 14.

36. Ibid., 1.

37. Negroponte, *Being Ditigal*, 228.

38. Sassen, *Globalization and Its Discontents*, xxii. See also Saskia Sassen, *The Global City: New York, London and Tokyo* (Princeton, N.J.: Princeton University Press, 1991), our emphasis.

39. Sassen, *Globalization and Its Discontents*, 196.

40. James J. O'Donnell, *Avatars of the Word: From Papyrus to Cyberspace* (Cambridge, Mass.: Harvard University Press, 1998).

41. Walden Browne, *Sahagún and the Transition to Modernity* (Norman: University of Oklahoma Press, 2000), 26–36. See also Barbara Miller "Indigenous Visions of the Book," in *Technology, the Environment and Social Change* (Albuquerque: SALALM Secretariat, 1995).

42. <http://www.rose-hulman.edu/~delacova/florentine-codex.htm>. Accessed January 5, 2004.

43. Saskia Sassen, foreword, in *Latno Metropolis*, ed. Victor Valle and Rodolfo Torres (Minneapolis: University of Minnesota Press, 2000), ix.

44. Manuel Pastor, Peter Drier, J. Eugene Grigsby, and Martha Lopez-Garza, *Regions that Work: How Cities and Suburbs Can Grow Together* (Minneapolis: University of Minnesota Press, 2000), 134.

45. Karen Hossfeld, "Divisions of Labor, Divisions of Lives: Immigrant Women Workers in Silicon Valley" (Ph.D diss., University of California at Santa Cruz, 1988).

46. Sassen, *Globalization and Its Discontents*, xxiv.

47. These were later published in Frank Bonilla et al., *Borderless Borders: U.S. Latinos, Latin Americans, and the Paradox of Interdependence* (Philadelphia: Temple University Press, 1998).

48. CTCNet electronic list.

49. Al Gore's appropriation of the highway was preceded by a long history, which is detailed in Mark Surman, "Wired Words: Utopia, Revolution and the History of Electronic Highways," http://www.isoc.org/inet96/proceedings/e2/e2_1.html>. Accessed December 3, 2003.

50. Eric R. Avila, "The Folklore of the Freeway: Space, Culture, and Identity in Postwar Los Angeles," *Aztlan* 23, no. 1 (Spring 1998): 15–31.

51. Blanca Estela Gordo, "The "Digital Divide" and the Persistence of Urban Poverty," *Planners Network Newsletter*, 2000.

52. Sassen, *Electronic Space*, 9–11. Examples of cybersegmentation focus on mergers, deregulation, and the drive to be the sole data, voice, and digital pipe into homes that will increase market share.

53. For example, see Jorge Reina Schement and Scott C. Forbes, "The Persistent Gap in Telecommunications: Toward Hypotheses and Answers," in *Competition, Regulation, and Convergence: Current Trends in Telecommunications Policy Research*, ed. Sharon Gillette and Ingo Vogelsang (Mahwah, N.J.: Lawrence Erlbaum, 1999), 179–93; Jorge Reina Schement, "Divergence Amid Convergence: The Evolving Information Environment of the Home," <http://www.benton.org/publibrary/policy/Schement/HomeMedia/home.html>, accessed January 5, 2004; and California Telecommunications Policy Forum, *Unfinished Business: Extending Connectivity to All Americas, A White Paper*, 1998.

54. National Telecommunications and Information, *Falling Through the Net: A Survey of the "Have-Nots" in Rural and Urban America* (Washington, D.C.: NTIA, 1995); see also NTIA, *Falling Through the Net II: New Data on the Digital Divide* (Washington, D.C.: NTIA, 1998); NTIA, *Falling Through the Net: Defining the Digital Divide, (Washington, D.C.: NTIA, 1999); NTIA, Falling Through The Net: Toward Digital Inclusion, A*

Report on Americans' Access to Technology Tools (Washington, D.C.: NTIA, 2000). The latest report issued under the Bush administration is *A Nation Online: How Americans Are Expanding Their Use of the Internet* (Washington, D.C.: NTIA, 2002).

55. National Telecommunications and Information, *Falling Through the Net: A Survey of the "Have-Nots" in Rural and Urban America* (Washington, D.C.: NTIA, 1995).

56. Norris Dickard, "Federal Retrenchment on the Digital Divide: Potential National Impact," Benton Foundation *Policy Brief*, No. 1, March 2002, <http://www.benton.org/publibrary/policybriefs/brief01.pdf>. For a view that dismisses the idea of a digital divide and lays the groundwork for the Bush administration's position, see Benjamin M. Compaine, ed., *The Digital Divide: Facing a Crisis or Creating a Myth* (Cambridge, Mass.: MIT Press, 2001).

57. Aki Helen Namioka, "Negotiating Open Access with AT&T—The Seattle Experience," *Community Technology Review*, 1999, 9–10.

58. For $120 Yahoo promises to review an Internet site for possible inclusion into their portal.

59. Romelia Salinas, "CLNet: Redefining Latino Library Services in the Digital Era," in *Latino Librarianship* (Jefferson, N.C.: McFarland, 2000); and Romelia Salinas, "Building Virtual Communities: Latino Organizations in an Urban Setting," *Community Networking Conference Proceedings*, Taos, New Mexico, May 1996, 121–24.

60. Octavio Romano, "The Historical and Intellectual Presence of Mexican Americans," *El Grito*, 2, no. 2 (Winter 1969): 32–46. See also his essay "The Anthropology and Sociology of the Mexican American: The Distortion of Mexican-American History," *El Grito* 2, no. 1 (Fall 1968): 13–26.

61. This is the most comprehensive bibliographic resource for information about Mexican American topics and the only specialized database for Chicano reference. It identifies, in one place, all types of material about Chicanos and provides uniform subject access to this constantly growing body of literature.

62. In Williams's terms, they were not considered part of the selective tradition.

63. Harry Cleaver, "The Zapatistas and the Electronic Fabric of Struggle" <http://www.eco.utexas.edu/faculty/Cleaver/zaps.html>. Accessed December 3, 2003.

64. John Arquilla, David Ronfeldt, and Michele Zanini, "Networks, Netwar, and Information-Age, Terrorism," in *The Changing Role of Information in Warfare*, ed. Zalmay M. Khalilzad and John P. White (Santa Monica: Rand, 1999), 82. This study pointed to the Zapatistas' use of the Internet as potential international security risk.

65. Sassen, *Electronic Space*, 12.

66. Paulo Freire, *Pedagogy of the Oppressed* (New York: Continuum, [1970] 1982).

67. American Library Association Presidential Committee on Information Literacy.

68. Computer Science and Telecommunication Board, National Research Council, Committee on Information Technology Literacy, *Being Fluent with Information Technology* (Washington, D.C.: National Academy Press, 1999).

69. Freire, *Pedagogy of the Oppressed*.

70. The final document *Principles for a Networked World* (Washington, D.C.: American Library Association, 2003) can be found at <http://www.ala.org/Content/

NavigationMenu/Our_Association/Offices/ALA_Washington/Publications16/ principles.pdf>.

71. Guillermo Gómez-Peña, "The Virtual Barrio @ The Other Frontier," in *Clicking in: Hot Links to a Digital Culture*, ed. Lynn Hershman Leeson (Seattle: Bay Press, 1996), 179.

72. <http://www.pocho.com>. Accessed October 1998.

73. Oscar "Zeta" Acosta, *The Revolt of the Cockroach People* (San Francisco: Straight Arrow Books, 1973).

74. Zukin notes "Despite its ideology of resistance, postmodernism suggests a similar accommodation with the culture of market transactions. It decorates the city with legible, local, 'friendly' emblems of economic power while real economic structures are more abstract, more influenced by international flows, and less likely to be understood as they appear in public view." Sharon Zukin, *Landscapes of Power: From Detroit to Disney World* (Berkeley: University of California Press, 1991), 28.

75. Gómez-Peña, "The Virtual Barrio @ The Other Frontier," 178.

76. Mark Warschauer, "Language, Identity, and the Internet," in *Race in Cyberspace*, ed. Beth E. Kolko, Lisa Nakamura, and Gilbert B. Rodman. (New York: Routledge, 2000), 156.

77. OCLC Web Characterization Project, <http://wcp.oclc.org/stats/intnl. html>. Accessed January 5, 2004.

78. Quoted in Warschauer, "Language, Identity, and the Internet," 156.

79. Balsamo, *Technologies of the Gendered Body*, 3.

80. Ibid., 9.

81. McDowell, *Gender, Identity and Place*, 30.

82. <http://www.cmp.ucr.edu/students/glasshouses/>.

83. Jacalyn Lopez Garcia, "Glass Houses: A View of American Assimilation from a Mexican-American Perspective," *Leonardo* 33, no. 4 (2000): 263–64.

84. For another construction of mixed identity, see Angie Chabram Dernersesian, "'Chicana! Rican? No, Chicana-Riqueña!' Refashioning the Transnational Connection," in *Multiculturalism: A Critical Reader*, ed. David Theo Goldberg (Malden, Mass.: Blackwell, 1994), 269–95.

85. Gómez-Peña, "The Virtual Barrior @ The Other Frontier," 173–74.

86. Massey, *Space, Place, and Gender*, 254.

87. Sassen, *Globalization and Its Discontents*, xxi.

88. Raymond A. Rocco, "Citizenship, Civil Society and the Latina/o City: Claiming Subaltern Spaces, Reframing the Public Sphere" in *Transnational Latina/o Communities: Politics, Processes, and Cultures*, ed. Carlos Vélez-Ibáñez and Anna Sampaio (Lanham, Md.: Rowman & Littlefield, 2002), 201.

89. *Falling Through the Net: Defining the Digital Divide*, 1999.

90. Computers In Our Future, "A Policy Agenda for Community Technology Centers: Assuring That Low-Income Communities Benefit from Technological Progress in the Information Age," (Los Angeles: Computers In Our Future, 1999).

91. Anthony Wilhelm, *Democracy in the Digital Age: Challenges to Political Life in Cyberspace* (New York: Routledge, 2000), 37.

92. Blanca Estela Gordo, "The "Digital Divide" and the Persistence of Urban Poverty." Douglas Schular describes six core values that are marks of successful community technology centers: conviviality and culture, education, strong democracy, health and well-being, economic equity, opportunity, sustainability and information, and communication. Douglas Schular, *New Community Networks: Wired for Change* (New York: Addison-Wesley, 1996), 11–22.

93. Linda Fowells and Wendy Lazarus, *Computers In Our Future: What Works in Closing the Technology Gap?* (Los Angeles: Computers In Our Future, 2000).

Jennifer L. Gibbs, Sandra J. Ball-Rokeach,
Joo-Young Jung, Yong-Chan Kim, and
Jack Linchuan Qiu

18 The Globalization of Everyday Life

Visions and Reality

Terms like *information superhighway, Internet revolution, global village,* and *globalization* have become buzzwords that liberally season the discourse of the media, corporate communications, advertising, political speeches, and everyday interpersonal conversations. As with past innovations in communication technology (the newspaper, the telegraph, television, the personal computer), the Internet is heralded by many as bringing about new freedoms, democracy, and increased opportunity to society at large. New communication technologies are regarded as driving forces of globalization, in that e-mail and the World Wide Web provide instantaneous access to information and communication with Internet-connected persons located anywhere in the world. The Internet is heralded by some as overcoming space and rendering physical place unimportant.[1] Others worry that Internet connections are displacing local social contacts and traditional mass media (e.g., newspapers, radio, and television), thus reducing civic participation in social communities.[2]

Despite such proclamations, we have very little grounded evidence about how the Internet and globalization are affecting people's everyday lives. Globalization tends to be studied as a macro economic, political, or socio-demographic process taking shape in the relations within and between multinational corporations and governments, and in the migratory flows of large populations across traditional state borders. We feel it is important to include the largely unheard voices and experiences of everyday people of diverse ethnic and cultural backgrounds in the broader public debate on globalization and the Internet. What meaning does globalization have for everyday people? How does the phenomenon of globalization play out in their lived behavior?

A difficulty in grounded analyses of globalization is that the term does not have a consensual meaning. Globalization is defined broadly as the growing interconnectedness and interdependence of the world. Beyond that, however, the term refers to many different and sometimes contradictory visions of how our world is changing and being reorganized. We do not seek to resolve this definitional dilemma. Rather, we examine whether globalization visions are part of the everyday person's repertoire of understanding the changing world about her or him, and whether any of these are evidenced in the realities of everyday communication behavior. As Anthony Giddens observes, "globalisation isn't only about what is 'out there,' remote and far away from the individual. It is an 'in here' phenomenon too, influencing intimate and personal aspects of our lives."[3]

In the Metamorphosis research project, which addresses communication technology and community in the twenty-first-century urban context, we have examined the visions and realities of globalization in the everyday lives of people living in seven diverse residential areas of Los Angeles.[4] We focus upon communication behaviors as reflections of how people negotiate their changing worlds. We refer to these communication behaviors—the everyday conversations and stories that people, old and new media, and grassroots organizations create and disseminate—together with the resources that afford a conducive or constrained communication environment for the conduct of daily life, as *communication infrastructures*. These negotiations afford grounded insights into serendipity or why people usually surprise us in defying the proclamations of how new communication technologies will change our world, insights not available in macro studies of economic and political globalization. We assume people, individually and collectively, give sense to globalization, and in so doing, become both reactive and proactive participants in the process. This is part of the reason why the shape and consequences of the present communication revolution (i.e., change in the communication infrastructure) are no easier for people to grasp ahead of time than past communication revolutions were for the people going through them.[5]

We cannot reach firm judgments about where we are going, but we can make observations about how much change in the communication infrastructure has occurred at this point in time. How much is globalization eroding traditional lines dividing social interaction? Are people, for example, incorporating the Internet to do new things (e.g., break down ethnic and cultural barriers), or are they using it to do old things in new ways (maintain or extend family and friend relationships)? To what extent does the Internet really bring people in closer contact with the rest of the world? Is the communication opportunity structure of daily life changing more rapidly for some groups than others? Are there more than digital divides in access to the tools of the global era—are there profound inequalities in the breadth and depth of incorporation of these tools?

These are the major questions we address in this essay. In the first section, we explore the various symbolic meanings the term *globalization* has for culturally diverse groups of everyday people. This is followed by an examination of the extent to which people's global visions are grounded in the realities of their everyday communication behavior.

Visions of Globalization

David Held and his colleagues observe, "Indeed, globalization is in danger of becoming, if it has not already become, the cliché of our times: the big idea which encompasses everything from global financial markets to the Internet but which delivers little substantive insight into the contemporary human condition."[6] One point of contention among scholarly visions is whether globalization involves a process of convergence, divergence, or both. From Bill Gates to George Soros, from Marshall McLuhan's "global village" to Immanuel Wallerstein's "world-system," globalization is envisioned by convergence theorists as the emergence of a global market that transcends local economies,[7] a power structure or even "transnational civil society" that supersedes nation-states,[8] and a homogeneous global culture dominated by media conglomerates.[9] Convergence theories characterize a large part of the literature, including a whole spectrum of arguments ranging from neo-liberal celebration of world unification[10] to Neo-Marxist critiques of oppressive global capitalism.[11] Other scholars are skeptical of globalization as a process of homogenization and regard divergence and fragmentation as the fundamental features of the contemporary world.[12] Those who focus on divergence argue that, in addition to the digital divide of information haves and have-nots, Third World economies are increasingly marginalized and separated from the global market,[13] and the resurgence of nationalism and religious fundamentalism leads to conflicts among civilizations rather than world integration.[14] Still other theorists conceptualize globalization as an uneven process of both convergence and divergence, in which new patterns of global stratification arise and reinforce certain power hierarchies while undermining and reconfiguring other ones.[15]

We explored whether any of these scholarly visions resonated with everyday people who are connected to the Internet. These "high-digitals" are most likely to be aware of and affected by globalization. We asked them (in a mail survey) about the words they associated with the term *globalization*. Their responses were coded into several broader themes.

There was a great degree of similarity in the language used by diverse ethnic groups to describe globalization. High-digitals in African American, Caucasian, Chinese-origin, Central American-origin, Korean-origin, and Mexican-origin groups associated the term *globalization* with the ideological themes that permeate public, scholarly, and commercial discourse. The main themes that emerged were classified into four major categories: *utopian, dystopian, neutral,* and *meaningless/hype.* Any one participant could make associations that fit into more than one category.

Utopian views of globalization associated it with a process of unification or breakdown of cultural, economic, or political borders that make the world smaller and bring people closer together. Common responses included "one world," "inclusion," "cohesiveness," "instant communication," and "worldwide expansion." Other positive qualities were mentioned, such as "advance," "opportunity," "freedom," "equality," "weakening of dictatorship," and "the opening of communist countries." This vision echoes the neo-liberal celebration of globalization as bringing about world harmony and progress. This was by far the largest category of associations, with a total of 64 percent of the 136 respondents ascribing to this positive ideology. Positive visions were especially prevalent among the African American respondents (83 percent) and Central American respondents (74 percent).

The next most prevalent type of association, however, was *dystopian* (33 percent of respondents). Three major subthemes emerged: 1) digital or socioeconomic divide comments such as "increasing gap between rich and poor" and "less equality"; (2) corporate control through associations with multinationals, business, capitalism, and commerce; and (3) negative feelings such as fear, annoyance, and feeling overwhelmed or out-of-control. This vision taps into Neo-Marxist convergence discourse where globalization is a totalizing process that further exacerbates world inequalities and corporate control. This theme was strongest among the Caucasian respondents from South Pasadena (67 percent) and the Westside (38 percent).

The third category, *neutral* views (20 percent of respondents), contains responses that could not be easily classified as either positive or negative, but which still considered globalization a meaningful term. Comments in this category include references to the Internet and new technology, foreign languages, the importance of the English language, the environment, diversity, and standardization. These do not fit neatly into any of the ideological camps, partly due to the nonevaluative nature of the responses. These sorts of associations were most common among Chinese-origin respondents (41 percent).

Skeptics who consider the term *globalization meaningless* (13 percent) regarded it as a utopian "one world" notion that they rather cynically dismissed as merely political rhetoric or hype. This antivision regards the term *globalization* as not grounded in reality and was most common among the Korean-origin respondents (27 percent).

While these mail survey responses suggest the success of efforts to promote utopian visions of globalization, focus group discussions afforded more nuanced and ambivalent associations. The *Chinese-origin* focus group participants, for example, had ambivalent feelings about globalization. On the one hand they associated it with "unity, peace, trust"; on the other hand, it was thought to be the "Americanization of other cultures" and to entail "gaps between rich people and poor people." This largely middle-class group also associated globalization rather neutrally with new technology tools, such as the Internet, fiber optics, digital cameras, cell phones, biotech, satellites, and pagers.

As with their mail survey responses, *Korean-origin* focus group participants tended to be the most skeptical of the term *globalization*. This is apparently due to their associations of the term with the political rhetoric of former president Young Sam Kim, who has been held responsible for leading South Korea into economic crisis. For this reason, they considered it an unattainable, utopian term. Nonetheless, some participants noted that the Internet had helped open communist countries such as China and potentially, in the future, might do so for North Korea.

The following quote reflects the skepticism among Korean-origin focus group participants.

> I think globalization is impossible, as racism is not disappearing. It is an ideal concept. Each race has its own world.

Both the *Mexican-origin* and *Central American-origin* participants felt that globalization was generally positive. They saw it uniting humanity, generating open communication and a free flow of ideas, information, and trade, spreading democracy, and opening closed societies. They predicted widespread use of the Internet, but were also aware of the digital divide. There was a sense of solidarity in both groups that the Latino community should help each other out.

> The Internet will become a tool to have humanity become more united, to be able to get along, to communicate and become closer. To have borders become blurred, countries are getting closer. (Central American–origin)

> Globalization means that those who know computers and know English will be able to get ahead. My niece in El Salvador begs me to send her a computer. El Salvador wasn't using bar codes on products, if Central America isn't on bar codes, how can it be in the age of the Internet? (Central American–origin)

> People in our communities need to learn about the Internet and that it exists. (Mexican–origin)

Although they gave the most positive spontaneous associations, *African American* participants were most negative when making more considered judgments in the focus group discussion. They were the most concerned about social inequalities and the political and economic implications of globalization, indicting globalization as exacerbating culture clashes and threatening their job security. They associated it negatively with ethnic conflict, increased immigration to the United States, and outsourcing of labor. This group was the most cynical about the utopian "one world" vision and did not buy into it.

> Globalization is like the melting pot theory gone bad, the end result is going to be a catastrophe. Globalization, there are too many different views from different people, different cultures, and there are people that have had wars for hundreds of years, they've been warring, and you don't just come in with that "global community" because there is a buck in it and say "stop all of this now."

> As we move forward in the technological era, can you imagine how many people will be locked out?

The *Caucasian* groups were ambivalent about globalization, concluding that the Internet was a double-edged sword. Coming from residential areas with the highest socioeconomic status, these participants evidenced a strong sense of self-efficacy and were optimistic, yet critical of globalization. South Pasadena residents felt they could participate effectively as citizens through appropriate e-mail communications, and some saw the Internet as a potential tool for revitalizing democracy. While they noted the global village and the breakdown of cultural boundaries as positive aspects of globalization, they also saw negative aspects, such as problems with hackers or pornography, or more macro consequences with regard to economic control and cultural imperialism. Westside participants also revealed ambivalence: on the one hand, they felt that global access to information and communication would expand horizons, spread democracy, open up communist countries, and keep politicians accountable; on the other, they feared that global technologies could be used to increase social and corporate control and they voiced ethical concerns about globalization.

. . . increases my availability to the world and the world's intimate presence in my own life. (South Pasadena)

It's one world, it's not different continents. The world is everybody and we're all part of the same universe. (Westside)

I think the Internet will function in whatever language people choose to express themselves. Coca-Cola, Disneyland, TV have already eliminated a lot of diversity, but it also allows me to compete with them. I cannot open a Disneyland in my backyard, but I can do it on the Internet for a couple thousand dollars. (South Pasadena, English is her third language, speaks eight languages)

I think globalization is really elitist. Only a few multinational corporations really know what is going on. . . . this idea of "one world" . . . if you get the wrong group in there, the wrong message, with people's gullibility and short attention span, it could be very dangerous, we could be screwed if not enlightened . . . there is a tremendous amount of power in relatively few hands. (Westside teacher)

Our diverse groups of "high-digital" participants are well aware of both utopian and dystopian visions of globalization that appear in public, commercial, and academic discourse. While the meanings they associate with globalization differ, most groups expressed a mixture of positive and negative visions. The most prevalent vision assumes that globalization entails the unification of the world, racial harmony, social justice, and equality; however, some people (in all of the areas) uncritically buy into and celebrate this notion of global village, while others are skeptical (e.g., Koreans) or cynical (e.g., African Americans and Caucasians). More affluent old immigrants generally tend to be more critical of the possibilities and consequences of globalization than less affluent new immigrants from Central America, Mexico, and China. Interestingly, though, Caucasian critiques were more reflective of macro problems affecting society at large and ignored the digital divide issue. All ethnic minority groups, on the other hand, made comments reflecting an awareness of social inequalities in access to new technologies and suggesting desire for equality of participation in the global era by members of their communities.[16] The question now is how well these visions of globalization correspond with everyday-life realities.

REALITIES OF EVERYDAY COMMUNICATION BEHAVIOR

We classified our study samples along lines of immigration generation into two main groups, old/established and new, according to whether the study sample consisted of predominantly first- and second-generation immigrants or immigrants of third generation or more.

Table 18.1   Immigration Generation

Old/Established Immigrants	First or Second Generation
Caucasian/Protestant	16.8
Caucasian/Jewish	30.5
African American	21.8

New Immigrants	First or Second Generation
Mexican-origin	75.7
Central American-origin	96.7
Korean-origin	98.3
Chinese-origins	95.1

Inspection of everyday-life communication behavior in a number of ways suggests that cultural globalization occurs by way of what Arjun Appadurai has called "ethnoscapes,"[17] shifting landscapes of people due to immigration or other population movements, or diasporic spaces in which culturally displaced groups reconnect to their homeland through communication contacts via the Internet and traditional media, as well as through work and economic ties.[18] These connections are global in the sense of disembedding or lifting cultural experience out of local spaces;[19] however, they appear to follow the contours of ethnicity, rather than crossing such boundaries.

GLOBALIZATION OF CULTURAL IDENTITY

Our particular conception of cultural globalization rests on the possibility that the contemporaneous emergence of NAFTA and Pacific Rim political economies as well as substantial immigration of people from countries in and near these political/economic sectors may afford a new and dynamic pattern of cultural attachment. Specifically, we wonder if new immigrants from NAFTA and Pacific Rim regions will depart from traditional patterns of progressive assimilation by maintaining closer cultural and social ties to the country of origin. This may be so because the existence of a political economy advantages immigrants from these areas (e.g., via career and business opportunities) in a way that was not the case prior to the emergence of NAFTA and Pacific Rim economic sectors. Thus the basic unit of cultural globalization would be a sustained co-identification (e.g., over three or more generations) with both the country of residence and the country of origin. These diasporic spaces or ethnoscapes may or may not extend to encompass larger cultural identities that are inclusive of other NAFTA or Pacific Rim countries.

While it will take generations to know if our hunch has merit, our study groups of new immigrants were chosen, in part, to lay the groundwork for an examination of the strength of ties between Mexican-origin, Central American-origin, Korean-origin, and Chinese-origin immigrants and their respective NAFTA and Pacific Rim home countries. Old immigrant study groups afford a base of comparison. Thus far our data indicate the existence of multiple identifications among old and especially new immigrant groups with both residential community and their country of origin, rather than evidence of the formation of larger regional communities among our sample groups. We interpret these findings as evidence of ethnoscapes connecting people around the world along ethnic lines.

We see the resilience of ethnicity reflected in a number of ways, through cultural identity and communication behavior. The countries of origin mentioned by each ethnic group largely represent cultures of the same ethnicity, for example, Western European countries for the Caucasian study groups, or Mainland China, Taiwan, and Hong Kong for the Chinese-origin group. Similarly, when respondents were asked to describe their cultural heritage, moderate numbers gave more than one cultural description of themselves, but these descriptions were, for the most part, not multiethnic. Although regional ethnic descriptions were given by some, country of origin descriptions seem to be more salient for new immigrants (e.g., Mexican, Korean, El Salvadorian, Chinese) than regional descriptions such as Hispanic or Asian. Old immigrants from Greater Crenshaw overwhelmingly classified themselves as African American, while Caucasian respondents described themselves as American and, to a lesser extent, Jewish or European. Perhaps the most striking finding was that, out of more than 1,800 respondents to a phone survey, a mere twelve of them claimed to be of more than one ethnicity (despite our efforts to encourage multiple responses to this question).

GLOBALIZATION OF EVERYDAY BEHAVIOR

Our indicators of everyday communication behavior are based on survey responses from our new immigrant study groups only. We focus on new immigrants because we are particularly interested in their roles as possible constructors of new kinds of associations. We asked all new immigrant groups (1) whether they had business or work connections with their country of origin, (2) whether they sent money to people in their country of origin, and (3) whether they stayed on top of recent natural disasters in their home country.

Both class and cultural differences are evident with regard to work associations and money transfer. We find strong work associations with the Pacific Rim: 55 percent of the Chinese-origin group have work ties to Mainland China, Hong Kong, or Taiwan, while approximately twenty percent of the Korean-origin group have work connections with Korea. This may be attributed to class differences between the more affluent Chinese-origin group and the lower-middle-class Korean-origin group.[20] Slightly less than 10 percent of the Mexican-origin and the Central American-origin respondents have work ties to their home countries, which may again be due to their relatively lower class status. These findings suggest evidence of cultural globalization in the sense of lifting cultural experience out of localities, although the work ties identified are specifically with the country of origin. The percents reporting any work connection are reported in Figure 18.1.

The trend observed in work connections is dramatically reversed when comparing the extent of money transfer among the new immigrant groups (see Figure 18.2). Approximately 80 percent of the Central American-origin, and more than half of the Mexican-origin study groups, report sending money to their country of origin. The Korean-origin and Chinese-origin groups report lower frequencies, 45 percent and 31 percent, respectively. These findings are consistent with our field observations of the study areas,

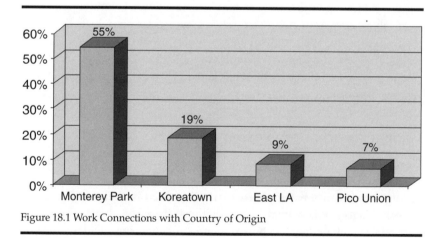

Figure 18.1 Work Connections with Country of Origin

in that we observed many money-transfer businesses in the Latino study areas, but not in the Korean and Chinese study areas. These findings reflect the well-known pattern of many new immigrants from Mexico and Central America coming to Los Angeles for the purpose of earning money that they can send to their families in the home country. These financial ties are again suggestive of ethnic ties back to the country of origin.

Another means of building regional community by reconnecting with one's country of origin is by staying on top of major news events that happen there. The level of concern with events such as natural disasters in one's home country can be indicative of the strength of new immigrants' attachment to these regions. We included questions in our phone survey about two relevant natural disasters that occurred just prior to data collection in the Central American and the Chinese study areas: Hurricane Mitch in Central America and the 1999 earthquake in Taiwan.

Nearly half (44 percent) the Central American respondents had family or friends in Central America who were involved in the Hurricane Mitch disaster. Of the 84 percent of Central Americans who followed news coverage of this event, the great majority (78 percent) did so by watching television (mainstream and Spanish-language channels). Only 13 percent of the Chinese-origin respondents had family or friends in Taiwan who were involved in the earthquake. Despite this small percentage, most (88 percent) followed the event through some form of media. Of these, 77 percent connected to television and 12 percent connected to the Internet. While

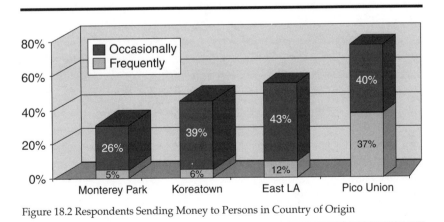

Figure 18.2 Respondents Sending Money to Persons in Country of Origin

Central Americans connected to mainstream and Spanish-language media at the same rate, Chinese-origin respondents connected more to Chinese-language community media.[21] These findings can be seen as reflective of mediascapes[22] that disembed local media events from their immediate context and enable these new immigrant groups to reconnect with their home culture—although once again, along strict ethnic lines.

Globalization of Communication Behavior

High-digital focus group participants provided us with information that we employed to map their identification with countries of the world, as well their degree of communication contact with these countries. We asked them to list the names of countries that they identified with, and to tell us whether they had any communication with people living in those countries—through visits, phone, letter, e-mail/Internet, or fax. We then translated their responses into scores that reflected the total degree of contact with each country mentioned. These scores were then transformed into socio-spatial mapping algorithms that allowed us to visually examine intensity of contact on a world map, and to analyze statistically differences in scope and intensity (see Figures 18.3 and 18.4).

Overall, there are no substantial differences between the scope or intensity of contact between new and old immigrants. New immigrants mentioned a total of forty-three countries, and old immigrants mentioned forty

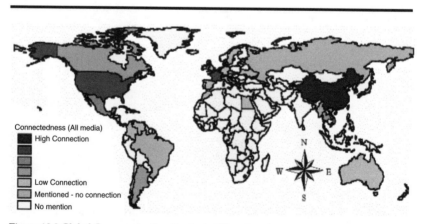

Figure 18.3 Global Communication Contact of New Immigrants

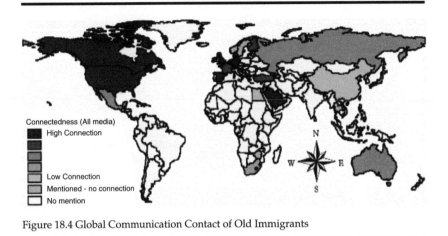

Connectedness (All media)
High Connection

Low Connection
Mentioned - no connection
No mention

Figure 18.4 Global Communication Contact of Old Immigrants

countries with which they had some degree of contact. The actual countries with which they have the most contact closely mirror their countries of origin. New immigrants tend to have the most contact with NAFTA countries (the United States, Mexico, Central America) and some Pacific Rim countries (Korea, China, Taiwan, Thailand). Old immigrants, on the other hand, have the most contact with countries in Europe (the United Kingdom, Ireland, Spain, Germany, France, Finland) and the Middle East (Turkey, Saudi Arabia), as well as Liberia, the United States, and Canada. This suggests, once again, that globalization as indicated by the pattern of communication contacts follows along lines of shared ethnicity. Intraethnic communication patterns are clearly illustrated by the scores for the average degree of contact old and new immigrants have with their countries of origin (including the United States) versus other countries. A higher score indicates stronger intensity of contact. For old immigrants, the average contact score for their countries of origin (plus the United States) is 416.83, while the average score for contact with other countries is 80.09. For new immigrants, the average score for contact with their countries of origin (plus the United States) is 665.87, while their average contact score with other countries is 65.13.

These results suggest at least two conclusions. First, new immigrants understandably have stronger connections with their countries of origin, while old immigrants are more connected with the rest of the world. Second, the communication contact of both new and old immigrant groups is largely confined to those of the same ethnicity. Thus the ethnoscapes of both new and old immigrants differ significantly and trace intraethnic communication patterns rather than being truly globally dispersed.

Further evidence of ethnoscapes is evident in responses from our high-digitals concerning the five people with whom they communicate most often. A homophily effect is evident in that 77 percent to 93 percent of the high-digitals communicate most with people of the same ethnicity. There is, however, a difference between new and old immigrants in the locations of these people: for Koreans, Chinese, and Central Americans, 37 percent, 34 percent, and 22 percent of their most frequent communication contacts, respectively, live outside the United States, while less than 5 percent of the most frequent communication contacts for the other four groups live outside the United States.

How Global Are People's Internet Connections?

As previously discussed, our focus groups revealed an awareness of the Internet's globalizing potential to overcome cultural and geographical borders and unite people from different parts of the world. When asked whether they felt the Internet brought them in greater touch with the rest of the world, the initial reaction of focus group participants was that it did. However, when probed further on how they actually used the Internet, it turned out that their communication was primarily to maintain and extend social relationships with friends and relatives, rather than developing new social relationships online. New immigrants tended to have stronger contacts with their home countries by e-mailing people there or reading online newspapers to stay on top of news events in these countries, while old immigrants used the Internet to enhance communication with relatives and friends in different states, and a few who were temporarily living abroad. Thus, Internet communication tends to be limited to preexisting social relationships, rather than relationships originating from the Internet.

The main reason for the resistance to developing new online relationships seemed to be a high degree of suspicion and doubt as to their credibility. Concerns ranged from fear for personal safety to cynicism about the depth and intimacy of such social bonds. Virtually no one felt they belonged to any kind of virtual community online. Several people participated in interactive games with players from all over the world or had international e-mail correspondence with people they had never met in person; however, none of these relationships were regarded as meaningful "friendships" and were generally discounted.

> [Online relationships are] not credible. People may cheat you. In Taiwan there was a woman who cheated lots of guys to mail her money by sending out beautiful pictures. But she was actually ugly and fat. (Chinese-origin)

> I'm not sure you can make a friend on the Web. There is so much that goes into personal compatibility . . . You are going to wait and discuss personal stuff in person anyway, you are not going to do it in a letter or over the phone. (Caucasian)

Parents were particularly concerned about their children meeting undesirable people in chat rooms.

> My daughter is very open and less reserved than my older son. She used the user name "Aphrodite." One time she was saying she was twenty-five years old and I had to explain to her she was only eleven and must never do this. (Caucasian)

Interestingly, the tendencies mentioned earlier of respondents to communicate within the same ethnicity and for new immigrants to maintain ties with their countries of origin are once again evident with regard to patterns of Internet use. We examined the five Web sites visited most often by our adult high-digital participants. Among high-digital new immigrants, few access Web sites located in places other than the United States or their countries of origin. This phenomenon is particularly obvious among people of Korean and Chinese origins: 36 percent of Web sites mentioned by the Korean-origin participants are located in Korea and 24 percent mentioned by Chinese-origin respondents are based in Mainland China, Hong Kong, or Taiwan. However, none of the Korean-origin and Chinese-origin people listed any Web sites located any place other than the United States and their home country. Thus the much-heralded globalizing potential of the Internet, at least for now, seems problematic in so far as everyday life is concerned.

Do Internet Connection Patterns Correspond with People's Global Visions?

Our focus group discussions revealed that the Internet is not, for the most part, having a globalizing effect on everyday people's communication patterns. Confirming this observation, we find that degree of Internet connectedness does not account for differences in people's visions of globalization. The depth and breadth of people's experience with the Internet do not predict variations in their visions of globalization (utopian, dystopian, neutral, or meaningless). This suggests that people internalize global visions from exposure to traditional media and their interpersonal contacts, but not directly from their online experiences.

We also, however, asked high-digital participants to fill in a set of self-anchoring scales where they indicated the extent to which they saw *themselves* as "global." From these items we created a multidimensional index of global self-perception that included being multilingual, having culturally diverse friends, being technologically savvy, being a citizen of the world, and having "global thinking" skills. This "global self-perception index" is significantly correlated with Internet connectedness, especially among new immigrants. This means that, although high Internet connectors may have mixed feelings about globalization, the more strongly they are connected to the Internet, the more likely it is that they will attach the global label to themselves. These findings hold when controlling for age, education, and income.

INEQUALITIES IN INTERNET CONNECTEDNESS

A part of the everyday experience of the temporal and spatial dimensions of globalization comes by way of using new communication technologies. In this sense, people with broad access to and use of these technologies have a different experience of the everyday-life aspects of globalization than people lacking access. Concerns about inequality of access to new communication and information resources have been widespread.[23] Most of these have focused upon a growing digital divide in computer and Internet access.[24] Some researchers, however, challenge claims of increasing disparities in class and ethnic/racial characteristics of digital haves and have-nots. Norman Nie and Lutz Erbring, for example, largely dismiss such concerns and predict "everybody is going to be a (Internet) user soon."[25]

We examine this issue in detail elsewhere.[26] For present purposes, suffice it to say that there are broad inequalities among our study groups. These go well beyond sheer access to computers and Internet connections. Inequality does not dissolve with sheer access; rather, it persists in the form of lower-quality Internet connections. Poor new immigrants who are Internet-connected, for example, evidence less breadth and depth of incorporation of the Internet into their everyday lives. In short, such connections are less likely to advance their and their families' struggles to move up the class ladder. This is further evidence against the "one unified world" global vision:

rather than bringing people together in a single global village, the Internet may be perpetuating and even exacerbating divisions between ethnic groups through differences in access and the quality of Internet connections.

CONCLUSION

In sum, the prevalent "one world" vision of globalization held by our respondents does not appear to reflect the realities of their actual communication behavior. Some evidence of cultural globalization can be seen through the diasporic reconnection of new immigrants with their home country through work and money ties, staying on top of news, communication contact, and Internet use. However, these diasporic cultural communication ties take the shape of ethnoscapes that remain largely ethnically bound. Thus we can conclude that although diasporic movements may be bringing diverse peoples closer together geographically, they are not really coming into greater communication contact with one another. While the world may be becoming increasingly interconnected in many ways and certain boundaries are breaking down, ethnicity remains a major dividing line between people. The Internet so far is not doing much to alter these engrained patterns of social interaction. Despite its globalizing potential, the Internet does not seem to be significantly altering the everyday person's worldview or reconstituting cultural and social practices. Interestingly enough, people with the broadest and deepest connections to the Internet are just as likely to hold positive as negative perceptions of globalization. Our findings suggest that the Internet is being incorporated into everyday life by people who proactively tailor its meaning and its utility to their everyday lives.

NOTES

1. See Nicholas Negroponte, *Being Digital* (New York: Alfred A. Knopf, 1995).

2. See Norman H. Nie and Lutz Erbring, *Internet and Society: A Preliminary Report* (Stanford, Calif.: Stanford Institute for the Quantitative Study of Society, 2000).

3. Anthony Giddens, *Runaway World* (London: Profile Books, 1999): 12.

4. A detailed description of the larger Metamorphosis Project research design is presented in the Metamorphosis Project Technical Report (May 2000). A documentary video is also available. We draw on a rich set of interrelated quantitative and qualitative databanks in our in-depth study of seven historically significant residential areas in Los Angeles: (1) Mexican-origin residents of East Los Angeles, (2) African American residents of Greater Crenshaw, (3) Korean-origin residents of

Greater Koreatown, (4) Chinese-origin residents of Greater Monterey Park, (5) Central American-origin residents of Pico Union, (6) Caucasian and dominantly Protestant residents of South Pasadena, and (7) Caucasian and dominantly Jewish residents of the Westside. This essay draws on data from a forty-three to forty-seven-minute telephone interview with approximately 250 randomly selected households in each area, focus groups with "high-digital" or Internet-connected telephone respondents, and a supplemental mail-out survey to cover a larger "high-digital" database.

5. See Sandra J. Ball-Rokeach and Melvin L. DeFleur, *Theories of Mass Communication*, 5th ed. (White Plains, N.Y.: Longman, 1989); James W. Carey, *Communication as Culture: Essays on Media and Society* (Boston: Unwin Hyman, 1989); David J. Czitrom, *Media and the American Mind: From Morse to McLuhan* (Chapel Hill: University of North Carolina Press, 1982); Carolyn Marvin, *When Old Technologies Were New: Thinking About Electric Communications in the Late Nineteenth Century* (New York: Oxford University Press, 1988); Armand Mattelart, *Networking the World: 1794–2000*, trans. Liz Carey-Libbrecht and James A. Cohen (Minneapolis: University of Minnesota Press, 2000); and David E. Nye, *Electrifying America: Social Meanings of a New Technology, 1880–1940* (Cambridge, Mass.: MIT Press, 1990).

6. David Held, Anthony McGrew, David Goldblatt, and Jonathan Perraton, *Global Transformations: Politics, Economics and Culture* (Stanford, Calif.: Stanford University Press, 1999), 1.

7. See Manuel Castells, *The Rise of Network Society* (Cambridge, Mass.: Blackwell, 1996); Mattelart, *Networking the World*; Majid Tehranian, *Global Communication and World Politics: Domination, Development, and Discourse* (Boulder, Colo.: Lynn Rienner, 1999); and Malcolm Waters, *Globalization* (New York: Routledge, 1995).

8. See Sandra Braman and Annabelle Sreberny-Mohammadi, eds., *Globalization, Communication, and Transnational Civil Society* (Cresskill, N.J.: Hampton Press, 1996); Kevin R. Cox, ed., *Spaces of Globalization: Reasserting the Power of the Local* (New York: Guilford Press, 1997); and Tony Spybey, *Globalization and World Society* (Cambridge, Mass.: Polity Press, 1996).

9. Benjamin Bagdikian, *The Media Monopoly* (Boston: Beacon Press, 1997).

10. See Marshall McLuhan and Bruce R. Powers, *The Global Village: Transformations in World Life and Media in the 21st Century* (New York: Oxford University Press, 1989); Negroponte, *Being Digital*; Kenichi Ohmae, *The End of the Nation State* (New York: The Free Press, 1995); and Roland Robertson, *Globalization: Social Theory and Global Culture* (London: Sage, 1992).

11. See Herbert I. Schiller, *Mass Communications and American Empire*, 2nd ed. (Boulder, Colo.: Westview Press, 1992); Leslie Sklair, *Sociology of the Global System: Social Change in Global Perspective* (Baltimore: Johns Hopkins University Press, 1991); and Immanuel Wallerstein, *The Modern World System* (New York: Academic Press, 1974).

12. See Hazel J. Johnson, *Dispelling the Myth of Globalization: The Case for Regionalization* (New York: Praeger, 1991); Michael McGee, "Text, Context, and the Fragmentation of Contemporary Culture," *Western Journal of Speech Communication* (1990): 274–89; Alan Scott, ed., *The Limits of Globalization: Cases and Arguments* (London: Routledge, 1997); and John H. Simpson, " 'The Great Reversal': Selves, Communities, and the Global System," *Sociology of Religion* 57 (Summer 1996): 115–25.

13. Paul Hirst and Graham Thompson, *Globalization in Question: The International Economy and the Possibilities of Governance* (Cambridge, Mass.: Polity Press, 1996).

14. See Benjamin Barber, "Jihad Vs. McWorld," *The Atlantic Monthly* 3 (1992): 53–63; Samuel Huntington, *The Clash of Civilizations and the Remaking of World Order* (New York: Simon & Schuster, 1996); Joel Kotkin, *Tribes* (New York: Random House, 1992); and Nick Stevenson, "Globalization, National Cultures and Cultural Citizenship," *The Sociological Quarterly* 38 (Winter 1997): 41–66.

15. See Arjun Appadurai, "Disjuncture and Difference in the Global Cultural Economy," *Public Culture* 2, no. 2 (1990): 1–24; Mike Featherstone, *Global Culture: Nationalism, Globalism and Modernity* (London: Sage, 1990); Jonathan Friedman, *Cultural Identity and Global Process* (Thousand Oaks, Calif.: Sage, 1994), Roger Silverstone, "Finding a Voice: Minorities, Media and the Global Commons," paper presented at Managing the Global Conference, University of Southern California, October 26–27, 1999; John B. Thompson, *The Media and Modernity: A Social Theory of the Media* (Stanford, Calif.: Stanford University Press, 1995); and John Tomlinson, *Globalization and Culture* (Chicago: University of Chicago Press, 1999).

16. There is a close correspondence between class and ethnicity in our study samples, such that the two Caucasian groups have significantly higher average income than the two Latino groups; the African American and two Asian groups fall somewhere in between. Although our focus groups had differing proportions of females, we find no evidence of gender differences in the global visions expressed.

17. Appadurai, "Disjuncture and Difference in the Global Cultural Economy."

18. Silverstone, "Finding a Voice."

19. See Giddens, *Runaway World*, and Tomlinson, *Globalization and Culture*. See also Anthony Giddens, *Modernity and Self-Identity* (Stanford, Calif.: Stanford University Press, 1991).

20. Although such differences are not reflected in the average household incomes for these two groups, the actual total income for the Chinese-origin group is likely to be higher than reported due to the number of people holding stock in China or Taiwan.

21. Respondents were allowed to choose multiple media to which they connected. For example, one person may have connected to both English and Chinese/Latino media.

22. Appadurai, "Disjuncture and Difference in the Global Cultural Economy."

23. See Benton Foundation, "Resolving the Digital Divide," *The Digital Beat* <http://www.benton.org/DigitalBeat/db111299.html>, November 1999, accessed November 11, 2001; Children's Partnership, "Online Content for Low Income and Underserved Americans: The Digital Divide's New Frontier," <http://www.childrenspartnership.org>, March 28, 2000, accessed January 30, 2002; Consumer Federation of America, "Transforming the Information Superhighway into a Private Toll Road: The Case Against Closed Access Broadband Internet Systems," <http://www.consumerfed.org/internetaccess/>, December 20, 1999, accessed November 13, 2001; George A. Donohue, Clare N. Olien, and Philip J. Tichenor, "Media Access and Knowledge Gaps," *Critical Studies in Mass Communication* 4 (1982): 87–92; William H. Dutton, *Society on the Line: Information Politics in the Digital Age* (Oxford: Oxford University Press, 1999); Larry Irving, "Refocusing Our Youth: From High

Tops to High Tech," National Urban League and the National Leadership Council on Civil Rights Urban Technology Summit (Washington, D.C.: July 1998); Thomas P. Novak and Donna L. Hoffman, "Bridging the Digital Divide: The Impact of Race on Computer Access and Internet Use," <http://ecommerce.vanderbilt.edu/papers/race/science.html>, Project 2000, Vanderbilt University, February 2, 1998, accessed October 19, 2001.

24. See NTIA, *Falling Through the Net: Defining the Digital Divide* (Washington, D.C.: U.S. Department of Commerce, National Telecommunications and Information Administration, 1999); Pew Research Center, *Online Newcomers More Middle-Brow, Less Work Oriented: The Internet News Audience Goes Ordinary* (Washington, D.C.: Author, 1999).

25. Norman H. Nie and Lutz Erbring, *Internet and Society: A Preliminary Report* (Stanford, Calif.: Stanford Institute for the Quantitative Study of Society, 2000).

26. See Joo-Young Jung, Jack Linchuan Qiu, and Yong-Chan Kim, "The Internet into Everyday Community Life: Beyond the Digital Divide," working paper (Los Angeles: University of Southern California, 2000), and Jennifer L. Gibbs, Sandra J. Ball-Rokeach, Yong-Chan Kim, and Joo-Young Jung, "The Globalization of Everyday Life: Visions and Realities of Social Justice in the Internet Age," paper presented at Rochester Institute of Technology conference on "Social Justice, Peace, and International Conflict Resolution: Civic Discourse beyond the Millennium," July 20–22, 2000, Rochester, N.Y.

About the Contributors

Sandra J. Ball-Rokeach is professor of communication and sociology, and director of the Communication Technology and Community Program at the Annenberg School for Communication, University of Southern California. She is the author, with Robert Baker, of *Violence and the Media*; with Melvin DeFleur, *Theories of Mass Communication*; and, with Milton Rokeach, *The Great American Values Test: Influencing Belief and Behavior through Television*; and co-editor, with Muriel Cantor, of *Media, Audience and Society* and, with Margaret Gatz and Michael Messner, *Paradoxes of Youth and Sport*.

Sarah Banet-Weiser is assistant professor at the Annenberg School for Communication, University of Southern California. She is the author of *The Most Beautiful Girl in the World: Beauty Pageants and National Identity* (1999), and has written on media, popular culture, and national identity. She is currently working on a book on the Nickelodeon cable network that explores the relationship between youth, media, and citizenship, entitled *The Kids-Only Zone: Nickelodeon, Youth, and Citizenship*.

John Perry Barlow co-founded and co-chairs the Electronic Frontier Foundation. He has written about the Internet for a broad array of publications, including *Communications of the ACM*, *Mondo 2000*, the *New York Times*, and *Time*. He has written for *Wired* magazine since it was founded, and has been a Berkman Fellow at Harvard Law School since 1998. He is also a former Wyoming rancher and Grateful Dead lyricist.

Asa Briggs is former provost of Worcester College, Oxford University, and former chancellor of the Open University. He is a member of the House of Lords, and the author of numerous books, including the five-volume *History of Broadcasting in the United Kingdom*, *Victorian Things*, *Victorian Cities*, *A Social History of England*, *The Power of Steam*, and, with Peter Burke, *A Social History of the Media: From Gutenberg to the Internet*.

Richard Chabrán is chair of the California Community Technology Policy Group and former director of the Center for Virtual Research at the

University of California at Riverside. He is a co-editor of *Biblio-Politica: Chicano Perspectives on Library Service in the United States* and the *Latino Encyclopedia*. He is a founder of the Chicano Database and Chicano/Latino Net (CLNet).

Jennifer L. Gibbs is a senior research fellow at the Center for Research on Information Technology and Organizations (CRITO) at the University of California, Irvine. She has a Ph.D. in communication from the Annenberg School for Communication, University of Southern California. Her research interests include culture and identification in global and virtual teams, the implementation of new technologies in organizations, and the social impact of new technologies on cultural identity and community.

Larry Gross is director of the School of Communications and professor at the Annenberg School for Communication, University of Southern California. He was formerly the Sol Worth Professor at the Annenberg School for Communication, University of Pennsylvania. His most recent books are *Up From Invisibility: Lesbians, Gay Men, and the Media in America* and *Image Ethics in the Digital Age*, edited with John Stuart Katz and Jay Ruby.

Wendy M. Grossman is a freelance writer based in London. She has written extensively about technology for the *Daily Telegraph*, *Wired*, and *Scientific American*. She is the author of *net.wars* and *From Anarchy to Power: The Net Comes of Age*, and the editor of *Remembering the Future: Interviews from Personal Computer World*.

Katie Hafner writes about technology for the *New York Times*. She is the author of *The Well: A Story of Love, Death & Real Life in the Seminal Online Community*; *The House at the Bridge: A Story of Modern Germany*; with Matthew Lyon, *Where Wizards Stay Up Late: The Origins of the Internet*; and, with John Markoff, *Cyberpunk: Outlaws and Hackers on the Computer Frontier*.

Joo-Young Jung recently completed her Ph.D. at the Annenberg School for Communication, University of Southern California, with a dissertation entitled "Internet Connectedness and its Social Origins: An Ecological Approach to Communication Media and Social Inequality." Her research interests include post-access digital divides in the ways that people connect to the Internet and the globalization of people's everyday communication behaviors. Her work has appeared in journals such as *Communication Research*, *New Media and Society*, and *Prometheus*.

Yong-Chan Kim is an assistant professor of telecommunication and film at the University of Alabama. He has a Ph.D from the Annenberg School for Communication, University of Southern California, where he worked as research associate for the USC Metamorphosis Project. His research addresses the role of communication resources in building community/civil society, the importance of communication infrastructure in the welfare of families with young children, and the role of ethnic media in the context of diverse urban communities.

Peter Lyman, who trained as a political theorist, is professor at the School of Information Management and Systems, University of California at Berkeley. He is currently working on an ethnography of the cultural and organizational dynamics of startups in the Silicon Valley.

Carolyn Marvin is Frances Yates Professor at the Annenberg School for Communication, University of Pennsylvania. She is the author of *When Old Technologies Were New: Thinking About Electric Communication in the Late Nineteenth Century*, and, with David Ingle, *Blood Sacrifice and the Nation: Totem Rituals and the American Flag*.

David E. Nye is professor of American history and chair of American Studies at the University of Southern Denmark. His books include *American Technological Sublime*, *Electrifying America: Social Meanings of a New Technology, 1880–1940*, *Narratives and Spaces: Technology and the Construction of American Culture*, *Consuming Power: A Social History of American Energies*, and *America as Second Creation: Technology and Narratives of New Beginnings*.

Jack Linchuan Qiu is a research fellow at the Annenberg School for Communication, University of Southern California, where he recently completed his Ph.D. His research interests include Internet and society, IT and the public sphere, new capitalism, globalization, and China.

Romelia Salinas is the social sciences librarian at California State University, Los Angeles, and is currently working on a doctoral degree in Information Studies at the University of California at Los Angeles. She was formerly the Internet development librarian at the Center for Virtual Research at the University of California at Riverside, where she was involved in the establishment of the Community Digital Initiative, a university-based effort to develop information and computer literacy in the local community.

Jeffrey Sconce is associate professor in the Radio/Television/Film Department at Northwestern University. He is the author of *Haunted Media: Electronic Presence from Telegraphy to Television*, and currently at work on a book, *Either/Or/Whatever*, on irony in popular culture.

Vivian Sobchack is professor and associate dean in the School of Theater, Film and Television, University of California at Los Angeles. She is the editor of *The Persistence of History: Cinema, Television, and the Modern Event* and *Meta-Morphing: Visual Transformation and the Culture of Quick-Change*, and the author of *Screening Space: The American Science Fiction Film, The Address of the Eye: A Phenomenology of Film Experience*, and *Carnal Thoughts: Embodiment and Moving Image Culture*.

Lynn Spigel is professor in the School of Communications, Northwestern University. She is the author of *Make Room for TV: Television and the Family Ideal of Postwar America* and *Welcome to the Dreamhouse: Popular Media and Postwar Suburbs*, and has edited numerous anthologies, including, with Michael Curtin, *The Revolution Wasn't Televised: Sixties Television and Social Conflict*, and the forthcoming *Television After TV: Essays on a Medium in Transition*.

Marita Sturken is associate professor at the Annenberg School for Communication, University of Southern California. She is the author of *Tangled Memories: The Vietnam War, the AIDS Epidemic, and the Politics of Remembering*, a British Film Institute monograph on *Thelma & Louise*, and, with Lisa Cartwright, *Practices of Looking: An Introduction to Visual Culture*.

Douglas Thomas is associate professor at the Annenberg School for Communication, University of Southern California. He is the author of *Hacker Culture* and editor, with Brian Loader, of *Cybercrime: Law Enforcement, Security and Surveillance in the Information Age*.

Sherry Turkle is Abby Rockefeller Mauzé Professor of the Social Studies of Science and Technology and director of the MIT Initiative on Technology and Self at the Massachusetts Institute of Technology. She is the author of *Psychoanalytic Politics: Jacques Lacan and Freud's French Revolution, The Second Self: Computers and the Human Spirit*, and *Life on the Screen: Identity in the Age of the Internet*.

Langdon Winner is professor of political science at Rensselaer Polytechnic Institute. He is author of *Autonomous Technology* and *The Whale and the Reactor: A Search for Limits in an Age of High Technology*, and editor of *Democracy in a Technological Society*.

INDEX